Critical Conventions

Oklahoma Project for Discourse and Theory

Critical Conventions

*Interpretation
in the Literary
Arts and Sciences*

By John O'Neill

University of Oklahoma Press : Norman and London

By John O'Neill

Perception, Expression, and History: The Social Phenomenology of Maurice Merleau-Ponty (Evanston, 1970)

Sociology as a Skin Trade: Essays Towards a Reflexive Sociology (London and New York, 1972)

Making Sense Together: An Introduction to Wild Sociology (London and New York, 1974)

Essaying Montaigne: A Study of the Renaissance Institution of Writing and Reading (London and Boston, 1982)

For Marx Against Althusser and Other Essays (Washington, D.C., 1982)

Five Bodies: The Human Shape of Modern Society (Ithaca, N.Y., and London, 1985)

The Communicative Body: Studies in Communicative Philosophy, Politics, and Sociology (Evanston, 1989)

Plato's Cave: Desire, Power, and the Specular Functions of the Media (Norwood, N.J., and London, 1991)

Critical Conventions: Interpretation in the Literary Arts and Sciences (Norman, 1992)

O'Neill, John, 1933–
      Critical conventions : interpretation in the literary arts and sciences / by John O'Neill.
      p.   cm.—(Oklahoma project for discourse and theory : v. 8)
      Includes bibliographical references and index.
      ISBN 0-8061-2378-8
      I. Title.   II. Series.
PN81.05   1992
801'.95—dc20   91-50868
                                                                                  CIP

Text and jacket design by Bill Cason.

The paper in this book meets the guidelines for permanence and durability of the Committee on Production Guidelines for Book Longevity of the Council on Library Resources, Inc. ∞

Critical Conventions: Interpretation in the Literary Arts and Sciences is Volume 8 of the Oklahoma Project for Discourse and Theory.

For my daughter
Daniela

My *God*, my *God*, Thou art a *direct* God, may I not say, a *literall God*, a *God* that wouldest bee understood *literally*, and according to the *plaine sense* of all that thou saiest? But thou art also (*Lord* I intend it to thy *glory*, and let no *prophane mis-interpreter* abuse it to thy *diminution*) thou art a *figurative*, a *metaphoricall God* too: A *God* in whose words there is such a height of *figures*, such *voyages*, such *peregrinations* to fetch remote and precious *metaphors*, such *extentions*, such *spreadings*, such *Curtaines of Allegories*, such *third Heavens of Hyperboles*, so *harmonious eloquutions*, so *retired* and so *reserved expressions*, so *commanding perswasions*, so *perswading commandements*, such *sinewes* even in thy *milke*, and such *things* in thy *words*, as all *prophane Authors*, seeme of the seed of the *Serpent*, that *creepes*; thou art the *dove*, that flies. O, what words but thine, can expresse the inexpressible *texture*, and *composition* of thy *word*; in which, to one Man, that *argument* that binds his faith to beleeve that to bee the Word of *God*, is *the reverent simplicity* of the Word, and to another, the *majesty* of the Word; and in which two men, equally pious, may meet, and one wonder, that all should not understand it, and the other, as much, that any man should.

John Donne,
Devotions upon Emergent Occasions,
Nineteenth Expostulation

Contents

Part One. Literary Politics

Part Two. Disciplinary Theory and Practice in a Post-Kuhnian Economy of the Arts and Sciences

Part Three. Symptomatic Texts

Figures

Tables

Series Editors' Foreword

The twentieth century is in many ways shaped by its awareness of science and technology's encroachments as decisive influences on Western culture. This is the basis, for example, of the loud and public debate by C. P. Snow and F. R. Leavis over the ethical orderings of "two cultures"—Snow and Leavis's disagreement over the exact separation of humanistic and scientific cultures and the degree to which science supersedes humanistic values and ethics. These terms for debate continued into the 1960s. It is by now a commonplace, however, that a second great wave of reconception followed after 1968 and the political and cultural upheavals in Western Europe and America. After 1968, in the wake of undermined political orientations and displaced communal values, scores of Western intellectuals began to recast the relations of the humanities to the sciences far more extensively than had been conceived earlier in the century. This recasting by Jean-François Lyotard, Noam Chomksy, Julia Kristeva, Luce Irigaray, Michel Foucault, Jacques Derrida, and others provided justification and momentum for a conception of the "human sciences," by which was meant the critical engagement with a broad spectrum of social and humanistic "texts" as articulations of cultural discourse, social formation, and epistemic systems.

In the 1960s, as John O'Neill advances in *Critical Conventions: Interpretation in the Literary Arts and Sciences,* Western culture is now arguably entering a third phase of relation for the sciences and humanities. "The establishment position" in the human sciences, as O'Neill says, "is that we operate *two languages* [for social and cultural inquiry], science and literature, each achieving identity through what the other lacks." This stance has gradually been eroded as contemporary discourse analysis and cultural studies have deconstructed the category of pure metacommentary, of scientific notation as impermeable to the probings of critique and—as a language—having no intrinsic relations to culture and history. One effect of contemporary discourse, as O'Neill writes, is that "we can no longer take as a starting point for the phenomenology of science the simple demarcation adopted by Heidegger, Schutz, and Habermas, who argue, no less than the positivists, that the community of scientific reason sets itself off from the community of everyday reasoning and relevance." In the aftermath of quantum mechanics and postmodernism—not to mention May 1968 uprisings, Viet Nam, Watergate, and even Paul de Man's Belgium papers—it is no longer possible to separate the observer from the observed, to "treat the philosophy of science [for example] as a privileged gloss upon the practice of the sciences."

The logic of O'Neill's poststructuralist position on scientific observation can be seen in a text by Maurice Merleau-Ponty that O'Neill does not quote but which *as science* accurately suggests O'Neill's own cultural-studies project for a humanistic science. About objective observation, Merleau-Ponty argues that

> as long as I keep before me the ideal of an absolute observer, of knowledge in the absence of any viewpoint, I can only see my situation as being a source of error. But once I have acknowledged that through it I am geared to all actions and all knowledge that are meaningful to me, and that it is gradually filled with everything that may *be* for me, then my contract with the social in the finitude of my situation is revealed to me as the starting point of all truth, including that of science and, since we have some idea of the truth, since we are inside truth and cannot get outside it, all that I can do is define a truth within the situation.

It is precisely this sense of a "truth within the situation," within the situation of a local culture and historical frame of inquiry, that O'Neill pursues as the boundaries of his reformulated "scientific" inquiry. Like many contemporary social scientists and humanists—in light of the loss of a discourse of "natural" critical distance, or unproblematic objectivity—O'Neill engages the prospect of reformulating scientific inquiry as participation "within the situation" instead of enacting the distanced monitoring of a specimen of observed culture.

The implications for a cultural-studies project in O'Neill discourse are clearly evident. Like Jon Stratton, J. Fisher Solomon, Jonathan Culler, Christopher Norris, Marjorie Perloff, and Shari Benstock, O'Neill explores the interconnectedness of the human sciences. In this way, following what Gilles Deleuze and Felix Guattari call the rhizomic paths that move across disciplinary lines, and like the Oklahoma Project for Discourse and Theory itself, O'Neill attempts not to mark and rename well-worn cultural routes but to discover emergent channels of interdisciplinary inquiry for which we as yet have few maps.

ROBERT CONN DAVIS
RONALD SCHLEIFER

Acknowledgments

I should first thank the unknown reviewer for University of Oklahoma Press whose critically constructive reading of earlier versions of my manuscript is largely responsible for its present form and definition. Susan C. Philip, of Founders College, and Larry Hamberlin and Sarah Morrison at University of Oklahoma Press gave the manuscript more care than it may deserve. Some of the chapters derive from earlier publications that have been reworked for the purposes of the present volume, and I give their original sources as follows: chapter 4 appeared first in *Theory, Culture, and Society* 5, nos. 2–3 (June 1988); chapter 5 in *The Structural Allegory: Reconstructive Encounters with the New French Thought,* edited by John Fekete (Minneapolis: University of Minnesota Press, 1984); chapter 6 in *Philosophy of the Social Sciences* 11, no. 3 (Autumn 1981); chapter 7 in *The Canadian Journal of Sociology* 6, no. 2 (Spring 1981); chapter 8 in *Philosophy of the Social Sciences* 16, no. 1 (March 1986); chapter 9 in *Postmodernism and Continental Philosophy,* edited by Hugh J. Silverman and Donn Welton (Albany: State University of New York Press, 1988); chapter 11 in *New Literary History* 14 (1982–83); chapter 13 in *Practical Reasoning in Human Affairs: Studies in Honor of Chaim Perelman,* edited by James L. Golden and Joseph J. Pilotta (Dordrecht: D. Riedel, 1986); chapter 15 in *University of Ottawa Quarterly* 55, no. 4 (October–December 1985); chapter 16 in *Hermeneutics: Questions and Prospects,* edited by Gary Shapiro and Alan Sica (Amherst: University of Massachusetts Press, 1984) and chapter 17 in *Vico and Joyce,* edited by Donald Phillip Verene (Albany: State University of New York Press, 1987). I am grateful to the faculty and students who listened to earlier versions of these arguments at York University; the universities of Alberta, Ottawa, and Toronto; the University of York, England; Trinity College, Dublin; the universities of California, Berkeley, of Kansas, and Nebraska; the University of Notre Dame, Indiana; the State University of New York, at Buffalo; the Ohio State University, Columbus; and Emory University, Atlanta; as well as the International Center for Post-Graduate Studies at Dubrovnik, Yugoslavia, the Institute for Advanced Studies in Vienna, Austria, the Institute for Vico Studies, New York and Venice, Italy, and Keio University, Japan.

PART ONE Literary Politics

CHAPTER 1

**On the Practice of
Literary Politics**

Contemporary critical thought in the arts and sciences is flirting with
the idea that it makes as much sense to declare the fruitlessness of
looking for the meaning of human affairs as it once did to pronounce
upon the patterns of ultimate order. Our cultural intelligence now
professes to be acosmic and ahistorical, and yet not apolitical. This
new cultural sublime sits on the American horizon in the form of a
self-styled ironic liberalism, derisive of any other historical or political
romance than the game of intellectuals' redescribing themselves *pour
encourager les autres:*

> The difference between a search for foundations and an attempt at
> redescription is emblematic of the difference between the culture of
> liberalism and older forms of cultural life. For in its ideal form, the culture
> of liberalism would be one which was enlightened, secular, through and
> through. It would be one in which no trace of divinity remained, either
> in the form of a divinized world or a divinized self. Such a culture would
> have no room for the notion that there are nonhuman forces to which
> human beings should be responsible. It would drop, or drastically reinter-
> pret, not only the idea of holiness but those of "devotion to truth" and of
> "fulfillment of the deepest needs of the spirit." The process of de-diviniza-
> tion . . . would, ideally, culminate in our no longer being able to see any
> use for the notion that finite, mortal, contingently existing human beings
> might derive the meanings of their lives from anything except other finite,
> mortal, contingently existing human beings. In such a culture, warnings of
> "relativism," queries whether social institutions had become increasingly
> "rational" in modern times, and doubts about whether the aims of liberal
> society were "objective moral values" would seem merely quaint.[1]

Since Richard Rorty claimed to have cracked the mirror of nature—
as well as the reflecting mirrors of society and the self—we are all
urged to keep calm by maintaining a conversation whose conviviality
will be guaranteed by Rorty's rule that we not get metaphysical
about language. Under these conditions "decency" and "kindness" will
prevail, with an allowance for getting worked up over "cruelty." Our
political life will be ruled by an ironic citizenry whose virtue lies in

its commitment to the contingency of all-prevailing laws and its expectancy that its poets will continuously overthrow its philosophers of truth, justice, and beauty. History ends in America not because of its promise but because of its practice—and not because of its common sense but because of its cultivated irony. What America practices best is "literary criticism." Admittedly, this is stretching the practice of literary criticism somewhat. But Rorty claims that this has been the secular trend in the high culture of those democracies that appear not to have fallen apart by replacing the hope of paradise with *social hope*. America is that earthly place where we can best construct the political scenarios that realize rather than frustrate the present hopes of our fellow citizens:

> The metaphysician's association of theory with social hope and of literature with private perfection is, in an ironist liberal culture, reversed. Within a liberal metaphysical culture the disciplines which were charged with penetrating behind the many private appearances to the one general common reality—theology, science, philosophy—were the ones which were expected to bind human beings together, and thus to help eliminate cruelty. Within an ironist culture, by contrast, it is the disciplines which specialize in thick description of the private and idiosyncratic which are assigned this job. In particular, novels and ethnographies which sensitize one to the pain of those who do not speak our language must do the job which demonstrations of a common human nature were supposed to do. Solidarity has to be constructed out of little pieces, rather than found already waiting, in the form of an ur-language which all of us recognize when we hear it.[2]

What is remarkable in these assertions is their determination to ride the surface of things, forbidding distinctions that might shatter the liberal's shop window. Rorty's own mirror is full of things he can't see about America because he can't see how it is that others see America with another eye for its divisions and exclusions. From his position, softened by its authority in a comfortable university niche, he can no longer remember the vulgar economy of Babbittry, robber capitalism, and colonialism for which neopragmatism provides an American gloss—hence his pretence of modest reasoning in a world its practices have driven crazy. Like a teenage surfer, Rorty rides the waves of cultural contemporaneity, dumping on the past, shrugging his shoulders at philosophical seriousness or spiritual urgency—

laughing at any other politics than his own as if it were a flint stone operation. What Rorty fails to see in the American mirror is that the specular effect of American ideology is to erase the distinction between public and private life, between materialism and idealism, between America and the world, and, of course, between *he* and *she*. The academic consequence of this process of specularization—which I treat at length in my book *Plato Cave*—is the *light-minded aestheticism*[3] that Rorty seeks to disavow on the grounds that its superficiality belongs to that complex of the rise of the market economy, increased literacy, disenchantment, tolerance, and practicality. Ignoring America's nuclearism, Rorty concludes that even if the American "experiment" with those values fails us, the show will have been instructive to watch. Such philosophical sangfroid may be appealing against the background of the world's fundamentalism—much of which is produced in America—but its weakness is that it is only the other side of a coin whose moral value has collapsed.

Rorty goes to some length to assign a female persona to his liberal ironist. Unfortunately, "she" isn't "scrappy" enough for Barbara Herrnstein Smith, for whom life in the ethical supermarket has induced the firm belief that we struggle over scraps for which there is no overall moral menu. One man's meat is another woman's poison. "There is no *bottom* bottom line anywhere, for anyone or for 'man,' " she says.[4] And Rorty is just dozing if he tries to invoke "solidarity," however nice the company:

> Since the relativist knows that the conjoined systems (biological, cultural, ideological, institutional, and so forth) of which her general conceptual taste and specific conceptualization of the world are a contingent function are probably not altogether unique, she expects some other people to conceptualize the world in more or less the same ways she does and, like her, to find objectivist conceptualizations more or less *cognitive, distasteful,* unsatisfactory, and irrating along more or less the same lines. She may have found it worth her while to seek out such *fellow relativists,* to promote conditions that encourage their emergence, and where she has had the resources, to attempt to cultivate a few of them herself: "worth her while" because since she cannot herself live any other way, she is glad for a bit of company.[5]

So, after a hard day's battle in the critical arena developing the virtues of "scrappiness," it is nice to withdraw into the good company of one's fellow relativists, that is, into the company of established criticism grounded in the "tough" market metaphors and semireal pragmatism that account for its own place in the academic "world."

I have chosen these extraordinary versions of contemporary "literary politics" in part to show how a sociologist can be at home in literary studies and in part to show how literary studies appropriate the central metaphors of the social sciences, so that we cannot remain comfortably behind our disciplinary barricades. Today's intellectual common market has brought down the walls of philosophy, literature, and the sciences so that we must all trade in the common currency of text/discourse, cultivating rhetoric and irony, or else be dismissed as cultural Luddites. As a sociologist of sorts, I suppose I should welcome the contemporary alliance between literature and the social sciences. Indeed, I do. Moreover, one can be quite happy that this alliance is not based on the reductionist model of an earlier sociology of literature.[6] The latter sought to fulfill an equally reductionist program of a Marxist sociology of knowledge, ideology, science, and the arts. The same might be said of the early program of the psychoanalytic study of the arts and sciences. Fortunately, these externalist approaches have been largely abandoned for more reflexive, internalist approaches to the social sciences themselves, as well as to Marxism and psychoanalysis, as I show in chapters 6 and 14.

In a sense, we are now all literary sociologists and literary psychoanalysts because we have lost our fear of the patristic texts that once guarded our intellectual borders, preventing interdisciplinarity and intertextuality. The canon now stands like the Berlin Wall—a shameful edifice unable to rid itself of the critical graffiti it had accumulated in the last forty years or so. The destruction of the canon has, of course, involved the destruction of its language. Raising the level of rhetoric, abstraction, dialectics, and the unconscious, criticism now rejects every trace of representation in order to rework the writer-text-reader triad and to recontextualize it historically and politically in the light of contemporary models of productive—that is, antirealist—criticism.

This unmooring of the text has been accompanied by a similar loosening of aesthetic values from the elite values of the broader society within which literary criticism operates. In part, this has involved the separation of criticism from itself, that is, the shift from the New Criticism to what we might call sociophilosophical or Continental criticism, a move that pluralizes criticism. But caution must be exercised on this front, since much depends on which elements of the literary community we appeal to and how their values are constituted, if we are not to lose all sense of an ideal critical community concerned to advance knowledge and emancipation. Here what I have in mind is the double claim of writers and readers to specific competences derived from and (re)productive of a literary community whose observances (empirically and ritually speaking) are obliged to, analytic of, and emancipatory for the larger political community invoked in their own institution. In this regard, I am adopting a framework that is broader than either leftist criticism or pragmatist neo-liberalism, since I think their practitioners may be just as liable to violate the reading and writing practices of an ideal critical community as any other interpretative group (see chapters 2, 3, 5, and 16).

In short, literary alienation is not the exclusive product of elite culture. Yet the very idea of an ideal critical community will fly in the face of current postmodernism while we remain under the ban on narrative and its bias toward social consensus. But it is one thing to produce an oedipalized narrative, as I shall show in Freud's case (chapter 14), or an arbitrary narrative of episodic history, as I show in Fredric Jameson's treatment of Baudelaire (chapter 3), and it is quite another matter to reduce literary practice to "just gaming" (Jean-François Lyotard) or a "market" (Herrnstein Smith), as though our culture could withstand every assault in which imagination and reality lose respect for their difference.

My proposal—that we consider literary and scientific writing and the critical community of artists and social scientists as two sides of the economy of the disciplinary organization of knowledge—goes in the direction of a post-Kuhnian sociology of the arts and sciences. My own practice of the rhetorical analysis of the written procedure in the arts and sciences we employ in the production of recognizable or "good enough" disciplinary knowledge sits somewhere between the interpretative programs elaborated by Rorty and Stanley Fish. I shall say enough in chapter 2 to show that Fish's reliance on the consensus in the interpretative community is both a critic's prejudice and one that may be exclusionary in its own way. It is essential to my perspective on disciplinarity and its relevant body of literature that it is not achieved uniquely through adherence to scientific method, despite the attempts by both humanists and social scientists to achieve professional identity in this very way. Moreover, since these alternatives leave open a "third way," namely, the exercise of a relatively autonomous "criticism" whose own exclusionary force may be overlooked, I have expressed some difference of opinion over whether we can abandon the romance of an ideal critical community. To do so, in my opinion, would be to exact from ourselves too high a price for antipositivism and anti-idealism. Rather, I believe that the arts and sciences are each to be regarded as human institutions whose current practitioners are doubly obliged to treat them as techniques of preservation as well as of innovation, as I show in chapter 11, where I discuss the Renaissance problematic of self and society. The critical tradition, as I understand it, has never been wholly oppressive, any more than it can ever become entirely irrelevant. Indeed, any such conceit of contemporary criticism would represent a new mode of spiritual alienation. It would not be a finding of literature but rather the founding of illiteracy. That in turn would deepen the levels of cultural ignorance required by the new information apparatus of late capitalism.

I must, however, say something more on what I consider to be the "perverse Kuhnianism" that underwrites contemporary literary politics—aggravated even further by Lyotard's "wayward Wittgensteinianism." Curiously enough, these two "misreadings" constitute the very bedrock of the antifoundationalists' insistence that, since neither science nor language can be cleansed of rhetoric and fiction, all that remains is to choose decent "poets"—American pragmatists and French anti-Communists—who will rid politics and literature of "theory" and thus save liberalism—apparently turning America into a new Amazonia, if Rorty's prose is to be believed:

> Even in the sciences, metaphoric redescriptions are the mark of genius and revolutionary leaps forward. If we follow up this Kuhnian point by thinking, with Davidson, of the literal-metaphorical distinction as the distinction between old language and new language rather than in terms of a distinction between words which latch on to the world and those which do not, the paradox vanishes. If, with Davidson, we drop the notion of language as fitting the world, we can see the point of Bloom's and Nietzsche's claim that the strong maker, the person who uses words as

they have never before been used, is best able to appreciate her own contingency. For she can see, more clearly than the continuity-seeking historian, critic, or philosopher, that her *language* is as contingent as her parents or her historical epoch. She can appreciate the force of the claim that "truth is a mobile army of metaphors" because, by her own sheer strength, she has broken out of one perspective, one metaphoric, into another.[7]

Ironically, Rorty, despite his use of the feminine gender, seems hardly to please women. Thus Nancy Fraser, a feminist philosopher, takes strong exception to Rorty's poeticizing of Thomas S. Kuhn's concept of a paradigm-breaking discourse because it reduces the public discourse of science to the private monologue of the romantic. The result is that, whereas Rorty might have employed Kuhn to pluralize political discourse, his romanticism runs away into bourgeois narcissism at the expense of the efforts of workers, peasants, women, and the "hard-core" unemployed to get a hearing in the public realm as the arena of oppositional rather than consensus politics:

> Rorty's conceptions of politics and theory are obverses of one another. If theory is hyperindividualized and depoliticized, then politics is hyper-communalized and detheoreticized. As theory becomes pure *poiésis,* politics approaches pure *techné.* Moreover, as theory is made the preserve of pure transcendence, politics is banalized, emptied of radicalism and desire. Finally, as theory becomes the production ex nihilo of new metaphors, politics must be merely their liberalization; politics must be application only, never invention.[8]

Properly understood, Kuhn's theory of scientific change has very little to do with any larger theory of social and political change, even though it may well alter how we think about social change in institutions other than science. To make this point, I have developed in chapter 6 a complex model of the exchanges between science, technology, economy, and polity, and I have spent considerable time on the question of the interaction between science and society. In chapter 7, I have expanded on Kuhn's concept of the disciplinary matrix by showing how we observe its practices in writing, reviewing, and commenting within our respective disciplines. But, beyond Kuhn, I have also tried, in chapter 16, to link the disciplinary matrix to literary desire and in turn to link that desire with the body politic as the larger work of art in which we shape our lives. To do this, I have tried to show how disciplinarity must subvert itself and its temptation to fall into elite consensus even while proclaiming its own liberal romance.

What makes Rorty's practice "unruly" is the way he rides a crest supported, on one side, by the discovery of the fictionality of science—which I consider more carefully in chapters 8 and 14—and, on the other side, by the current flirtation with ethical nihilism and its romance of tradition busting in the arts. Rorty is, of course, a moderate in all this, and that accounts for his critical authority in a discontented world of ambitious but guilt-ridden academics. It does make a good American yarn to tell how philosophy is, after all, humbug and badly in need of sensible Americans to conduct its business. But does the success of burger capitalism in deluging America and seducing the Soviet Union justify us in selling off the classics of philosophy, religion, and literature and filling our laboratories with Rorty's poets? How *does* Rorty read "our" literature not to leave any impression that it has never ceased from the first day to struggle with these questions or that it has remained "classical," "lively," and "essential" precisely because it has never given in to any easy fiction? What may imperil my own position is the extent to which it risks falling outside of the current disciplinary celebrations of leftist and neoliberal criticism, even though all my thinking and writing is, broadly speaking, socialist. Yet as I write this, the term *socialist* has acquired a quaint ring. But while Lyotard appears to have scared everyone off the socialist path and Jameson tries to shepherd everyone along it, I believe that Marx never had in mind either the iron road of communism or the broad avenue of utopia that are supposed to represent his thought on the relations between history, economy, and politics.

Because a little Freud is enough to scandalize French communism and because Louis Althusser imagined that Marx was not a Hegelian hardly renders either Lyotard or Jameson keepers of our "political unconscious" except as we imagine we have read Marx through them. One wonders how our current discussions of Marx came to pass. In part, I think Jürgen Habermas is to be blamed for giving us a Marx who did not understand that we are communicative as well as productive beings. That allowed the culture vultures to eat away at Marx, spitting back at us his undigested corpus.[9] Surely, Marx had invented ideological criticism, discourse analysis, and genealogical deconstruction in the footnotes of the first volume of *Capital* and in the fourth volume, where he engages in the critique of the major classical economists, not to mention *The German Ideology* and *The Holy Family?* The whole point of Marx's analysis of the commodity fetish is that capitalism speaks from a place where it cannot be understood. Above all, it is from Marx—and not from Jean Beaudrillard—that we first learned that capitalism has no culture of its own that it is not prepared to garbage in the drive for profits. As I show in chapter 4, postmodernism—despite Beaudrillard and Jameson—has nothing to do with the seduction of the signifier, but is entirely an effect of the signified, namely, capitalist enterprise, into which the whole world is unceasingly drawn. By the same token, every new phase of capitalism creates new orders of exploitation, cruelty, disease, and ignorance. Postmodernism is not "post" anything—it is decidedly a reflection of the current intellectual foreclosure of the signified, namely, *power,* and its effects of national and global stratification. Marx's iconoclasm is not improved by lining it up with Andy Warhol's glitter unless critics have completely surrendered to cultural junk.

Lyotard's "waiting game" is really nothing more than a gesture toward indeterminacy.[10] But without the contrastive structure of rules it hardly makes sense. It is, of course, flattering to artists to speak of themselves as antinomians—hardly daring to title their own work! Lyotard's embrace of this community overrates both its intelligence and its radicalism. Artists are generally minor thinkers who experience as much difficulty in breaking paradigm-art as workers in any other field. Indeed, one might even argue that artists are even weaker as a community the more they embrace the internalist pragmatics of art offered to them by Lyotard's minimalism.[11] Outside of the grand narratives on which Lyotard conducts his postmodern dance, everything withers. Having lost their vital relation to the tradition, the minor arts fail to resist their commercial reinscription in the collage-collection of postmodern art, architecture, and literature.

Lyotard merely makes a virtue out of the poverty of minor art and its minor politics. Even worse, he reinscribes the exhaustion of art and politics in a new "paganism," despite our complete loss of any sense of the sacred invoked in pagan practices, which have nothing to do with secularism. Lyotard's phraseology reverses history, pushing us back into perilous institutions whose organizational structures are not yet complex yet no longer simple. The effect is an imaginary one where we have to restart all civilizational linkages. Does Auschwitz require such a restart, as Lyotard claims? Or does it not point to the evil in separating our story from God's story—an evil made worse by our "accounts" of Auschwitz, whose horror cries out only to God because we have no truth and no justice for it, any more than we have for any of the countless atrocities we commit against every people in the world. The horrors of human history exceed our prayers. we blaspheme them in trying to conscript their horror into a theory of the sublime. Here we not only come to a limit of the aesthetic but also to the limits of aestheticizing politics.

It remains a common assumption of "literary politics" that the operation of language in all its forms is central to our political lives. Indeed, it appears that linguistic alienation has replaced economic alienation as the principal object of critical thought in both the literary and the social sciences. Thus, "the tradition," "the canon," "the classics," "the paradigm" have come under scrutiny in every field of thought. Usually, the methods of analysis employed in that task result in a blurring of the genres on which they are brought to bear. Of course, the particular positions adopted from that perspective are enormously varied. In part, this is because one may choose different sites of discursive production according to one's sense of what is crucial and one's competence with the relevant materials of analysis.

Superficially, it may appear from all this that critics are more clever than they used to be since no one shrinks from interdisciplinarity and intertextuality any more than from the unconscious, desire, and power. Today, critical studies in the arts and social sciences are unashamedly moral and political. They are moral in the sense that critics exercise a keen eye for the exclusions, privileges, and presumptions of the canonical texts—at least insofar as this affects themselves. Yet critics claim to practice their trade on behalf of readers rather than writers. These two attitudes may well overlap, inasmuch as critics are conscious of working in universities whose pedagogical politics must favor "immigrant" students, teaching them, at least for a few years, to acquire some point of view on the extraordinary "in-mixing" of high and low culture that characterizes our society. All of this is valuable. My previous remarks regarding our need for a more profound grasp of political economy are not meant to subordinate critical studies to political economy. Quite the contrary, they call for an end to criticism's presumption that it knows political economy and that it conveys enough of it by invoking the shibboleths of "power," "ideology," "repression," "sexism," "racism," and like notions. This is a practice that conveys ignorance in the name of emancipation.

The double discovery that language is ideological and that ideologies are languaged or discursive has taken the time it took because it was hard to break the spell cast by "science" on rhetoric and the human sciences. That may have been a serviceable spell—potentially enlightening and possibly democratic—for as long as science itself seemed serviceable. But we now know that science as an institution must accommodate itself to its surrounding political and economic institutions and that as a consequence scientific discourses become rhetorical and ideological in exactly the same fashion as literary and social scientific discourses. There is no loss in this; indeed, there is a considerable gain, inasmuch as we no longer accord a blind faith to the "value-free" pronouncements of science. This strengthens both our morals and our politics without necessarily weakening either our sciences or our arts. For we really should set aside the contrast between the natural and hermeneutical sciences, as I show in part 2. Contemporary antirealist or constructionist accounts of scientific fact and theory, derived from laboratory ethnographies inspired by phenomenology and ethnomethodology, increasingly recover the hermeneutical features of practical scientific reasoning and inquiry. It is in fact much more difficult for science practitioners to neglect the ties between the community of science and the practical, natural attitude than its hitherto official ideology has allowed. We now know that science, literature, and philosophy as human institutions are fields of endless interrogation, as Maurice Merleau-Ponty would say, or fractured enterprises in which, like Orpheus, we are forbidden to look back on the truth or origin to which we believe ourselves allied.

From this standpoint, realism in the arts and sciences is hopelessly inarticulate about its necessary choices. Realism is obliged to repress its alliance with the unreality of language through which art works its very realism. Actually, literary realism is rather a *via negativa* when practiced by such artists as Flaubert. Indeed, as may be seen from

Flaubert's *Bouvard and Pecuchet,* the separation between literature and science—presumed on in the subordination of literature to science and in such scientific methods of literary analysis as structuralism—collapses under its own weight. It is a distinction practiced upon the assumption that we have *two languages.* Thus, *scientific* language is purely instrumental or self-effacing in allowing content to dominate form. *Literary* language, by contrast, is autonomous because its rhetorical properties determine content.

Both Merleau-Ponty and Roland Barthes, to name a couple, rejected this myth of scientific discourse. They regarded objectivism and realism as rhetorical affectations of scientific neutrality whose grammatical decoys—absence of first-person reference/third-person agency—can just as well be employed in literary discourse. In turn, so far from being a purely subjective achievement, literary discourse can be analyzed in terms of objective units of discourse and intelligible progression and resolution, as well as conventional taxonomies and classifications of things, persons, and events that fulfill its sense and expressivity. But, as Barthes and Michel Foucault saw, structuralist discourse itself lacks any privilege in its own use of language:

> The logical continuation of structuralism can only be to rejoin literature, no longer as an "object" of analysis but as the activity of writing, to do away with the distinction derived from logic which turns the work itself into a language-object and science into a meta-language, and thus to forego that illusory privilege which science attaches to the possession of a captive language.[12]

Thus, as I see it, the "crisis in the human sciences" has less to do with the forgetfulness of science than with our irresolution in assuming responsibility toward what might be called the *poetics of thinking* in the arts and sciences. To recover the work of the text, without falling into either frivolity or constrained pedagogy, structuralism turned into deconstruction, revealing to science and philosophy the scandal of language; its resilient sovereignty, which undercuts literary positivism no less than positivist science and philosophy. This is the point at which Marxism and phenomenology can fruitfully be brought together, as I try to show. In other words, here, as in the field of science, there is the beginning of the realization that rational argument, discovery, and criticism must not be abstracted from the tradition and community of philosophers, artists, and scientists who refuse to adopt the posture of unsituated and unhistorical subjectivity, whether of History, Science, or the Party. Thus, by the time of *Die Krisis der Europäischen Wissenschaften,* Edmund Husserl himself had come to realize that the *telos* of Western rationality is undermined by its transcendental posture and that the philosopher must reestablish his ties with the historical tradition and community within which he dwells "poetically." Merleau-Ponty remarks on how the Husserlian notion of *Stiftung* embraces simultaneously the anxiety and fecundity of cultural institutions:

> It is thus that the world as soon as he has seen it, his first attempts at painting, the whole past of painting all deliver up a *tradition* to the painter—*that is,* Husserl remarks, *the power to forget origins* and to give to the past not a survival, which is the hypocritical form of forgetfulness, but a new life, which is the noble form of memory.[13]

In other work on Merleau-Ponty, I have emphasized this shift in the concept of reflection as institution rather than trade on the metaphor of transcendental "constitution."[14] I hope thereby to recover the field of coexistence in which truth is historically sedimented and renewed without the bond between tradition and self-improvisation ever breaking, any more than the mind can escape its embodiment, as I have tried to show in chapter 13, where I consider Descartes' foundationalism. But this means that the human arts and sciences are obliged to dwell within the temporal horizons of the body politic they elicit and serve. To this end, I have elaborated on a conception of sociological relevance that I have called sociology as a skin trade[15] whose incarnate grounds I later developed under the phenomenological notion of wild sociology.[16] Both of these concepts scandalize the fractured language of sociology because they treat social science as another faith to be suffered by the great body and family of society whose repetitions furnish the surplus value exploited by the human sciences. In chapter 17 I repeat this exercise, reading Giambattista Vico against James Joyce against Sigmund Freud.

Since I have gone to such trouble to call attention to the literary body and its ties with the body politic, I am encouraged by Susan Horton's prediction with regard to the possible future of literary criticism: "It would seem, then, that at the most radical end of the continuum, the *most* oppositional critic is the one who suggests that three things may be in style again: *the body,* action, and teaching—

the last representing, not coincidentally, one of the finer marriages of body and action."[17]

Horton's nice observation on the teaching body deserves further comment. As I see it, what is potentially oppressive in current literary criticism is its possessive attachment of critical practice to professional bodies whose sensibilities we are asked to trust despite what we know about them as ideological organizations. Rather, I believe that anyone who loves reading and writing must be awakened to the disappearance of literature, increasingly abandoned by its fashionable authors on the one side and its comfortable critics on the other.

The proliferation of signs does not, as some might argue, quicken the life of literature. On the contrary, the flickering electric life of the sign merely runs on after the death of literature, equally indifferent to the dignity of art and life. In such circumstances, we must try to reconnect literature with its embodied life, with the soul's senses awakened in words whose life has never existed anywhere else than in the gesture of writing and in that fold of the flesh wherein writing and reading are consummated, loving literature. We must set aside the ideologies of literature that render it stillborn, that make of it the lifeless debris of a dead society or clique, just as we must refuse those whose criticism serves only to orphan their students, committing them to the poorhouse of literary criticism, where they end their days with wretched minor texts.

Rather, we must espouse writers who, like Montaigne and Barthes, write from a habit of the body that is achieved only through its improvisation of the sounded-sense of its being and who seek to write one-self and to be received in a responsive reading answerable to its invocation of the living word. Such writers—like Gertrude Stein and Joyce—seek to avoid linearity, to escape the compulsion of argument, surrendering rather to the landscape of words that nudge up against the writer like wild animals who have never known the captivity and domestication of prose. To achieve this, they are obliged to escape their own ordinary sensibilities, to wait elsewhere, to travel away, to seek their literary body in an act of rebirth in which the soul's guest is language enjoying itself in them as its witness, as *jouissance,* as *gynema*[18] and *homotextuality*:

> *Text of pleasure:* the text that contents, fills, grants euphoria: the text that comes from culture and does not break with it, is *linked to a comfortable*

practice of reading. Text of bliss: the text that imposes a state of loss, the text that discomforts (perhaps to the point of a certain boredom), *unsettles the reader's* historical, cultural, psychological *assumptions,* the consistency of his tasks, values, memories, *brings to a crisis his relation with language.*[19]

Writing demands not that we avoid either the body of death or the body of bliss but that we incorporate them, as a woman quickens with her child, life-within-life, waiting, moving, self-sounding witness to all life. To read is to pray that literature will not fail us, any more than those other places in our life where we owe to one another our inner being.

CHAPTER 2 Is There a Class in This Text?

I am going to raise O'Neill's question, namely, "*Is there a class in this text?*" The *class question,* of course, displays all the artifactual troubles that Stanley Fish claims to have settled when he chose to explicate his theory of interpretative communities around an anecdotal question, "*Is there a text in this class?*"[1] I shall work from Fish's question because I think it offers us a path into the contemporary text of humanist studies, where we are faced with the postmodern celebration of the disappearance of the subject, that is to say, the disappearance of any subject of history, whether an individual or a class, and thereby the collapse of any grand narrative text arising from and giving shape (*Bildung*) to the adventures of the individual or class hero.

The humanist text now lies in ruin, destroyed by its logocentrism and paternalism. Whether the postmodern fragmentation of the text and the consequent pluralization of the interpretative community to accommodate new critical voices will liberate the literary canon in favor of more charismatic communities of knowledge and action or whether this is merely a phantasmic projection of the minor politics of academic criticism remains to be seen. So much is at stake in this question that we shall have to be content with trying to keep the question alive well beyond what small answers we may fit to the puzzle it opens on this occasion.

I am going to be very schematic with Fish's question, since by now it constitutes a commonplace of critical argument. Even as I say this, of course, I am already invoking a concept of interpretative community by working within the range of interpretative options offered by Fish's text-class (*TC*) question:

> *TC 1:* "Is there a text in this class?" may be taken, when raised by a student and answered by a teacher, to be asking whether the class is taught around a textbook, such as the *Norton Anthology of Literature.*

TC 2: "Is there a text in this class?" may, in view of the student's sense of current literary criticism, be taken to ask the teacher's position on whether he or she considers criticism to have priority over the authority of the text.

Fish spends a great deal of time showing that these two questions are not specimens of the kind of undecidability of literary interpretation his opponents believe to have undermined the literary canon—at least among those poor fish in the tank of New Criticism and its Continental variety. Nothing is made of the student's class position—which might be inferred from her attendance at Johns Hopkins University, where Fish's question was first raised—nor from what might be the case for students receiving the current answers at Duke University, where the leftist literary elite engages in skillful deconstruction of the canon.[2] Because Fish's question is silent about the social class in the class, we shall risk impertinence by reformulating his question as a class question with respect to the texts that operate as the totems of interpretative community, or of affiliation and utopia, to introduce the perspective of Edward Said and Fredric Jameson on the class question and the canon.

Now whereas TC 1 is perfectly well answered by telling the student that the teacher does use a textbook, it nevertheless might well have been answered with the exclamation:

No, there isn't a text in this class!

Had the teacher employed this pedagogic strategy with respect to TC 1, then the student might not have been obliged to get her teacher to start thinking by offering him something like:

TC 3: So, no *Norton Anthology?* Thank God, I'm really opposed to the canon myself.

Had this exchange transpired, the teacher might then have saved face with some such rejoinder as:

Yes, the canon has collapsed. There are only texts, or intertextuality. I'm looking for strong readers in this class!

Thereafter, the student would have been free to return to the coffee shop to contemplate the chaos in Fish's class and the prospect of leaping into the arms of his literary authority, or else she may have gone off to the library to contemplate the silent appeal of those texts that have survived generations of interpretations so well that they still wait for her and some gentler hermeneutician to lead her through the garden of thought and feeling they lay open.

I have already remarked that although Fish's question serves to make the ethnomethodological point that the interpretative community does not paralyze itself with undecidability, Fish nevertheless forecloses the class question that can be discerned as soon as we take *TC 1* to be a question about cultural authority posed by a student to a professor whose status derives from his or her commitment to the reproduction of the cultural apparatus. In that case, Fish's question may be replaced with O'Neill's question:

> *CT 1:* Is there a class in this text?

Now, of course, this class-text (*CT*) question needs to be disambiguated in at least the following ways, since any of the students might have asked:

> *CT 2:* Is class analysis the interpretative approach in this text?

Here the student may want to know whether or not the teacher insists on a strictly Marxist interpretation of the texts in the class. To this the teacher might reply, depending upon how he or she conceives of the issue of interpretative authority, in a number of ways:

- No, class analysis is not a useful critical tool in literary studies, though it may be in the social sciences ;
- Yes, class analysis is employed as a critical tool, but with no greater claim than other methodologies such as psychoanalysis, structuralism, or semiotics;
- Yes, class analysis is the basic tool in the class, since it deals with texts that show the interpretative power of Marxist literary criticism.

We can now imagine that our student will rephrase the first class-text question (*CT 1*), at least with respect to the second and third responses, so that it becomes:

> *CT 3:* Well, I mean, do you have to be class conscious to be in your class?

We now see that whereas Fish's question (*TC 1*) reduces the student's concerns to a question of organizational practice, O'Neill's question

(*CT 1*) identifies the student's concern with class membership in a classroom where the teacher's interpretative ideology is the decisive link to the world beyond the text, that is, to history and politics. In addition, the class-text question (*CT 1* and *CT 3*) asks of the teacher how it is possible for that question to be raised as merely a *possible* interpretative strategy, one that would leave the class uncommitted to the Marxist politics of a classless society and culture.

Fish pays insufficient attention to the vicious circle in the history of his own position: in view of interpretative criticism having risen as part of the dissensus within formal criticism, does not Fish's community overemphasize its own ability to achieve consensus? Fish's students are likely to be attracted to reader-response criticism because it apparently blends with their own narcissistic culture. The latter may in turn prove difficult to bring to order and even subvert the liberal consensus in the productive community of criticism. Here I think Fish's wish that his pedagogical practice avoid authoritarianism is salvaged by an unrecognized appeal (Robert Scholes calls it a "bribe," offering an illusory power to the reader in exchange for becoming the servant of Fish's autonomous readings)[3] to the authority of the literary consensus he and his "school" are institutionalizing at this moment.

Fish claims that his students are not coerced because they "already have" the values and abilities that bring about communication by itself, confidently and without infringement on their conventional sense of things. But Fish does not explore whether that bias to consensus exists in his class as a social class and what would happen to it in the context of a broader conception of America as a class society. In reality, conflict is the order of the day outside the classroom, but its expression is channeled into discourses that foreclose the class question[4] by talking about crime, drugs, homelessness, inflation, ageing, and the like. In this context, Ted Koppel can play Fish's umpire sitting among ABC's panel of experts, whose expertise consists in not naming the class system and its colonial extensions. Within these parameters Koppel gets the answers by which he is paid to be puzzled. Here Koppel is the all-American critic, relaying the game of interpretation without seeing that that game is utterly violated by the information industry's expropriation of alternative stories.

In this regard, Jean-François Lyotard's disingenuous report on the postmodern condition is surely one of the great curiosities of the contemporary critical scene.[5] Precisely when it was time to resist the collapse of the grand narratives, in view of the power of the global information industry to shape events by suppressing and foreshortening their historical economic and political contexts, Lyotard glibly announced a minoritarian view that, like that of Michel Foucault, Gilles Deleuze, and Félix Guattari, puts the mind in a handicapped parking spot until the corporate traffic has rolled by. Lyotard's "report on knowledge" was in fact its death certificate. Lyotard's belated discovery that in practice scientists are fictionalists whenever they see the chance of paradigm-breaking discoveries hardly justified the abandonment of all our social and political poetics except for the cheap cultural tropes of corporate postmodern architecture. Why Fredric Jameson should have been tempted to put Lyotard's Humpty Dumpty together again remains a mystery to me. One would have thought his Frye would have saved him from his French, since he really does not believe there is any *au delà du marxisme*. But we shall consider those issues in later chapters.

In *Fish* vs. *O'Neill* what is at dispute is the concept of community invoked in all such expressions as the interpretative community, the ideal speech community, and the socialist or religious community, which I take up in later chapters. This may be hard to believe in view of the postmodern insistence upon fragmentation, self-consuming artifacts, hyperreality, and the fall of history into the black hole of signifiers that never return any local sense. But Fish and Co. have too good a sense of the sociolegal conventions that constitute intelligibility and value to do more than flirt with challenging the literary community with arguments that it will not eventually establish as its own. In this, of course, they represent everything that is successful about the combination of professional competence and the establishment of the academic critic. We therefore cannot expect the tropes of postmodernism to do more than rattle our university cages.

Fish engages the pleasure of his own text, at least, but he does so in a way that hides its subjectivity by adopting the underlaborer role in an interpretative community whose practices he neither grounds nor questions. Fish's sociolegal propriety, however, hides the history and politics of the (leftist) community of criticism that he invokes in quasi-democratic fashion, as opposed to Roland Barthes, for example, whose pleasure and self-indulgence are unruly elements of his critical practice. Fish poses as a common reader, one empowered to dispossess the text of its priority and to assign it a sense that is average and shareable, because the reader's practices are never his or her own but are constitutionally productive of a shared world sustainable and reparable without either extraordinary insight or affect. The interpretative competence that Fish has in mind, however, is really that of the not so average academic, one as capable of changing an opinion as of reaching one.

Even so, Fish probably overlooks the power of the paradigm that binds the majority of academics in any discipline so that at the end of the day the say-so goes to the Fishes of the world. Indeed, it must do so, since Fish employs a "perverse Kuhnianism" to make the paradigm a machine for revolution according to its own internal design but otherwise impervious to external change. Much like Freud, whose similar strategy he opposes—as we shall see in chapter 14— Fish deprives the young bloods of a "theory" of critical change by arguing that there is no such thing as a change that has not *already* been made by the literary community:

> A theoretical pronouncement is always an articulation of a shift that has in large part already occurred; it announces a rationale for practices already in force; it provides a banner under which those who are already doing what it names can march. . . . [Theory] does not even cause critical self-consciousness or make one aware of one's assumptions (these are the usual claims); first, because self-consciousness is a necessary condition for any activity even if one cannot produce its informing principles on demand; and second, because if one were to produce those principles— that is, make one's assumptions explicit—that activity would itself occur within assumptions of which one was not and could not be aware. All of which is to say that theory's project—the attempt to get above practice and lay bare the grounds of its possibility—is an impossible one.[6]

It is interesting to note that while Fish brilliantly identifies Freud's rhetorical substitution of his own interpretative authority for the Wolf Man's reconstruction of the primal scene, he fails to see that Freud's procedure is identical with his own arguments against theory and its young pretenders in the school of literary criticism. The primal scene of interpretative practice has the same seductive hold on any young theoretical Fish as Freudian rhetoric has on its disciples. It withholds "assumptions" in just the same way Freud withholds "origins"—now you see them, now you don't—according to the father's anal pleasure. Thus, Fish controls "change" in his community by claiming that for anything to count as change—oh, you theorists!—it must *already* have occurred in his community. Here is *Nachträglichkeit* with a paternal vengeance. In the name of rhetoric, Fish and Freud exercise the same anal control over the history of their respective professions. They seduce readers in the same fashion. "The thesis of psychoanalysis is that one cannot get to the side of the unconscious; the thesis of this essay [Fish on Freud] is that one cannot get to the side of rhetoric."[7]

But surely Fish is aware of his own elite position in the critical community? And does this not result in a higher form of leftist critical consensus that is exclusionary in its own way? If we were to dispute the practices of Fish's interpretative community we should surely need to appeal to the text, if not to the author—and why not, since we argue with Fish and his text? After all, to appeal to the text does not eliminate the differences of interpretation as though they were coffee stains. Rather, it makes interpretative difference arguable and, for a time, may settle them. We can erase neither the text nor the minds of the writer and reader, however much this might suit the conceit of the critic. Moreover, I think that in the end we would be worse off as writers and readers if critics were able to lord it over us as they do in the university, where reason and freedom are not especially the order of the day. Rather, I believe that both writers and readers enjoy the switching back and forth between the "readerly" and the "writerly" aspects of the text, such as occurs in Montaigne's *Essays* (see chapter 12), where the image of the scale captures how the author and the reader weigh themselves against the measure of the text.

Fish's metaphor of "self-consuming artifacts" may be intended to save the productivity of the reader, but to do so it reinstates the imbalance created by the destruction of the text by weighing the reader's affections in the scale of the interpretative community. Here, in fact, Fish loses the common sense of Montaigne's reader in preference for the sociological consensus subscribed to by the ethnic or professional reader despite the rhetoric of textual and interpretative free play. Ultimately, Fish's reader is "read by" the interpretative community within which he or she chooses a text for this exercise of critico-legal competence:

> Intention and understanding are two ends of a conventional act, each of which necessarily stipulates (includes, defines, specifies) the other. To construct the profile of the informed or at-home reader is at the same time to characterize its author's intention and vice versa, because to do either is to specify the *contemporary* conditions of utterance, to identify, by becoming a member of, a community made up of those who share interpretive strategies.[8]

Indeed, Fish's sociologism—actually his confident professionalism—raises not only the question whether there is a text in the class but also whether there is a reader in the class. The answer to both of Fish's questions is that for a given class (of readers) there are texts that are occasions for the display of "class" consciousness of the rules of the current literary game. In this way O'Neill's question is spirited away. Given the perversity of the current cultural scene, we may have to wait until the announcement of the death of the class question reanimates the literary community as much as it was fired by Nietzsche's posting of the divine obituary.

Having confronted Fish's question with O'Neill's question in a rather crude way, I propose to rephrase the contrast with Fish's question with two variants of the class-text question as they might be taken from the critical works of Edward Said[9] and Fredric Jameson.[10] Again with some violence, I shall reformulate their respective critical questions as follows:

CT 4: What are the lines of affiliation in this text?
CT 5: Where is the utopian class in this text?

As a "traveling theorist" himself, Said's critical task is to keep abreast with every literary movement that permits him to reformulate the class-text question (*CT*) as the question of the exclusion of all other cultural groups than those organized within the colonial canon or museum (*CT* 4). The canon of world literature that has been taught in Europe and North America as the foundation of a humanist culture is now revised as an instrument of expropriation, prejudices, and oppression, inasmuch as it silences the voice of the greater part of humanity. Indeed, if postmodernism reflects anything it expresses the current failure of nerve—the failure of "filiation" as Said would say—among those charged with handing on the imperial and patriarchal canon. The crisis of filiation that haunts modernist literature (Joyce, Eliot, Mann, Proust) gives rise to the critical question of discerning a shift from weak filiation to new bonds of "*affiliation*":

> Childless couples, orphaned children, aborted childbirths, and unregenerated celibate men and women populate the world of high modernism with remarkable insistence, all of them suffering difficulties of filiation. But no less important in my opinion is the second part of the pattern, which is immediately consequent upon the first, the pressure to produce new and different ways of conceiving human relationships. . . . What I am describing is the transition from a failed idea or possibility of *filiation* to a kind of compensatory order that, whether it is a party, an institution, a culture, a set of beliefs, or even a world-vision, provides men and women with a new form of relationship, which I have been calling *affiliation* but which is also a new system.[11]

Since I share Said's broadly Viconian concept of social institutions, and I have elsewhere developed my own views on communicative sociology in this vein,[12] I shall limit my comments to showing how Said's vision of an institutional history moving from filiation to affiliation, or from *Gesellschaft* to *Gemeinschaft,* simultaneously involves revising the critical practice of literary institutions. Affiliative criticism, therefore, challenges the following assumptions built into the literary canon:

> (i) . . . the almost unconsciously held assumption that the Eurocentric model for the humanities actually represents a natural and proper subject matter for the humanistic scholar. Its authority comes not only from the orthodox canon of literary monuments handed down through the generations, but also from the way this continuity reproduces the filial continuity of the chain of biological creation. What we then have is a substitution of one sort of order, in the process of which everything that is nonhumanistic and nonliterary and non-European is deposited outside the structure.[13]
>
> (ii) . . . the assumption that the principle relationships in the study of literature—those I have identified as based on representation—ought to obliterate the traces of other relationships within literary structures that are based upon acquisition and appropriation . . . none of which can be accounted for in the framework rigidly maintained by the processes of representation and affiliation doing above-ground work for the conversation of filiation.[14]

Because affiliative criticism challenges the canonical principles of exclusion and filiation, it necessarily reworks the methodological elements in Fish's question that have to do with the relative weight of subjective and objective criticism, or the ratio between textual authority and the critical reader's implied community of interpretation. Thus the affiliative critic will want to be concerned with the following set of questions with regard to the potential class in the text:

> How does the critic approach, choose and enter the text?
> How does the critic take a stance—identifying with the text, or with the reader or neither—that fulfills the critic's intention?
> How does the critic deal with the marginality of criticism to its text—is it a text itself, an intervention between texts, or a movement relating the world, the text, and the critic?[15]

The critical essay is inevitably caught in the ironic insufficiency that separates its form and practice from the life-and-death questions and the world historical context into which it seeks to insert itself as a revisionary mode of human relationships. Today, moreover, criticism is in serious danger of disappearing into its own labyrinth, incapable of returning to furnish the world with even a temporary shelter, let alone a home for the mind. Criticism, Geoffrey Hartmann observes gleefully (even if from that side of Yale that does not see black New Haven), is busy creating a "wilderness." All the same, the wilderness is mappable, and Said provides us with a useful grid in which to locate the principle issues:

> (1) Criticism as scholarship, humanism, as "servant" to text, mimetic in its bias, *versus* criticism as revisionism and as itself a form of literature . . .
> (2) The role of critic as teacher and good reader: safeguarding the canon *versus* subverting it or creating a new one . . .
> (3) Criticism as detached from the political/social world *versus* criticism as a form of philosophical metaphysics, psychoanalysis, linguistics, or any of these, *versus* criticism as actually having to do with such "contaminated" fields of history, the media, and economic systems . . .
> (4) Criticism as a criticism of language (language as negative theology, as private dogma, as a historical metaphysics) *versus* criticism as an analysis of the language of institutions *versus* criticism as a study of the relationships between language and nonlinguistic things.[16]

The question is whether we are to regard these options as an open shelf of possibilities constituting no single class perspective for criticism—in which case the classroom is served cafeteria style and the teacher is in line with the students, his or her own tastes forbidding either first or last place at the literary banquet. That scenario is a more than likely one, inasmuch as the postmodern critic will want to "play" with the canon, either to encourage the critical powers of youth or because today's classroom is no longer filled with the children of a culturally confident white elite whose loss of nerve makes it a poor reader of Northrop Frye's biblical code. It will be remembered how, earlier, Marshall McLuhan had hoped that postliterate youth would leap through the eye of the TV set into global tribalization, affiliation, or ecumenism.[17]

In Canada, our double marginality with respect to Franco-German and Anglo-American culture—the framework of my entire intellectual life—allows us to waver between lamentation over and sudden conversion to cultural free trade—as I show in my *Plato's Cave*. It is therefore remarkable to us that Jameson should have drawn such inspiration from Frye's allegory of the civilized mind in refurbishing his own version of the class-text question as the definitive question in humanist studies and as such the unabridged legacy of Marxist literary criticism. Let us repeat our reformulation of Jameson's question:

CT 5: Where is the utopian class in this text?

It is, of course, surprising if not reckless of Jameson to raise the class-text question in the midst of postmodernism, where he is as much embroiled as anyone else. In fact, he is capable of losing his way on this scene as much as anyone else even when he acts as a guide, as we shall see in the following chapter. Yet amid all the critical debris, in the din of deconstructionism and the glitter of diamond dust shoes, Jameson sounds out the sacred trumpet of a transcendental truth: "It is the proposition that *all* class consciousness—or in other words, all ideology in the strongest sense, including the most exclusive forms of ruling-class consciousness just as much as that of oppositional or oppressed classes—is in its very nature *Utopian*."[18]

The extraordinary catholicity of Jameson's formulation of the class question must be emphasized, since it means to avoid any narrow model of class conflict or a reductive socialist realism. Yet his utopian formula is underwritten by a number of subtheorems that ought not to be overlooked:

(i) The oppressed class realizes its solidarity before the dominant class;

(ii) the *truth* of ruling-class consciousness is to be found in working-class consciousness;

(iii) It is unnecessary to argue these quite correct propositions;

(iv) the achieved collectivity or organic group of whatever kind—oppressors fully as much as oppressed—is Utopian not in itself, but only insofar as all such collectivities are themselves *figures* for the ultimate concrete life of an achieved Utopian or classless society.[19]

These interpretative theorems then permit us to ask of a specific text the following subset of questions in exploration of the utopian marriage between individual and collective desire:

(a) Where is *desire* in the text?

(b) Where is the *collective body* in the text?

(c) Where is the *political unconscious* in the text?

As Jameson argues, the unavoidable relationship—the family romance, one might say—between Marxism and post-Freudianism requires that the body politic be the shaping element of love's body, so that we really need a sociology of the body—which I have developed elsewhere[20]—in order not to repeat the errors of a regressive political psychology deriving from the culture of narcissism and the corporate agenda that underwrites it. In this respect Jameson and myself are unrepentant medieval Marxists: "A social hermeneutic will . . . wish to keep faith with its medieval percursor in just this respect, and must necessarily restore a perspective in which the imagery of libidinal revolution and of bodily transfiguration once again becomes a figure for the perfected community."[21]

Said and Jameson deserve equal credit for not shying away from the ultimately religious question that lies behind the secular scriptures even when they have been refigured as class or affiliative texts. Said never shrinks from an appeal to the religious concepts of authority in which all civil culture is grounded. He, of course, starts from a Viconian or what we might call an Orphic perspective—which I develop in chapter 17—whereas Jameson starts from what we shall call a promethean perspective: culture as theft restored, a hope that few of us will want to abandon. Of course, there is a considerable danger here that leftist, secular criticism will turn into the path of neoconservatism, just as there is a danger that the elite cultural groups within neoconservatism will find themselves in alliance with the most irrational regressive elements of fundamentalism. Only philistines will turn away from these difficulties:

> It would be a great relief to break with the idea of the sacred, and especially with institutions that claim to mediate it. Yet the institution of language makes every such break appear inauthentic. It keeps us in the "defile of the word," meeting, staying, purifying what is held to be sacred or sublime again and again. The very persistence, moreover, of so many and various ideals of language purification betrays something religious in spirit, if not in name.
>
> Yet if we turn from religion, philosophy, psychoanalysis, linguistics, and so forth to literary criticism, and acknowledge its separate status, it is because we need that garden in the wilderness.[22]

For the rest, we have to consider how far secular culture can exhaust its religious capital, however carefully it is spent on cultural surrogates. For a while, it seemed that elite culture could underwrite the social bond in class societies and that it could resist the charge that it has in fact contributed to the barbarization of large elements of humankind that it excluded from its purview. If postmodernism reflects anything, it reveals the double impact of a failure of nerve at the level of hitherto elite culture and a proliferation of (in)difference on the level of mass culture. Since the university now functions as one more shopping mall, we can expect it to operate with the same deep discount values offered elsewhere. To do so, it will employ, and it already does, a wide range of languages that will effectively fragment its culture and internal politics even further. At some point, the effort to translate those languages will cease, since no one will have any memory of our first community.

The critical voice, then, currently insists on the abandonment of a separatist aesthetics with its comfortable expectancy of an eventual marriage of beauty and justice in the political realm. Despite the unhappy results of the shotgun marriage with socialist realism and the obvious commercialization of wall art, corporate sculpture, and touristic museums, literary critics remain convinced that "texts" would somehow survive and that they would even thrive on their frontline use in politics and social reform. Obviously, to debate the issue in these broad terms is pointless. We need to know which books, poems, and works of art—and what specific strategies they display—could possibly prove to be effective instruments with respect to ideological criticism, political reform, and social change in equally specific sectors of society. That academic critics know how to answer this question with respect to curricular and current conference programs has about as much relevance to the democratic political process as free food and drink at Las Vegas. By the same token, the low stakes make academic literary politics a rough business.

In short, we can say that the less real are politics outside of the classroom the more real they become inside the class. But the more the classroom becomes political while social classes become less political, the more academic politics of the right and left acquire conservative and establishment functions, babysitting themselves and the student body. Consider how few people ever read a book, much less buy one, after leaving the university. Think how few of them can think critically, remember how inarticulate they are before, during, and after the time they are in school, or college and university.

Just as the corporate world was beginning to expand the university system and to reconstruct it on the model of the multiuniversity, the Pax Americana disintegrated in the unsuccessful and unpopular wars of the 1960s and 1970s. Like everyone else, students and professors discovered the killing end of history and politics packaged for American hard sell. The distance between middle-class white Americans, Vietnamese peasants, and American blacks seemed to narrow, and indeed, in the university the erasure of such differences became the order of the day. A minoritarian ethic was espoused, enabling a larger number of people to politicize their social needs. Women became one half of the visible society. It is these changes that have reworked the curriculum and changed the professional face of America. With incredible speed, a resistance literature has emerged and in fact now operates its own canon, curriculum, and career institutions. The result is a brilliant spectacle of people who are increasingly knowledgeable about how institutions think and speak and how to capture and rechannel institutional discourses. Society appears to be a text, and the text to be alterable by means of fresh readings. Literary criticism, and not philosophy, wins the political crown. Moreover, even the business of philosophy is best taught by literary critics, as Rorty urges, since they can be relied on to eradicate the essentialism, realism, and holism that have reduced our lives in favor of totalitarian institutions wearing the false face of universal humanism.

Now, we ought never to lose the political insights we have won from the critical analysis of official discourses. By the same token, we cannot ignore the broader political economy in which official discourses are produced, that is, the bureaucratic, corporate, and governmental institutions that command national and global economies. It really is time for us to take up this "intertext." Otherwise, criticism right and left remain equally suspended in a phantasmic conception of the irreality of institutions as self-consuming artifacts of the postmodern and now post-Communist world. The world may not be "outside" the text, but it certainly is not "inside" it. We will have recreated an even more perverse idealism if, after all we have learned from discourse analysis and rhetorical deconstruction, we expropriate political economy in the name of "textual power," as Scholes calls it. In short, the critic must be a Janus figure, able to face both ways, because it is necessary to be able to switch the bias of power and interpretation as required by the real political and historical situation that confronts us.

We currently impose on ourselves the bad sublime of a moral height from which, in the midst of our own postmodern rubble, we consider critical studies to rule all past history, politics, and morality. That sublime is rendered all the more vertiginous by Lyotard's destructive gesture toward the stories of the past and his blindness toward the global political economy now disembarrassed of any countercultural narrative than the new minoritarian ethics it can so easily subsidize. The success of Lyotard's pronouncements—like Rorty's ironic liberalism—do not reflect the ascendancy of criticism's own intelligence so much as the achieved exhaustion and irrelevance of criticism in a world where anything goes and anything does. Rather, these speculative options only continue to appear open because in fact a violent closure is imposed elsewhere in practices that are still grounded in class, race, and imperial exploitation. But these lack a fashionable discourse. Nor is anything helped by placing them under the banner of (anti)apartheid or of "the" holocaust in the hope that those events will be the last of humanity's bad memories. Such gestures are sacrilegious because we have no single atrocity to which history can be reduced. Rather, literature must remember the story that each one of us is trying to tell.

CHAPTER 3

Baudelairizing
Postmodernism
Hyperreading

The less we understand a poet, the more he is compulsively misinterpreted and oversimplified and made to say the opposite of what he actually said, the better the chances are that he is truly modern; that is, different from what we—mistakenly—think we are ourselves. This would make Baudelaire into a truly modern German poet and Wordsworth and Yeats into truly modern English poets.

—Paul de Man[1]

Fredric Jameson has recently urged that we read Baudelaire as a postmodern lyricist like himself.[2] Now whereas both Baudelaire and Walter Benjamin insist on the need to bind modernity to "times out of mind," Jameson separates them. He makes no reference at all to Benjamin in his essay, although his own program in *The Political Unconscious* would in fact need to recognize a common insistence on modernity's need to preserve cultural memory in order to fuel its utopian future. Here I propose to examine how such a reading of Baudelaire is produced. Since I consider Jameson's practice to be arbitrary and self-indulgent, I should explain why I think so in the interest of readers whose "response" to such virtuoso performances is likely to be lost in dissonance. In part, as I shall show in the following chapter, Jameson's errant criticism derives from his reliance on Jean Baudrillard's semiotics of political economy[3] rather than Benjamin's more relevant literary criticism. But my concern is not to teach Jameson what he already knows. It is to show what Jameson teaches others who may not know the price they pay (the opportunity cost) for consuming his critical product. I want therefore to show how Jameson produces a reading of a fragment from Baudelaire, since by now he has patented his version of a considerable number of texts with which we all work.[4] My purpose is to show how leftist criticism must be careful in what it teaches precisely because it raises great expectations.

How do we read lyric poetry? The question pays deference to our own historicism in the sense that it offers to limit our understanding with our understanding of limits. Our sense of the limits of our categories of thought may be due to Immanuel Kant; our sense of limit as the limits of our language might be due to Ludwig Wittgenstein, or the Martin Heidegger and Jacques Derrida. Inasmuch as our modernity is conditioned by the double limit of thought and language, or by our inextricable blindness and insight, we might understand our modernity as a difficult lyric, with Baudelaire its major poet and Benjamin its major literary critic. Modernity, literature, the self, and history are moments in an ebb and flow that confirms the weight of literature and history on the self's poetry through its very denials.[5] Or rather, in each case, the modalities of truth and error do not separate in any absolute way; neither achieves priority anywhere in the self, in history, or in literature.

In such circumstances, only an extreme synecdochal strategy can save things from fragmentation—and such is the lyrical gesture in Baudelaire and Benjamin, two of modernity's ragpicker poets.[6] Yet whereas these two believed that their artistic goal was to make modernism worthy of antiquity, to preserve the historical tension between forgetfulness and memory:

> Paris change! mais rien dans ma mélancolie
> N'a bougé! Palais neufs, échafaudages, blocs,
> Vieux faubourgs, tout pour moi devient allégorie,
> Et mes chers souvenirs sont plus lourds que des rocs.

> Paris changes . . . But in sadness like mine
> nothing stirs—new buildings, old
> neighbourhoods turn to allegory,
> and memories weigh more than stone.[7]

Jameson insists nonetheless upon reading Baudelaire as a postmodern lyricist. In order to fix upon such an interpretation of Baudelaire's "postmodernism," it is essential for Jameson to multiply the text, to spin it so that his reader is on the merry-go-round of postmodern criticism, giddily flying past the sober interpretations of Baudelaire that wait for the stomach once the ride is over.

But first, let us see how we are enticed onto Jameson's fairground. How are we drawn away from what we thought we knew until Jameson made his pitch? Well, the first temptation would be to deal with the old coconuts of modernist interpretation which Jameson knocks down with a single throw:

1. a second-rate post-Romantic Baudelaire . . . (247) the Baudelaire of
   diabolism and of a cheap frisson . . . the poet of blasphemy (247)

Here we leave Ezra Pound and Henry James in tears. But they should
have grown up. We hesitate at another stand before dashing on:

2. Baudelaire contemporary of himself (247)

This one, Jameson confesses, is too hard to get at, and instead he
proposes we move on to two more mock-ups or "Baudelaire-simula-
cra"—"Jameson grotesques" might be more accurate—which are
identical with item 2 while distinct in themselves (supposing that
makes sense):

3. Baudelaire, inaugural poet of high modernism (247)
4. The Baudelaire of postmodernism (245)

Jameson confesses that he feels safer riding the third hobbyhorse,
since its pleasures and pain could be argued about, like everything
else in the realist world of high modernism. But he appeals to our
sense of adventure to engage with his own prophetic loss of the
referent and asks us to jump on the image machine and to spin with
it until we have gained sufficient interpretative momentum to re-
experience the postmodern sublime. Once this is achieved, we shall
have distilled Baudelaire from modernism and released him for the
postmodern spectacle. Or shall we have lost all sense of each? After all,
Jameson's contrast between modernism and postmodernism requires
considerable indulgence. Why should we accord it to him? He asks
that we allow him to define modernism in terms of naïve realism
rather than the exploration of realist fiction and that we then permit
him to exclude Baudelaire from his own exploration of these issues
by setting him down on the side of postmodernism, where, as I
believe, fiction is the new realism precisely because of its lack of any
vision. After all, Andy Warhol's soup cans are hardly flowers of
evil! We shall need to return later to the considerable issue of the
indulgence Jameson begs from the reader in order to float his anachronistic and violent readings of the text, or rather, the simulacra spun
off the text to service Jameson's will to reinterpretation (or is this
Jameson's one-man class war on the canon?)

At this point, we need to turn to the texts of Baudelaire on which
Jameson builds his argument for a postmodern reading. The first item

is the first part of "Chant d'automne." No reason is given for the exclusion of the second part (I return to this question and its interpretative consequences later on). Furthermore, the translation by Richard Howard cannot be accepted without some commentary.[8] In order to mark this effect, then, let us add a fifth Baudelaire-simulacrum, even though its full treatment would overextend our argument:

5. The Baudelaire translated by Richard Howard

It is surprising that a critic as sophisticated as Jameson should indicate no awareness of the issue of interpretation in translation. It is, however, a strategic oversight, since Howard's translation often sacrifices a referential reading for a subjective reading rather than preserve Baudelaire's tension between those fictional options. Such effects service Jameson's theory of the postmodern shift in Baudelaire's sensibility. Nevertheless, it is necessary to give the text as Jameson uses it, except to give it in full:[9]

Chant d'Automne

Bientôt nous plongerons dans les froides ténèbres;
Adieu, vive clarté de nos étés trop courts!
J'entends déja tomber avec des chocs funèbres
Le bois retentissant sur le pavé des cours.

Tout l'hiver va rentrer dans mon être: colère,
Haine, frissons, horreur, labeur dur et forcé
Et, comme le soleil dans son enfer polaire,
Mon coeur ne sera plus qu'un bloc rouge et glacé.

J'écoute en frémissant chaque bûche qui tombe;
L'échafaud qu'on bâtit n'a pas d'écho plus sourd.
Mon espirit est pareil à la tour qui succombe
Sous les coups du bélier infatigable et lourd.

Il me semble, bercé par ce choc monotone,
Qu'on on cloue en grande hâte un cercueil quelque part.
Pour qui?—C'était hier l'été; voici l'automne!
Ce bruit mystérieux sonne comme un départ.

2
J'aime de vos longs yeux la lumière verdâtre,
Douce beauté, mais tout aujourd'hui m'est amer,
Et rien, ni votre amour, ni le boudoir, ni l'âtre,
Ne me vaut le soleil rayonnant sur la mer.

Et pourtant aimez-moi, tendre coeur! soyez mère,
Même pour un ingrat, même pour un méchant;
Amante ou soeur, soyez la douceur éphémère
D'un glorieux automne ou d'un soleil couchant.

Courte tâche! La tombe attend; elle est avide!
Ah! laissez-moi, mon front pose sur vos genoux,
Goûter, en regrettant l'été blanc et torride,
De l'arrière-saison le rayon jaune et doux!

Autumnal

Soon cold shadows will close over us and
summer's transitory gold be gone;
I hear them chopping firewood in our court—
the dreary thud of logs on cobblestone.

Winter will come to repossess my soul
with rage and outrage, horror, drudgery,
and like the sun in its polar holocaust
my heart will be a block of blood-red ice.

I listen trembling to that grim tattoo—
build a gallows, it would sound the same.
My mind becomes a tower giving way
under the impact of a battering-ram.

Stunned by the strokes, I seem to hear, somewhere,
a coffin hurriedly hammered shut—for whom?
Summer was yesterday; autumn is here!
Strange how that sound rings out like a farewell.

2
How sweet the greenish light of your long eyes!
But even that turns bitter now, and nothing
—not love, the boudoir, nor its busy hearth—
can match the summer's radiance on the sea.

Love me still, my darling! I am your naughty boy.
Sister and mistress! be the fleeting warmth
of a sumptuous autumn or a setting sun.

Your chore will be brief—the grave is covetous!
so let me rest my forehead on your knees
and relish, as I mourn white summer's lapse,
the yellow favor of the waning year.

Jameson starts us off gently, pointing to his own "modest" use of "the commonsense language of everyday life." Such an approach permits the claim that the poem conveys three experiences, of which the first is

a. "a feeling of some kind, strong and articulated, yet necessarily nameless" (249)

This "vague but articulated [sic]" feeling could be "anxiety" or something quite different, like "sadness." Whichever it is, the feeling would not sit well with the feeling of "anticipation" in the poem. Yet it does not matter, since such questions belong to:

6. The Baudelaire of an aesthetic of expression (249)

But then we are not to be beguiled by the game of hunt the psychological referent ("emotion"), because Jameson is simply ("virtually by definition") not interested in it. So we turn to the remaining two experiences, to the "banal informing presence" of:

b. "a season—*fall*" (250)
c. "a physical perception, an auditory event or experience, *the hollow sound of logs and firewood being delivered*" (250)

Here we should note that Jameson reduces autumn, the season of harvest and maturity, to its American association with the fall of leaves. This is unfortunate, since "Chant d'automne" is concerned with what we reap from our youthful passions, that is, with a more universal and appropriate imagery and sensibility of autumn than that aroused by the fall of leaves, as Americans experience it.[10] Actually, it is the *fall of the chopped logs* that carries the experience here. Unfortunately, Jameson again misinterprets this as the sound of *logs being delivered*—more prosaic and quite wrong, unless we project Baudelaire into Jameson's postmodern consumer high in a New York apartment house. The same is true of the image of "fall." Nothing is required of us for the trees to lose their leaves, whereas the harvest is not reaped apart from what we have sown, and old age not reached without cutting us off from our youth. Furthermore, Jameson's gloss on the activity of chopping logs in a Parisian courtyard sharply opposes the orders of Nature and the City, whereas the very charm of old Paris is their overlap, a certain modus vivendi, and not the violent antithesis rendered by Jameson's American urbanism.[11]

Having gratuitously introduced his own conflictual imagery of

Nature and the City, in abstraction from their complementary status in the wood-heated apartments of nineteenth-century Paris and from their remetaphorization in Baudelaire's response to the shift in the seasons of nature and of his own life, Jameson proceeds to extrapolate this interpretative divergence through an extraneous commentary on Heidegger's use of the imagery of World and Earth. Of course, Jameson immediately permits himself to "rewrite" the Heideggerian pair in terms of his own Marxist pair, History and Nature. As Jameson reads "Origins of the Work of Art," Heidegger tells us that we inhabit two worlds, one of which is meaningful, while the other is meaningless. Even if we suppose Heidegger to have taken such a view of History and Nature (in fact, this is definitely not his understanding of the relation between Earth and World),[12] and however refined the contrast might actually be in Heidegger, what is to be gained from alleged reflections on the work of art as the work of reminding us of its inability to heal this "rift"? Given that Jameson has to apologize for Heidegger's own naturalization of history in the politics of *Blut und Boden*, one might wonder about the advisability of this interpretative gesture. This is all the more the case when one recalls that if Jameson had appealed to Marx at this point, he would have found a flat rejection of the concept of the two histories of society and nature: "Nature as it is formed in human history—the birth process of human society—is [the] real nature of man and thus nature as fashioned by industry is true anthropological nature, though in an alienated form."[13]

Furthermore, had Jameson traded less on Heiddeger for flash effect and more on Marx, he might also have approached Baudelaire's view on these issues. That is to say, rather than proceed to the assertion that "Chant d'automne" can be read *both* as the staging of the gap between nature and society *and* as their nomadic interface (Jameson does express a worry about the "price" of such a reading), one could just as well show that neither Baudelaire nor Marx believed in a concept of nature outside of history. Baudelaire's views on this probably owe as much to his Christianity as to his preference for the urbanity of that artificial paradise to be found in the cafés and boudoirs of Paris but which Jameson can view only in terms of later theories of kitsch, *toc,* and the Victorian sublime.

Withdrawing from his Heideggerian meditation, Jameson proposes to tackle the "drearier humdrum sense" of Baudelaire's historical context. It should be observed that Jameson's use of pejorative characterization is a subterfuge for any proper methodological discussion of the interpretative contexts he constructs in order to float his own theories. From a pedagogical standpoint, they are exploitative of readers without the resources to check the referents, although, of course, they may serve to bind his own interpretative community. With this in mind, I shall comment on Jameson's next move. He begins with a characterization of high modernism as it is to be found in the conventional wisdom (and here he refers to Roland Barthes, of all people). Thus high modernism is framed as a breakdown in the constitution of public rhetoric and reading and, in the midst of general fragmentation, as a flight into style and the private self. Jameson's "tradition," presumably his Marxism, locates the shift from rhetoric to style in terms of the logic of capitalism, more specifically, in its increasing capacity for the refraction of experience. Jameson then claims that Baudelaire's experience as a poet can be conceived as a linguistic struggle with an ever-transcendent referent that escapes the poet, much as the commodity escapes labor. At this point the reading of "Chant d'automne" begins, and here we need to pay particular attention to how Jameson ascribes to it an aesthetic that he believes renders the poem a precipitate of postmodernism:

> The referent in "Chant d'Automne" is not particularly mysterious or difficult of access: it is simply the body itself, or better still, the bodily sensorium. Better yet, it is the bodily perception—better still even more neutral a term, the sensation—which mobilizes the body as its instrument of perception and brings the latter into being over against it. The referent here is then simply a familiar sound, the hollow reverberation of logs striking the courtyard paving. Yet familiar for whom? Everything, and the very mysteries of modernism itself, turn on this word, about which we must admit, in a first moment, that it no longer applies to any contemporary readership. But in a second moment, I will be less concerned to suggest ways in which, even for Baudelaire's contemporaries, such a reference might have been in the process of becoming exotic or obscure, than rather to pose as a principle of social fragmentation the withdrawal of the private or the individual body from social discourse. (252)

Since Terry Eagleton[14] finds Jameson's prose admirable, I think it is worth remarking on it, if only with respect to this passage (Robert Scholes has commented on Jameson's use of mediation to the same damaging effect)[15] rather than attribute to it a sense that is hardly found there prima facie. Consider, then, how Jameson sets up the search for the referent of the poem in order to lose it. The referent is

> Simply the body itself—"or better still"
> The bodily sensorium—or "better yet"
> The bodily perception—or "better still"
> The sensation (253)

While it is nice to watch Jameson improve his mark, at least in his own eye, it cannot be said that this progression of terms—which lacks, incidentally, any attempt to consider their phenomenological complexity—is appropriate to Baudelaire's vocabulary of "my soul," "my heart," "my mind" (Howard's translation) and the sense of hearing or *imagined* hearing. But then Jameson turns around to say that the referent is

> Simply a familiar sound (252)

However, the truth of this start, or restart, is too obvious. So we must try to lose it. Jameson thus raises the critical question, "Yet familiar for whom?" (252). Jameson proposes the question on behalf of Baudelaire's postmodern readership, apparently already unable to find any familiar resonance in the sound of logs being chopped in a Parisian courtyard on an autumn day in preparation for winter's cold, if not already for the autumn nights. (There really can be no mystery in this for anyone who knows how much Paris, London, and Rome, which still offer chilly accommodation all year round!) So "Chant d'automne," as we have it so far, is not a poem whose opening lines are about the sun's withdrawal at the end of the summer and preparations to keep body and soul together with a little heat from a log fire. So far from invoking such immediate bodily perception and working from a familiar visceral experience, those opening lines are considered by Jameson to initiate the postmodern problematic of the isolation of bodily sensation, and thus their referent becomes

> The withdrawal of the private or the individual body from social discourse (252)

Through this progression of referents from the familiar to the unfamiliar, Jameson has managed to accomplish the following readings:

A gratuitous attribution of psychological vocabulary whose positivism he
will proceed to criticize

A return to the obvious referent, although with no sense of its status in
the poet's own imaginary sensibility

A loss of that referent in favor of an interpretative hypothesis drawn from
Marxist social theory concerning the loss of any public or familiar
discourse of experience due to the logic of fragmentation and isolation
in capitalist society

Having attributed to Baudelaire a positivist psychology of sensory
experience quite alien to his usage, Jameson proceeds to employ this
move to "sharpen the problem of reference," again overlooking his
own fudging of it. Thus the alleged unfamiliarity of namelessness of
the sound of the logs being chopped is assimilated to an (in)describ-
able body pain, which challenges the arts of medical semioticians and
their literary counterpart.

Having assigned them to hunt for a nameless sensation, Jameson
then proceeds to put the game into its proper historical perspective,
with due weight assigned to its objective and subjective dimensions:

> I would like to make an *outrageous* (or at least, as they say, unverifiable)
> generalization, namely, that before Baudelaire and Flaubert there are no
> physical sensations in literature. . . . It does mean, *more modestly,* and on
> the side of the object (or the literary raw material) that free-floating bodily
> perception was not, until now, felt to be a proper content for literary
> language. . . . And it means, on the side of the subject, or of literary
> language itself, that the older rhetoric was *somehow* fundamentally nonper-
> ceptual, and had not yet "produced" the referent in our current sense.
> (253, my emphasis)

I have chosen to emphasize Jameson's modifiers in order to mark
how he employs a sheer assertion, which he then criticizes as though
to correct someone else's rash judgement. Here the claim is that there
is no psychological literature or literary psychology before Baudelaire.
The obvious distortion in this self-aggrandizing remark moves Jameson toward his own modesty so that his observation is apparently
reduced (in fact, it is no less extraordinary) to the claim that we have
a literary psychology only when sensations are not merely signs of
external referents, such as wealth or social status, but are irreducibly
scandalous and resistant to symbolic reunification.

Jameson then adopts the strategy of interpreting "Chant d'automne"
in terms of two grids: metonymy and metaphor. In the first move-

ment, autumn's positive associations (of maturity, harvest) are associated with an ominous loss (end of summer, death). The poem, according to Jameson, oscillates between metonymy and metaphor so that the sound of wood being chopped into logs is like the sound of a scaffold being erected or of a coffin being nailed up. In either case, he says, the poem ends in negativity. Here I note that Jameson neglects part 2 of the poem, whereas its consideration would alter such a premature conclusion. To this I return later. Meanwhile, Jameson reverses his conclusion:

> This is of course not altogether true: and a complete reading of the poem (not my purpose here) would want to underscore the wondrous reappearance of the place of the subject in the next line—the naive and miraculous, "Pour qui?" and the utter restructuration of the temporal system, in which the past is now abandoned, the new present—now defined, not negatively as the end of summer, but positively as autumn—reaffirmed to the point at which the very sense datum of the sound itself becomes a promise rather than a fatality. (254)

Why Baudelaire's "For whom?" should be read as the point of "naive and miraculous" reversal in the poem is not obvious, especially since the second half of the poem has been omitted (why excuse Jameson from "a complete reading"?).

Phenomenologically considered, "Chant d'automne" reverberates from the very beginning in the ear of the poet/reader alerted to autumn's sounds of preparation against winter's silence. Such sounds—and sights, though these are not the perceptual modality in question here—are part of a traditional experience, communal and cyclical, that has not yet been destroyed.[16] Moreover, that experience is saved and not lost in the poem, any more than the ritual of execution and burial that resonates in it. Thus the poem turns upon three interwoven cycles: the cycle of the seasons, the life cycle of the poet, and the love cycle with Marie Daubrun. Each cycle is overlaid with the others, so that the body's warmth and cold are modes of the seasons of summer and winter and of woman, who is quite absent from Jameson's lexicon. In turn, those seasons are mediated by autumn and the preparations within which the life and death of the tree give warmth and life to those huddled around the hearth in winter. Despite Jameson's fiction of the conflict between Nature and the City, home heating has to be fueled by oil or gas to lose its traditional symbolism—except where gas heaters are sculpted into log fires, or unused logs sit in the unused fireplaces of gas- and oil-heated homes. Such observations require an unpardonable appeal to the real world of work and consumption, which unfortunately lies without honor in Jameson's hermeneutics. Having said as much, I should add that none of this has much to do with anything *in* the poem, but much to do with what is *about* the poem, once Jameson gets hold of it.

But Jameson demands further indulgence for his interpretation of "Chant d'automne." He insists that our understanding of two phenomena that we have sufficiently examined—namely, the production of the referent (the hollow sound) and the emergence of modernism—be related to the crisis of the reading public ("For whom?"). According to Jameson, it is the public, itself a consequence of social fragmentation, that makes it impossible to identify the poem's referent—the hollow sound. But, of course, the sounds are not "hollow." Nor are they a "dreary thud," as translated by Richard Howard, since "dreary" loses specificity unless associated with what is gloomy about funerals. The sounds (*chocs funèbres*) are mournful, that is, like the measured steps of a funeral march, and thus funereal. In addition, the wood that warms life, when the blood is less able to do so in old age, will one day hold the cold corpse in the fires of heaven or hell that once inspired its youth. The loss of the referent is actually the work of Jameson and Howard in tandem. It is not the poem, therefore, that pursues endless metonymy but Jameson's own text, which unnecessarily struggles to fill in voids that it has itself created. In fact, we may reject Jameson's imputation of a crisis in the reading public of "Chant d'automne." The latter is nothing but an effect of Jameson's own desire to sweep away referents, in fact, to "eclipse" (255) them while claiming that they thereby reappear.

> This crisis in readership then returns us to our other theme, namely the production of the referent: a paradoxical way of putting it, you will say, since my ostensible topic was rather the "eclipse" or the "waning," the "disappearance" of the referent. I don't want to be overly subtle about all this, but it seems to me very important to understand that these two things are the same. The "production" of the referent—that is, the sense of some new unnameable ungenerizable private bodily sensation—something that must necessarily resist all language but which language lives by designing—is the same as the "bracketing" of that referent, its position-

ing as the "outside" of the text or the "other" language. The whole drama of modernism will lie here indeed, in the way in which its own peculiar life and logic depend on the reduction of reference to an absolute minimum and on the elaboration, in the former place of reference, of complex, symbolic, and often mythical frameworks and scaffolding: yet the latter depend on preserving a final tension between text and referent, on keeping alive one last shrunken point of reference, like a dwarf sun still growing feebly on the horizon on the modernist text. (255)

Before we allow Jameson to take us over the brink, let us retrace our steps. What, after all, is the poet saying in "Chant d'automne"? A poet enunciates poems. Everything in a poem is there to accomplish the poet's expression of his or her thoughts and feelings as responses to the source and sense they find in themselves and the world around the poet, which is always "poetically" a world within the poet mediated by the poem's composition both formal and material. So much for the bare bones of it, since we need no very elaborate theory of poetics in order to argue with Jameson's reading of Baudelaire— though we may need to know much more to deal with his Marxist hermeneutics.

I shall be brief. The steady chopping that Baudelaire hears in the courtyard repeats the maternal rhythms, or *chora,*[17] that bind the poet in original fascination with the mother-body and "sa douce langue natale," so that in responding to the question *Pour qui?* he can answer as a child, mother, lover, sister, anyone in need of love. Again, despite Jameson's theory of loss, I must insist on the constitutive power of repetition on the phonemic, syntactic, and semantic levels of the poem, which give it its quality as a *song* of autumn. Thus, it is only within the rise and fall of the song that the absence and presence, the *fort/da,* of the mother-body[18] floats toward the horizon and returns like the sun on Baudelaire, who in turn wanders, while rooted in fascination—*voyeur* and *voyageur:*

Invitation au Voyage

Mon enfant, ma soeur,
Songe à la donceur
D'aller là-bas vivre ensemble!
Aimer à loisir,
Aimer et mourir
Au pays qui te ressemble!

Les soleils mouillés
De ces ciels brouillés
Pour mon esprit ont les charmes
Si mystérieux
De tes traîtres yeux
Brilliant à travers leurs larmes.

Invitation to the Voyage

Imagine the magic
of living together
there, with all the time in the world
for loving each other,
for loving and dying
where even the landscape resembles you:
the sun dissolved
in overcast skies
have the same mysterious charms for me
as your wayward eyes
through crystal tears,
my sister, my child!
(Trans. by Richard Howard)[19]

"*Chant d'automne*" belongs to the love cycle for Marie Daubrun, the lady with green eyes: "J'aime de vos longs yeux la lumière verdâtre."[20] In this cycle, Baudelaire's love moves from an initial intoxication, greater than even wine or opium, which exudes from his lover's lips and eyes and which at its very height is poetry itself. By the same token, there lies at the heart of that intoxication a certain indifference, if not exhaustion, so that the moment of youth is never far from the time of old age, beauty never far from ugliness, and love on the turn to hatred. Indeed, in the heart of the poet light and darkness turn into one another, like the day into night or as the season of summer turns into winter through autumn's song. In such a cycle, Jameson notwithstanding, everything is renewed and not simply destroyed by spleen.[21] Above all, poetry itself is renewed in the poet as long as he is able to dedicate himself to his muse, madonna, or angel guardian, as to those green eyes in which like Narcissus he caught himself. And so the passion of the poet and his lover could rise and wane like the seasons of warmth and freezing cold for which the poet's heart and love is at once the free and falling log in the cycle of passion's life and death. If there is any connection here to "La mort des amants," to which Jameson appeals later on, it is through the mirrors of love loving itself in the poet like a woman with green eyes. Because that love never goes outside of itself it is also ambiguously maternal and sisterly—autumnal:

> Et pourtant aimez-moi, tendre coeur soyez mère
> Même pour un ingrat, même pour un méchant;
> Amante ou soeur, soyez la douceur éphèmere
> D'un glorieux automne ou d'un soleil couchant.

> Love me still, my darling, mother me,
> ungrateful though I am, your naughty boy
> Sister and mistress! be the fleeting warmth
> of a sumptuous autumn or a setting sun.[22]

Here, too, it might be as well to recall that, whatever Jameson makes of the referents in terms of his theory of Baudelaire's aesthetics of bad taste, the referent is Woman as an invitation to happiness, a voyage, a dream that emanates from her eyes, lips, movements, clothes, and perfume to carry the poet away and toward himself as poet of such flights of imagination and sensation. Moreover, it is always Baudelaire who is ravished in these moments. Himself the woman-she-cat:

> Quand mes yeux, vers ce chat que j'aime
> Tirés comme par un aimant,
> Se retournent docilement
> Et que je regarde en moi-même.

> Je vois avec étonnement
> Le feu de ses prunelles pâles
> Clairs fanaux, vivantes opales
> Qui me contemplent fixement.

> and when my spellbound eyes at last
>   relinquish worship of
> this cat they love to contemplate
>   and look inside myself,

> I find to my astonishment
>   like living opals there
> his fiery pupils, embers which
>   observe me fixedly.[23]

Thus a fire burns in the green eyes of Marie Daubrun, of the cat of the poet, each warming in the other a narcissism à deux, heartless and cold like the winter sun of "Chant d'automne." Or, to vary the metaphor slightly, there is no approach between Baudelaire and his lovers that does not keep their distance, no passion generated that is not cold, no similarity without difference—no child without its distant mother (see chapter 15, "The Mother Tongue").

Despite all this, Jameson presses on with his postmodern reading of Baudelaire. Again, he takes an extraordinary leap off Heidegger to argue that in Baudelaire language "is only the apartment of Being," and no longer "the house" of Being, due to the urban conquest of nature. Once more, Jameson's vision fails to capture the nature enclosed in the Parisian courtyard, not to mention the great boulevards and parks that gave nineteenth-century Paris its glory, whatever the strategic intentions of Georges Eugène Haussmann. Moreover, Baudelaire was more at home in the salons, galleries, cafés, and boudoirs of Paris than in any apartment. Furthermore, he is the poet of that public intimacy that draws everyone to Paris for its special bouquet. Yet Jameson wants to see in Baudelaire an apartment dweller, shut in like a corpse in the coffin he imagines he hears being nailed together in his courtyard. Indeed, he so insists on Baudelaire's fascination with furniture and the handicraft in coffin building that he entirely misses that "Alchimie de la douleur" from which he gives the following excerpt:

> Et sur les célestes rivages
> Je bâtis de grands sarcophages.
>
> to shroud my cherished dead,
> and on celestial shores I build
> enormous sepulchres. (256)

That poem is about Baudelaire's poetic capacity to so transform things that he can weave winding sheets from clouds and build sepulchres on heaven's shores—something quite beyond the capacity of any labor force, especially under late capitalism.

But there is a further aspect of this alchemical theme in Baudelaire to which we can only draw brief attention, whereas Jameson ignores it. It is the desire to conquer otherness,[24] to make of something what it is not, above all to eradicate the shock of sexual difference by prostituting the self in other selves, at the same time being prostituted by them:

Qu'est-ce que l'amour?
Le besoin de sortir de soi.
L'homme est un animal adorateur.
Adorer, c'est se sacrificier et se prostituer,
Aussi tout amour est-il prostitution.
What is love?
The need to go outside of oneself.
Man is an adoring animal.
To adore is to sacrifice oneself and to prostitute oneself.
Thus all love is prostitution.[25]

Baudelaire seeks to extract his virility from his feminity as much as to sublimate his feminity from his virility. Thus Baudelaire's projected sterility and frigidity are simultaneously the molten fires of his poetry and self-making. The same transformation is, of course, repeated in the very title of Les Fleurs du mal, in which the poet blossoms amid death. It is the cycle of good and evil, like the cycle of the seasons repeated in the internal cycles of love and death, that is the setting of Baudelaire's poetry. This, and not Jameson's postmodern exhaustion of nature and the city, is the sublime in The Flowers of Evil.

In order to strengthen his claim that he is offering us a more "objective" analysis (the quotation marks presumably warn us not to take this effort too seriously, so playful is Jameson's Marxism) of the social history of the materials that apparently provide the referents (after all?) in Baudelaire's postmodern apartment, Jameson exhibits "La Mort des amants":

Nous aurons des lits pleins d'odeurs légères,
Des divans profonds comme des tombeaux,
Et d'étranges fleurs sur des étagères
Ecloses pour nous sous des cieux plus beaux.

Usant à l'envi leurs chaleurs dernières,
Nos deux coeurs seront deux vastes flambeaux,
Qui réfléchiront leurs doubles lumières
Dans nos deux esprits, ces miroirs jumeaux.

Un soir fait de rose et de bleu mystique,
Nous échangerons un éclair unique,
Comme un long sanglot, tout chargé d'adieux;

Et plus tard un Ange, entr'ouvrant les portes,
Viendra ranimer, fidèle et joyeux,
Les miroirs ternis et les flammes mortes.

The Death of Lovers

We shall have richly scented beds—
couches deep as graves, and rare
flowers on the shelves will bloom
for us beneath a lovelier sky.

Emulously spending their last
warmth, our hearts will be as two
torches reflecting their double fires
in the twin mirrors of our minds.

One evening, rose and mystic blue,
we shall exchange a single glance,
a long sigh heavy with farewells;

and then an Angel, unlocking doors,
will come, loyal and gay, to bring
the tarnished mirrors back to life. (257–58)

To produce a postmodern reading of this poem, Jameson suffers a number of self-inflicted temptations—and succumbs to all of them:

> I am tempted to be brutally anachronistic, and to underscore the affinities between this curious interior scene and the procedures of contemporary photorealism, one of whose privileged subjects is not merely the artificial—in the form of gleaming luxury streets of automobiles (battered or mint)—but above all, interior scenes, furnishings without people, and most notably bathrooms, notoriously of all the rooms in the house the least supplied with anthropomorphic objects. . . .
>
> Baudelaire's sonnet is also a void of human beings: the first person plural is explicitly displaced from the entombed chamber by the future tense of the verbs: and even where that displacement weakens, and as the future comes residually to fill up the scene in spite of itself, the twin protagonists are swiftly transformed into furnishings in their own right—candelabra and mirrors, whose complex fourway interplay is worthy of the most complicated visual illustrations of Jacques Lacan. (258)

The devils whispering in the critic's ear lead Jameson, perhaps against his better sense, to declare, "I am tempted to go even further than this and to underscore the *evident paradox*—even more, the *formal scandal*—of the conclusion of this poem (258; my emphasis).

As if it were not enough to indulge the anachronistic comparison between photorealism and Baudelaire's invocation of the transfiguration of two lovers, each mirrored in the other as much as in a room furnished with the poet's flowers, torches, mirrors, and delivering

Angel, Jameson then turns the poem inside out. He reverses the poem's conclusion to empty the lover's bedroom once and for all—whereas the lover's room is nowhere else than "in the twin mirrors of our minds," which the Angel brings back to life and thus to their world. Despite this, Jameson prefers to elaborate on the temptation—whispered to him by Jean Paul Sartre, Susan Sontag, Jean Cocteau, Hart Crane, Jack Spicer, and David Bowie—to introduce us to yet another Baudelaire simulacrum:

7. Baudelaire, refined master of the raw material of bad taste, of *toc*, camp, the hysterical sublime.

Baudelaire's lovers, then, are intoxicated with the fallen and irredeemable trash of postmodern capitalist culture, within Biedermeier furnishings and kitsch. Once again, Jameson tears a poem from both the larger cycle of *Les Fleurs du Mal* and the smaller cycle of death in which the two lovers figure along with the poor, the prostitute, and the artist in Baudelaire's great anthology of the spirit, which triumphs over all the world's evils, among which a preoccupation with bad taste is perhaps the least:

Camp, better than anything else, underscores one of the most fateful differences between high modernism and post-modernism, and one which is also, I believe, operative in the strange poem of Baudelaire: namely what I will call the disappearance of affect, the utter extinction of that pathos or even tragic spirit with which the high moderns lived their torn and divided condition, the repression even of anxiety itself—supreme psychic experience of high modernism and its unaccountable reversal and replacement by a new dominant feeling tone: the high, the intensity, exhilaration, euphoria, a final form of the Nietzschean Dionysiac intoxication which has become as banal and institutionalized as your local disco or the thrill with which you buy a new-model car. (260)

Jameson is, unfortunately, rather more interested in the metonymies of contemporary literary fashion—Jacques Lacan, Gilles Deleuze, Félix Guattari—than in Baudelaire, whose obliteration is required to support their parade of subjectlessness and his own flight into the hysterical (unhistorical) sublime. Not content to stretch Baudelaire on the rack of poststructuralism, Jameson also turns the wheel backward to Edmund Burke's aesthetics of "the sublime," which he interprets as the disappearance of affect, imputing to Burke the cool posture of postmodernism struck in the eighteenth century:

Burke's problem, as he confronted an analogous and historically equally new form of affect—the sublime—was to find some explanation—not for our aesthetic pleasure in the pleasurable, in "beauty," in what could plausibly gratify the human organism on its own scale, but rather for our aesthetic delight in spectacles which would seem symbolically to crush human life and to dramatize everything which reduces the individual human being and the individual subject to powerlessness and nothingness. (261)

So far from contemplating either nascent capitalism or the rise of urbanism, Burke found the sublime in nature, and his influence was, if anything, upon English gardens, William Wordsworth's view of the Lake District, and Thomas Hardy's image of Egdon Heath.[26] Having indulged in yet another brutal anachronism, Jameson then changes the sign on Burke's imputed affectlessness so that it becomes the invitation to a Nietzschean affirmation of anxiety as the highest gratification in a world without genuine pleasure. Swallowed by our machines and cities, reflected in the mirrors of our glassy corporate windows, we continue the ghostly parade of Baudelaire's dandy. At this point, Jameson exits with a line that betrays just a little sympathy for what time and interpretation have done to Baudelaire and his postmodern simulacra:

8. In that then, as in so much else, he is, perhaps unfortunately for him, our contemporary. (263)

We have turned full circle. Consider again Paul de Man's observation on our modernity with which we began and recall how much we lose Baudelaire by projecting him into postmodernity.

CHAPTER 4

Religion and Postmodernism

The Sense of an Ending, with an Allegory of the Body Politic

Since I have complained that literary politicians must take more care with the social sciences they invoke through one or two central metaphors of "power" or "economy," I propose to show what happens when we look closely at how a sociologist and a literary critic analyze the current state of culture in late capitalist society.

In contemporary cultural criticism, whether the figures are neoconservative or neo-Marxist, it is generally agreed that our cultural malaise is at its height in postmodernism. But whereas Daniel Bell would argue that the collapse of the modern temper is to blame for the incivility of postindustrial society,[1] Fredric Jameson would consider late capitalism itself to be the source of the postmodern fragmentation of its cultural values. Despite this analytic difference and their opposing political values, however, both Bell and Jameson are inclined to call for a renewal of religious symbolism to restore the social bond against postmodern values, which undermine equally the conservative and Marxist traditions. Postmodernism appears, therefore, to create a neomodern opposition from both left and right. In turn it inspires a Durkheimian reflection on the sacred value of the social bond, which is either backward looking, as in Bell's neoconservatism, or else resolutely utopian, as in Walter Benjamin, Ernst Bloch, Herbert Marcuse, and Jameson.

I think it is not unfair to Bell's argument to put it as follows: Capitalism has successfully changed itself and the world without destroying itself through the class and ideological conflicts predicted by Marxists. Indeed, capitalism has successfully moved into a postindustrial phase in which its information sciences continuously revise its technological future, thereby solving the problem of crisis and again disappointing its Marxist critics. The postindustrial phase of the capitalist economy appears, however, to be threatened more by the contradictions that derive from its postmodern culture and policy than early capitalism was endangered by the cultural tensions of modernism. In short, late capitalism may prove unable to integrate its postmodern culture with its technological base. This is because the efficiency values of the latter are difficult to reconcile with a culture of narcissism and a politics of egalitarianism. While Bell insists that previous cultural critics were naïve in supposing that modern society can collapse at any single point, his own articulation of the triplex of economy, policy, and culture nevertheless envisages the possibility of the postindustrial technoculture being sapped by postmodern hedonism and self-gratification. For, despite the contempt that modernist artists expressed towards bourgeois scientism and materialism, they nevertheless shared the same "bounded" individualism exemplified in the Protestant ethic and its affinity for industrialism. That is to say, there existed a tension in modernism between its religious and its secular values as well as between its attitudes toward the self and toward society. But this tension has collapsed in postmodernism and its lack threatens to bring down postindustrialism. Bell, however, is quite unclear whether it is modernism or the collapse of modernism (and thus postmodernism) that undermines late (postindustrial) capitalism. How do we choose between the following observations?

> Today modernism is exhausted. There is no tension. The creative impulses have gone slack. It has become an empty vessel. The impulse to rebellion has become institutionalized by the "culture mass" and its experimental forms have become the syntax and semiotics of advertising and *haute couture*. As a cultural style, it exists as radical chic, which allows the cultural mass the luxury of "freer" life-styles while holding comfortable jobs within an economic system that has itself been transformed in its motivations.[2]

Here, then, modernity is damned if it does and damned if it does not underwrite capitalism. In the next passage, however, we can hear more clearly Bell's neoconservative lament for the moral values of a solidly bourgeois society in which the bond of religion is strong and resilient enough to bear the creative tensions of bounded Protestantism and spirited capitalism. At bottom, Bell attributes the crisis of capitalism to a crisis of religion, to a loss of ultimate meaning, which undercuts its civic will. By this he means that the obligations of collective life are reduced to subjective rights, the will to endure calamity is softened into the demand for instant gratification, and religion is replaced by the utopiates of progress, rationality, and science:

> The real problem of *modernity* is the problem of belief. To use an unfash-
> ionable term, it is a spiritual crisis, since the new anchorages have proved
> illusory and the old ones have become submerged. . . . The effort to find
> excitement and meaning in literature and art as a substitute for religion
> led to modernism as a cultural mode. Yet modernism is exhausted and
> the various kinds of postmodernism (in the psychedelic efforts to expand
> consciousness without boundaries) are simply the decomposition of the
> self in an effort to erase individual ego.[3]

Bell's conception of postmodernism seems to turn upon a rejection of everything in modernism except its puritanism as the matching ethic of bourgeois culture and mass industry. Everything else is thrown into a catchall of hedonism, neurosis, and death that exceeds the bounds of "traditional modernism," whose subversion, remained aligned with "a rationality of form, if not of content." But, he contin-ues, the vessels of art are smashed in postmodernism and religious restraint has vanished from the civil scene. Humanity itself disappears as a transcendental value. Worse still—for Bell is not worried so much by philosophical extravaganzas—postmodernism ushers in a crisis of middle-class values. Here bathos is the result of Bell's attempt to combine historical, philosophical, and sociological generalities to create a vision of cultural crisis that is universal and yet decidedly American.

What he gains in assigning a certain grandeur to the diagnosis of American problems, Bell loses when it comes to tackling them in any specific institutional setting. For example, he claims the road to postmodernism involves three stages. In the first, we encounter a natural world; in the second, we deal with a fabricated world; whereas, in the third, our world is ourselves and our social interaction. Although one might have expected Bell to celebrate this last stage of sociability as a sociologist's (Georg Simmel, Erving Goffman) para-dise, he finds instead that we have lost all sense of the social bond due to our progressive secularization:

> The primordial elements that provide men with common identification
> and effective reciprocity—family, synagogue and church, community—
> have become attenuated, and people have lost the capacity to maintain
> sustained relations with each other in both time and place. To say, then,

that "God is dead" is, in effect, to say that the social bonds have snapped and that society is dead.[4]

Because he is at pains to avoid a Marxist (even a Critical Theory) analysis of the sources of "instability" in the American social order, Bell is obliged to leave things at the level of a neoconservative lament over contemporary neoliberalism, hedonism, and postmodernism. Thus America's final crisis is blamed on a moral crisis whose sources are found in any number of situations (ignorance, poverty, and now AIDS) that exceed the social compact and the proper arbitration of public and private goods. Without naming the excesses of the corporate culture and its willful barbarization of the masses, and by keeping silence with regard to the industrial-military adventures that enraged American youth, Bell falls into dismissing the critical culture of the 1960s in the same vein that Christopher Lasch trashes the culture of narcissism. Because they both suppress relevant distinctions regarding the systems of corporate power, whose production of the culture they despise determines its mass consumption,[5] Bell and Lasch cannot avoid the voice of a genteel modernism lamenting its own lost contexts of value with the fall into postmodernism.

Overall, Bell seems worried that the project of modernity will be overwhelmed by its own antinomianism. The latter may have served a positive good in its break with patriarchal and feudal authority, but without such authorities to kick against, antinomianism soon loses all sense of its own limitations and the result is that liberty turns to liberation against which we lack any overarching principle of legitimation. The death of God and now the death of man, rather than his expected resurrection, leaves society without value. This is the terrible price of the antibourgeois assault upon modernism. The curious thing, however, is that, despite Bell's vision of the erosion of authority, we have not seen any expansion of social revolutions other than in the name of the very bourgeois and Christian values discounted by postmodernism. The reason may be, as the Grand Inquisitor well knew, that the masses retain that coherence of meaning and value which Bell believes it is the task of his own exhausted elite to reimpose. Thus, whatever the changes in the institutions and rites of religion, its basic existential responses are perhaps less endangered because they are more necessary than ever.

Bell seriously underestimates the popular resistance (if not indifference) to the elite culture of unrestrained individualism, impulsive art, and moral nihilism, which he defines as modernity's gift to postmodernism. Apart from remarking upon the resurgence of idolatry in the Chinese and the Soviet Communist, he does not make enough of the power of religious values to sustain resistance among intellectuals as well as old women. Of course, one is not appealing to the current prevalence of cults and sects of one sort and another which flourish whilst official religions appear to wane. Yet Bell is bold enough to forecast the appearance of three new religions or types of religious practice:

(1) Moralizing religion: Fundamentalist, evangelical, rooted in the "silent majority"
(2) Redemptive religion: Retreating from (post)modernity, rooted in the intellectual and professional classes; and the growth of "mediating institutions" of care (family, church, neighborhood, voluntary associations) opposed to the state
(3) Mystical religion: Anti-scientist, anti-self, past oriented, rooted in the eternal cycle of existential predicaments[6]

If Bell's prediction were to be borne out, then we might hope for (post) modernism to erase the "beyond" of modernity, returning to the limits that the great civilizations have imposed upon themselves. To do so, however, (post) modernism would need to revive sacred institutions while not sacrificing our commitment to cultural pluralism. So far, no theorist has appeared with any positive vision of such a society.

In the meantime, we may turn to Jameson's reflections on postmodernism and his attempt to restore Marxism to what Bell would call a redemptive religion, since each of them is in fact aware of his respective appeal to Walter Benjamin's insistence on the indestructibility of the aura of religion in human history. Ordinarily, social scientists, and Marxists in particular, are not kind to messianism. This has made the reception of Benjamin slower on that score than the adoption of his studies of culture and society. In short, Benjamin's analysis of commodity fetishism and his messianic response to modernism have been separated, either to be expropriated in the analysis of postmodernism or else left to those whose sympathies lie with the unhappy consciousness deprived of any hope of redemptive institutions. It is to Jameson's credit, therefore, that in a phrase reminiscent of Benjamin he entertains the possibility of a "two-way street" between religion and Marxism. And we shall look at this argument more closely in our conclusion. Meantime, as an unrepentant Marxist, Jameson draws some of the necessary distinctions we found lacking in Bell's account of the role of mass culture in late capitalism. Yet it can also be shown that, despite their opposing political values, Bell's neoconservativism and Jameson's neo-Marxism derive equally from a Durkheimian lament on the dissolution of the social bond. But whereas Bell's ancient liberalism separates him from the Marxist vision of community, Jameson can enthusiastically invoke that communal vision as the ultimate emancipatory drive in the political unconscious of our culture.

Postmodernism certainly reflects the sense of an ending. The question is, what has ended? Is it industrialism? In that case both capitalism and socialism are finished. Bell would probably take this view. Yet he can find nothing to celebrate in postindustrialism because in the end he remains a high priest of modernism. But then, Bell, Jürgen Habermas, and Jameson, despite their differences, are all open to the taunts of Jean-François Lyotard, who finds everything to celebrate in the postmodern dissolution of a consensus between right and left.[7] For Habermas, too, is unwilling to abandon the modernist project to which Marxism is committed. With quite different values from those of Bell, Habermas has also set about the destruction of the French branch of postmodernism, which currently infects North America and Western Europe.[8] Between such figures, Jameson's position is a little difficult, since certain aspects of postmodern cultural criticism continue to appeal to him, inasmuch as it belongs to the received radicalism of literary studies, art, and architecture with which he identifies himself.[9] Overall, however, Jameson manages to extricate himself from the postmodern dissolution of grand narratives and to oppose it with an eloquent, even if surprisingly religious, appeal on behalf of Marxism as the transcendental ground of all human culture and community.

It might well be argued, as I do in *Plato's Cave*, that such sociologies as those of Bell's postindustrialism, Lasch's culture of narcissism, and Alvin Toffler's third wave are themselves prime examples of the postmodern exorcism of ideology and class struggle essential to the culture industry of late capitalism. Thus Jameson insists on drawing a number of distinctions in order to avoid both cultural homogeneity and cultural heterogeneity as twin aspects of postmodern mass culture. He therefore argues that:

Cultural analysis always involves a buried or repressed theory of historical periodization.
Global and American, postmodern culture is the superstructural expression of American domination.
Under late capitalism aesthetic production has been integrated into commodity production.
Postmodernism cannot be treated as part of modernism without ignoring the shift from early to late capitalism and the latter's redefinition of the culture industry.

These distinctions enable Jameson, like Habermas, to argue that Marxism must survive as the neomodernist opposition to late capitalism, absolutely opposed to its superficiality, its imaginary culture, and its total collapse of public and private history. Jameson and Habermas are therefore insistent that Marxist discourse cannot flirt with contemporary fragmentation and subjectlessness. Marxism is the transcendental story, a utopian gesture without which humanity is unthinkable.

However incapable it has become of shocking the bourgeoisie, postmodernism certainly seems to *épater les marxistes*. Consider how Jameson contrasts Andy Warhol's *Diamond Dust Shoes* with Van Gogh's *Peasant Shoes*, or rather, Heidegger's reflections on them.[10] Warhol's shoes are colorless and flat; they glitter like Hollywood stars, consumed by a light that bathes them in superficiality, denying them all interiority, making them appear crazy for want of any gesture that is rooted in a world beyond artifice. By contrast, Heidegger claims that the peasant's shoes tell a story that involves ordinary people; they are continuous with institutions whose meaningful history is the broader framework in which they figure as human artifacts. According to Jameson, all this is lost in the world of video space-time, in the hyperspatiality of postmodern architecture, and in the self-consuming arts of postmodern literature and music.

Like Bell, Jameson refuses the postmodern celebration of the fragment, the paralogical and paratactical arts that dissolve the modernist narrative, dancing on the grave of identity, rationality, and authority. Yet Jameson insists that postmodernism should not be considered solely as a phenomenon of style:

It [postmodernism] is also, at least in my use, a periodizing concept whose function is to correlate the emergence of new formal features in culture with the emergence of a new type of social life and a new economic order—what is euphemistically called modernization, post-industrial or consumer society, the society of the media or the spectacle, or multinational capitalism.[11]

Here, as so often, Jameson's piling up of alternative epithets for the description of the socioeconomic system leaves it unanalyzed in favor of its exploration in terms of two cultural phenomena—pastiche and schizophrenia—to which I now turn.[12] The fascination of these phenomena for postmodernist theorists is itself a sign of the inextricable sense and non-sense that characterizes the ahistorical and anecological predicament of late capitalism. Pastiche involves the intertextuality, the intermodishness of codes-without-context, whose inappropriateness suggests they never had even a local value and hence always prefigured the contemporary value chaos. As I see it, such codes create the illusion that Humphrey Bogart experienced his screen persona and his social institutions with the same affectation as that exhibited for *The Rocky Horror Picture Show* by today's kids without a society, for whom character cannot mean anything else than caricature. The illusion of recycled popular culture is that bourgeois capitalism never created the institutional settings in which Bogey was taken by himself and others for real. This is appealing because in the bureaucratic contexts of late capitalism Bogey could only be a pastiche/parody of lost subjectivity or individualism. Postmodern sophisticates would, of course, claim that Bogey is all there was from the beginning, that is, the essential myth of individualism. Hence all that remains is to democratize the myth—everyman his own Bogey, everywoman as Bacall. All we can aspire to is auto-affection through style, fashion, fad, with everyday life as an open museum, a junk store, a replay.

While drawing on the evaluative connotations of schizophrenia as a diagnostic concept, Jameson nevertheless disavows any intention to engage in cultural psychoanalysis beyond the confines of the literary community. Thus, schizophrenia, as Jameson takes it from Jacques Lacan, is a linguistic pathology, the inability—due to faulty oedipalization—to assign signifiers any temporal and spatial fixed points of identity and reference. Everything floats in an imploded present; action, project, and orientation collapse in the literal, nauseous, and real present in which teenagers are typically trapped. To keep them in this docile state is a task for our education system as a part of the larger system of mass culture to which it occasionally opposes itself, as I have argued elsewhere regarding the functions of the disciplinary society and its therapeutic apparatus.[13]

What Jameson (like Bell and Habermas, but from a different interpretation of the same materials) finds at work in pastiche and literary schizophrenia is the collapse of the oppositional culture of modernism so that these two cultural elements of postmodernism now feed the cultural style of late capitalist consumerism:

> I believe that the emergence of postmodernism is closely related to the emergence of this new moment of late, consumer or multi-national capitalism. I believe also that its formal features in many ways express the deeper logic of the particular social system.[14]

By foreshortening the production process to the management of consumerism, the more difficult analysis of the social relations of production, power, class, and racism is reduced to the operations of an imaginary logic of the political economy of signifiers, where everything floats on the surface of communication. Here Jameson's reliance on Jean Baudrillard's *For a Critique of the Political Economy of the Sign* commits him to the company of Daniel Bell in a lament over the flood of narcissistic consumerism deprived of the mirrors that reflected the old order identities of societies that subordinated exchange value to the higher symbolisms of gift, sacrifice, and community. Rather, postmodern consumers find themselves as mere switching points at video screens that miniaturize their lives in order to speed them up. The result is that their everyday lives are left devastated by the contrast between the archaic symbolic orders that consumers nevertheless inhabit and the imaginary flux in which they drift.

Thus, inside those soft bodies that wander through our shopping malls, whose minds are operated upon from the outside world, desire is deprived of all intelligence:

> This is the time of miniaturization, telecommand and the microprocession of time, bodies, pleasures. There is no longer any ideal principle for these things at a higher level, on a human scale. What remains are only concentrated effects, miniaturized and immediately available. This change

from human scale to a system of nuclear matrices is visible everywhere: this body, our body, often appears simply superfluous, basically useless in its extension, the multiplicity and complexity of its organs, its tissues and functions, since today everything is concentrated in the brain and in genetic codes, which alone sum up the operational definition of being.[15]

Here, then, we have a curious effect. How can analysts as varied as Bell, Jameson, Lasch, Baudrillard, and Habermas join common chorus against late capitalism when their politics vary so widely from right to left? The answer seems to be that as cultural critics of late capitalist consumerism they are all neomodernists. In turn. Marx's own modernism may well be the guiding influence. The centrality of Marxism to the project of modernity, as argued for by Habermas and Jameson, can also be claimed on the consideration of Marx's writing, his imagery, style, and narrative conventions. Thus Marshall Berman and myself have drawn attention to the modernist reading required in order to grasp Marx's polyvalent writings without reducing them either to narrow science or to mere mythology.[16] I have also argued that because Marx's text so obviously turns upon its modernist aesthetics, the Althusserian reading of it as a text of science must be rejected, but without surrendering to Lyotard's reading of it as a lunatic text, or a pure work of art.[17]

What unites Bell and Jameson, despite the different nuances in their response to the culture of postmodernism, is the will to order. In Bell the order is backward-looking; in Jameson it is forward-looking. Both are in search of a new social bond and both believe that it cannot be discovered by severing our links with the past as the most mindless forms of postmodernism imagine. In this regard, even Lasch and Habermas share the same modernist sentiment, despite different ideas about its historical sources. Although orthodox Marxism and neoconservatism are as opposed to postmodernism as they are to one another, with respect to the value of the past each is shot through with the contradictory impulses of modernism. Each may blame the self-consuming artifacts of postmodernism for their cultural malaise, but the fact is that it is industrialism which institutionalizes discontent and, so to speak, condemns us to modernity. Yet the neo-Marxists seem just as unwilling as the neoconservatives to switch their gods. As Marcuse saw, both continue to cling to the old god Prometheus. Both fight to keep out the young gods Orpheus and Narcissus, whose premodern and postindustrial figure still fails to seduce Habermas and Bell. This is so, even though the social forecast of postindustrialism calls for a more creative divinity:

> In the light of the idea of non-repressive sublimation, Freud's definition of Eros as striving to 'form living substance into ever greater unities, so that life may be prolonged and brought to higher development' takes on added significance. The biological drive becomes a cultural drive. The pleasure principle reveals its own dialectic . . . the abolition of toil, the amelioration of the environment, the conquest of disease and decay, the creation of luxury. All these activities flow directly from the pleasure principle, and, at the same time, they constitute *work* which associates individuals to "greater unities"; no longer confined within the mutilating dominion of the performance principle, they modify the impulse without deflecting it from its aim. There is sublimation and, consequently, culture; but this sublimation proceeds in a system of expanding and enduring libidinal relations, which are in themselves work relations.[18]

Given the neo-Marxist and neoconservative refusal of the new god Eros, a void is created in which Jameson can work to refurbish the Marxist vision of a collective utopia. Thus he argues that the death of the subject, the end of man, the migration of reason into madness, the collapse of social and historical narratives into schizophrenic case histories, are only acceptable visions of postmodern critique if we work for a renewal of Marxist history and hermeneutics. Jameson, still apprenticed to Marcuse and Bloch, assumes the Promethean task of binding his own myth to the utopian future of industrialism. He thereby seeks to retain the historical identity of the original Promethean myth with its utopian science of action and community bound by hope and memory:

> Now the origin of Utopian thinking becomes clear, for it is memory which serves as the fundamental mediator between the inside and outside, between the psychological and the poetical. . . . The primary energy of revolutionary activity derives from this memory of prehistoric happiness which the individual can regain only through its externalization through its reestablishment for society as a whole. The loss or repression of the very sense of such concepts as freedom and desire takes, therefore, the form of a kind of amnesia . . . which the hermeneutic activity, the stimulation of memory as the negation of the here and now, as the projection of Utopia, has its function to dispel, restoring to us the original clarity and force of our own most vital drives and wishes.[19]

Whereas capitalism displaces its own myths with secular science, utopian Marxism keeps the bond between myth and science as a history-making institution. Utopianism, then, is not a romanticism or nostalgia that refuses to learn from history. Rather, what can be learned from history, which preserves rather than represses its own genealogy, is that romanticism and myth cannot be contained by secularism and that in the end they are to be joined to the sciences of action and collectivity that they prefigure:

> Thus, to insist upon this term of Breton which corresponds both to Freudian usage and to our own hermeneutic vocabulary . . . a genuine plot, a genuine narrative, is that which can stand as the very *figure* of Desire itself: and this not only because in the Freudian sense pure physiological desire is inaccessible as such to consciousness, but also because in the socio-economic context, genuine desire risks being dissolved and lost. . . . In that sense desire is the form taken by freedom in the new commercial environment.[20]

In short, Jameson argues that every genre of thought (myth, literature, science) has to be grasped as a psychohistorical master narrative (the political unconscious) which when properly interpreted, is Marxism. Postmodernism cannot be a stage in that narrative because it abandons history as a human motive, that is, as the motive to make ourselves human individually and collectively.

Whereas Bell and Lasch lament the dissolution of the social bond, Habermas and Jameson continue to affirm its ultimate historical, normative, and analytic primacy. Jameson's particular strength, it must be said, lies in his will to carry the burden of the dialectical switching between the secularization and the reenchantment of the life-world and its modern vocation while seeking to avoid Weberian pessimism as well as Nietzschean cynicism. He does so fully conscious that the age of religion has passed and that for this very reason we are tempted to produce an "aestheticized" religion, an imaginary or hallucinated community, in an age that is neither religious nor social. How, then, can Marxism exempt itself from such sentimentalism? Jameson's reply is that Marxism and religion can be embraced as elements of "marital square" in which history and collectivity join individual and community action and understanding against inaction and ignorance that dispossess the community and exploits it in favor of its masters. Jameson's fundamental claim is that all forms of social consciousness—both of oppressor and of oppressed—are utopian, inasmuch as these groups are themselves figures for an unalienated collective life. Jameson is at pains to deny that such an affirmation merely represents a return to a Durkheimian symbolics of social solidarity, or to a neo-Marxist marriage of aesthetics and social hygiene. Marxism needs both a positive and a negative hermeneutics of social solidarity if it is not to degenerate into postmodern fragmentation, or into an absurd negativity that would separate forever its scientific utopianism from its primitive myth of communism:

> Only Marxism can give us an adequate account of the essential mystery of the cultural past, which, like Tiresias drinking the blood, is momentarily returned to life and warmth and allowed once more to speak, and to deliver its long forgotten message in surroundings utterly alien to it. This mystery can be re-enacted only if the human adventure is one; only thus—and not through . . . antiquarianism or the projections of the modernists—can we glimpse the vital claims upon us of such long-dead issues as the season alternation of the economy of a primitive tribe, the passionate disputes about the nature of the Trinity . . . only if they are retold within the unity of a single great collective story . . . Marxism, the collective struggle to arrest a realm of Freedom from a realm of Necessity . . . It is in detecting traces of the uninterrupted narrative, in restoring to the surface of the text the repressed and buried reality of this fundamental history, that the doctrine of a political unconscious finds its function and its necessity.[21]

Such passages are among the best in literary Marxism. Yet Jameson's claims are clearly exorbitant. He cannot identify any specific social forces to carry his utopianism—his proletariat is everywhere and nowhere—and so he throws the holy water of Marxist utopianism over any group, whether oppressor or oppressed, insofar as they are "figures" of an ultimately classless society!

In effect, Jameson achieves a remarkable inversion of the position of both Louis Althusser and Jean-François Lyotard with respect to the allegorical cathexis of master narratives or ideologies. History, in the large sense, is taken by Jameson to move through four levels—from the collective to the individual and from the individual to the collective story, thereby refurbishing Marxism as the master narrative, albeit as the "absent cause" or the political unconscious of our times.

The shifts involved between the collective and biographical figures and between the individual and communal levels of the social are achieved through the ideological categories of class discourse insofar as its antagonistic figures are always framed in an ultimately utopian reversal that results in a transcendental community. The stages along the way, so to speak, require that nature never be outside the romance in which it can respond to our desires in figures of good and evil, or wildness and civilization through which we, in turn, educate our imagination, as Northrop Frye would say. Giambattista Vico and Marx, as I understand them, would have said something similar. That is, each would have insisted on the positive continuity in the hermeneutics of the past and the present in recognition of the social debt that capitalism represses (as the basis of its unconscious) and which socialism recognizes as its humanist *point d'honneur*. From this standpoint the Marxist critique of reification and fragmentation is not simply an exercise in dialectical epistemology. It represents an ethical rejection of every possessive appropriation of values and relationships that breaks off, interrupts, and represses the recognition of exchange, intergenerationality, and collective debt. It is from this point of view that we understand the affinity between capitalism and secularism. That unholy alliance is constituted precisely through its suppression of the sacred and its rituals for the redemption of humankind's debt to the creation. The shift from Gemeinschaft to Gesellschaft represents the reduction of social debt to the social contract as a device for the individual appropriation of the precontractual values of reciprocity and communal indebtedness.

It is time now to look a little closer at Jameson's attempt to open a "two-way street" between religion and Marxism. In turn, this will oblige us to formulate an alternative allegory of the body politic in response to Jameson's efforts on these lines:

> I have throughout the present work implied what I have suggested explicitly elsewhere, that any comparison of Marxism with religion is a two-way street, in which the former is not necessarily discredited by its association with the latter. On the contrary, such a comparison may also function to rewrite certain religious concepts—most notably Christian historicism and the "concept" of providence, but also the pretheological systems of primitive magic—as anticipatory foreshadowing of historical materialism within precapitalist social formations in which scientific thinking is unavailable as such.[22]

One might charitably interpret such passages as Jameson's effort to maintain solidarity with past societies and to recognize a certain indebtedness to them. But his benchmark of science in fact breaks the bond between them because it is still necessary for Jameson to consider Marxism a science, however riddled with hermeneutics and psychoanalysis. This is all the more curious since he is also engaged in the restoration of the sacred values that underwrite the Marxist text to make it central to humanity. By the same token, it should be noticed that Jameson treats only a very generalized concept of Christian history, abstracting from the rituals and communities in which Christian doctrine is practiced—and the same can be said of his concept of Marxism and mass culture. In each case, Jameson holds to the utopian position that, however degraded these forms of human culture may be, they never quite erase the aspiration toward individual and collective transfiguration that constitute class consciousness:

> All class consciousness of whatever type is Utopian insofar as it expresses the unity of a collectivity; yet it must be added that this proposition is an *allegorical* one. The achieved collectivity or organic group of whatever kind—oppressors fully as much as oppressed—is Utopian not in itself, but only insofar as all such collectivities are themselves figures for the ultimate concrete life of an achieved Utopian or classless society.[23]

In this extraordinary embrace of class consciousness, Jameson appears to have exceeded even his own understanding of Durkheim's inscription of religious solidarity as the subtext of all culture. His utopianism demands an absolutely sublimated culture entirely free of any functionalist or ideological usage. Ultimately, this is achievable only on behalf of a totally collective subject who would entirely escape the arrows of the poststructuralist critique of subjective subjectivism. The only figure of such a collective subject that Jameson can produce at this point is the "body of the despot" contributed by the Asiatic mode of production:

> In most of the *Asiatic* land forms, the *comprehensive unity* standing above all these little communities appears as the higher *proprietor* or as the *sole* proprietor. . . . Because the *unity* is the real proprietor and the real presupposition of communal property . . . the relation of the individual to the *natural* conditions of labor and of reproduction . . . appears mediated for him through a cession of the total unity—a unity realized in the

form of the despot, the father of many communities—to the individual, through the mediation of the particular commune.[24]

Despite the potentially regressive features in this figuration of "Orientalism," Jameson contents himself with noting the attendant controversy but does not consider whether any other figure of the symbolic enactment of social reciprocity might be drawn from elsewhere in our cultural heritage. Here I think we need to rethink the allegory of the body politic, as I have done elsewhere,[25] and to show how Jameson lets slip a figure that might well have served his purposes better than that of the despotic body.

The body politic certainly emerges from a long allegorical history of the desire for the representation of unity and difference in a just society. It contains both a myth and a metaphysic which have been appended to it throughout the history of social and political conflict both for revolutionary and restorational purposes. It is a transgressive figure when opposed to caste interpretations of social division of labor, as well as a figure of difference and charismatic justice when opposed to the forces of rationalization and homogenization. It is above all, a figure operative on both levels of synchrony and diachrony, demanding reciprocity on the social level and intergenerational indebtedness on the level of history. Thus it may be said that the political community thinks itself a community of difference and exchange, both avoiding any extreme naturalization of its difference and rejecting any hardened organic or totalitarian conception of its species existence. The body politic is not a purely natural figure because it already figurates the desire for political community, whose infrastructures are already in place at the levels of work, family, and society. It is therefore an act of interpretative violence for any theorist to treat the body politic as anything less than a mode of collective knowledge. It is not a mode of unconscious or of natural desire. Yet it is a transgressive figure because of its power to integrate what has been separated and to differentiate what has been homogenized.[26] The body politic is a civilizational concept, to use the language of Frye, and it functions on the highest level of allegory to transfigure society in terms of the human body itself imaginatively conceived as the universe of human potentiality.

Here, however, Jameson loses nerve and objects that the figure of the body politic is reprivatized and can reflect only itself, losing its

Table 4.1 Levels of the Body Politic

Levels	Institutions	Discourse
(1) Bio-body	Family	Well-being
(2) Productive body	Work	Expression
(3) Libidinal body	Personality	Happiness

analogical power as a collective organism. But Marx never conceived of the natural body as the subject of history for the very reason that he considered nature part of human history: "History is the true rational history of man."[27] Thus the history of the human body belongs to a collective history in which the figures of the body politic and of the *sensus communis* sketch out strategies of community and difference in the articulation of social life, economy, and policy. Vico's two basic axioms provide an initial formulation of the hermeneutic principles of the allegory of the body politic:

> Common sense is judgment without reflection, shared by an entire class, an entire people, an entire nation, or the entire human race.
> Uniform ideas originating among entire peoples unknown to one another must have common ground in truth.[28]

Viewed in this fashion, the body politic requires that we construct scenarios for the mutual accountability of the communities of natural and social science within the larger democratic community of commonsense political and legal practice. The metaphor of body-politics, in keeping with Vico's own views, would therefore replace the scientistic metaphor in the dominant imagery of the polity. In this way, we might restore the public functions of rhetoric in the rational advocacy of knowledge and values that address the three basic domains of the body politic (see table 4.1).

By differentiating these three levels of the body politic, we further separate ourselves from naturalistic accounts of the political legitimacy problem by introducing a logic of ethical development as the fundamental myth of political life. The three levels of family, economic, and personal life represent a historical-ethical development and also permit it to identify contradictions or constraints and regressions in the body politic. Thus, we can identify alienation as a complex phenomenon that affects not only the productive body but also the bio-body and libidinal body. Conversely, alienation is not solved merely by satisfying organic needs, nor by the smooth engineering of productive relations, since these do not meet the demands of the libidinal body. By the same token, we cannot abstract the dreams of libidinal life from our commitments to familial and economic life. Thus a critical theory of the legitimacy problems of the body politic is simultaneously a constitutive theory of social development and of members' recognition of the places in their lives where this development is blocked and even deteriorating. Members' expression of their experience with the underlying logic of development that sustains political legitimacy will not be limited to official electoral conduct. It will include such subversive practices as strikes, family breakdown, crime, protest, lampoons, neighborhood and street gatherings, music, songs, posters, and wall art. A critical theory of political legitimacy does not discount the rationality of members' ordinary accounts of their political experience in terms of the vocabularies of family, work, and person. Moreover, it does not presume upon either the found rationality or irrationality of such accounts.

Each of the three levels of the body politic is represented in a characteristic institution which is in turn allocated its proper domain of discourse. Although the various institutional and discourse realms of the body politic are only analytically differentiated, they may be said to constitute an evolutionary process in which the congruency of the three discursive orders maximizes the commonwealth. Every society must reproduce itself biologically and materially. These needs are articulated at the institutional levels of work and the family where discourse focuses on the translation of notions of well-being, health, suffering estrangement, and self-expression. Here we cannot deal with the institutions that are generated at these two levels of the body politic. In the later evolutionary stages, the articulation of the libidinal body generates discourse demands that impinge differentially upon the institutions of family and work. To date, the institutionalization of these "revolutionary" demands represents a challenge to all modes of scientist, social, and political knowledge. Meantime, we can envisage an extension of Habermas's program for the rational justification of the ideal speech community in terms of the specific discursive contexts of the tri-level body politic. It would be necessary to generate a topology of knowledge and evaluation claims with regard to the bio-body, the productive body, and the libidinal body at each appropriate institutional level, with further criteria for urgency, democratic force, and the like.

The libidinal body politic represents a level of desire that fulfills the order of personality insofar as it transcends the goods of family and economy. So long as human beings continue to be birthed and familied of one another, then the bodily, social, and libidinal orders of living will not be separable pursuits. But the same token, the body politic cannot be reduced to purely economistic satisfactions any more than to the dream of love's body. A distinctive feature of the metaphor of the body politic is that it allows us to stand away from the system, that is, the machine, cybernetic, and organization metaphors that reduce the problem of political legitimacy to sheer cognitivist sciences. This shift in turn recovers the plain rationalities of everyday living, family survival, health, self-respect, love, and communion. Members are aware of the necessary interrelationships between their family, economic, and personal commitments. They judge the benefits of their labor in the productive sector of the body politic in terms of the returns to their familial and personal lives. They are willing to make trade-offs between the demands of family life and the ambitions of their personal and libidinal lives. In short, members have a fairly complex understanding of their corporate life that is not reducible to the single pattern of utilitarian or decisionistic reasoning that governs calculations in the productive sector.

On the right and on the left, we are still waiting for history to deliver itself. Whether politics or religion will be the midwife remains undecided. After a bitter lesson, the sociologist puts his money on religion. Jameson, in the meantime, perseveres with the alchemy of a hermeneutics that will delivery history, politics, and religion. And so the stage of history takes another turn. The Ghost of Marx returns; there is much talk about talk in which Jameson is apparently more agile than Habermas, who waits for a chance to articulate a final economy of truth, sincerity, and justice. Bell is silenced, but offstage the laughter of Lyotard still reaches us. Marcuse, Bloch—and perhaps ourselves—remain saddened.

CHAPTER 5

Breaking the Signs
*Roland Barthes and the
Literary Body*

With the preceding sketch of the body politic in mind as our larger
context, I now want to move through the battle lines in the body of
literature as reviewed by Roland Barthes and then to introduce his
conception of the literary body, which I will elaborate in the studies
of the symptomatic text in part 3, where I finally set forth the concept
of homotextuality/gynema.

Any strictly Platonist or historicist attempt to grasp the shift from
structuralism to poststructuralism involves "misreading" what each
analytic strategy brings to literary and semiological criticism. There
can be no general estimate of this yield apart from what one can
ground in the practice of individual thinkers such as Barthes, whose
encounter with the lively intellectual movements of his day was
continuously revised or "revisioned" from work to work. Situated
between Claude Lévi-Strauss and Jacques Derrida, and with some
reference to Jacques Lacan and Michel Foucault—though lacking
the stamina of any of them—Barthes' itinerary consciously, if not
indulgently, takes us over the difficult ground lying between a science
of literature (structuralism) and the permanent revolution or atopia
of language (deconstructionism). Thus, at one level, it seems best to
think of structuralism and deconstructionism as absolutely relative
analytic strategies. Where thought is settled, its objects achieve an
individual and reified status—one might say, they acquire a reality
and a morality that is hard to question. Yet things and relationships,
realities and values, are never quite solidary. They may be placed
within larger frames of space and time that suspend their individual
weight, refloating them as changing values of an underlying
structure, pattern, or myth. For a time, thought will again be
trapped in fascination with the permanence and universality of
structure freed from evanescent detail. Inevitably, however, every
structure seems to oscillate and, never having achieved perfect
closure, once again to open up to the tide of history, social change,

and individual appropriation. All human institutions seem to reveal a similar cycle, as may be seen from the great testaments of Vico, Hegel, and Marx. This is not to deny, of course, that at a different level of ideological and historical concreteness it may be appropriate to view structuralism and deconstructionism as a continuous strategy, project, or tradition.

At first sight, literature as an institution might appear to be indifferent to such observations. After all, literature is demonstrably the work of individuals creating artifacts whose power to describe human reality, society, and nature resides in a competent use of language. Literary realism combined with literary individualism seems to capture the essence of our literary institutions. Such, at any rate, was the case until it could be argued that these were merely oppressive fictions of the literary establishment. To destroy such an establishment, literary structuralists began to find texts without authors, as well as intertextuality and the coproductivity of writing and reading freed from linguistic realism. The excitement of these discoveries very quickly, if not from the very start, hastened structuralism into post-structuralism—or deconstructionism. As a matter of fact, something very similar occurred in the social sciences. Here the constructivist attack on positivism could not be controlled by phenomenology, whose formalism quickly yielded to a variety of deconstructionist strategies in pursuit of the social production of meaning and order.[1] We cannot investigate those connections here. Yet in following Barthes' itinerary, we shall be very close to those developments, at least as they influenced the life of a figure who met them with different degrees of enthusiasm, practicing and revising their precepts according to his own best sense:

> In short, structuralism will be just one more "science" (several are born each century, some of them only ephemeral) if it does not manage to place the actual subversion of scientific language at the center of its programme, that is, to "write itself." How could it fail to question the very language it uses in order to know language? The logical continuation of structuralism can only be to rejoin literature, no longer as an "object" of analysis but as the activity of writing, to do away with the distinction derived from logic which turns the work itself into a language-object and science into a meta-language, and thus to forego that illusory privilege which science attaches to the possession of a captive language.[2]

STRUCTURALISM AND DEMYTHOLOGIZATION

Although Barthes on two occasions at least seems to have espoused what he later saw as the myth of the scientificity of literature, even his most structuralist studies appear as mocking, self-consuming artifacts. In *Le Système de la mode* (1967), for example, he submerged himself in the world of women's fashion and apprenticed himself to the fictions whereby those who, like himself, seek to be loved cover themselves in words, fabrics, and fabrication. This world of fashion prefigures the world of Balzac's castrato La Zambinella, in which truth and appearance are no more solid than male and female. Like a child, or like Jules Michelet, he wanted to get into the secret of words, into the secret of women, to assume their fascination before a public. Hence *Le Système de la mode* will appear to be a forsaken intellectual enterprise unless we understand its forbidden motive, its pleasure in the erotic spaces between the flesh and the word, between the exoticism of the language of clothes and the language of science when juxtaposed:

> Is not the most erotic portion of a body *where the garment gapes?* In perversion (which is the realm of textual pleasure) there are no "erogenous zones" (a foolish expression besides); it is intermittence, as psychoanalysis has so rightly stated, which is erotic: the intermittence of skin flashing between two articles of clothing (trousers and sweater), between two edges (the open-necked shirt, the glove and the sleeve); it is this flash itself which seduces, or rather, the staging of an appearance-as-disappearance.[3]

In every case, language and the flesh exceed the attempt to classify and organize them. On Barthes's account, it is as though language can no more be completely classified than a woman can ever be fully dressed: hence the failure of structuralism. By the same token, neither language nor a woman can ever be completely stripped: hence the impossibility of deconstructionism and of demystification. With women, as with language, style is taken to be everything: it held Barthes in endless fascination. This, however, anticipates Barthes's itinerary, and we should now follow him without the privilege of his continuously revised program.

In his preface to the 1970 edition of *Mythologies*, Barthes provides the retrospective standpoint from which this phase of his work is to be considered. It represents a combination of Saussureanism and *semioclasm*, that is, an attempt to break the signs, to demythologize by means of a detailed analysis of the sign system that fulfills the ideological function. Later on, Barthes abandoned the "euphoric dream of scientificity" with which the current state of linguistics seduced semiology and literary criticism. His *Système de la mode* is exceptional for the attempt to devise an abstract, monological system of clothing signs that never steps outside the world of women's fashion into the social and economic system upon which it is floated. By contrast, in *Mythologies*, Barthes never pursued the analytic strategy at the expense of the critical task of unveiling the operation whereby bourgeois myths naturalize the objects, events, and relationships that underwrite the status quo, essentializing it and removing it from historical and political change. Here we can present only a single example given in some detail rather than try to capture the variety of topics pursued in *Mythologies*. The example is that of a magazine cover which, during the Algerian war of independence, shows a black soldier saluting the French flag.[4] In formal semiological terms the elements of the myth of imperial France may be analyzed in terms of fig. 5.1.[5]

The image presents a self-sufficient whole, in which the soldier's salute and the greatness of the French Empire overlap and leave no room for anticolonialism. The signified is swallowed in the signifier,

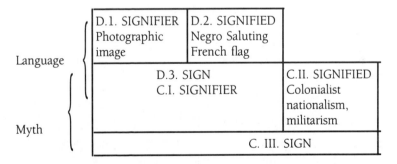

Fig. 5.1. The myth of imperial France

and an unhistorical sign closes the circuit of meaning to constitute an irreproachable myth of imperialism. In order to deconstruct the myth in this case, it is necessary to perform the following "readings":

    a. By focusing on the empty signifier, the reader allows the black soldier saluting to stand as a *symbol* of French imperialism. This is the standpoint of the journalist who must find a form for the concept he has to convey.

    b. If the reader focuses upon the full signifier, distinguishing denotation and connotation, the myth is decoded and the black soldier becomes an *alibi* for French imperialism. This is the standpoint of the mythologist engaged in deconstruction.

    c. If the reader responds to the signifier as an inextricable whole of denotation and connotation, the black soldier is the very *presence* of French imperialism. This is the naïve standpoint of the reader of myths.

Myths escape decoding by bypassing language, avoiding the critical unveiling or liquidation of their meaning by naturalizing it so that the reader remains in the natural attitude, so to speak, of the myth consumer. Because language is never at the zero degree, it cannot avoid feeding myths:

> Now in a fully constituted myth, the meaning is never at zero degree, and this is why the concept can distort it and naturalize it. We must remember once again that the privation of meaning is in no way a zero degree: this is why myth can perfectly well get hold of it, give it for instance the signification of the absurd, of surrealism, etc. At bottom, it would only be the zero degree which could resist myth.[6]

From this standpoint, Barthes considered that in *Writing Degree Zero* he had in fact been concerned with the demythologization of literature. We may indeed take this to be the case for that light it throws on his later work and, in particular, on the much bolder critical strategies devised to carry out his project. The symbiosis between language and myth is such that it is impossible for literary criticism, linguistics, or structuralism to avoid their own mythologies. Barthes was aware, of course, of having succumbed to these mythologies in his proposals for a science of literature, that is, the most general discourse on the plurality of meanings ever attributed to a work. In practice, he withdraws from such a project in favor of the exploration of the ties between the literary text and the literary body.

THE QUESTION OF STYLE

With the benefit of Lacan's powerful revision of Freud, Barthes found himself turning away from the politics of criticism toward the pleasures of the text. How this shift was accomplished may be seen from his transformation of an early, if awkward, terminology in which he distinguished the two modes of transitive and intransitive writing— the work of the *écrivant* and of the *écrivain*. Throughout the classical period, there existed an official discourse shared by the writer (*écrivant*) and the preachers. These were "transitive" men whose task was to instruct and explain without any concern for the reflexive features of language, which they assumed to be an unambiguous instrument of communication. This separation of language and literature arose from the suppression of rhetoric, and it lasted until Mallarmé, Proust, and Joyce—those "intransitive" men—restored the reflexivity and productivity of language to the author (*écrivain*), making him inseparable from the act of writing:

> The modern verb *to write* is becoming a sort of indivisible semantic entity. So that if language followed literature—which, for once perhaps, has the lead—I would say that we should no longer say today "*j'ai écrit*" but rather, "*je suis écrit*," just as we say "*je suis né, il est mort, elle est éclose.*" There is no passive idea in these expressions, in spite of the verb *to be*, for it is impossible to transform "*je suis écrit*" (without forcing things, and supposing that I dare to use this expression at all) into "*on m'a écrit*" ["I have been written" or "somebody wrote me"]. It is my opinion that in the middle verb *to write* the distance between the writer and the language diminishes asymptotically. We could even say that it is subjective writings, like romantic writing, which are active, because in them the agent is not interior but *anterior* to the process of writing. The one who writes here does not write for himself, but, as if by proxy, for a person who is exterior and antecedent (even if they both have the same name). In the modern verb of middle voice *to write*, however, the subject is immediately contemporary with the writing, being effected and affected by it. The case of the Proustian writer is exemplary: he exists only in writing.[7]

So conceived, the author (*écrivain*) withholds himself from the social commitment of language and official literary discourse: the best an author can do is to be responsible to literature as a failed commitment, neither true nor false. In practice, or in our age, writer and author are rarely separable identities, and we find ourselves engaged in writing for our own sake as well as that of society, simultaneously using a language we seek to emancipate from common usage, earning a living in universities, laboratories, and bookstores while half-excused from life.

Yet Barthes also conceives of the author as a productive worker, forging a native language whose strength lies in his own body, from which language acquires a surplus value beyond anything the writer could intend because he is wholly given up to the immaterialism of language and the body.[8] Such a concept of language and embodiment required Barthes's later theory of the text and, in particular, the method of fragmentary writing that became the very mark of Barthes's pleasure in and of texts. We are required now to abandon the notion of the literary work as a sort of Newtonian object and to conceive of it as an endlessly relativized text between texts—as intertextuality.

Viewed from this perspective, the text loses its essential significance and becomes a radically symbolic play of language whose efficacy involves us in a hermeneutics and psychoanalysis of the polyvalent meanings from which it is woven. The literary game of influence is thereby exhausted and must be replaced by a materialist criticism, analogous to Freud's interpretation of dreams, following Lacan. Such a practice equalizes reading and writing after their long subordination. It also liberates the author from the oedipal contract, which, so to speak, underwrites all the literary conventions of the readerly text, but not the text of pleasure, which is engendered only through *différance* à la Derrida.[9]

From the very start, in *Writing Degree Zero*, Barthes was concerned with the writer's freedom and commitment within the quasinatural environment of language and literature. At this stage, namely, prior to his encounter with structuralism and Saussurean linguistics, Barthes represented language as a historical burden, a collective legacy, apparently only to be overthrown in an act of literary violence, rejecting realism in favor of magic, placing poetry beyond prose. Since Barthes's argument presupposes familiarity with Jean-Paul Sartre's *What Is Literature?* (1948), it may be well to recall that essay briefly.[10]

The intention of Sartre's survey of the history of literature is not to separate its future from its past or near-present. Indeed, Sartre is not surveying the history of literature in any ordinary sense at all. It is only in the light of a literature that is for itself that its separation from its modality as action identifies it as having been a literature of *hexis* and consummatory destruction. The task of literature is to reveal the human situation in order to surpass it toward a community of freedoms. Its proper history is internal to the ideal relationship of generosity and freedom that it forges between the writer and the public. In the past, literature fell into the category of consumption because it had adopted a metaphysics in which being and having were identical. Thus literature professed to offer through indulgence the fulfillment of being, the appropriation of being through the spectacle of being. By contrast, the literature of praxis starts from the metaphysical assumption that being is appropriated only through the act of making itself. The literature of praxis is always a literature *en situation*. It inserts itself into the world of gestures and instruments that reveal the world in the act of transforming it. The writer engaged in such a task must create what Sartre calls a total literature, which is simultaneously a literary and political activity in which the writer and the reading public communicate man to man, on the model of a socialist society.

Thus we are in language as we are in the body; that is, as a vehicle of expression, an excarnation of particular purposes or detotalizations of the total human project. In speech we unveil the world, name its objects, and describe the situations in order to transcend them. According to Sartre, it is the poet who does not pass beyond words to the practical utilities they furnish. To the poet these connections are purely magical. He uses words to produce word-objects or images of the world, but not to express a certain situation like the writer of a political pamphlet who intends to transform the situation in the light of his description. Every creation of the genuine artist, far from being a finished object, opens onto the entire world, calling forth the freedom of his public.

The artist's creation, therefore, appeals to a kingdom of ends for which terror and beauty are never simply natural events but simultaneously an exigency and a gift to be integrated into the human condition. Whenever the artist is separated from his public, his work loses its quality as an imperative and is reduced to a purely esthetic object. In turn, the artist is forced to substitute the formal relationship between himself and his art for the relationship of commitment and transcendence between the artist and the public. Under these conditions, works of art function not as outlines of the total man but as treasures whose scarcity is the measure of the absolute poverty of man, whose eternity is the denial of human history.

Not yet having embraced structuralism, Barthes appears to be uncomfortable with the closure in various historical modes of writing—revolutionary, bourgeois, Marxist, even the writings in *Les Temps modernes*. Barthes's objection is that political commitment violates the necessary ambiguity of language, the fundamental inability of the writer who respects language to push it to either pole of society or the individual. As we shall see, he never really altered this view, even though he realized it kept him out of politics. Yet he admired Bertold Brecht enormously, even as a political writer. What he loved in Brecht was his ethical combination of intellectual clarity and pleasure, of theatrical distance, judgment, and enjoyment. Barthes was absolutely overwhelmed by *Mother Courage*. "Basically, Brecht's greatness, and his solitude, is that he keeps inventing Marxism."[11] Above all, Brecht's formalism dissolved the "petty bourgeois realism" of socialist art, as well as its morality, unable to adapt to its own history. He established the productivity of the gestural and theatrical signifier while simultaneously setting it in an ideological context that did not overwhelm its autonomy, its constitutive ambiguity. In Brecht, Barthes saw that fundamental respect for the suspense of language that he himself observed and loyally cultivated:

> One could say that literature is Orpheus returning from the underworld; as long as literature walks ahead, aware that it is leading someone, the reality behind it which it is gradually leading out of the unnamed—that reality breathes, walks, lives, heads toward the light of meaning; but once literature turns around to look at what it loves, all that is left is a named meaning, which is a dead meaning.[12]

With regard to bourgeois writing, he objected to its use of the narrative past (the preterite) to confer a universal reality on events and characters (in the third person) who were otherwise imaginary and local fictions. Above all, the bourgeois novel is a mythological device for suppressing existential history in favor of society:

> This is strictly how myths function, and the Novel—and within the Novel, the preterite—are mythological objects in which there is, superimposed upon an immediate intention, a second-order appeal to a corpus of dogmas, or better, to a pedagogy, since what is sought is to impart an essence in the guise of an artefact.[13]

Unlike Sartre, Barthes seems to have understood from the very beginning the significance of modern poetry for the autonomy or productivity of language. He never accepted the realist view of language and thought, or the classical euphoria in the clarity of ideas and unencumbered prose. He saw in these assumptions the subordination of Nature to Society, and the very same violence in which Marx saw the essence of capitalism. He positively ridiculed the practices of socialist realism. Yet he was unwilling to conspire with Stéphane Mallarmé's murder of language or with Albert Camus's degree zero writing, for example, because he refused to believe in any successful escape from language and its responsibilities.

> Writing therefore is a blind alley. The writers of today feel this; for them, the search for a non-style or an oral style, for a zero level or a spoken level of writing is, all things considered, the anticipation of a homogeneous social state; most of them understand that there can be no universal language outside a concrete, and no longer a mystical or merely nominal, universality of society.[14]

Barthes saw in the proliferation of literary language a utopian quest for an Adamic language that might name things prior to all divisions and all conflicts. While he may never have been tempted to the political versions of that vision, I believe that, in spite of his apprenticeship to a transcendent structuralism, this utopia of language remained a personal vision. It deepened with that carnal knowledge that characterizes his later writings. Yet, here again, there are powerful beginnings of this development in *Writing Degree Zero*, contained in certain distinctions drawn by Barthes which he employed to underwrite his differences with Sartre. Where Sartre opposed language and style in analogy with the contrast between collective determination and individual decision, Barthes needed a further distinction to avoid the pitfalls of an instrumentalist view of language, upon which he felt Sartre fell back.

As a matter of fact, we can see that Barthes's usage differs from Sartre's even with respect to the two terms they seem to share in the chapter each wrote called "What Is Writing?" Barthes was concerned with the productivity of language as a historical phenomenon whose historicity is given a quasinatural form in the literature of any given period of society. Although he already had certain structural linguistic formulations of this phenomenon, he was basically concerned with the ethical question it raises. Yet, like Maurice Merleau-Ponty later,[15] he was unwilling to resolve the problem in a Sartrean decision, to politicize language as preeminently a social object. Most of us dwell in language without making its usages thematic and can never hope to expropriate all of its wealth. Much of the time a writer will similarly trust the great scaffold of his language even when trying, as he must, to overreach it. Indeed, the writer must, so to speak, suspend himself between two languages—between the common language into which he is born and a second language, or *style*, which is, so to speak, his body language, the resonance of his sounded being to which he must listen if his *writing* is to be productive of something else than the commonplaces of language and *literature*, which is language pointing to its official mark as *belles lettres*:

> A language is therefore on the hither side of literature. Style is almost beyond it: imagery, delivery, vocabulary spring from the body and the past of the writer and gradually become the very reflexes of his art. Thus under the name of style a self-sufficient language is evolved which has its roots only in the depths of the author's personal and secret mythology, that subnature of expression where the first coition of words and things takes place, where once and for all the great verbal themes of his existence come to be installed.[16]

Here we can see that Barthes's attachment to what he called the "great verbal themes of his existence" is rooted in a deeper phenomenology of language than anything Sartre espoused. Indeed, this original remark strikes the theme of all Barthes's later investigations into everyday mythologies, the structural semiotics of fashion, his study of Michelet, Sade, Loyola, Fourier, Balzac, and himself. At first his linguistic body, so to speak, was given a deterministic formulation that would later relax under the influence of Lacanian psychoanalysis, opening the *literary body* to the defiant pleasures of the text, resolutely set against the literary and political establishment of his day. Barthes never lost sight of the writer's solitude, which derives from the obligation to listen to and cultivate the literary sensibilities that are a writer's unchosen and therefore uncommitted being-in-the-world.

Style, then, is the writer's resistance to society and politics and not a Sartrean will. Style is indifferent to society and choice; nor is it a literary instrument:

It is the decorative voice of hidden, secret flesh; it works as does Necessity, as if, in this kind of floral growth, style were no more than the outcome of a blind and stubborn metamorphosis starting from a sub-language elaborated where flesh and external reality come together.[17]

In Barthes's view, style is outside the pact between the writer and society. It utterly precedes the writer's choice of language, being a marriage of thought and body conveyed in rituals of metaphor and gesture that are the natural product of time and the condensation of living. Between language and style so conceived, Barthes located the distinctive function of writing (*écriture*). The writer links language to society in accordance with its great historical epochs, which he may celebrate or reject. But although the writer conceives of his freedom as a historical project, it remains a utopian use of language that forever falls back on its own society. Barthes, therefore, ultimately separates himself from Sartre's literary project, remaining, like Merleau-Ponty, a philosopher of ambiguity:

> Writing is an ambiguous reality: on the one hand, it unquestionably arises from a confrontation of the writer with the society of his time; on the other hand, from this social finality, it refers the writer back, by a sort of tragic reversal, to the sources, that is to say, the instruments of creation. Failing the power to supply him with a freely consumed language, history suggests to him the demand for one freely produced.[18]

How Barthes understood the body of language and style may be seen from his discussion of Michelet's historical writing. As we know from *Mythologies*, Barthes was fascinated by the smooth, sleek, silken surfaces of things, of toys, food, and automobiles—above all, of women dressed, undressed in never-ending fashion, clothed in words, exalted, impenetrable, glossy, and glorious.[19] Language of women, for women, in service of women, a service into which Barthes allowed himself to enter like Michelet, whom Barthes studied like himself. No conventional biography results: what is undertaken is another display of the procedures and insights of what in chapter 16, I call *homotextuality*—that is, literary conduct displayed in the corporeal practices of writing and reading that exceed both a plain physiology and any reduction of textuality to sexuality.

Barthes's life of Michelet is concerned only with the incarnations of the man who lived and wrote history, who could not live apart from writing history, and whose own life set the parameters of his *History of France*, each otherwise incomplete. Accordingly, the man is presented as voluminous, like the very histories to which he devoted his life. By the same token he had always to worry that his strength should last, his days be long enough to match the histories he was making. Thus, his body became the battleground of history, so to speak; he devoured history and was eaten away by history's demands upon his strength: "Michelet's sickness was migraine, a mixture of dizziness and nausea. Everything was like migraine to him: the cold, a storm, spring, the wind, the history he was narrating."[20] Michelet's body never ceased to struggle under the massive, encyclopedic historical corpus that he pitted himself against. He was always at work, long hours, at grips with immense projects from which, if he were ever free, he feared to die. He therefore lived off history's own lifeblood like a parasite, suffering its calamities and exuberances—above all, its deaths. He made himself a corpse of history, donned its masks, and moved in and out of its stages, always approaching an end he needed to delay in order to confer upon it its proper due:

> Work—history in other words—being a nursery place where every weakness was assured of its value; his migraines settled there, that is, were rescued and endowed with meaning. Michelet's whole body becomes a product of his own creation and he established in himself a surprising sort of symbiosis between the historian and history. The nauseas, the dizzy spells, and the depressions no longer come only from the seasons and climates; it is the very horror of narrative history that provokes them: Michelet has "historical" migraines.[21]

History was Michelet's body. He devoured it, he lived from it. He could do this because whether from the origin of reptiles, the Battle of Waterloo, or the feeding of English infants, he, like Vico, regarded history as itself a living corpus, a body in which we have our very humanity:

> Michelet described with predilection all the intermediate stages of matter, savoring those ambiguous zones of development, where silex gives place to wheat, then to the French who feed themselves from it; where the plant extends itself into an animal, the fish into a mammal, the swan into a woman (Leda in the Renaissance), the Jew into a stone, the goat in a prophet (the Moses of Michelangelo); where a child's brain is nothing else than the milky flower of the camelia; where man even can substitute himself for the woman in the transhumanization of marriage.[22]

Michelet, writes Barthes, loved the world's body, its waters from which the fish are born and everything slippery, sliding, and silken like a woman's body, a woman's skin. Like the world's body, Michelet's history is also gendered and moves in accordance with the rhythms of birth, life, and death. History's body is male and female. The world-woman is moved, overthrown, and renewed by history's heroes. The two figures in Michelet's web are Grace and Justice, or Christianity, the woman as environment, and Revolution, the male as forceful entry, overthrow, rebirth. History is flesh. Thus the ultimate task of the historian is to discover the principle of corruptibility in the living flesh of each historical period. Here, again, we connect with the portraits of history, with history-as-portrayal, written into the faces, the eyes, modes, and posture of its principal actors, who are historical because they are embodied, humored, fleshed, and fed.

FRAGMENTATION, PERVERSITY, AND THE PLEASURE OF THE TEXT

From the very beginning, Barthes struggled to break the signs, to proliferate meanings, to exceed structure, classification, and stereotypes. With every step away from the conventional mode of writing, with each transgression of the codes of established literary criticism, as in *On Racine*, and above all in *S/Z*, he pushed writing back into the text of pleasure, back into the textual body that underwrites the atopia of meaning. Thus the liberated text became increasingly an icon of the liberated body, without center, hierarchy, or division:

> Who knows if this insistence on the plural is not a way of denying sexual duality? The opposition of the sexes must not be a law of Nature; therefore, the confrontations and paradigms must be dissolved, both the meanings and the sexes be pluralized: meaning will tend toward its multiplication, its dispersion (in the Theory of the Text) and sex will be taken into no typology (there will be, for example only *homosexualities*, whose plural will baffle any constituted, centered discourse, to the point where it seems to him virtually pointless to talk about it.[23]

He therefore employed literary criticism to disperse a work, to multiply its meaning through hundreds of fragmentary comments, each indulging its own purpose, and altogether excessive, like the countless stars of the night sky. In fact, every work of Barthes prefigures Barthes on Barthes, deepening the reflexive pleasure toward

which he pushed reading and writing. Barthes's fragments are therefore deliberate play, promiscuous and excessive openings and foreclo-
sures of literary desire drawn from nowhere, *hors-texte*, incomprehen-
sible to the conventional commentator. He slipped through
classifications, oppositions, and divisions of logic, drifting in language, ignoring alibis, the natural, the narrative as much as law, sex,
and marriage. This resolute inability to master his ideas according to
the divisions of the day rendered him incapable of violence and
therefore incapable of politics. If Barthes's writings nevertheless collect, they do so as a personal encyclopedia of topics indulged for their
own sake, as pleasurable incidents in a life compelled to find meaning.
The futility in this compulsion to meaning is exonerated only through
the author's surrender to the tide of words washing up their own
meanings for him to decipher—like a child on the beach.

Barthes wanted to use political philosophy and scholarship generally in the same way. That is, he would surround himself with them
and then, with an eye on his own body, pick and choose among them
what suited him. In this, the mirror image is essential. He saw
language; first the language of others, then his own language naked,
and then several languages from which to keep his writing in love
with his own body:

> The *corpus*: what a splendid idea! Provided one was willing to read *the
> body* in the corpus: either because in the group of texts reserved for study
> (and which form the corpus) the pursuit is no longer of structure alone
> but of the figures of the utterance; or because one has a certain erotic
> relation with this group of texts (without which the corpus is merely a
> scientific *image-répertoire*).[24]

Writing, then, would become an atopia; it would consist of sentences
whose sexuality would not be phallocentric expressions of the violence between the sexe˙ (in accordance with legal convention), and
it would be quite unpreoccupied with conquering meaning, mastering
it, reducing it to a system or to a calculus. Such writing would be
dedicated to foreplay and postponement rather than consummation.
Therefore he wrote introductions, sketches, outlines, histories of
writings—rhetoric, stylistics, unfinished, unfinishable works, mock
systems of intelligence and pleasure (see chapter 16 below).

In every case, he struggled to escape the conventional scenarios
that it was his misfortune to see in the words around him. His body's

capacity for seeing words deprived him of his political body: he did not enjoy the abstract, disembodied discourse of politics. There was nothing for him to try on, nothing to touch, nothing that suited him in it. Political gestures did not suit his corporeal style. He lacked convictions because he could not use language to convince himself—let alone others. In short, he was unable to make a scene, since the essence of such staging is the violence in ordinary language:

> violence always organized itself into a *scene*: the most transitive of behavior (to eliminate, to kill, to wound, to humble) was also the most theatrical, and it really was this kind of semantic scandal he so resisted (is not meaning by its very nature opposed to action?); in all violence, he could not keep from discerning, strangely, a literary kernel.[25]

THE LITERARY BODY AND THE BODY POLITIC

In the last analysis, Barthes remained pessimistic about our chances of limiting violence either at the collective level or in our individual lives. The only way he saw to resist society was to retreat from it, to struggle against death and disintegration as a writer. Here he hoped to sow seed, to be regenerated among other writers and thinkers. What appealed to him in his position at the Collège de France was that it is an institution outside of power (*hors-pouvoir*). At the same time, like Foucault, he did not see power in monolithic terms but as consisting of innumerable social strategies. He therefore considered that he could attack and displace power wherever it lodged in the discourse of domination and servility. For this reason, he hoped for a plurality of language without subordination, free from the conventional *topoi* in which power sediments. Barthes's dream of a language in which knowledge and pleasure might circumvent the language of power remains a literary fantasy. This is not to say it should be set aside as worthless. Rather, it needs to be combined with the kind of analysis of discourse production attempted by Foucault, Pierre Bourdieu, Jürgen Habermas, and Paulo Freire,[26] and even Barthes's own studies of mythology.

While we can concede the anti-establishment pathos of Barthes's theory and practice of literary pleasure, and its poststructuralist direction, it is necessary to be clear about its political and sociological limitations. Barthes really did not concern himself with anything but the faults of political writing (its stereotypes, realism, false antitheses, and violence). He seems to have forgotten his own contributions to a sociolinguistic analysis of political discourse. Any future work would, in my view, have to consider how the literary community is located within the larger communicative community as both an ideal speech atopia and as a practical pedagogy working at the level of literary initiation. Cultural politics would then be less a matter of artistic sublimation than the work of decoding the discursive production of the body politic on three institutional levels—family, work, and personality. Thus it may be said that the counterculture has prematurely identified political emancipation with the level of the libidinal body politic in terms of cultural and sexual emancipation of the personality, but without any strategy for connecting with the reproductive level of the bio-body and the working level of the productive body politic. Thus literate, middle-class, bourgeois counterculture fails to connect with working class and family culture, and thus fails to situate the literary community and libidinal emancipation within the broader project of emancipation strategically articulated to embrace the different levels and larger communicative community of a resurrected body politic. Barthes's literary deconstruction, like so much else in the counterculture, ironically remains locked within the establishment of knowledge and culture. Since most revolutionary regimes have been peculiarly puritanical in practice, it is hopelessly ill-conceived to imagine that there is any direct social nexus between polymorphous perversity and socioeconomic emancipation. Indeed, as Foucault reminds us, the link between power and sexuality in the modern biopolitical economy is endemic.

It seems best, therefore, neither to neglect nor to abandon the struggle to situate the problematics of the literary body and its community within the larger body politic. We must, however, refrain from the imaginary extrapolation of the ideal language or speech community to the total political community. We must learn to deal with a Babel of tongues. The humanities and the social sciences produce discourses that are mutually hostile and far from intelligible to the laity. We lack contexts in which the variety of institutional and practical discourses can confront one another to practice translation and dialogue. The university and the media are the institutions where this exercise is currently located. But media differ widely in their pedagogical possibilities, and both university and media are increasingly instruments of mass culture. Nevertheless, it remains true that the university, notwithstanding the external and internal constraints on its engagement with the larger issues in the polity, is the institution of last resort when it comes to the production of emancipatory knowledge and subversive discourse.

Barthes did not ignore these issues. We may not share his response to them. But we should recognize Barthes's personal courage and his resolute freedom in the pursuit of his craft and the creation of his own corpus:

> If I managed to talk politics with *my own body*, I should make out of the most banal of (discursive) structures a structuration; with repetition, I should produce Text. The problem is to know if the political apparatus would recognize for very long this way of escaping the militant banality by thrusting into it—alive, pulsing, pleasure-seeking—my own unique body.[27]

I think Barthes did not believe that any political regime could tolerate the pleasure of the text. Yet like many others he considered the writer's freedom an essential institution in any occasion of a good society. Inasmuch as this freedom must be fought for within the literary community, he may be considered a radical. That he was unable to find the linkage between literary emancipation and a broader social emancipation merely reveals the present political condition of all intellectuals.

PART TWO Disciplinary Theory and Practice in a Post-Kuhnian Economy of the Arts and Sciences

CHAPTER 6

Marxism and the Two Sciences

A Post-Kuhnian Economy of Cultural Production

I have been conducting a skirmish along several fronts—starting from a disagreement with Richard Rorty's neoliberalism, on to Jean-François Lyotard's postnarrative sublime and its effects on Fredric Jameson's utopianism, and with shots at Stanley Fish and Barbara Herrnstein Smith's combination of sociologism and economism in literary criticism. What divides us is whether or not we take post-Kuhnian science to legitimate a free-for-all in literary and social studies hitherto trapped in the normal paradigm of an essentialist hermeneutics and its totalitarian politics. To make further headway on these issues, I think it necessary to look closely at the economy of science rather than to trade on Thomas Kuhn's substitute metaphor of a "paradigm"—since with the latter we simultaneously lose the appropriate institutional concept of a sociology of science and the arts, as I shall argue in the following chapter, and are too easily seduced into a political metaphor of revolution, which in the case of critical studies of the arts and sciences is extremely difficult to connect with political change. To do this, however, I am obliged also to rethink the grounds for a Marxist approach to these issues—avoiding Louis Althusser's help since I think it did little good for Jameson's efforts on these lines, or anyone else's, as I have argued in my *For Marx against Althusser*.

The problem I wish to identify is an ambiguity in the demarcation of the sociology of the arts and sciences as understood by Marx and followers. The "two sciences" problem, incidentally, does not refer to the demarcation of the natural and social sciences—nor to the *double hermeneutic* of the natural and social sciences.[1] It refers to the inadequacy of the Marxist topology of superstructure and substructure to accommodate a sophisticated understanding of scientific, literary, and artistic inquiry. The result is that the arts and sciences are both subject to and exempt from social determination; furthermore, they function in both the substructure and the superstructure according to historicized stages of capitalist development. A Marxist sociology of knowledge, therefore, cannot avoid the problem of its own demarcation.

While it is generally conceded that Marxism has given a considerable impetus to the sociology of literature, it is undeniable that the Marxist conception of science is ambiguous, if not ambivalent. In very simple terms, Marx launched what we may call an externalist sociology of art and science, inasmuch as he stressed the social determination of knowledge and belief, rejecting the idealist or ideological view that society is driven by dominant ideas and values:

> Political, juridical, philosophical, religious, literary, artistic, etc., development is based on economic development. But all these react upon one another and also upon the economic basis. It is not that the economic position is the *cause*, solely while everything else is passive effect. There is, rather, interaction on the basis of economic necessity, which *ultimately* always asserts itself.[2]

Whether Marx or Engels is to blame for the equivocation here, we have not to decide. Engels' recognition of the interaction between the ideological superstructure and the economic infrastructure—even with a certain primacy accorded to the economic base—makes it necessary to draw further analytic distinctions in order to construct a working sociology of science within which a place is provided for the distinctive analytic enterprise of Marxism as a science of society. Otherwise, an ambiguity dogs Marxist sociology, namely, the uncertainty of whether to locate itself as a relatively autonomous ideological enterprise or to ground itself in the deterministic springs of the economic infrastructure. The seriousness of that ambiguity appears once we also see that Marx was tempted both to exempt the natural sciences from economic determinism and to claim that the Marxist analysis of the economic infrastructure is itself a natural science:

> With the change of the economic foundation the entire immense superstructure is more or less rapidly transformed. In considering such transformations the distinction should always be made between the material transformation of the economic conditions of production which can be determined with the precision of natural science, and the legal, political, religious, aesthetic or philosophic—in short, ideological forms in which men become conscious of this conflict and fight it out.[3]

The ambiguity I refer to as the "two sciences" stand consists in the sociology of science having to define science as both the object of its study and as its own method of research.[4] The demarcation of the sociology of science vis-à-vis the natural sciences is resolved by the "two sciences" stand only if we can assume that the philosophy of science is more descriptive of scientific practice than prescriptive; or that scientific practice is to be treated as an approximation of its idealized methods; or, finally, that the social sciences in principle, if not in practice, aspire to meet the standards of the natural sciences characterized in either of the preceding ways. The "two sciences" stand settles the demarcation problem by trading on a realist and empiricist view of science grounded in a correspondence theory of truth. According to this view, scientists seek causal relationships that hold with respect to society and nature independently of their procedures for constructing contexts in which these relationships are found to have local dominance. However, this is seriously challenged wherever it can be argued that the categories through which we construct facts are not context-free with respect to their usage.[5] This does not rule out objectivity in science. Rather, it calls for an empirical study of the constitutive practices and conventions of scientific inquiry as a laboratory and literary enterprise.

A difficulty here for sociologists of science who presume upon their own grounding in the methods of science is that the practice of the natural and social sciences differs widely from its members' own idealized accounts of their procedures. If the "two sciences" stand is to be avoided, then the sociology of science must drop any distinction between the natural and social sciences, inasmuch as each offers a domain of interpretive and discursive inquiry whose practical adequacy furnishes the sociology of science with its topics of investigation. On this view the phenomena for sociological study are the linguistic, conceptual, and technical practices that are for practitioners of discipline-specific domains of inquiry pragmatically adequate and competent achievements of sense, fact, generalization, confirmation, refutation, and the like. It is premature, if not mistaken, to tax such practices and their study with claims for absolute internal consistency, since this only reintroduces the demarcation problem regarding the ultimate grounds for the distinction between rational and nonrational beliefs in purely metaphysical terms. The paradox here is that we are committed in the name of empirical science to an a priori conception of what shall count as science. Perhaps it is on this score that we can be sympathetic to efforts by Jürgen Habermas and Karl-Otto Apel[6] to historicize the grounds of the natural and social sciences in a hierarchy of human knowledge interests and ideological criticism.

PARSONIAN EXCURSUS ON THE SUBSYSTEM OF SCIENCE

On the strong *externalist* program of the sociology of science, Marxist sociology and political economy is itself subject to determinism from the economic infrastructure. But that subjection renders superfluous the distinctively political and voluntarist nature of Marxist social science. If we weaken the Marxist program to a thesis on the *interactive* nature of ideology and the material substructure of society, however, Marxism is reduced to a hermeneutical exercise without benefit of the claim to constitute a scientific reading of social structure and historical process. It is here that the Weberian option for a *historical-hermeneutical sociology of science* opens up. Thus, Talcott Parsons argues that, rather than debate whether or not ideas in general determine or are determined by the material substructure, we need to distinguish three types of ideas, which will then allow us to adjudicate between a Marxist and a Weberian sociology of science:[7]

> *Existential Ideas.* These are frameworks for the analysis of the external world. They may be divided into (a) empirical ideas, verifiable by scientific method, and a residual class of (b) nonempirical existential ideas.
>
> *Normative Ideas.* These refer to valued states of affairs that an actor may seek to preserve or to bring into existence. Normative ideas may not be verifiable in terms of empirical scientific method.
>
> *Imaginative Ideas.* These are possible states of affairs that no actor is obliged to realize; for example, Marcuse's idea of a "New Science," which we shall take up later.

With regard to existential ideas, there exists a large consensus that valid empirical knowledge is best achieved, for given ends, by means of instrumentally rational action. This is the dominant scheme in economics and technology and even in commonsense, nonscientific knowledge. It was Max Weber's contribution to show that certain nonempirical existential ideas (the interest in salvation, for example) could favor empirically rational-legal accounting behavior. The question of the relative causal status of normative and existential empirical ideas in the relation between Protestantism and capitalism is itself decidable in principle through the comparative method of empirical social science and, as Parsons would claim, a generalized theory of action. On this basis, then, Parsons argues that Marx's super/substructure scheme is too simple. It is incapable of differentiating the role of empirically verifiable ideas at work in the processes of technology as well as in the processes of law, art, and science, which it is obliged to locate in the ideological superstructure.

Just as the division between superstructure and substructure proves to be too rough to handle the differentiation of meaning systems, so we need to refine the distinction we began with, namely, that between the externalist and internalist programs in the sociology of science. Those labels will undoubtedly remain useful as broad characterizations of contemporary directions of research. But each is capable of overlapping with the other at so many points, as well as at different levels of analysis, and with respect to quite different subsystems of the institutions and conduct of science. It may be useful, therefore, to offer at least a brief summary and map of the main lines of inquiry that occupies the sociology of science as a cultural system that permits us to identify the *analytic sense* in speaking of the internal and external *economy of science* or of the internal and external values of *science as a social system*.[8] Readers can check for themselves the ways in which the various arguments I shall consider make adequate analytic distinctions or presume upon boundary exchanges within the subsystem of science without articulating what levels of the system are in question. I am not, of course, proposing to settle differences through this device. Rather, I think it may serve to identify both persistent differences of approach and areas of complementary inquiry.

I am not demanding an instant mastery of the Parsonian four-function scheme. Here it has no other purpose than to facilitate recognition of the "boxes" left in the dark if one tries to trace the specific analytic domains recognized in any particular argument drawn from either an internalist or externalist sociology of science.[9] To speak of overlaps or gaps between these two approaches is a clumsy way of trying to identify their specific capacities for dealing with subsystem processes of differentiation and boundary exchanges between science as a subsystem and its environment of cultural, economic, and political subsystems. This system of exchanges can, of course, be addressed from the standpoint of any other subsystem, thereby relativizing the others as environmental-exchange subsystems. This contingency bears, for example, on the issue of whether we regard science as dependent on politics and technology, or vice versa. It also allows us to see that we need to be clear that science as a subsystem has its own economic and political subsystems, to which we refer later. We therefore cannot presume that the internal and external subsystems of science are the same thing throughout.

What the four-by-four system of functions (figure 6.1)[10] reveals to us is that we cannot regard science in abstraction from such other elements of the cultural system of a society as its arts, law, religion, and cosmology. Thus science is an *adaptive system* (A) analogous to the *economy* in its standing to society. As such, it has its own fourfold structure. Its primary goal (G) will be the production of knowledge, accomplished mainly in the research subsystem (A_G). The system

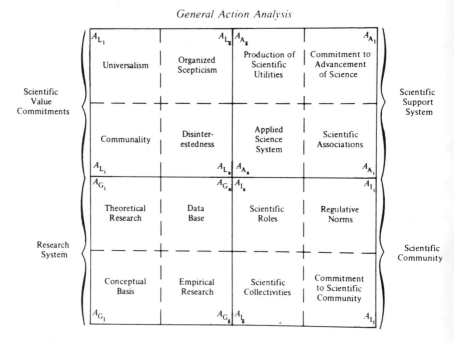

Fig. 6.1. The subsystems of science. Reproduced from *Explorations in General Theory in Social Science: Essays in Honor of Talcott Parsons,* ed. Jan. L. Loubser et al.; copyright © by The Free Press, a Division of Macmillan, Inc.

requires whatever resources are needed for its function; this provision constitutes the adaptive scientific support subsystem (A_A). Faced with the integration (I) of its internal goals and its need for external resources, there is a need to integrate the units involved and this falls to the *scientific community* (A_I). Finally, there is a need for an overall normative structure (L) to preserve the commitment to science within it members and within the broader society. This identifies the fourth subsystem, scientific value commitments (A_L).

Each of the four subsystems of science may be further differentiated according to the four-function (A, G, I, L) system. Thus, with respect to the subsystem of scientific value commitment, we can identify the specifically integrating values described by Robert K. Merton—universalism, organized scepticism, communality, and disinterestedness—which may be at odds with, or enhanced by, the wider cultural value system. Similarly, the cognitive values of the science subsystem may be threatened by the values at work within its own adaptive quest for research money and by the external economy's or the political system's adaptive quest for scientific knowledge of one sort or another. Here we can identify a number of issues with respect to claims for the "public" and/or "autonomous" nature of scientific inquiry. We can differentiate either claim with respect to its ideological, adaptive, and community functions. More important, we can imagine that any of these issues will have empirically distinctive features as soon as we differentiate field-specific sciences with their respective technologies and adaptative systems, which will certainly offer variable degrees of immunity from and dependence on "influence." Again, therefore, if we differentiate the research subsystem into its fourfold component functional systems, any assertion regarding the political or economic determinism of science will have to be made specifically with regard to its theoretical research, its data base, its conceptual basis, its empirical research, or any combination of the four, as we shall see in the final section of this chapter. Likewise, it is with respect to the scientific support system that we look for factors shaping how the science community sets itself problems and research programs, how it acquires its hardware, how it socializes its research personnel—in general, how it translates general societal needs for knowledge into specific science research problems that motivate and reward science personnel. Finally, the science system maintains more or less permeable boundaries with the rest of the sociocultural system of arts, law, and cosmology and with the social, political, and economic subsystems that surround it. In the following sections of this chapter I propose to take up these abstracted and generalized considerations in the context of arguments over the internal and external relations between science, technology, and politics in Marxist and Mertonian sociology of science.

SCIENCE, TECHNOLOGY, AND IDEOLOGY

Modern technology is largely based on scientific knowledge. Thus, we may infer that Marxists would have to save their own theory of ideology by arguing that in "advanced capitalism" the relation of super- to substructure is "reversed," namely, that the economy and technology become "science driven," operated and managed by "intellect workers."[11] But then, apart from its obvious difficulties as an explanatory variable that moves back and forth from substructure to superstructure, natural science loses the exemption accorded to it in a Marxist sociology of science, which in turn needs this exemption for its own identity. That this is not a purely imaginative possibility is to be seen in Habermas's attempt to remedy the Marxist schema through a corrective move that nevertheless preserves the "two sciences" distinction. The difficulty in this is that the natural sciences, on the one hand, are exempt from a sociology of science, while Marxism itself as a critical science, on the other, is confined to a superstructural activity of communicative and emancipatory hermeneutics designed to contain the disembedded logic of a science-driven technical and instrumentally rational political economy.

Habermas has argued that Marx failed to develop a unified critical science of man because, in splitting the natural and social sciences, he reduced historical materialism to the laws of the natural science of production and failed to develop any adequate theory of ideology-critique other than a simplistic materialist reduction of knowledge interests:

> If Marx had reflected on the methodological presuppositions of social theory as he sketched it out and not overlaid it with a philosophical self-understanding restricted to the categorial framework of production, the difference between vigorous empirical science and critique would not

have been concealed. If Marx had not thrown together interaction and work under the label of social practice (*Praxis*), and had he instead related the materialist concept of synthesis likewise to the accomplishments of instrumental action and the nexuses of communicative action, then the idea of a science of man would not have been obscured by identification with natural science.[12]

Here, then, we must notice a distinctive version of the "two sciences" argument. Habermas sees in Marx only one science of man reduced to a materialist science of the forces of production, ultimately the natural sciences. I have cited Marx to show that he held the "two sciences" view, that is, that science is socially determined and that the natural sciences are exempt from social determination. Moreover, in a later citation I shall show that Marx also held out the possibility of the historical unification of the natural sciences and the social sciences of man. Against this view, and in particular against Herbert Marcuse's remarks on the third option of a "New Science," Habermas himself holds to the "two sciences" view, arguing that human knowledge is guided by a triple structure of technical, hermeneutic, and emancipatory interests. At the technical level, scientific rationality is exempt from strictly sociological determination, although at the transcendental level of the constitutive interests of knowledge, science appears to lose its exemption.[13]

I propose now to examine this argument to show that it misses the opportunity to treat science as a single but highly differentiated communicative meaning system analyzable without any exemption clause to set it apart from other subsystems of society. In short, a Marxist sociology of art and science cannot exempt the natural sciences from sociological analysis and at the same time try to embed scientific inquiry with the hermeneutical, emancipatory pragmatics of universal communication. Rather, I think that recent developments in the sociology of science indicate that once we adopt an antirealist view of science, thereby becoming fully conscious of the socially constructed nature of science, the exemption clause is removed and the "two sciences" become one community of knowledge. It is with respect to this single community of knowledge that a Marxist sociology of science must propose studies of the human sciences and social policy.

It is always possible to assemble texts from Marx in order to refine what we have called the "two sciences" problem. To avoid such assembly, I propose the schema in table 6.1. We then have in Marx a functionalist schema of four subsystems—technology, science, economy, and state—each with obvious overlaps or boundary exchanges, and with no subsystem reducible to a simple sub- and superstructure dichotomy between the processes of transforming nature and the transformation of ideas. It is hard to deny, however, that Marx tends to identify science and technology as a system of man's domination over nature that reinforces (causes or is caused by?) the social domination of man by man.[14] Yet insofar as Marxism is the social science that looks to man's social emancipation, it looks toward the end of science:

> Industry is the real historical relationship of nature, and therefore of natural science, to man. If then it is conceived of as the open revelation of human faculties, then the human essence of nature or the natural essence of man will be understood. Natural science will then lose its one-sidedly materialist, or rather idealistic, orientation and become the basis of human science as it has already, though in an alienated form, become the basis of actual life. *And to have one basis for life and another for science would be in itself a falsehood.*[15]

The end of science flies in the face of the end of ideology not only because it rejects the ideology that science ends ideologies but also because it envisages an new science that would not be the instrument of the scientization of social and political life. It is over this "imaginative idea" of science that Marcuse differs equally with Parsons and Habermas. Marcuse, then, proposes that in any Marxist redefinition of social labor, it would be necessary to redefine not only economic and political labor but also scientific labor. In other words, he challenges the residual "two sciences" thesis in Marx, as well as in Ha-

Table 6.1. Marx's system of science and economy

Tools	technology
Technology (applied science)	
Theoretical natural sciences	science*
Economic relations of production (economic science)	economy
Social relations of production (law)	
Political relations of production/reproduction	state

*See figure 6.2, Model of "science production and reproduction," below.

bermas, since he proposes to take science out of the realm of necessity. According to Marcuse, natural science is part of our historical amnesia.[16] The "two sciences" stand represents an unnecessary concession to surplus repression and alienation. Unfortunately, Marcuse himself was not consistent in his conception of science. He had only the shakiest idea of the actual practice of the natural sciences.[17] Yet he is of interest to us because he tried to bring the "two sciences" argument to a utopian solution in his vision of a New Science made possible by the very social dominance of positive science:

> The point which I am trying to make is that science, by virtue of its own method and concepts, has projected and promoted a universe in which the domination of nature has remained linked to the domination of man—a link which tends to be fatal to this universe as a whole. Nature, scientifically comprehended and mastered, reappears in the technical apparatus of production and destruction which sustains and improves the life of the individuals while subordinating them to the masters of the apparatus. Thus the rational hierarchy merges with the social one. If this is the case, then the change in the direction of progress, which might sever this fatal link, would also affect the very structure of science—the scientific project. Its hypotheses, without losing their rational character, would develop in an essentially different experimental context (that of a pacified world): science could arrive at essentially different concepts of nature and establish essentially different facts.[18]

Here it is not to the point to explain in any detail how Marcuse's reduction of the methods of the natural sciences to behavioralism, operationalism, functionalism, and instrumentalism needs to be complemented by more contemporary research into the conduct of scientific research. What is to be remarked in the preceding passage is how Marcuse seems to move the natural sciences from the substructure into the superstructure. He attributes social domination to the method and concepts of science, while it is substructural force, and then tries to reverse the process, calling for a socially emancipated science that would, nevertheless, not lose its conceptually rational character. This equivocation is a perfect example of the "two sciences" stand in Marxism.

Now, Habermas rejects out of hand any notion of a unified science of both human beings and nature. Interestingly enough, his argument against Marcuse also preserves the "two sciences" stand. Habermas argues that the psychosomatic organization of humankind makes it historically impossible for us to conceive of an end to instrumentally rational action. In other words, we cannot conceive of science and technology as anything but natural science. Consequently, Marcuse's proposal, if any sense is to be made of it, requires a distinction between two subsystems of society—*work* (instrumental action, typically science and technology) and *language* (symbolic interaction, typically politics and ethics). Habermas's two subsystems[19] are defined in terms of a gloss on the Parsonian-Weberian schema of rational and nonrational orientations, which yields the contrastive structure in table 6.2.

It should be noted that Habermas's own schema preserves the exemption of scientific rationality from the rationality of the ideal language community. Scientific discourse and communicative discourse are separable subsystems of meaning production. It is an error to address either system in terms of the logic and relevances of the other:

> The alternative to existing technology, the project of nature as opposing partner instead of object, refers to an alternative structure of action: to symbolic interaction in distinction to purposive-rational action. This

Table 6.2 Habermas's two subsystems of society: work and language

	Institutional Framework: Symbolic Interaction	Systems of Purposive-Rational (Instrumental and Strategic) Action
Action-orienting rules	Social norms	Technical rules
Level of definition	Intersubjectivity: shared ordinary language	Context-free language
Type of definition	Reciprocal expectations about behavior	Conditional predictions conditional imperatives
Mechanisms of acquisition	Role internalization	Learning of skills and qualifications
Function of action type	Maintenance of institutions (conformity to norms on the basis of reciprocal enforcement)	Problem-solving (goal attainment, defined in means-ends relations)
Sanctions against violation of rules	Punishment on the basis of conventional sanctions: failure against authority	Inefficacy: failure in reality
"Rationalization"	Emancipation, individuation; extention of communication free of domination	Growth of productive forces; extension of technical control

means, however, that the two projects are projections of work and language, i.e., projects of the human species as a whole, and not of an individual epoch, a specific class, or a surpassable situation. The idea of a New Science will not stand up to logical scrutiny any more than that of a New Technology, if indeed science is to retain the meaning of modern science inherently oriented to possible technical control. For this function, as for scientific-technical progress in general, there is no more "humane" substitute.[20]

Like Parsons, Habermas finds the super-substructure distinction too unwieldy. Rather, he historicizes it. In early capitalism, science and technology may be said to drive the social system from below. In late capitalism science enters the "steering system" as the principal arm of the legitimacy function, redefining all the ethical problems of the communicative subsystem of science and technology.[21] Critical theory resists the scientization of politics.[22] But it is not our present task to follow these arguments.[23] It is the other side of the coin with which we have to deal. Is critical theory concerned to analyze the politicization of science, or is that the same thing as the scientization of politics, and are these two phenomena together the basic issues in a Marxist critical sociology of science?

There is much to be said for such a conclusion. Thus, it can be argued that the positivist methodology of the natural sciences functions not only to demarcate the technical rationality of science from the interpretative understanding proper to the historical and social "sciences" but also, through the program of unified science, to recommend the scientization of politics and society:

> It is its (instrumental) conception of the relation of theory to practice that gives the scientific conception of truth its meaning and therefore sets the conditions for the validity of a scientific explanation. It is just this conclusion which supports my claim that a positivist conception of the knowledge of social life contains within itself an instrumentalist-engineering conception of the relation of this knowledge to social action; for one is committed to this engineering view of theory and practice in the very act of adopting the positivist view of theory—indeed, it is this engineering view which supports and gives meaning to this view of social theory.[24]

That this is not a one-sided Marxist view is clear enough from Karl Popper's counterclaim that all that stands between an "open society" and totalitarianism is a commitment to a "falsificationist" view of science.[25] The consequence of this view is that politics is defined as a field for piecemeal social engineering rather than for any holistic planning. At issue, too, is a definite sociology of science, inasmuch as Popperians consider the scientific community to be the heart of liberal social values as well as the seat of the Western commitment to critical rationality. By contrast, Marxism only imagines it is a science—or a political science, for that matter—because it has a mistaken view of the concepts and procedures of the natural sciences and a keen view of the concepts and procedures of the natural science and a wholly erroneous view of the kind of lawful system a society might be.

Indeed, there are others who would argue that inasmuch as a modern society is by definition a "knowledgeable society,"[26] any form of ideology and dogmatism such as Marxism ought to recede in favor of the rule of scientific logic and evaluation. In other words, the critics of Marxism and Marxists themselves seem to agree that to have any notion of an alternative sociology of science than a descriptive version of the knowledgeable society is sheer utopianism. Habermas rejects that agreement, yet he is unwilling to support the Marcusean alternative of a New Science[27] because, although he is critical of the postivist program in the social sciences, he nevertheless uncritically accepts it as an adequate version of the natural sciences. He therefore remains caught in the "two sciences" stand. By contrast, Popper has a subtly differentiated view of the unified-science approach that allows the method of science to vary with its specific subject matter, but is always consistent with a critically rationalist view of science as an antirealist or constructionist enterprise. This means, however, that Popper also rejects the instrumentalist view of science, which goes unchallenged in the "two sciences" view adopted by Marxists:

> Popper is firmly against the instrumentalist view of the role of theories in science which argues that theories ought to be regarded as tools in research, and judged strictly in terms of their differential utility or functional capacity to this end. He believes that such a focus is appropriate only to technological rules, where this sort of success orientation is warranted. With Bunge, he views the long-term effects of this attitude as potentially and actually injurious to science, and therefore technology as well.[28]

Whether or not one accepts the details of Popper's philosophy of science, it is important to see that without the distinction it draws between theoretical science and applied science Marxists are driven to locate the instrumentalism of applied science in science generally. They are then caught in the quandary of a sociological critique of applied science that seems to involve a rejection of scientific rationality as such. Scientific rationality and scientific practice may in fact each be open to a constructionist or antirealist sociology of science—for which there is much contemporary evidence, as we shall see in chapter 8. If Marxists were not obliged to the "two sciences" stand, they could then avail themselves of a unified constructionist interpretation of scientific inquiry and social inquiry. They could recognize a subsystem of applied science and technology whose instrumentalism may well be its defining methodology. However, where the subsystem of applied science and technology exchanges with other subsystems of science, economy, society, and politics, they could properly avoid any scientific formulation of the logic of those discourse systems. Incidentally, this is precisely what is involved in the critique of Marxist scientism.[29]

THE MERTONIAN ECONOMY OF SCIENCE

We may speak generally of the social factors in the vocation of science,[30] or else we may wish to argue that the cognitive procedures, hypotheses, and methods as well as the objects/objectives of scientific research are also socially, economically, and politically determined. Here sociologists of knowledge have generally backed off into what we have called the "two sciences" stand, that is, the position that the natural sciences are exempt from social determination, at least with respect to their cognitive structure, if not to their community structure. Yet, as Merton observes, the social sciences, with the possible exception of "proletarian science," are not accorded any similar exemption. They are identified with the sphere of ideological knowledge—despite the difficulties that identification raises for the conceptual status of the sociology of knowledge itself. In practice, Merton has himself shaped most of the working options:

- The sociology of knowledge
- The sociology of scientific knowledge
- The normative structure of science
- The reward system of science
- The processes of evaluation in science[31]

Thus, at the level of general social determinism of science, he showed the nonlogical (not irrational) sources of science in puritanism. Then, with reference to the community of science, Merton initiated an internalist or interactionist sociology of science built on the "two sciences" exemption clause with respect to the cognitive structure of science (logical positivism) but otherwise opening up the sociological study of the conduct of science. He thus made it possible to ignore cognitive questions regarding the production of knowledge generally and in the particular sciences.[32] Today, however, these are areas of concern for several sociologists of science.[33]

In the meantime, Mertonians could construct a sociology of science as a social institution. Here the emphasis lay in spelling out the functional relationships between the conduct of critical, empirical science and its institutional norms of universalism, communism, disinterestedness, and organized skepticism. A next major step lay in the study of the internal economy of science so to speak. Here I refer to studies by Merton and many others who have analyzed the problems of scientific priority, recognition, unequal reward competition and deviancy, evaluation procedures, and related topics.[34] The studies constitute a huge literature, easily available to anyone interested in the sociology of science. Here I seek only to characterize the Mertonian approach as a "rival enterprise" that Marxist sociologists of science cannot afford to ignore, one that confronts Marxists with a concrete version of the economy of science analyzable in terms of specific schemas of the production of knowledge and status that go far beyond any programmatic invocation of the economic determinism of science. Thus, in an approximation to the model economy of science, we may understand science as the socially organized production and consumption of knowledge and recognition according to a schema that we offer as a device for bridging Mertonian and Marxist sociology of science (fig. 6.2).

It is clear from the literature that scientific theories are not easily abandoned merely on account of disturbing facts. The scientific community, particularly at field-specific levels, or within heavily capitalized research programs, will hold tenaciously to paradigm-bound inquiry. None of this rules out scientific opportunism, competition, secrecy, ambition, or exclusivity.[35] In short, the science community is not nearly so "free floating" as Karl Mannheim claimed. Rather, it

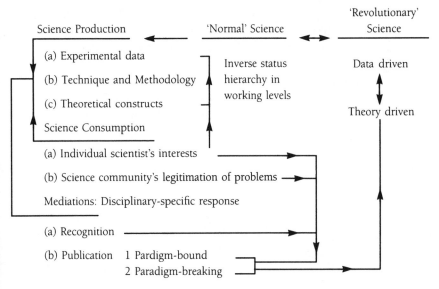

Fig. 6.2. A model of science production and reproduction

reflects the average vices and virtues of the general community, while nevertheless getting the business of science done. To the extent that we accord any autonomy to science that is not simply due to our ignorance of its practice, we refer to what Warren Hagstrom calls the "gift" in science. That is, we recognize that the production of scientists is to a certain extent self-generated in its choice of problems, its methods and its procedures for evaluation. Even in the worst science fiction this is a recognized attribute of science, though sometimes equated with its madness and open capacity for good and evil.

It should be noted that Merton generally presumes upon the "two sciences" exemption clause with respect to the cognitive structure of science. In terms of the more recently sociology of science, it is questionable to what extent the philosophy of science describes or prescribes the actual pragmatics of science inquiry. Here it suffices to refer to the arguments over the critical and consensus-oriented functions of scientific paradigms, falsificationism, or research programs.[36] As a matter of fact, Merton is committed both ways, that is, both to Popper and to Kuhn, although the Popperians reject any sociology of science. Of course, Popper's situational logic of scientific conduct presupposes the values of individualism and critical rationality in the open society. Yet Popper's view of science is decidedly antipsychologistic, at the same time that it is opposed to Kuhnian consensualism as a potentially irrational sociologism.[37] The Mertonian accommodation, however, is managed by allowing Popper's critical positivism to rule in the *validating* processes of science and regarding the Kuhnian program as a natural ally in the sociology of *discovering* science.[38]

THE POLITICAL ECONOMY OF SCIENCE AND SOCIAL POLICY

Following Pierre Bourdieu,[39] Karin D. Knorr and Dietrich Knorr have argued that scientific inquiry, when studied through an ethnography of practices of a large research laboratory, is best viewed as a constructive process aimed at "successful" research careers.[40] The pragmatics of science opportunism are not caught by the perspective of a correspondence or realist theory of knowledge. Rather, the scientific field must be regarded as locus for the competitive struggle to achieve recognition while the laboratory is then understood as the investment site for the symbolic and material capital accumulated by means of successful scriptural recognition (publication). The input-output relationships in the production and reproduction of scientific knowledge may then be formulated in the way shown in figure 6.3[41]

The benefit of Knorr's model is that it permits us to focus empirical research in the sociology of science on three levels:

1. *Laboratory Production*—the pragmatics of laboratory inquiry
2. *Literary Production*—the pragmatics of written inquiry in the sciences
3. *Historiographical Reproduction of Science*—the historicity of science achieved through literary reconstruction

It is at the first level that we discover the "two sciences" stand to be misconceived. It is not necessary to concede either simple realism or simple idealism in order to account for science's working relation with the world it simultaneously constructs.[42] Similarly, at the scriptural level, the literary production of natural and social science inquiry turns upon local laboratory interpretations of a discipline-specific literature as well as upon intertextual practices that call for empirical study as the organizational matter of public knowledge. It is only on

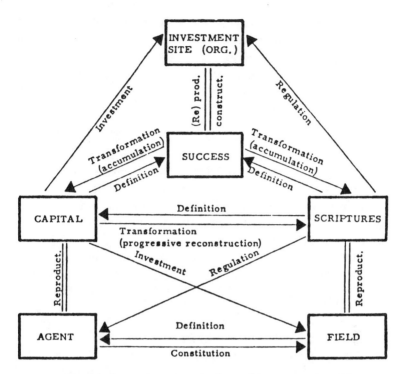

Fig. 6.3. A model of research production. The model represents the predominant relationships as seen from the respective entry. For example, the scientific field is *constituted* by the agents, while the position of the agents is *defined* by the field. Double lines represent relationships of *production,* single arrows represent phenomena in the area of *production,* and arrows combining relationships of transformation with those of definition represent the level of *historicity.* The model is proposed as an analytic tool to facilitate our understanding of the relationship between the concepts chosen and *not* as a somewhat mechanistic description of research production.

the basis of such studies that we may be able to fill out the Kuhnian paradigm as something more than a gloss on the scriptural regulation of science. Needless to say, such studies would differ entirely from studies of written inquiry as an organizational object.

It cannot be denied that there is a tendency in the Mertonian program to concede a certain autonomy to the science subsystem analogous to the autonomy of the self-regulating competitive market system. This is so, even though everyone knows, Parsons and Merton included, that the subsystems of science, politics, and economics have highly permeable boundaries (though not unregulated exchange in terms of the norms ruling each subsystem). Similarly, although Habermas speaks of the scientization of politics, it is probably erroneous to see this in terms of a conspiracy of scientists rather than as the divisive effect of the particular political objectives upon specific fields and technologies of science.[43] Here it is possible to argue that the professional and technical expertise of the sciences, so far from being the arm of democratic enlightenment, render them less and less accountable to lay political authority. This is aggravated to the extent that politicians turn more and more to the social sciences rather than to the natural sciences, though there are powerful and dangerous biosocial cross-fertilizations that have even more frightening prospects for the citizenry.

In this regard, Van den Daele and Weingart distinguished between the external influence of social policy upon science—aimed at promoting science on its own terms with a general presumption of its influence, say, on the quality and productivity of personnel—and policy controls that bear directly on a specific science discovering process, say, cancer research.[44] The latter direction offers the possibility of pursuing in some detail the otherwise general but nonspecific claims of the externalist program in the sociology of science. To render adequately the case where social policy seeks to foster a specific science specialty, Van den Daele and Weingart point to a triple structure of analysis:

The *policy* level—definition of science policy objectives
The *cognitive* level—definition of the structures of science as a working enterprise
The *institutional* level—definition of science in terms of a system of social action.[45]

It then becomes possible to locate the influence of social policy on science in terms of the empirically specific receptivity or resistance to a given specialty enterprise in cognitively and institutionally specific terms. Thus, at the *policy* level we may distinguish whether the objective is, for example, to facilitate description or assessment of the demographic or health characteristics of the population. Alternatively, the policy objective may be for the production of constructed theory and data in the implementation of some systems' control operation, for example, water fluoridation or pest control. At the *cognitive* level, exchanges with the policy level requirements may be generalized, specific, possible, or severely restrictive, or else unattainable without redefinitions and negotiations on either side. Within the cognitive level, it would be necessary to examine, for a given specialty, the extent to which change or resistance to policy directives effect singly or cumulatively its subdimensions of method and technology, theory construction, and disciplinary relations with other fields of research. Finally, at the *institutional* level, the strong sense of policy influence exists when we have evidence of science specialty with distinctive differentiation of its research area, membership, and reproduction mechanisms. Clearly, the process of differentiation in each subsystem on the institutional level involves exchange differentiation on each of the other levels and their specific subsystems.

In order, then, to speak of the social policy determination of science, Van den Daele and Weingart argue that it is necessary to be able to demonstrate a mutual convergence, so to speak, of politics and science. In other words, political objectives must increasingly adopt the form and methodology of technical or applied science, while science itself must be correspondingly organized to be capable of serving policy demands for description, measurement, and functional and causal explanations. The typology in table 6.3 may then be sketched as a device for locating the differentiation of levels of policy and science exchange:[46]

What this typology permits is the location of specific areas in which it is possible to analyze, with respect either to policy objectives or to the distinctive rhetorical and discursive practices within a given science specialty, the factors that bear upon desired or undesired chances of influence, cooperation, lag, and resistance. It remains to be said that thereafter it is a question of empirical ethnographic investigation and discourse analysis to examine the historical course of the differentiation, demarcation, and boundary exchanges institutionalized in specific uses of a policy-fostered science specialty. Moreover, such rhetorical studies would not only contribute to deepen our sense of the sociology of science; due to their power to pursue the system exchanges between levels of policy objectives and science practice, they promise to demonstrate the reciprocal scientization of politics

Table 6.3 Typology of degrees of "scientification" of political problems, functions of knowledge, and levels of development of science

Political objectives of control according to the degree of "scientification"	Scientific capacity (cognitive level of development)	Political objective of control according to function of demanded knowledge
"Analytical" politics (rationalizing initial conditions of political problem solving)	Assessment (description)	Basic structural concepts, operations analysis and measurement
"Means-end" rationalization (production of technical means of political intervention)	Systems control	Functional explanation; macro-theory of the subject matter
	Construction	Causal explanation; micro-theory of the subject matter
Systems politics (reflexive process of goal definition for political intervention)	Systems formation	Integrated science; fusion of natural and social sciences theory of complex system

as well. They thereby fulfill an important part of the program of a critical theory of science discourse and practice.

I have argued that a post-Kuhnian sociology of knowledge and culture does not need to respect the distinction between superstructure and substructure in analyzing the domains of science, art, technology and policy. Indeed, any attempt to preserve such a distinction leads only to further troubles in such practices as the exemption clause, the demarcation problem, the reflexive question, and the utopianization of science. In my view, the "two sciences" stand can be avoided if the sociology of knowledge drops any distinction— such as the "double hermeneutic"—between the natural and the human sciences. Each activity offers a domain of interpretive and discursive inquiry whose practical adequacy furnishes the sociology of knowledge with its proper topics of investigation.

CHAPTER 7 The Disciplinary Production of Natural and Social Science Arguments

We need to revise the practice of segregating science and literature as though it were the only way to preserve logic from the intrusions and distractions of rhetoric. On the contrary, we may achieve a more adequate understanding of our practices of competent social science accounts by drawing explicit attention to their pervasive rhetorical features.

Joseph Gusfield[1] has argued, as have many others by now,[2] that we cannot trust the wall we have set up between the interpretative communities of science and literature. What sociologists have discovered about written science is readily confirmed by Gerald Holton, who like Thomas Kuhn is a knowledgeable physicist and historian of science. Holton argues that we cannot readily understand how scientists produce their work if we rely solely on the procedures for rendering the events of science in empirical and analytical language:

> The technical report of, say, the analysis of a bubble chamber photograph is cast largely in terms of a life-cycle story. It is a story of evolution and devolution, of birth, adventures, and death. Particles enter on the scene, encounter others, and produce a first generation of particles that subsequently decay, giving rise to a second and perhaps third generation. They are characterized by relatively short or relatively long lives, by membership in families or species.
>
> Listening to these village tales told by physicists, one is aware that the terminology may initially not have been "seriously" meant. Yet the life-cycle thema works and so do a number of other themata imported into the sciences from the world of human encounters.[3]

The practice of normal science is surely as much a literary or documentary phenomenon as it is a laboratory practice.[4] We cannot, therefore, speak of science as though its "real" events or its "real" practices are to be found only in its laboratory settings. It may well be that one cannot learn laboratory practice uniquely from reading science in the journals.[5] It turns out that literary and laboratory science are linked practices; orientation within the laboratory is not independent of what the laboratory itself is oriented toward, namely, published science, the documentary correlate of laboratory crafts.[6] It seems reasonable, therefore, to extend Kuhn's notion of the paradigm control of normal science by reminding ourselves of the complex documentary organization of discipline-specific written procedure in scientific inquiry, which renders the literary gloss contained in the area of the paradigm into a set of further inquiries regarding its written practices. After all, as any schoolchild will testify, paradigms are far more rigid and sanctionable affairs than are the practices to be found in the formulation of reasoned argument and refutation in the scientific literature, as I shall show.

Instead of considering the consensus that prevails in normal science as due to the dominance of a theoretical paradigm, it has been argued that we should view areas of knowledge as loosely related, adaptive models of inquiry, whose written formulation includes self-evaluative practices concurrent with the production of knowledge claims.[7] Scientific models are inherently fallible, or controversial; they permit gradual, overlapping changes without hardening until only a revolution can liberate their adherents. Users and interpreters of models are always free to adapt them according to need. Nevertheless, there are temporary alignments of professional understanding between writers and readers, and it is these that constitute scientific knowledge. In fact, this gradualist view of scientific development is more faithful than Kuhn's use of the political term *revolution,* which he substituted for Ludwik Fleck's sociological concept of the thought structure (*Denkzwang*) that constrains the paradigm as an exemplar of work identifying a given scientific community (*Denkkollectiv*).[8] Fleck's sociological preference for the term *collective,* rather than *school* or *community,* seems in fact to have caused Kuhn to suppress the sociological term in favor of the grammatical term *paradigm,* but then to have gratuitously substituted Fleck's conception of sociologically constrained change with the ideologically progressivist notion of "revolution." Thus Fleck was Americanized behind his back, and his landmark in the sociology of science became available in English only in 1979, when, as I believe, it inaugurated what I call a "post-Kuhnian" sociology of the arts and sciences.

WRITTEN SCIENCE

The inadequacy of logico-inductive metaphysics of science[9] as an account of the pragmatics of either laboratory "discovering" science or of published science is stressed by the distinguished physicist John Ziman in his reflections on the social bases of science. Ziman is emphatic on the primacy of written science in fulfilling the distinctive task of science as the production of public knowledge. Furthermore, Ziman stresses that scientific discourse even in the natural sciences cannot be characterized in terms of any unified language, far less by logically or mathematically precise formats in total abstraction from everyday language and reasoning: "The reasoning used in scientific papers is not very different from what we should use in an everyday careful discussion of an everyday problem."[10]

I am not concerned to find in Ziman's remark any popularist argument for the reduction of scientific logic to commonsense argument. Rather, what I find to be necessitated by Ziman's observation is a post-Kuhnian program of study whereby we discover the order of pragmatic reasoning, refutation, evidence, and generalization that are constitutive of the discipline-specific arts and sciences as vernacular and written achievements. Moreover, I am not entering the simple claim that science is published knowledge. Rather, this is a fact consequent upon, or inseparably tied to, the socially organized practices of documentary argument, confirmation, and refutation that relate scientific writers and readers in the critical community of science. Furthermore, this is the underlying feature of public knowledge in the arts and social sciences, no less than in the physical and natural sciences.

The phenomenon, then, that I think deserves the current consideration of the sociology of the arts and sciences is the ordinary practice of written argument, evidence, corroboration, and refutation whereby "discovering" laboratory and field sciences establish new findings as relevant to discipline-specific contexts of argumentation located in the core journals of any science. Ziman's remarks can be taken to challenge the extraordinary abrogation of logic and rationality to the natural sciences. Despite the prejudice in favor of the scientific monopoly of logic and rationality, it is readily apparent that the daily practice of science in laboratories, journals, and conferences contradicts the normative accounts of science. But such findings usually remain anecdotal features of practitioners' lives. Inasmuch as practitioners generally gloss their experience in the very terms of normative sociology, whose abstractive procedures fail endemically to provide for the issues of the local production of its merely legislated orders, practitioners come to terms with what normative theory misses as "deviance," "everyday life," "latent functions," and the like. By contrast, I propose that the question, What are the communicative practices of logic and argumentation in written science? is entirely empirical. How these phenomena may be made a matter for sociological and literary inquiry may be seen from a look at a variety of complementary analytic procedures in contemporary studies of cognitive and discursive structures of scientific reasoning.

THE DISCIPLINARY ORGANIZATION OF SCIENTIFIC INQUIRY

A number of practices witness to the socially organized formatting of written science, which renders it an object for sociological study according to a variety of rival strategies. I shall review these briefly in order to locate some specific claims and procedures that have emerged in studies of written science. There is, first of all, the commonplace phenomenon of journal science and a growing practice of reporting on its troubles for editors, reviewers, and authors.[11] All professional scientists are held responsible for the communication of their findings, whether these are the findings of laboratory discovering science or, as is extensively the case, the findings of textual inquiry that is generated in typically academic settings such as the library and study. It is a curious feature of written scientific communication that its professional practitioners are held to a competent performance in writing, reviewing, and editing articles, papers, books, texts, and reports without specific instruction. In calling attention to this phenomenon, I am not for the moment concerned with possible studies of the pragmatics of sanctionably adequate or inadequate science editing and review, although I think it is worthwhile exploring ties with research in this area. I note, in passing, that the literary production issues involved here are merely glossed in remarks about science journals' preferences for positivism and avoidance of bias. Such glosses miss entirely what is involved in the occasioned practice of a competence acquired only through its very exercise, and employed with respect to discipline-specific issues in the theory and practice of the natural and social sciences. Moreover, any analysis of the conventions of science in general would be specifically vague on the issues in each occasion of its practice.

Quite another mode of analysis—concerned with such sociological features of the scientific community as its system of influence, reputation, and reward—has been developed on the basis of the phenomenon of written science employed as an abstractive resource for such findings. Robert Merton and Harriet Zuckerman locate the phenomenon of a science literature in three basic factors, given the general accumulation of all cultural practices:

1. The institutionalized pressure for public diffusion of scientific work is reinforced by the institutional goal of advancing the boundaries of knowledge and by the incentive of recognition contingent upon publication.
2. there is the correlative obligation within the institution of science for the user of published knowledge to make reference to his sources and to avoid sanctions of theft or plagiarism.
3. The institutionalized reciprocity of incentives for conformity and sanctions for nonconformity were necessary for science to function as part of the public domain via the imperative to communicate findings.[12]

Among the incredible variety of topics pursued in the Mertonian program, attention has been paid to the corpus of scientific literature as an empirical resource for studies of the hierarchies of scientific influence,[13] and to scientific networks in articles, journals, and textbooks attested to by means of quantitative studies of citation indexes.[14] Citation analysis has become a specialty-specific quantitative procedure in the sociology of science.[15] These studies, however, do not analyze the endogenous textual organization of scientific influence in specific contexts of argumentation. Citations are treated as external evidence of literary networks that carry the collegial practices of the scientific community.

I believe that current work in the analysis of written practice in the sciences will go some way to correct Merton's own complaints with regard to the inability of citation analysis to capture the fine-grained social and cognitive interactions that compose scholarly scientific work. In particular, I think it can be shown by detailed textual analysis how scientific writers locate their work in a discipline-specific context of argument and accumulated findings, and how they provide textual resources for a copractitioner's competent reading and evaluation of their own contributions. Of course, at this point I can only report on preliminary findings. Indeed, along such lines I can envisage treating the Mertonian pattern of institutional norms for the conduct of science[16] as a set of directives for tracing the literary and rhetorical correlates of universality, communism, disinterestedness, and organized skepticism. Such an approach would, I think, strengthen the findings claimed for these normative principles by showing them to provide compliance features with respect to written scientific formats. The discussion of some of the analytic features of science articles later on provide a sense of what is at issue here.

THE RHETORICAL ANALYSIS OF SCIENTIFIC WRITING

As mentioned earlier, Gusfield has argued that we cannot overlook certain rhetorical features of the production of written science. In particular, he argues that it is possible to discover a basic dramaturgical structure in the communication of social science findings. Karin Knorr and Dietrich Knorr have advanced a related argument to the effect that a story-grammar model yields the underlying structure of a natural science article.[17] Gusfield's use of dramaturgical method constitutes a pioneering effort to raise the issue of the analysis of natural-language sociology.[18] I propose therefore to examine some issues in Gusfield's rhetorical formulation of a science article, J. J. Waller's "Identification of Problem Drinkers among Drunken Drivers,"[19] in order to suggest where its program can be extended in the light of more recent proposals for the sociological study of written inquiry in the natural and social sciences.

The rhetorical analysis of science raises the following production issues in the sociology of documentary knowledge:

1. What is the meaning of knowledge within a rhetorical perspective?
2. Through what process is written scientific knowledge developed?
3. What is the relationship between rhetoric and morality in the process of documentary knowledge construction and formation?

Like any other communicative act, written science involves a sender/receiver, speaker/hearer, author/reader relation.[20] Thus the author of a scientific report will be concerned to establish his or her authority (science agency), professional credibility and competence, and adherence to adequate methods of finding and reporting—and he or she will require of the reader an orientation to just those features of the report (scientific key). Hence the reader is either a novice or co-competent recipient of just those literary performances that make up a recognizable, ordinary science article.

What is involved here is not simply that the disciplinary journal provides a home for the relevant paper. The journal legitimates, and its authority is in turn reinforced by, the submission of articles conformable to its theoretic and methodological standards. Inasmuch as the article Gusfield chose to analyze appeared in the *Journal of the American Medical Association,* and just as his treatment of it appears in the *American Sociological Review,* a prospective reader is already cued not to be in search of recreational reading. Indeed, just as the author of such articles is expected to know the relevant disciplinary journals for the submission of his or her work, so the reader will ordinarily consult such journals only in the course of study and research, and very often with the purpose of contributing further such writing. Outside of such relationships, science journal writing and reading soon loses its "interest."

In the production of the science article every effort must be made to impersonalize the communication so that nothing is traded on in virtue of extrascientific attributes of the author. Thus the science article typically provides data on the author's scientific credentials, mentioning the author's academic auspices, university, research institute, sources of agency funding, collegial support, and the like (science agent/agency). Further information of this sort may be distributed in footnotes and citations of the author's previously published work. As Gusfield notes, these items function to mobilize the reader's trust in the professional competence at work in the paper and to invite rival competence regardless of unequal reputation and the like. The literary production of the science agent is to be found in such typically impersonal and passive-voice formulations as "it has been argued" and "the results of such and such a test indicated." The cumulative effect of these expressions is to attribute agency in scientific research to the observance of scientific method, descriptive procedure, and implications of findings.

The science author, by the very means of constructing the narrative to make it the work of scientific method, thereby simultaneously widens the distance between the author and the subjects under study, while narrowing the distance between the author and presumably collegial readers. The prominence given to research design and methods enhances the recipient design of professional scientific writing and reading, while rendering the professional/lay relationship increasingly asymmetrical.

As Gusfield recognizes, the method of rhetorical analysis puts a strain on devices for an adequate representation of the text under discussion. A number of procedures have been adopted, ranging from reproducing the full article as an appendix, to quoting full-length abstracts and introductions or, as we are now doing, trying to give as representative an idea as possible of the structure, principal divisions, and salient arguments of the analyzed text (Gusfield on Waller) by ample delineation and quotation. For his purposes Gusfield adopts a "quick and dirty" overview of Waller's text drawn from its very first page:

> Information about previous contact with community agencies, particularly contact involving drinking problems, was compared for 150 drunken drivers, 33 accident-involved drivers who had been drinking but were not arrested, 117 sober drivers involved in accidents, 131 drivers with moving violations, 19 drivers with citations plus arrest warrants, and 150 incident-free drivers. Screening criteria for problem-drinkers were two or more previous arrests involving drinking or identification by a community agency as a problem-drinker. These criteria were met by the following: drunken drivers, 63 percent; drivers with an accident after drinking, 50 percent; drivers with warrants, 30 percent; non-drinking drivers with an accident, 14 percent; persons with driving violations, 8 percent; and drivers with no accidents, 3 percent. High correlation was found between two or more arrests involving drinking and an impression of problem drinking. Eighty-seven percent of the drunken drivers were known to community agencies, most with multiple contacts starting before age 30.[21]

Gusfield speaks of this summary version of the article as a device for providing the reader access to its expanded form by treating the whole article as a narrative, a story involving a transformation.

The summary from Waller functions to accomplish a disciplinary reduction of the activity of "driving" to that of "drunken driving," and of "drinking" to "problem drinking." These two reductions are achieved through a chemico-mechanical test that measures blood alcohol count and two or more arrests involving drinking while driving. The two reductive moves produce an agent characterized specifically as a science-produced agency that can now be enlisted in a drama of social problem and social science control or administration. In order to exert some control over "drunken drivers" a method is employed—"high correlation was found between two or more arrests involving drinking and an impression of problem drinking"— to separate ordinary "social drinkers" from "problem drinkers." The scene is then set for the transformation of the "drunken driver" from a "social drinker," as commonly supposed, into a "problem drinker," that is, a shift from the ranks of ordinary citizens whose drinking is responsible even if foolish, to a place among the antisocial and unhealthy elements of society. The characters are now in contrastive place, although the rest of the report to take the narrative form of a morality play, which turns upon what Gusfield nicely terms "the rhetoric of social hierarchies." In other words, despite changes of scene and many an upheaval, a good play generally leaves the audience where it was when it came in.

Put differently, it is a finding of ethnomethodology[22] that, so far from discovering society, the social sciences trade on a presumed knowledge of society for the sense of their particular findings. In terms of dramaturgical analysis this means that, while initially Waller's study threatens to degrade social drinkers as members of normal society, it ends by assigning them their own rightful sense of being above the sick, criminal, and pathological members of that same society. In short, what is moral about society is one's sense of relative but not absolute worth. Whatever the troubles of "social drinkers," they are not those of "problem drinkers"—and this view of things is upheld in law and medicine. Thus, the normative contrastive structure upheld in society is replicated in the contrastive categorization of the "social drinker" and the "problem drinker" as respectively comic and tragic figures who provide the narrative story of Waller's paper.

THE LOCAL PRODUCTION OR TEXTUAL ORDER: SOME EXAMPLES

Perhaps enough has been said in terms of our discussion of the preceding dramatistic keys for us to see that under this rubric of science agency we have only a summarizing gloss on the science writer's efforts to produce recognizable scientific reporting. Whether in fact that means a reduction of metaphor, or a reliance upon it, or a preference for impersonal and passive-voice formulations, for quantitative rather than qualitative measures, and for strictly logical formulation and the exclusion of all biographical and social bias, I think requires further empirical study. The purpose of such a study of written science is not to produce polemical or ironic contrasts between normative science and canonical procedure. It is simply to discover how in fact we produce and consume normal science literature without our practice being seriously faulted, even where it is remote from the idealized accounts of the philosophy of science.

To this purpose, I hold that written science must be treated as a structure of at least four elements:

1. Laboratory and field notes, measures, science artifacts
2. Competent assembly of intertextual sources, tradition
3. Disciplinary-specific production of a plausible text
4. Competent readers, reviewers of scientific discourse

Each of these domains calls for a program of empirical research into the social organization of written science. Thus we need studies of how it is that significant articles and rival journals come to challenge the disciplinary paradigms in the corpus of normal science. Here I locate contemporary interests in rival readings, and in the psychoanalysis of intertextuality.[23] The latter approaches to literary production have succeeded in raising reflective understanding of textual organization, although in my view Louis Althusser's analytic practices do not differ substantially from such analytic practices as those of Talcott Parsons[24] and Joseph Schumpeter.[25]

In view of the runaway risks of disengaged analysis in terms of elaborate dramaturgical and story-grammar models, we need methods of textual analysis more directly located within the written organization of the natural-language arts and sciences. Following Harold Garfinkel, I prefer to speak of the "local production" of science inquiry and its literary accomplishment of furnished arguments, assumptions, refutations, relevance, and topicality—of all the features of a plausible text. In view of the ethnomethodological finding that sociological descriptions achieve adequacy and conclusiveness only as practical matter,[26] and not as representative matter or as states of affairs "really,"[27] then it becomes a task to extend those findings from conversational and organizational settings to the discovery of the literary correlates of reasoned argument, and of reader/writer relations of topical coorientation, recipient design, closure, and repair.[28]

Of course, this does not mean that we can apply the findings of conversational analysis as disengageable rubrics in order to provide machinery for the organization of texts as documentary collections of warrantable sense, fact finding, cogent argument, practical refutation, and the like. With these qualifications in mind, it is possible to envisage studies of the sequential order, logic, categorizations, and contrastive structures in written scientific inquiry. These phenomena furnish the sociology of texts with issues of an orderliness that is a technical feature of discipline-specific written procedure, whose analysis it now seems will contribute substantially to the sociology of science.

To show how this method functions, I shall reproduce a passage from a text[29] analyzed by Digby C. Anderson and passages from an article[30] that I shall analyze for the sake of showing how refutations are constructed. In addition to certain general observations, attention may be drawn to two preliminary analyses.

TITLES AS READER'S INSTRUCTIONS

The Counsellor and Alienated Youth
D.H. Hamblin
Department of Education, University College of Swansea

This article is based on the writer's experiences with intelligent young men aged from 16 to 19 who rejected the values of home and school and disassociated themselves from contemporary society. It is argued that behaviour which appeared to be self-destructive to the outsider, serves important functions for these individuals. Their alienated behaviour masked an intuitive attempt to avoid the most damaging form of alienation—alienation from oneself. Some account is provided of the processes which occur when this is the case and the strategies used in creating satisfying identities.[31]

In his analysis of the work of the title, the abstract, and an excerpt from the article above, Anderson discovered three constitutive features of its textual order: (1) author authority (categorization of the writer), (2) age orientation (populating a page), and (3) investing purpose.

Notice that while these literary devices are comparable to Gusfield's dramatistic keys, Anderson's analysis is not obliged to any dramaturgical metaphors. Rather, we can treat these devices as interactional resources whereby each of the categories of author, reader and subject of study is framed in a recipient design of relevantly communicable, competent knowledge of experiences, differently distributed between what many of us know in general and what can be learned further through discipline-oriented reading in scientific journals concerned with youth problems and modern society. Within that allocative framework, the author is concerned to produce findings of cogent fact, generalization, and policy that a competent reader, commanding relevant intra- and extratextual resources, will find plausible, though perhaps questionable and corrigible in this and that respect, often enough as furnished by the text, and rarely wholly in contradiction of its argument.[32]

Anderson's discussion of textual authority tends to overlap with considerations that are allocated to the device he calls "investing purpose." In part, this is because he seems to suggest that the author/ reader relationship is unequal in some motivated way. I consider this a potential distraction. Much more to the point is Anderson's observation that that relation, while unequal in terms of discovering knowledge, tends to be repaired through the literary complicity of author and reader in the normative contrastive structure of those who are subjects of social science inquiry and those who produce and consume such inquiry. Since this is a finding with respect to the tropes of deviance literature similar to Gusfield's account of the function of the rhetoric of social hierarchies, I shall not expand on it any further. That it may be consequential for studies of *Ideologiekritik* goes without saying.

TITLES AS READERS' INSTRUCTIONS

In addition to these general constitutive features of the literary production of argument, Anderson raises some interesting observations with respect to the commonplace functions of titles. It is of course easy to overlook titles as merely handy tags to an article's contents, although as authors we are likely to give them considerable thought. In fact, the work of titles can be construed as productive features of a topic's organization, scope, methodology, and the like.

In other words, we may treat titles as instructions designed to orient the reader to the author's proposal to take such overlapping concerns as "youth," "alienation," and "counselling" in a preferred reading. Anderson's recommendation is that we read the title "The Counsellor and Alienated Youth" as follows:

(1) Treat "alienated youth" as a subcategory of youth.
(1a) Do not read "alienated youth" as a subcategory of alienation, i.e., as "youthful alienation."

With these rules in mind, we are in a position to resolve the ambiguity in the conjunction between "the counsellor" and "alienated youth" appearing in the title of the article. The title might foster the expectation that the article will deal critically with the activities of counsellors as further experiences that contribute to the subculture of alienated youth. We therefore need a way of deciding which is the relevantly troubled population. From the abstract we can gather that the troubles mentioned—"rejecting the values of home and school"— are more likely to categorize at least some of youth rather than counsellors, though some counsellors may favor abolishing the family. On the basis of this category-bound definition of troubles,[33] we can derive two further reading instructions:

(2) Treat the topical troubles as category-bound activities of alienated youth.
(2b) Treat the conjunction between alienated youth and counsellors as a duplicate organization of category-bound activities with the ordering that counsellors are authorized and socially positioned to treat alienation among youths rather than themselves.

Thus, if counsellors, like so many other professionals in human relations, experience themselves as part of the alienation they allegedly help to dispel, then any article with such a focus ought to be titled in a way that avoids generating other expectations in its readers.

REFUTATIONS AS A PRACTICE OF WRITTEN SCIENCE

The locus of refutation in science is the article note, or reviewer's comment written in response to an article submitted for appraisal or after publication. According to the Popperian view of science, any claim to knowledge must: (a) specify, actually or in principle, "criteria of refutation" or factual propositions such that, (b) when observed, these criteria succeed in refuting the claim; thus (c) knowledge is any claim that stands the list of (a) and (b). To this Imre Lakatos adds the observation that, since factual propositions are asserted only in the light of an observational theory, challenges to propositions of fact can always be met by revising the observational theory by means of auxiliary hypotheses.[34] As Nigel Gilbert observes, Lakatos's position seems to capture better the exchanges in the scientific literature where refutation and response are concerned.[35] Thus he quotes the exchanges between E. J. Opik and A. C. B. Lovell, in particular, the charge that Opik's claims for the hyperbolic velocity of meteors was dependent on a mode of measurement whose findings could not be replicated by radar measurements. Gilbert found that the exchange of claim and counterclaim remained undecided, with each experimental group sticking to its observational theory, though modifying it with auxiliary hypotheses to survive flat refutation. Here, Gilbert surely discovers in written science a practice one would not expect if refutation were conducted according to the logical canons of idealized science. However, the local production of the phenomena of artifactual troubles, agreements and disagreements, escapes him. It is here that work by Michael Lynch and myself is especially relevant.

In an analysis of a historian's article I have found that a historian's way of dealing with rival frames of interpretation, regarding the significance of the feminization of religious language in medieval texts, consisted in a practice of "discounting" contrary evidence. The written practice, however, proceeds in accordance with no clear imitation of any idealized account of logical refutation. By the same token, the refutation built up through heavily documented sources and the rhetorical accumulation of "negators" yields for all practical purposes a historian's refutation. This can be seen only in its full textual detail. Caroline Bynum seeks to reject arguments to the effect that medieval maternal imagery reflected changes in theological attitudes toward women rather than the use of female imagery to rethink roles of authority in the religious community. She appeals to specifically lacking documentation, or specifically undecidable evidence in cases where shared documents are at issue:

> "I have *not* found the idea of God as mother elaborated in any twelfth-century female writer."

"There is *no* evidence that women were especially attracted to devotion to the Virgin or to married women saints."

"*Neither* is there *any* evidence that the idea of God as mother was developed in writings which men addressed to women."

"And there is *little* evidence that the popularity of feminine imagery with cloistered males in the twelfth-century reflects an increased respect for actual women."

"It seems that the increase of feminine images in twelfth- to fourteenth-century religious writings does *not* tell us—at least *not primarily*—about the lives [of] (or even the attitudes toward) women."[36]

Through the accumulation of the *negators* (which I have italicized) and the rhythm of negative emphasis in each, Bynum produces a deep refutation whose strength derives not so much from logic or experiment as from its practical exhaustiveness. Its lengthy address, and the sense given that no relevant point is ignored, weigh in to close off further discussion. Both writer and reader gather audiovisually from everything said that this is all that needs to be said by way of adequate refutation. The list of points constitutes a notational order designed to achieve a cogent refutation whose seriousness is exemplified in the time and space allotted to it. In literally saying more against the rival interpretations of the trend in the feminization of religious language, and from notes 51–67, which add half as much again (three pages), the reader is led to presume that there is accountably more to favor Bynum's hypothesis that when the literary usage of maternal imagery is further specified it will be found to match Cistercian concerns with the relation between authority and community.

CONCLUSION: SOME ISSUES WITH RESPECT TO FORMAL ANALYSIS AND THE PRAGMATICS OF WRITTEN SCIENCE INQUIRY

There is now a growing body of work to challenge the conventional distinction between scientific and literary uses of language.[37] It may be argued instead that the social organization of the formats of inquiry in the arts and sciences is in every case specifically a matter for empirical study. I believe that such studies will deepen the issues in the opposing strategies of internalist and externalist sociologies of science.[38] Moreover, they should make it clear that the logic of argumentation is not the sole province of the philosophers of science, whose prescriptive versions of scientific method rarely consider the practices of laboratory and written science. Such normative or canonical versions for the formatting of good scientific writing according to models of inductive and hypothetico-deductive reasoning constitute formalizations of written inquiry rarely adhered to in practice, or else incompletely and without either explicit rebuke or contrition.

In view of this, I believe that we need to study how it is that such distinctions as those between (1) fact and theory, (2) scientific and personal voice, (3) fact and value, (4) context of discovery and context of validation, and (5) subjective and objective explanation consist of modes of practical reasoning whereby scientists produce documentary arguments whose formats circulate discipline-specific findings and generalizations for confirmation or invalidation by the very same procedures of written inquiry. It is plain that scientific discourse, especially in the social sciences, is not identical with the restricted codes of logic and mathematics. The language of written science suffices to carry all sorts of reasoned and documented inferences whose forms remain to be studied. In short, I believe that the pragmatic and rhetorical functions of scientific language require study by social scientists, and I do not think this task can be legislated as literary work only.

By the same token, it is not my argument that the production and consumption of scientific knowledge is wholly a textual phenomenon. Modern science is unquestionably a matter in its first stages, and repeatedly, of laboratory and field investigations. Indeed, it is imperative to accumulate studies of the social organization of the practice of laboratory science. We should distinguish between the vernacular settings of the sciences and their literary formats, in which the pragmatics of written inquiry and communication of documented or reasoned argument is the institutional focus. Just as scientific reports are not fully intelligible without access to practical circumstances of field-specific experimental research, so the latter is equally underinterpreted if we ignore its organizational ties to the scientific community through the discipline-specific production of reports, articles, and books that furnish the discursive objects of scientific inquiry.

A positivist account of science misses the phenomenon upon which the rhetorical and literary perspective focuses, namely, the phenomenon of audience elaboration in and by the design of rhetorical argument. It is perhaps better, as Kenneth Morrison has suggested, to speak of the 'recipient design' of written scientific inquiry, whose pragmatics are matters for empirical study in an internalist sociology of science. It is desirable that we begin with this restricted perspective, since at this preliminary stage the sociology of written scientific inquiry is obliged to deal with the analysis of the recipient-designed competences of professional science practitioners writing and reading within field specialities. It may therefore be necessary to postpone any interest in otherwise legitimate externalist approaches to the sociology of science. Rather than pursue issues of ideology, politics, and economy from the start, it may be advisable to pursue the literary production issues as a matter of the empirical discovery of the written practices that constitute writing sociology or writing history.[39] Of course, I do not envisage studies of sociological writing in general. Rather, I have in mind specific studies of introductory sociology texts, of sociological authors, prefatory practices, citation practices, of field note practices, and of science journal articles, such as I have undertaken in the present work. I reject the notion that scientific language is uniquely characterized by its features of logic, clarity, and simplicity, whereas literary productions are beset by an irreducible linguistic and rhetorical artifactuality. This is not a matter of the denigration of science, nor of any polemical irony on the difference between its ideals and its practice. Nor is it a matter of a gratuitous defense of literary practices, since we cannot treat them as found matters.

By contrast, the ideological issues in the externalist program of the sociology of science confront us pell-mell as soon as we understand the rhetorical production of written inquiry in terms of the sophistic arts of persuasion, dramaturgy, audience control, and the like. Rather than look to the more difficult pragmatics of nonrepressive communication,[40] it is a relatively easy move to generate idealized accounts of communicative community, by embedding speech-act theory within the emancipatory schema of a Marxist philosophy of history. Now, it cannot be denied that inasmuch as industrial democracies increasingly interpret themselves in terms of the documentary procedures of the social sciences, very difficult ideological, moral, and political issues are raised in relating commonsense and scientific accounts of society,[41] and especially of its power structure. By the same token, we need first to understand just how these ideological issues are translated into pragmatic documentary arrangements—whether to serve or to reform bureaucratic and exploitative relationships—that so often derive from the control of knowledge and communication media as much as from the control of labor power in the classical Marxist sense.[42]

CHAPTER 8 A Realist Model of Scientific Knowledge
With a Phenomenological Deconstruction of Its Model of "Man"

The present exercise itself trades on the linguistic competences whose techniques it proposes to make a topic for the sociology of the arts and sciences. The phenomenological turn here consists in treating taken-for-granted practices of scientific writing and communication as a family of practices required of "good enough" scientific publication. Those practices are conventional, highly sanctionable, and without explicit, formal pedagogy.[1] This work calls forth an empirical program of studies in the sociology of the arts and sciences whose direction is remarked upon with characteristic prescience by Alfred Schutz:

> It hardly needs to be stressed that in the systematization of a province of knowledge, in the "pedagogy" of the knowledge concerned, etc., the existence of a written tradition plays an important empirical role as against simply an oral one. . . . The detachment of theoretical areas of knowledge from life-worldly act-contexts, the progressive depragmatization, is a highly specific social-historical process, which is due to the institutional, economic-political establishment of the "theory" and "self-regulation" of the history of ideas.[2]

Rather than take a Mertonian turn with this last suggestion from Schutz, as I did in chapter 6, I propose to articulate the realist view of science generally espoused in the formulation of the knowledge/reality relation and its accompanying problem of interference effects. To do so, I shall deconstruct Roy Bhaskar's elegant account of the realist practice of science.[3] That text is chosen because it displays a highly competent and articulate account of scientific inquiry while simultaneously defending a realist ontology and a recognition of the social production of science. Bhaskar also espouses an emancipatory philosophical anthropology that cannot be ignored,[4] and thereby provides a necessary commentary on Richard Rorty's views on the fictionality of science and hermeneutics now so central to contemporary literary politics.

Since Bhaskar is highly critical of Rorty's reduction of ontology to epistemology on the grounds that it confines emancipatory science to narcissistic redescriptions of an already determined natural world,[5] it is important to see how he develops a double-entry account of science, distinguishing its "intransitive" (ontological) and transitive (sociohistorical) descriptions, or what the *world* must be like for our *sciences* to be possible. Bhaskar rejects Rorty's use of Thomas Kuhn, Carl Hempel, and Hilary Putnam to sink nature's determinism in the discursivity of the human sciences and the ethical priority of self-creation in a liberal society, because it loses the distinction between science (description) and nonscience (the world) along with the distinction between moral (paradigm) and abnormal (poetic) discourses. Human freedom takes on a poetic face rather than that of the scientist, engineer, or craftsman at grips with nature—or rather, the latter discover that they have been speaking poetry all along. Truth, power, and pain no longer eludes "woman" except as she lacks the will to redescribe herself within her own liberal practices. Rorty's pygmalionism is difficult to resist. After all, it even Americanizes Nietzsche. Admittedly, says Rorty, Americans will have to get used to such talk, which is presently marginal, abnormal, and clearer only *post festum*—after the party is over. The fact is, however, that Americans are born to swallow every such idea precisely because it suits their ideology of a freedom that makes no difference to American society. Such an ideology is all the more edifying in the university, where the class difference between being inside and outside of America is softened. In short, as we shall see later on, Rorty's American Woman turns out to be Martin Hollis's Plastic Man—but not the opposite of Autonomous Man, because these are two sides of an ideological fiction ruling liberal society.

Having displayed Bhaskar's theory as a principled account of the realist practice of science—with some attention to its own literary artifacts—I shall then consider Bruno Latour's parable on realism as a trope of normal paradigm science.[6] I then resume the analysis of the philosophical anthropology espoused by Bhaskar as it is found in Hollis's *Models of Man*,[7] a work by an author who is equally critical of Rorty's concepts of person and community.

It is a commonplace of phenomenology that knowledge is a vulgar sense-making practice present in the gestural, perceptual, and cognitive conduct of human beings.[8] Knowledge is languaged and articulated according to socially and biographically variable schemata of relevance into such finite provinces of meaning as myth, religion, science, art, economics, history, and sociology.[9] Social practices that govern the articulation and distribution of various modes of knowledge are the object of study for philosophers and sociologists of the natural and social sciences, as well as of literature and the arts:

> Knowledge is, to an empirically most significant extent, not only socially distributed, but also already *presupposed* in the relative-natural world view, and above all in the set types of the language. This involves neither a genealogy of logic, nor an empirical sociology of knowledge, nor a historical semantics. The findings about the basic forms of the requisition of knowledge and the basic structure of the life-worldly stock of knowledge should hold good for the natural attitude in general, whether a "scientific" or "magical" world picture is socially built up on it.[10]

Notwithstanding the general critics, phenomenology does not advocate the subjectivization of knowledge and reality, either with respect to nature or to society.[11] Such a view probably derives from certain countercultural extrapolations of the phenomenological differentiation of the world of everyday knowledge from the world of scientific knowledge, which is said to undermine or disvalue everyday knowledge.[12] This view concedes that positivism and realism are adequate accounts of the knowledge-reality relation in the production of natural science, but claims that the self-interpreting and self-organizing features (action and language) of the social knowledge–reality relation require a hermeneutical mythology peculiar to the human sciences. However, I believe no claim need be made for the so-called *double hermeneutic,*[13] as I have shown in the previous chapter. Rather, as Schutz has argued, the two sciences of nature and man are inconceivable without a necessary hermeneutical overlap within the community of science itself. We are otherwise committed to a quasi-natural concept of a community of scientists whose sense-making practices abjure reflexivity and practical reasoning in order to exemplify a canonical philosophy and sociology of science:

> We must proceed from the fact that the life-worldly stock of knowledge is not the result of rational cognitive events in the theoretical attitude. . . .

The structure of the life-worldly stock of knowledge resembles neither the logical systematic of a nonempirical science, as for instance algebra, nor the fabric of the interpretational schemata, taxonomies, laws, and hypotheses found within the empirical sciences. Insofar as there are similarities at all, they are to be traced back to the fact that the theoretic-scientific attitude is founded on the natural attitude.[14]

Once we see the prospect opened by the Schutzian perspective upon the social organization of the various finite provinces of meaning, ranging from everyday knowledge through to various disciplines of the arts and sciences, it remains a task for phenomenology to undertake the empirical description of the modalities of knowledge. In particular, it will be important to make much of the fact that all the sciences and arts involve a linguistic and symbolic competence whose taken-for-granted practice ought to be rendered thematic:

> Systems of signs, again especially language, are for their part a component of the social stock of knowledge and are the "medium" for the "objectiva-tion" of explicit elements of knowledge. They are thus the presupposition for the social cumulation of knowledge and for the development of "higher forms of knowledge."[15]

A REALIST THEORY OF SCIENCE

Bhaskar's realist theory of science starts from the assumption of two modes of knowledge: transitive (K_1) and intransitive (K_2). K_1 represents the social fact of the human production of knowledge on the same level as all other human work. K_2 refers to a knowledge of objects whose existence is available independently of any such intervention as K_1. As Bhaskar formulates it, the demarcation of the two K's requires an additional artifact, which I shall call imaginary science. Thus, it belongs to Bhaskar's account of a realist science that, in his words:

> We can easily imagine a world similar to ours, containing the same intransitive objects of scientific knowledge, but without any science to produce knowledge of them. In such a world, which has occurred and may come again, reality would be unspoken for and yet things would not cease to act and interact in all kinds of ways. In such a world the causal laws that science has now, as a matter of fact, discovered would presumably still prevail, and the kinds of things that science has identified endure. The tides would still turn and metals conduct electricity in the

way that they do, without a Newton or a Drude to produce our knowledge of them.[16]

Bhaskar's imaginary science, then, is not only possible without K_1 and its socially produced objects of knowledge, it is also in his view a science possible without humans. Such a postulate is necessary, in Bhaskar's view, to liberate science from the limits of anthropocentrism and the epistemic fallacy. It is the world and not humankind that makes science possible.

Having said so, Bhaskar nevertheless makes a slight anthropocentric concession. Although science does not presuppose human existence, it nevertheless seems to require as a precondition human freedom. This is because, as Bhaskar argues, scientific activity requires the notion of an open world in which agents are capable of recognizing causes and bringing about change in their physical and, so to speak, intentional environments:

> For science to be possible men must be free in the specific sense of being able to act according to a plan e.g., in the experimental testing of a scientific hypothesis. Human freedom is not something that stands opposed to or apart from science; but rather something that is presupposed by it.[17]

Having opened the door on humanity's "essential powers," Bhaskar quickly extends the list to include the power to acquire and to use *language* (since pictures, diagrams, and iconic models play an indispensable role in scientific thought) and the capacity to design, manufacture, and use tools that increase human beings' powers of perception and intervention with respect to "the course of nature."

Finally, Bhaskar argues that in addition to these preconditions an adequate realist theory of science requires an adequate philosophical sociology. Such a sociology must answer the question, What must society be like if science (as K_2) is to be possible? Therefore it will need to account for (a) individual agency, (b) preestablished social structures, and (c) social change achieved through the interaction of (a) and (b). This conception of society and social change is absolutely required if we are to satisfy the final condition of an adequate realist theory of science, namely, the continuity of scientific knowledge.

My reconstruction of Bhaskar's realist theory of science is not intended to produce any irony upon its practices. Rather, my own practice is absolutely parasitic in relation to the competent articulation of Bhaskar's account, on which it relies for its own discovery that a realist account of science turns on the artifact of an *imaginary science,* and that an imaginary science requires a negative *anthropology* that nevertheless postulates free, rational, and practical agents. Such findings represent phenomenological claims with respect to the constitutive features of a standing, that is, a reasoned, competent, scientific inquiry that itself displays its own kind. With some apologies, then, I have used Bhaskar's account of the realist theory of science for its clarity and forcefulness in bringing to bear the "two sciences" issue, which underlies the separation of realist and idealist sciences.

Bhaskar, as we have seen, begins with a forceful separation of the two knowledges and gradually remarries them in a "complementarity thesis."[18] In the light of some recent work in the ethnography of laboratory science and its ties with written science, it can be argued that realism functions as a phased alternative with idealism in accordance with shifts in the articulation and consolidation of scientific arguments. In a word, realism produces the dominant rhetoric of scientific textbooks, while idealism governs the scientific journals wherever textbook lore is challenged.[19] This, I believe, gives us a better sense than Rorty's view of how we change scientific discourse.

REALISM AS A LITERARY ARTIFACT OF SCIENTIFIC ARGUMENT

We can hardly doubt that scientists speak of a world outside of their laboratories or beyond their instruments. Such realism, however, hardly distinguishes them from madmen, poets, and theologians. Indeed, it marks them off from no one. We are all realists. None of us imagines that we have the world in our heads. Whenever such a thought worries us, we are not likely to find consolation from either side of philosophy: realism fails to explain our worry and idealism fails to explain our doubts. What we want to know is how it is we are able to speak of a world "really" that, for want of our speaking and thinking, would lack this very objectivity, for we are not likely to think that nature echoes itself. Nature is "our" object, it is our rule. In submitting ourselves intelligently to nature, we submit ourselves to our own sciences of nature. Society is in our minds and in our bodies, but not like our brains or blood; society is a fact of our lives only because we can intelligently formulate the rules of conduct whereby we live together customarily or in accordance with laws to which we submit ourselves from a general and historical sense of the requirements of collective like and the common good.

In short, there is little we can do with the idealist or the realist position in general beyond recalling in our own way their rhetorical grounds. If we are to achieve anything more, we need to see how a particular community of scientists practices realism, idealism, or positivism with respect to its distinguishing or disciplinary-scientific objects of inquiry. I shall take as an example Latour's fable concerning the practices whereby paleontologists claim "real findings" with respect to the anatomical, physiological, and ecological characteristics of dinosaurs.[20] So far from being a simple natural object, the controversial dinosaur turns out to be a complex social construct. It consists of:

Realsaur—the dinosaur "really," unavailable to us for about 150 million years

Scientaur—a paleological reconstruction of Realsaur begun in the nineteenth century by William Buckland, Georges Cuvier, and others and continuing through current research.

As a function of field research, the introduction of disciplinary related findings, conference reports, and published articles, the status of "dinosaurs really" and "science dinosaurs" shifts back and forth:

Realsaur I	←	Scientaur I	1910
Realsaur I	→	Scientaur I	1910–20
Realsaur II	←	Scientaur II	1920
Realsaur II	→	Scientaur II	1920–30
Realsaur III	←	Scientaur III	1930
Realsaur III	→	Scientaur III	1930–40

(N.B.: Dates are fictional)

Whenever scientific inquiry produced a controversy, as in 1910, 1920, and 1930, it was science that defined dinosaurs "really." Once the controversy settled, the textbooks reversed things, so that it seemed as though the dinosaur set the standard for adequate scientific findings. In short, the real status of dinosaurs seems to vary with the state of the art of Scientaur. Finally, only in periods of professional slump do scientists speak of Realsaur as though he were in the world as seen in textbooks. At such times, scientists are akin to the rest of us realists who have seen Popsaur at Disneyland, in the museum, or in the movies.

We may perhaps draw from this example a proposal for further research. Let us keep to the metaphor of expansion and recession in the field of science. We might then say that realism is the governing shibboleth in periods of normal science—when textbooks hold sway—and that idealism or constructionism is the governing shibboleth in periods of controversy within any specific science. Hence we may expect shifts in epistemological rhetoric over the history of any particular science. It needs to be said immediately, however, that we can gain from this generalized view of things nothing with respect to the specific practices that obtain in either discovering science or written science and the ties between them. Thus the work of Bruno Latour and Steve Woolgar,[21] Michael Lynch,[22] and Karin Knorr-Cetina,[23] all of whom have conducted field ethnographies of laboratory scientists, shows that we can understand scientific realism only as a socially organized achievement of situated practices of laboratory inscription, hermeneutics, and craft skills. The brute facts of science, rather than any natural starting point, represent an achieved state whose rediscovery now exercises contemporary ethnography of science. Similarly, Kenneth Morrison,[24] Digby Anderson,[25] and myself have argued that the written practices of scientific communication involve discipline-specific employments of the grand notions that populate the philosophy of science in ways that require empirical study. We can no longer treat the philosophy of science as a privileged gloss on the practice of the sciences.

Scientists in the laboratory are involved in a daily encounter with the artifacts of their own instruments and logic of inquiry. They manage interference effects in terms of local practices of interpretation with respect to their specimens and measures, and within the framework of a social hierarchy of craft and theoretical skills specific to the laboratory and oriented toward competition in the discovery and publication of discipline-specific facts and findings. The local detail of the life of laboratory science is consequently unavailable to the idealizations of scientific logic and practice to be found in the philosophy of science. Indeed, the latter requires for its good sense that "what everyone knows" about science be traded on to remedy their own hopeless abstraction of the philosophy of science. However, it is precisely this resource, namely "what everyone (in science) knows" that we now take to constitute a topic of inquiry for the sociology of science without deference to philosophical prescription. In other words, we can no longer take as a starting point for the phenomenology of science the simple demarcation adopted by Martin Heidegger, Alfred Schutz, and Jürgen Habermas, who argue, no less than the positivists, that the community of scientific reason sets itself off from the community of everyday reasoning and relevance. Rather,

- The scientific community is unavoidably a community of practical reason and relevance.
- The community of everyday reasoning and relevance is inextricably caught up in the larger industrial, scientific-technological, state, and bureaucratic society.
- The social sciences, which may treat the problematic of the relation between the two communities of reason and relevance, are themselves integrated with the larger society they take as an object of inquiry.

This reflexive formulation should make it clear that the social production of the natural and social sciences is incompatible with any generalized adherence to the epistemolgial shibboleths either of realism or idealism, or of the subordination of commonsense knowledge and values to the discipline-specific standards of rationality and value that are constitutive of the professionalized communities of knowledge in the natural and social sciences. We would be blind to ignore the ties between science, industry, and democracy, which, despite varying degrees of blockage and disappointments, as well as outright failures, nevertheless reflect our social commitment to the mastery of nature in order to create a society whose scientific and technological achievements might furnish the infrastructure for the social, political, and moral equivalents of freedom from nature.

THE LITERARY PRODUCTION OF PHILOSOPHICAL ANTHROPOLOGY: A DECONSTRUCTION

Literary critics, philosophers, and scientists are united in their ambivalence toward language. The autonomy, creativity, and conceits of language have been the occasion for both celebration and exorcism. The establishment position is that we operate two languages, science and literature, each achieving identity through what the other lacks. If this standoff is unstable, it is only because there are literary practitioners and philosophers who consider that their own language might be more effective once it acquires the formal features of scientific language. Yet against this drift, it now appears possible to argue that the demarcation of science and literature can be questioned even from within the community of science. What is involved here is no new irrationalism. Nor is it a matter of poetry and rhetoric avenging themselves for the confinement placed on them by philosophy and science. Moreover, the recent understanding of the literary production of natural and social science inquiry is independent of all philosophical laments and denunciations of the picture theory of language and its relation to the world.[26] It is so because, at one extreme, Wittgensteinian speech therapy seems to ignore philosophy as written inquiry (although Wittgenstein's own textual innovations might be studied), while Rorty's broad historical sweep of the philosophical tradition still returns philosophy to a conversational enterprise.[27] Although Rorty calls for a new historiography, its written practices go entirely unexplicated, and that is what is at issue here.

Now, inasmuch as philosophy is a written enterprise, however much it yearns for the spoken voice,[28] I think the philosopher's page can be shown to be a lively, organizational object whose constitutive features can be empirically described as both a topic and resource for the competent production of reasoned inquiry.[29] It is therefore without any polemical or ironic purpose that I have chosen to examine how it is that a philosophical text makes reference to its own interpretative practices (with figures as occasioned illustrations), to construct a practical history and a prologue to a perennial problem in the philosophy of the social science. Martin Hollis is a philosopher with the specific task of examining, in his *Models of Man,* the nature of social action and its implications for the construction of the Good Society, an enterprise in which he differs from Rorty. He engages in this enterprise with considerable wit and self-conscious humor. These are not merely stylistic devices but derive from his practical sense of the inescapable ad hoc reasoning that characterizes the achievement of such studies. Unfortunately, I must set aside the analysis of his opening remarks, that is, how his initial remarks "open" his argument. I start with his use of three figures. It is on the work required of them and text that they clarify, and by which they are in turn clarified, that we focus attention. The first proposal is that we "think of man as a black box, whose inputs and outputs are before us but whose workings are an enigma."[30] This permits us "to pose the problem in picture form" (see fig. 8.1).

This proposal is no sooner made than its troubles are noticed. We are warned

- Not to read too much into it
- To treat it as at best an aide-mémoire
- To remember that figure 8.1 depicts not a single transaction but a fundamental process
- That the two inputs are Nature and Nurture

There is, of course, nothing about the figure that prevents it from being "misread," even though its proper function is to clarify what remains to be read. Hollis's next move, then, is to "fix" the figure with two contrastive models of man (figs. 8.2 and 8.3), one portraying human nature as *passive*, the other as *active*. Broadly speaking, this device captures most of the history of Western philosophy, as well as the interests of the main camps in the social sciences:

> In pictorial terms, passive conceptions of man give us what I shall call *Plastic Man*. . . . Plastic Man is a programmed feedback system, whose inputs, outputs and inner workings can be given many interpretations. Active conceptions of man, by contrast, present what I shall call *Autonomous Man*. . . . Autonomous Man has some species of substantial self within. But what species of precisely what is an open question and nothing should yet be read into the drawing of a little match-stick man inside.

Fig. 8.1. Black box man. Reproduced from Martin Hollis, *Models of Man*, fig. 1.

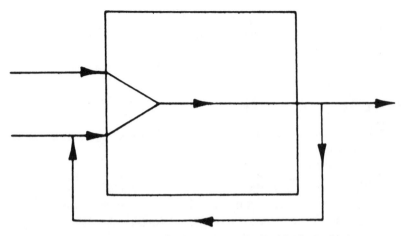

Fig. 8.2. Plastic man. Reproduced from Martin Hollis, *Models of Man,* fig. 2.

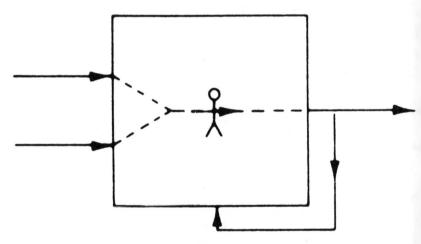

Fig. 8.3. Autonomous man. Reproduced from Martin Hollis, *Models of Man,* fig. 3.

It is to be noticed that, whatever their contrastive specifics, Figures 8.2 and 8.3 are as figures wholly uninterpreted. With regard to Figure 8.2, even the most unimaginative reader will be obliged to supply the following interpretative work, while nevertheless trying to comply with Hollis's *caveat* that he not read too much into things:

(a) The box is Man.
(b) The box is permeable.
(c) The inputs are Nature and Nurture.
(d) The inputs are equally identifiable outside of Man.
(e) The inputs seem to combine in equal (?) proportions inside Man.
(f) The feedback loop is carried by either Nature or Nurture.
(g) Given the amplification of one of the inputs in (f) the process in (e) would remain equiproportional.
(h) We may also read the input lines as arranged vertically, rather than horizontally, and as Nurture/Nature so that the feedback loop enhances Nature, in keeping with the passive model.
(i) In keeping with repair (h), we begin to think of further tinkering to display the way Man is more a creature of Nature than of Nurture.

With regard to Figure 8.3, we may suppose that the same interpretative work is required as in (a–f) for Figure 8.2, but also that

(j) Inside Man (a) there is "Matchstick Man".
(k) Matchstick Man is Man's "substantial self."
(l) Items (j) and (k) do not lead to the Russian doll problem.
(m) The feedback loop is carried through the substantial self (k).
(n) The feedback loop returns through Man (a) rather than either Nature or Nurture (c).

Hollis is quite aware that his figures can be considered illustrative only if they are allowed to trade upon a communal legend. They are otherwise lacking sense precisely because as spatial artifacts they necessarily sacrifice the temporal and embodied knowledge that renders them specifically sensible tokens of disciplinary discourse. Thus, Hollis is obliged to contextualize his amorphous shapes[31] by means of three textual devices:

(1) That there are two perspectives on human behaviour in society is a commonplace of sociology, although there are several different accounts of the divergence. The version I shall give reflects the distinction drawn in Alan Dawe's striking article "The Two Sociologies," *British Journal of Sociology,* 1970, reprinted in *Sociological Perspectives,* Penguin in association with the Open University Press, 1972. Debate between passive and active conceptions is conducted more obliquely in philosophy and many disputes about the explanation of action, the interpretation of experience or the nature of responsibility, for example, beat on it without always being directly addressed to it. But some works which do treat the issue in the spirit intended here are cited in the bibliography."

(2) A "cornflake-packet intellectual history."

(3) A bibliography characterized in note (1) as the corpus-relevant materials from which exemplary arguments are to be drawn.[32]

The cornflake history is, of course, Hollis's own gloss on his sense of the endemic artifactuality of his argument. It is an ad hoc history of the Enlightenment idea of the perfectibility of man through science. As such it cannot be diagrammatically portrayed, since it is essentially *written history* in the service of Figures 8.2 and 8.3. It can, however, be reduced to several points—though the achievement of this effect itself requires further written argument. The combination of figures and text constitutes a practical resolution of the lack of closure in either the text or figures as unique devices. Hollis's cornflake history, then, can be encapsulated in three points, which in turn reflect the two models employed to articulate the very history in which they are embodied. In particular, the internal modifiers (my emphasis in the quotation) function here, and as we shall see elsewhere, to undermine a frame that is nevertheless employed as a basic artifact in the construction of the author's argument:

> Faith in the perfectibility of man can be put, less bombastically and more in keeping with the political theories hailed earlier, as the belief that the laws of human nature can be harnessed to produce a society which satisfies human nature. Breaking the belief down further we find three presumptions, the last of which combines conflicting elements of the others. Firstly, there are *held to be*, in Hume's phrase, "constant and universal principles of human nature" (*Enquiries* VIII); secondly, social engineers are *deemed to have* a power of initiative and innovation, which somehow transcends these constant and universal principles; thirdly, human nature is *taken to be* fixed enough to have given needs or wants, yet mutable enough for those needs and wants to be satisfiable. These presumptions embody both the models of man, which are our points of departure.[33]

But this packet history is replete with troubles that derive from its inability to decide what is fixed and what is mutable in human nature. Philosophers debate this issue as the problem of freedom and determinism. Social scientists debate the issue in terms of the feasibility and desirability of an environmentally determined utopia versus self-induced change and moral progress: "There is thus a tension in the basic view of man, who is sometimes puppet and sometimes puppeteer, sometimes passive and sometimes active."[34] So Hollis returns to his models while noting that they seem to be infested with essentialism, a particular philosophical malady. Though Plastic Man is free of his virus, he is not Hollis's man. Autonomous Man, his favorite, is nevertheless a victim of the virus. Hollis is obliged to come to his aid. Consider the "reading effect" of the stressed phrases (even though not explicitly italicized by Hollis) in the following quotation:

(a) Autonomous Man, even if somehow possessed of a self, *need not* be a scholastic substance.

(b) I do not *quite mean* "substance" and "essence" to be taken as part of an ontology of necessary beings and subsistent attributes.

(c) But I do mean to stress the presence of *some* ontology and metaphysics in basic assumptions about human behaviour.[35]

The cumulative force of the "weak negators" is bolstered by two further points—a paradox and a plea:

(d) *Paradoxically,* any claim that Plastic Man has no essence will turn out to be an essentialist thesis.

(e) If the objector will agree that there is *some* basic distinction between passive and active conceptions of man, I will settle for calling them assumptions.[36]

In (e) it becomes clear that Hollis has indulged a dramaturgy of his own in which the artifactual troubles of his argument are assigned to the querulousness of a reader who is then pacified through the negators (a–d), whereby the author weakens the strong contrastive structure of Plastic Man and Autonomous Man, while at the same time preserving the contrast as the organizational frame of his book. (See the place of Plastic Man and Autonomous Man in the table of contents reproduced later in this chapter.)

Having tried to settle the issue of existentialism, Hollis returns to work on Plastic Man. The letter seems to be plagued with two further troubles—determinism and naturalism—which in turn help to clarify the sense of the vectors in figures 8.2 and 8.3. It is necessary, however, to delimit the claims of determinism if we are to have an acceptable version of naturalistic explanation. Hollis proceeds to list given classic elements of the idea of determinism with critical comments (which I include here in brackets):

1. Every event has an explanation.
   [Represents a generalized commitment to small-'r' rationalism.]
2. Every event has an explanation in the same mode. [Unspecified limit.]
3. Every event has a causal explanation. [Unspecified causation.]
4. Every event, together with some other event, is an instance of a natural law.
   [More useful, especially if amended to read, *every fact which has an explanation is, together with some other fact, an instance of a natural law.* (The "other fact" will be the *explanans.*)][37]
5. Every event is the only possible outcome of some other event being subject to laws which could not possibly be otherwise.
   [Glosses the notion of law with too strong a sense of necessity.]

The usefulness of item 4 is that Hollis thereby succeeds in blending naturalism and determinism so that they assert that there is a single, law-governed world and that, he claims, is just what is displayed in figure 8.2:

> The diagram for Plastic Man simply connects inputs to outputs by an arrow just like the other arrows, thus emphasizing the unity of scientific method and abolishing any ultimate hiatus between the inside and the outside of the box.[38]

What the diagram does "simply," of course, is only a *retrospective achievement.* Yet it was offered first, as though guiding the text through which it is itself deployed. Moreover, even when the interpretation of the figure has been amplified, Hollis makes no attempt to redraw them. Hence, they can never illustrate the text they apparently stand for, since it is the latter as (con)text that must be continuously referred to, whether to honor their figurative posture or to leave them behind as exhausted signs.

But there remains more trouble ahead. However well Plastic Man displays his allegiance to the unity of scientific method, he has two flaws. Although twice disclaiming any intention to "score an objection," Hollis remarks that Plastic Man's knowledge hardly seems to give him power rather than to subjugate him; and he is only the ghost of an individual. But since the Enlightenment and liberal tradition simultaneously embraced an active individual whose rationality enabled him to shape himself and his society, another figure is called for—and he is formulated in a single sentence: "The black box is equipped with a rational subject self, which we dub Autonomous Man."[39]

Once again, however, Hollis has to grapple with the conceptual overloading of his own phraseology. His artifactual troubles pile up, as evidenced by Hollis's resort (indicated by my emphases) to cumulative modifiers or weakening negators:

> The key to explaining social behaviour lies in the rational activity of the subject self. The black box is equipped with a rational subject self, which we dub Autonomous Man.
>
> The last sentence puts together three distinct themes, each too perplexing for more than a word of introduction here. There is to be a self, *whatever that may turn out to be.* The self is a subject, *in one or more of the senses which that term can take.* It is rationality which marks out man, *however rationality is to be construed.* We should note at once that the three elements are *not always all* present, even in active conceptions derived directly from the Enlightenment. Individualism *can be disavowed;* contrasts between subjects and objects are *often declared distracting;* rationality is *not the only contender.* In making Autonomous Man a rational subject self, I am generalizing *only very broadly* and, for the rest, giving warning of the line which I shall endorse myself. *Nevertheless the themes harmonize.* Whereas Plastic Man, being formed by adaptive response to the interplay of nature and nurture, is only spuriously individual, his rival is to be self-caused. Where Plastic Man is an object in nature, his rival is the "I" of the I and the Me. Where Plastic Man has his causes, Autonomous Man has his reasons.
>
> *The bare idea* is that Autonomous Man is the explanation of his own actions. But it derives from more sources than the Enlightenment and can be fleshed out in conflicting ways.[40]

When we consider Hollis's withdrawals on Plastic Man and Autonomous Man, we really are left with, unpardonably, "straw men." Yet inasmuch as each leans on the other, they stand for all practical purposes, namely, to articulate the divisions of Hollis's book displayed in its table of contents:

Contents

The table of contents, with the title and subtitles, functions to recruit readers willing to tolerate the ambiguities, undecidability, and perplexities of Hollis's text as a philosopher's delight. Moreover, these are not features that fault its author, since, like the reader, Hollis adopts an exemplary attitude toward them, displaying disciplinary wit and intelligence in their management. Not only Enlightenment thinkers but also theologues, commonsense thinkers, exchange theorists, anthropologists, and phenomenologists can be considered protagonists of Autonomous Man. Hollis is therefore in rich company. Like his predecessors, he espouses Autonomous Man. He does so at least as an *explanatory notion,* even if it is risky to burden anyone else with any attachment to a substantial self. Having come so far, there is no turning back. After several skillful moves with the "ordinary language" distinction between the language of action and the language of behavior, Hollis is able to employ the language of action to interpret the dotted lines inside the box of figure 8.3 or (Autonomous Man). In other words, the feedback loop to the box is direct rather than through the external inputs (Nature and Nurture) as in figure 8.2 (Plastic Man). And now we are given the key to the missing legend: "Bearing in mind the suggestion that rationality holds the key, we can propose that a man's reasons for acting can explain his actions, without being the cause of them."[41]

Then, at the heart of the matter, Hollis once again modifies his whole procedure. In the following quotations the contrastive structure between Autonomous Man and Plastic Man is further qualified (my emphases), undermined, and almost lost in the continuum from which it was drawn:

> I *may seem* to have spoken as if there were some sharp distinction in use between the language of action and the language of behaviour. . . .

and *as if* it reflected the distinction of active and passive.

That *is not* what I am after. . . .

I am trying to describe or analyze our everyday talk. . . .

Nor *am I* trying to claim that *the* language of action commits anyone to anything.

I have stated the difference between active and passive as a stark dichotomy, *but I have not* proved that there can be no continuum.[42]

Literal readers (here represented through the device of separating Hollis's actual remarks) might be tempted not to believe their eyes. Could Hollis not have been doing what he so deliberately did? Is this just a textual illusion? Can we correct things by a closer perusal of the diagrams? Perhaps it is better to read on.

In any case, Hollis is back at work, unrepentantly asserting (my emphases):

The contrast which I introduce *quasi-historically* is alive in current attempts at theorizing in the social sciences and philosophy.

. . . A historical setting was only introduced *for the sake of clarity* and *we are now ready to exploit the contrast* wherever we find it.[43]

With this prescription Hollis can then review the natural and social sciences, or the arts and sciences, and find in them nothing to permit their self-congratulatory differences. The standoff between "rat men" and "meaning men" is quite beside the real issue of the nature of rational explanation. The same is true in economics, where the concepts of rational man are divided between the activists and passivists. And, of course, in sociology there is hardly a topic that doesn't divide into the options of subjective and objective explanation.[44] Sensing that he is creating a philosophical monopoly, Hollis once again enters a set of disclaimers, distributed so as to partially appease the sociologists, on the one hand, and the philosophers, on the other:

(a) He recognizes a fondness for role theory at the expense of structuralist theory.
(b) He avoids much discussion of current ordinary-language philosophy.
(c) Both (a) and (b) may be justified if their constructive aim of finding a metaphysic for the rational social self is realized.[45]

These gestures are intended to set the tone for the conclusion of the opening chapter and turn naturally into a prospectus of the forthcoming chapters of the book:

Chapter 2   Parameters for a passive conception are sketched in chapter 2, which opens with nature vs. nurture but concentrates on what they have in common.

Chapter 3   Chapter 3 starts by rejecting Positive accounts (of causation). The central puzzle concerns "natural necessity," which I finally assimilate to conceptual necessity.

Chapter 4   In chapter 4 social action is set in a context of social positions and roles and a notion of "normative explanation" is introduced.

Chapter 5   In chapter 5, on personal and social identity, [actors] emerge as agents who satisfy strict numerical criteria of identity by rational choice of what *personae* to become.

Chapter 6   In chapter 6 the notions of purpose, intention, and rule offer something, but not enough and I conclude that only the actor's good reasons can be deemed to be inclined without necessitating.

Chapter 7   Epistemological debts are paid in chapters 7 and 8 with a defense of rationalism.

Chapter 8   The theme of chapter 8 is that rational action is a skill whose rational understanding depends on knowing necessary truths about the thing to do.

Chapter 9   Finally, the brief chapter 9 sums up and admits to large, unresolved problems, notably in the idea of the context of action.[46]

Thus Hollis concludes chapter 1 with a preface to his book. Here what is achieved is a new plane from which to survey the territory to be conquered, with the basic strategy mounted in the opening chapter and table of contents. Despite its weaknesses, patched here and there, but hardly logically tight, a frame has been constructed, and as the survey of the table of contents shows, much can be mounted on it. In any case, it is enough to bear a reasonable competent philosophical argument, especially if it is used with a little wit and a pinch of salt. Another effect of the chapter résumé, as well as of the table of contents, is to introduce the reader to its concepts as disengageable rubrics. However, their prima facie intelligibility is only a lure into the work of grappling with their artifactuality and radical contexture. Hollis cleverly sets the trap one last time:

A miser, summarizing the book by telegram, could do it in six words. *Rational action is its own explanation.* But since some will doubt the meaning or truth of this proposition, while others will quarrel with the sense I shall attach to "rational," six words seem too few. So let us press on.[47]

My analysis has hardly been equally telegraphic. For all that, it remains miserly with the explication of the art of written inquiry, which constitutes a thick field of empirical inquiry that can be opened up but hardly exhausted. Moreover, I should observe that it is a feature of the fine grain of written inquiry that its practices are not found at the level of transcendental criticism—nor are they nested in a Wittgensteinian family, awaiting armchair empiricism. On the present occasion I have looked at the work of opening a philosophical inquiry as a practical, ad hoc achievement realized through a contrastive structure (Plastic Man versus Autonomous Man) whose artifactual troubles can be remedied only insofar as the philosopher, like everyone else, keeps up the patchwork which is most of his work. Philosophical writing has not been singled out because it is peculiarly vulnerable to deconstruction, as Jacques Derrida and Richard Rorty might argue; philosophers are in the same linguistic predicament as any other writer in the arts and sciences. Their exposure to deconstruction is not due to the witless reliance upon any tradition or metaphysics, nor is it relieved by even the most perspicuous insights into the linguistic limits of reflective thought. In this respect, Wittgenstein's attempts to produce a "nontext," as in the *Tractatus,* are wholly unsuccessful. But he thought this was a failure of spoken language, and seems to have missed textuality as such. All written thought is the result of practical decisions within the limits and possibilities of its relevant mode of discourse. Such practices often point to themselves; in fact, this constitutes a mark of the better writers. Within the limits of philosophical discourse, Hollis is a lively writer and, in the sense I have just elaborated, he in turn provokes a lively reading. What more can be said, will be said. Such is the life of philosophy, literature, and the sciences.

A little more may be said here. I have tried to show how we may apply a persistent rhetorical analysis to a program of science and anthropology that is self-consciously deconstructive but nevertheless critically opposed to the literary politics espoused by Rorty's poetic scientist cum liberal poet. Thus Hollis and Bhaskar find it a mystery to understand how Rorty can appeal to the community to dignify persons whose status is very much determined by the extent to which they are included or excluded by the community. To answer such questions, one needs a vocabulary of class, colonialism, race, and sexism that will reveal the differential access to social goods and the avoidance of social evils, as I have argued in the opening chapters of the present book. Such a vocabulary is best acquired from the social sciences rather than from literature, as Rorty otherwise recommends. It involves the recognition that we need to discover the structural and historical determinants in our society if we are to modify the ratio of ignorance and justice that condemns a few to extraordinary freedom and most to debilitating disease, hunger, poverty, and ignorance. Between old-order scientific Marxism and new-order ironic liberalism, there must be a more thoughtful way.

CHAPTER 9

Deconstructing Fort/ Derrida:

The Convention of Clarity

I now propose to show how we respond to another interpretative task—that of commentary—required of us from time to time as professional critics but involving practices we are never taught except through their practice. On such occasions, we "do what comes naturally," as Stanley Fish might say. But only if nature is second nature can we be so sure of ourselves.

In the days when there was no writing and all texts had a single parent—due to His divinity rather than to the accidents of life— commentary involved honest work, like that of Saint Joseph. Today's texts, like the rest of the world, are orphaned by their modernity. Texts no longer echo their paternity, and genre is as outmoded as family. Honored neither in their beginnings nor their ends, texts come into their own from the margins, float on themselves, and proliferate with the least contact. Such is writing. What, then, of commentary? Upon what does it work? The text refuses to be the object of any steady craft such as commentary or illumination. Exulting in the freedom of its orphanage, writing runs away from the tutelage of commentary like a street kid fleeing from the flatfoot cop or social worker. Writing has no desire to be reflected in the father-text and is even less willing to look for its image in the mirror of commentary, however faithful.

This commentary should restrict itself to honest work and avoid any fancy of creation. It is beneath the copulation of writing and reading. The commentator's task is humbly to read and scarcely to write.[1] At best, a commentator reports on the scene of writing and reading—as a dutiful voyeur, whose place is ensured by the order of things fulfilling its authority from behind the scene. By an order that I hereby return to its senders, in order to reassure them of the correspondence of our intentions, and in order to keep everything that here transpires as commentary within the bounds of philosophical propriety, I hereby produce my letters patent:

Codirector
SPEP Executive Committee
Department of Philosophy
Any University
Anywhere, USA

Dear Codirector:
Please accept this letter as a symposium proposal for the 1984 SPEP conference. The title of the session is "Toward an Archaeology of Deconstruction."
This session is motivated by a general dissatisfaction expressed by a number of members of SPEP regarding the way in which recent French philosophy has been received by many of the American practitioners of Continental philosophy, and the purpose of this session is to explore a number of prefigurations within what might be called mainstream Continental philosophy of the method that has come to be called "deconstruction." The papers presented will not focus on any particular proponent of deconstruction. Instead, they will attempt to isolate certain methodological procedures which emerge within the works of such figures as Foucault, Derrida, Deleuze, Lyotard, etc., with an eye toward disclosing the continuity between these figures and their philosophical predecessors (Nietzsche, Freud, Husserl, Heidegger, Levinas, Merleau-Ponty, Blanchot). The papers' intentions are not to usher deconstruction into what a "Rortyan" might call the "normal discourse" of Continental philosophy. Rather, the intention is to show that deconstruction, while radical, has precursors within the Continental tradition and, as such, is deserving of serious consideration rather than the hostility and suspicion that it has to a large extent thus far.
Symposium participants will include the following persons:

Speakers	Professor A. D. Script Department of Philosophy Any University Any Town, USA
	Professor I. E. Trace Department of Philosophy Any University Any Town, USA
	Professor C. Cry Departmente de Philosophie Any French University Any French Town, Canada
Moderator/Commentator	Professor John O'Neill Department of Sociology Any English University Any English Town, Canada

Professor John O'Neill has agreed to moderate the session and provide a summary/commentary on the three papers presented. He will isolate certain threads that run through the three individual discussions of the method of deconstruction as well as raise critical questions and/or suggestions for the three speakers regarding the intertextual connections emerging within their respective presentations and the Continental tradition. In so doing, Professor O'Neill will initiate a discussion of the pertinent issues and open the dialogue between the speakers and the audience.

I have requested that this session be considered as a symposium. The individual papers will not exceed twenty-five minutes; Professor O'Neill's comments will be limited to fifteen minutes. Given the discussions and questions which have followed past sessions addressing deconstruction in general and Derrida in particular, I believe that our session should have ample time (forty-five minutes) for comments and discussion with the audience. Inasmuch as I am unclear as to what formal distinctions, if any, exist regarding the differences between symposia, panels, and workshops, I would be pleased to be placed on the program under any heading that the SPEP Executive Committee feels would be appropriate.

I hope I have included all of the relevant information. If you have any questions or suggestions regarding this proposal, please do not hesitate to contact me.

Thank you for considering this proposal, and I look forward to hearing from you.

Sincerely,
A. D. Script

I have presented my papers to show that we are committed to serious play in any of the sessions of a philosophical meeting. Our texts are from the very beginning ruled by an "outer text" (*hors texte*), which is oriented to the institution of philosophical authority, clarity, community, and concern for the tradition and the new. Any one of us might have made the submission (act of submission) presented here; any one of us might have received it and in turn have endorsed it. It is, then, common practice. As such, it can be overlooked as a formality, an initial move, necessary to bring forward what is valuable in our work, but otherwise insignificant beyond its sheerly instrumental value. Such documents are not considered part of the philosophical archive. They reflect the bureaucratic practices of our universities and are the means by which we escape them for a few days to seek the convivial company of our truth-seeking colleagues. Even Socrates had to get down to the marketplace. Yet we do not have direct access to the site of philosophical encounter. Indeed, the site of philosophy is never outside our work. Rather, we have to internalize it in the rhetoric of our methods, our topics, our citations, and our invocation of the relevant tradition and respectable novelty, which yields our philosophical vocation/vacation. There is, then, an act of submission, a prayer made before we begin our work. Admission to the practice of our philosophical rites requires that we formulate a certain *credo* in which the institution of philosophy is recognized, the practices of its authorities are honored and its power to patent local proceedings conceded. Thus, the inseparability of philosophical form and content are organized in the pretexts that initiate our papers and are their necessary preface. To make this practice explicit is neither to ironize it nor to wish apart the form and content of philosophy, as though it could be unlike our other institutions. And, certainly, philosophy could not be above the commitments of literary institution.[2] Rather, we argue as we do in order to see ourselves in and not through philosophy's mirror.

We may think of our "correspondence" as a device for specularizing the practice of philosophy, of matching its authority to our own authoriality within the limits of philosophy's discursive power. We write "on" or "about" philosophy's figures, *topoi,* and "aporia." We carry philosophy forward by restoring its future to its past; no problem is too difficult if it can contribute to this labor. On this occasion, our commentary labors under a triple oedipalization, a triple submission to the authorities:

(1) The Executive Committee of SPEP as presence/absence
(2) Derrida as absence/presence
(3) O'Neill as moderator, doubling the presence of Derrida and the absence of the Executive Committee of SPEP

Thus, a subordinate sense of commentary exists, a topology structured like the discourse of enlightenment, divinely psychoanalytic. The scene erupts with the father-text, Derrida, primal and iddish because he could not originate otherwise. The father-text, however, must constantly yield to the sense-making practices of its children, to the critical family involving w/ego where there was only id. In-the-name-of-the-father-and-of-the-sons-and-daughters, the commentator adjudicates between the id-text and its w/ego-texts, charged with giving words their due, fixing the page, allowing and disallowing interpretation—super-w/ego of meaning from page to page. Thus, the commentator is authorized, and thereby forswears his or her authorship, to find the sense by means of a line, in the triune papers, to set aside their individual errors, their wanderings, from the line, to discover in them the tradition. By means of such (im)pertinence, or permanence, the commentator sits to open a dialogue between the speakers, given their lines, and the audience, following the line. Beyond this, the moderator doubles as *chronos,* devouring the speakers a second time—his or her own allotted quarter of an hour completing their three-quarters of an hour—with equal time to the audience, guaranteeing the sacrificial dramaturgy of clarity and organization in the name of the philosophical community. A mass is as good as a miss.

Yet nothing in the scene of philosophy can prevent the irruption of its obscenities.[3] Despite our careful topology of authoritative discourses, and its insistence upon the serenity of interpretation and commentary in accordance with institutional practice, the copulation of thought and fury of creativity fathering before the critical family cannot be prevented. Nothing prevents commentary from wandering across borderlines, abandoning the coercion of super-w/ego to turn prodigal id, and reaching toward writing—Derridean dereliction. But commentary should withhold itself from speech and writing. Like Saint Joseph, its task is not to impregnate the text, which has received the word from elsewhere. Such Christian commentary, of course, disavows all contamination, shrinks from any transgression of the scriptures that have chosen it. To do otherwise makes commentary both master and servant of the scriptures, forever writing displaced, Derridean commentary, breeding rabbis and poets.[4]

Of course, in the ordinary way nothing prevents commentary from fulfilling its task. Indeed, everything serves it. The work of commentary presents itself under a rule of impartiality. It affects a self-effacing tone, so often discounting its own function that it is remarkable when commentary turns excessive and threatens to usurp the author-text, spilling unlimited ink where ordinarily a few remarks are sufficient to divide sense from nonsense.[5] Alternatively, where commentary adopts the voice of reason and justice, its complaints so proliferate that its own text risks outweighing the author-text, so that it were better the latter had never been born. Thus, one sees commentators at work busy with complaints about clarity, intentionality, priority, and the like. In the midst of such work, commentators record minor pleasures and satisfactions, substracting their disappointments and dissatisfactions like accountants. Commentators, then, must struggle with themselves not to appear more than they are, not to take more than their due. If they do speak, it is not with their own voices. Their task is to apportion things, to restore sense, to point out pitfalls.

When we do catch the sounds of their voices, we despise commentators for being prescriptive in place of the creative, for promising a better life without being able to bring to life the passions that suffer learning and unlearning. Commentators are literary parasites, incapable of renewing the literary corpus that hosts their insatiable appetite for a text beyond the fall into language. By the same token, they are invited to all our table talks. In fact, commentators have a curious way of inviting themselves to our symposia. Thus, they constitute themselves around a sacrificial text or topic invoked to collect a membership whose interested concerns they claim to represent. The proposal that originated our own symposium on deconstruction is perfectly in order in this regard. Nothing we say is intended to fault its practice. Rather, we wish to make its practices more visible. Consider, therefore, our abstracts, offered to seduce the executive committee into authorizing the sacrificial refragmentation of the father-text into the tradition-text restored by the sons and daughters of criticism:

> The papers that comprise this session (see enclosed abstracts) recognize the need to situate deconstruction within the context of Continental thought in a way that both acknowledges the continuity between this approach and the phenomenological/existential tradition, as well as marks the differences and contributions which deconstruction makes to Continental philosophy. In my paper, "Nietzsche between Foucault and Derrida: Genealogy as Deconstructive Technique," I show that both Foucault and Derrida have returned to Nietzsche's insight into the essentially critical function of philosophy. I trace the Derridean and Foucauldian rejections of philosophical binarism to Nietzsche's genealogical criticism of metaphysical hierarchization, and I argue that just as Nietzsche's particular genealogical analyses are informed by his general project of a transvaluation of values, the particular turns of the Derridean and Foucauldian texts are informed by one and the same project—the deconstruction of authority.
> Trace, in "The Trace of the Trace: Derrida, Husserl, Levinas, and Freud," attempts to articulate the limits of the Derridean notion of the trace in

relation to three precursors of this idea. Professor Trace addresses the Derridean critique of Husserl's notion of retention in his discussion of internal time consciousness for not being radical enough in its attempt to "represent" the past. She goes on to show that, although Derrida borrows heavily from Levinas's discussions of the "trace of the other," he recasts the discussion of the trace in a way that seeks to avoid the ontotheological presuppositions of Levinas's metaphysics. She concludes by contrasting the Derridean trace with Freud's conception of the trace as "deferred effect," arguing that Freud has incorporated into the "trace" a metaphysics that Derrida cannot accept.

Cry will present a paper on tonality and the cry in Blanchot and Derrida. Although the details of Professor Cry's presentation are not definite at this time, he will extend his past discussion of the cry in Nietzsche's *Birth of Tragedy* through Blanchot to the cry in Derrida as the excess of tone, an excess which moves language beyond meaning/*Sens*.

Professor Script proposes to aim our criticism at "method," i.e., at "deconstruction." Here he proposes to show that deconstruction is neither to be reduced to a normal paradigm of criticism nor touted as a completely radical innovation, quite without precedent in the philosophical tradition.

"Deconstruction" is neither fearsome nor familiar, and so our executive committee ought, as it did, to find the will to sponsor us. However, to reassure our executive committee that it could reasonably "underwrite" our activities, the submission contains summaries of each of the proposed papers designed to render them comparably intelligible and motivated by the concern to bring deconstructionism within the tradition. To clinch matters, the executive committee is further assured that Professor O'Neill will "moderate" the session, provide further "summary/commentary" on the three papers, isolating common threads and their intertextual ties with the Continental tradition. Having predigested the papers in this way, they are then presented to the present collectivity (audience, readership) for final communion. Finally, the executive committee is assured that the various segments of the symposium will observe conventional time allotments. *Ite, missa est.*

We see, then, that we are gathered in "general dissatisfaction" with the reception of recent French philosophy by even its sympathetic American practitioners. At the same time, we are concerned to avoid ad hominem argument, presumably out of respect for our irreverent sense of the nonexistence of authors—or is it our murderous wishes toward the father that renders Derrida beyond presence?

Is it possible for commentary to remain within its prescribed boundaries, to keep the panoptical promise of self-surveillance? Perhaps as a philosophical or literary collectivity we are rendered righteous in our sense of the conformity of deconstructionist practices with the discipline and punishment of the literary body, reassuring our executive committee that we have bravely avoided the pleasures of the text. Some such covenant is honored in Professor Script's paper. Derridean pharmacology may poison the inkwell, but it remedies the text, opening it up to a double writing carried on within and without the tradition. Although it leaves behind the superficial, the deep, the thorough, and the underground thinkers on the question of origins, Derridean deconstruction has antecedents in Kant's practice of critique and in Nietzsche's genealogical inquiries into the fetishism of words and values. But does this make a respectable tradition? Shorn of the grammatical subject, respecting no kingdom of ends and certainly no divinity nor any authority, how are we to assure our executive committee of philosophy that our proceedings nevertheless observe the herd instincts of subjection to institutionalized discourse? Will the committee not suspect the subversion of inverted commas, subjectless discourse, unauthorized texts motivated solely by the will-to-interpretation? Ought we to have made them any promises? Ought they to surrender philosophy to such scribble and not to dismiss us with shorter shrift, unshriven?

Professor Trace, although smuggling in quite a different paper than the one with which she solicited the executive's interest in the restoration of the tradition, also takes her departure from Derrida via Kant. She does so, despite Kant's un-Derridean concern with the search for a key, or criteriology, to the question of the limits of metaphysics. Kant nevertheless appears to be attractive as a rival father-text because of his intuition of a noumenal lack in the origins of reason. Thus in Trace's reading/writing, the Kantian critique labors to produce Nature as a ground of experience, to impregnate her with the transcendental categories of reason so as to have her bear particulars, "roots and peculiarity." At the same time, Trace argues, Kant fears that reason is impotent with respect to the critical task—is all too metaphysical—unless Nature can seduce reason to see/sense/sign her to bring forth things. In short, Kant sees that desire must be at the heart of reason, that the very history of metaphysics betrays this complicity, and that the scandal of metaphysics as history rather than science is the very condition of its possibility. In other words, the *nature* of reason is neither inside nor outside of reason, neither metaphysical nor physical. Rather, the transcendence of reason consists in the play of reason with itself whereby it becomes its own child, discovering the particulars of nature in a world it has seeded through itself as language, logos, sign. It is in the play of language that reason achieves both unity and difference, that openness and closure, which are movements in the articulation of desire and reason in historical nature:

> For metaphysics, in its fundamental features, perhaps more than any other science, is placed in us by nature itself and cannot be considered the production of an arbitrary choice or a casual enlargement in the progress of experience from which it is quite disparate.[6]

Here the Kantian critique, as Trace reconstructs it, approaches the very borders of deconstructionism, but remains blocked for want of an adequate conception of the semiotic play at the heart of things. This seminal move would release us from Kant's impossible metaphysical demands for the completeness of reason and the satisfaction of desire. Or would it? Ought not we to ask for the seriousness of play? Might it not be the case that the divinity, the feminity, of our play derives, overflows its limits, from the impossibility whose names are reason, God, desire, woman—all of which we pursue as the very condition of nature in us, that is, as embodied being, the conjecture of flesh, text, tissue? Perhaps Kant was, after all, married to such a conception of embodied reason, and he may well have realized that in pursuing metaphysics he experienced himself as father/mother of his own experience and reflection:

> That the human mind will ever give up metaphysical research is as little to be expected as that we, to avoid inhaling impure air, should prefer to give up breathing altogether. There will, therefore, always be a metaphysics in the world; nay, everyone, especially every reflective man, will have it, and for want of a recognized standard, will shape it for himself after his own pattern.[7]

Kant, then, accepted the embodied condition of philosophy, its essentially human and historical nature, its yearning for an impossible unity that is the driving force in each of us who takes up metaphysics according to his or her "own pattern," that is, according to our own patterns of seduction, our transgressive, linguistic, and corporeal difference. If this were so, we might trace another genealogy from Montaigne, through Maurice Merleau-Ponty to Roland Barthes, as I have done elsewhere,[8] according to my own pattern.

At this point, I must return to the margins, to correspond further with the natural history of our symposium:

Dear Professor O'Neill:

A problem has come up regarding our SPEP workshop in Atlanta. Professor Cry contacted me two days ago and said he would not be able to attend the meeting. I have been trying to get a replacement since then, and have invited Professor C. Supplement, who is now in the Department of Romance Languages at Another University. She has a paper on Derrida's resistance to empiricism which will fit nicely with Trace's paper on Kant and my paper on Nietzsche. However, she won't know until September 18 whether she can attend our meeting. She has another commitment in October, and the date of that commitment is still undecided. I told her it would be all right if she let us know on the 18th, since she was reasonably sure that her other commitment would not conflict with SPEP.

It turns out, then, that deconstructionists are substitutable and that for Professor Cry we can read Professor Supplement—from metonym to metaphor. Unfortunately, the proposed substitution of "The Cry and the Call in Derrida's Thought" by "Derrida's Resistance to Empiricism" did not meet the foolproof guarantees issued on its behalf. Thus, although I was prepared to read Supplement's paper in the light of either Cry's or Trace's paper, I was unable to read the latter papers in the light of Supplement's paper. So she was saved that impropriety—perhaps due to Canada Post's persistent purloining of the letters, which regularly destroys 10 percent of our mail—*hors texte*!

As a representative of the modest functions of commentary exercised on behalf of the executive committee's desire for order, clarity, and turnover, I have already exceeded my limits. I have done so to exemplify the claim that commentary that is or, rather, that is not simply translation cannot remain perched "on" whatever is offered for commentary. It necessarily falls into the "over" or "beyond" of the supplement of writing. It does so because, in the first place, Derrida refuses translation, or rather he makes writing difficult for those who live on by living off translation.[9] Now what is (who is) at stake here is Jacques Derrida, who refuses to accept his death warrant; that is, the claim made for him by his critics that he is ready to be reconciled with the tradition—provided we can divide his radical desire between us—we Kantians, we Nietzscheans, we traditional radicals, we deconstructionists, we DJs of university philosophy. By their obsequent logic ye shall know them, these scribes who hide their belatedness in the celebration of the tradition they themselves wish to survive by living on deconstructionism once they have cleaned it from its impropriety; that is, from what they desire in J/D, who must necessarily exceed them in order to go on living/writing.

The executive committee is asked to countenance a deed that the sons and daughters of criticisms cannot face themselves. They look to the executive committee because they cannot face Jacques Derrida, from whom they want deconstructionism without his radical signature. From all corners, they write on him, they imprint on him in order to write him off in commentaries that are nothing but a series of death warrants—literal overkill. In this way, the executive committee is called to appoint its philosophical firing squads so that no one need know who killed J/D, supposing anyone hits the mark. Why are the critics so bent on the mortification of Derrida? Why must they expropriate him in warrants bearing the collective signature of deconstructionism? I say (*J'ai dit*) it is to rid the executive committee of the scandal of J/D, to cleanse the community of philosophy driven by desire, to turn Derrida's self-refusal (*je/u*) into a collective "yes" (*oui*) uttered by the first person plural (*we/nous*) in which no one can be heard for himself or herself—to enter safely the normal paradigm/paradise of kitchen criticism (*heil/heimlich*).

The sons and daughters of criticism are, after all, capable of the deed, of the writ that prepares their own legacy as deconstructionists. They know how to celebrate the rituals, to organize the symposia, to collect anthologies in which the faded flowers of memory testify to the once-living moment when desire could not survive death, when it could only live on love. But now the notice is out, the program printed, the warrants signed. The officers are in; the proceedings are official. The time has come for Jacques Derrida, tried in his absence, to separate himself from deconstructionism, to avail himself of the tradition, to take the ashes in his mouth—memento mori. The scribes will bear him away the better to honor his science. That is the way of institutional recognition. *Fort/Derrida!,* the strength yielded through Derrida's absence from the group of deconstructionists, grows through the sacrifice of the presence of Derrida/*Da,* in unbearable love/hate. Such is the obsequious logic of institutions, as we know from Freud and ourselves—as so it is with philosophy and literature as institutions.

Now, the commentator is in just as much difficulty as the translator, whose troubles Derrida has self-consciously prepared. Both must proclaim fidelity in a world where nothing, and certainly not texts, honors such a notion, unless it be machines.[10] But commentators are not copyists—although much thinking aspires to little else. Yet if infidelity is no longer a textual virtue, it is just as empty to vaunt one's infidelity or even one's intertextual indecision. Perhaps, then, criticism and commentary are necessarily violent, murderous, or incestuous designs on the mother-text or father-text. Such anger broods on itself, given the fourfold sins of the parents against themselves, against their own accounts of their sins, against the style of their confessions, and against the penitential writing (*Schrift*) through which their sins are redeemed in blindness and wandering without return. But then the father-text cannot be brought home to the tradition. Worse still, it cannot be broken and shared among its critical sons in castrated communication of the tradition. Only those are fathers who prefigure their misdeeds. Therefore, it is only in turn that sons become fathers, but not through the father. This is the blind spot of criticism and commentary, still holding to an undeceived language, insane with the corrigibility of the absconding father to which sons are heir.

To come into its own, contemporary literary criticism must separate writing/reading from the body.[11] Criticism must dismember the original texts in commentary, separating their authors from the pleasures of their text, incorporating them in a collective history of dead names. Thereafter, literature keeps constant watch lest others repeat its improprieties—at least not without paying their dues! But Jacques Derrida has already sent us a prepaid "check" to underwrite our festivities. I, too, must sign my debt—J/O—for what "I owe" him/you. This, therefore, will not have been a commentary.

CHAPTER 10

Three Men in a Text
Autocritique

I am asked to review three books in the company of the authors of
the other two. I should confess that I have not read the third book
at all.[1] It is, of course, my own *Five Bodies* (FB). To compensate for
this, I have read Kenneth Joel Shapiro's *Bodily Reflective Modes* (BRM)
and David Michael Levin's *The Body's Recollection of Being* (BRB) as
carefully as possible. However, since it is the very notion of "review"
that is in question here—making my own practice atypical—I have
appended other reviews chosen simply because they repeat the present exercise (see the Appendix to this chapter). Nonetheless, Shapiro
and Levin will not be satisfied with this, any more than I expect to
be with their reading of *Five Bodies*. Perhaps this is what justifies the
current practice of literary criticism in which authors are disqualified
as writers—let alone as readers—of their own texts. Such literary
democracy is probably another elitist conspiracy since, after all, it
had to be invented for the largely passive public we call the university.
Authors are not in fact excluded from this argument, any more than
wild animals from a circus. They enter the ring, but at a safe distance—from us and from themselves.

Shapiro's book feeds upon itself in the name of a reflective phenomenology of the body. It is a curious mixture of introverted and
extroverted "concerns." I propose to deal with these in turn and in
the order which they provide the book with its textual constitution,
psychological temperament, and style. To start this way is to begin
phenomenologically with the explicit frame of the text as the very
structure of ambivalence toward science and the life-world that motivates its author. To start this way is definitely not a device to maintain
the external stance of a book reviewer. Rather, the concern is to
express the labor, the achievements and setbacks, experienced by the
author-in-the-text. This, then, is an exercise in what in chapter 16,
I shall call *homotextuality*. Its practice involves neither external criticism nor argument ad hominem. Rather, it takes up a structure that
is alive with its own implicit and explicit articulation of the topic,

method, and motives of BRM. I shall adopt the same approach to the other two books, trying to elicit the variations in the textual bodies at work rather than to evaluate their contributions to phenomenological social science in its struggles with other sciences or their response to the broader political and ideological institutions that frame the question of science. BRB and FB are more in tune than is BRM with the larger social context. But we shall not consider this an absolute advantage so much as a question of bodily style, an option that can be revised with the ratio of introverted and extroverted horizons of the body-text, as I hope to have shown in my discussions of Roland Barthes's critical practice.

Shapiro wants BRM to be both exciting and serious. He treats his relation to it as a challenge to himself and to his scientific colleagues. His hope is that he might succeed in showing them a fault in the scientific tradition that will permit them to shrug off the weight of its settled paradigms, which are no less oppressive in phenomenological psychology than elsewhere. Shapiro argues that whatever their former radicalism, Edmund Husserl, Jean Piaget, and Claude Lévi-Strauss remain trapped in rationalism and biologism. They refrain from taking the necessary methodological step that would ground their structuralism as a mode of embodied reflexivity.

Levin makes the same argument at length against Martin Heidegger, while he and Shapiro both turn to Maurice Merleau-Ponty to underwrite their turn in the tradition. (I note parenthetically that Levin's use of the term *deconstruction* has no technical or Derridean sense but invokes only the claim that the phenomenological tradition is not properly grounded until it comes to terms with the body's reflective being.) To do this, Levin struggles with a long preface and introduction (89 pages), while Shapiro spends more than half of BRM on "Introductory Concerns," "The Method," and "Toward a Phenomenology of Structure."

O'Neill seems to lack any such concern with either the sociological tradition or the philosophical tradition. If he exhibits any methodological anxiety at all, it is expressed in a challenge thrown down to philosophers and scientists that to resurrect "anthropomorphism," so far from being an act of folly, is in fact necessary to a critical and embodied intelligence faced with the complex moral and technical possibilities we now face in reshaping human life. O'Neill's basic concepts of "thinking bodies" and "familied intelligence" are bricolage concepts drawn from his earlier work on Merleau-Ponty[2] and Marx,[3] and more recently from Vico, Freud, and Joyce.[4] Sociology has provided little inspiration for these concepts, except as the works of Herbert Marcuse and Norman O. Brown influenced sociology in the 1960s. Otherwise, it is to anthropology—or his own "wild sociology"—that O'Neill has turned, and in particular to Marcel Mauss, Emile Durkheim, Claude Lévi-Strauss, Mary Douglas, and Marshall Sahlins. O'Neill does not, of course, lack professional pride or ambition. But he seems not to suffer his discipline in the same way that Shapiro and Levin do in their prolonged genuflections before the high altar of science and the tradition. The difference lies, I think, in O'Neill's "vulgarity"—his rhetorical vision of everybody as a thinking body not easily to be subordinated to the artificial intelligences of the professional bodies of science and the arts.

To be fair, I think O'Neill and Levin share a vision of the textual body that eludes Shapiro. But O'Neill has explored much further than Levin the dimensions of the body politic, its political economy, and the ethics of the biotechnology, whose practices are well beyond Levin's vision of nihilist or antinihilist philosophy.[5] Shapiro, however, is unable to extend his concerns to the broader context that shapes and reshapes the family haven that sustains him when at work in the world of science. BRM is caught in an ambivalence generated by the split between work and the family as conflicting ethical sites. Their integration appears to impose huge entropic demands on Shapiro's intellectual energy. By contrast, I think Levin and O'Neill celebrate the bond that ties them to the family and community, and they praise the temple in which their voice and labor sings the work and ornament of others with whom they are gathered.

In short, to use Shapiro's own phrase, these books differ because they derive from radically different "reflective postures." Levin and O'Neill can easily accept Shapiro's postulate that "the touchstone for a phenomenological method must be a reflective posture through which I experience myself engaged in a particular phenomenon while I am looking at myself so experiencing" (BRM, 9). Yet I think both would reject the visual, transcendentalizing reflexivity in Shapiro's formulation because it generates the very split it seeks to heal. In other words, Shapiro is caught in an oscillation between his posture

as a scientist and his posture as a family man. Shapiro's search for a
touchstone, namely, an embodied criterion of value in his professional
and family life, starts from a shapeless blur of words, as he describes
the early stage of his lectures. In his struggle to appropriate their
sense, he resorts to an entirely disembodied spatial artifact contained
in twelve figures that, it may be argued, exhibit the very rationalism,
biologism, and externalist posture that Shapiro tries to shrug off from
his forebears.

Consider figure 10.1, which is intended to resolve Shapiro's ambivalence toward "the present long-term writing project" (*BRM*, 197) in
which he risks losing the happiness, security, playfulness, and company of his family, whose "insignificance" and "incompetence" nevertheless weights upon him. By contrast, *BRM* offers him a world of
significance, risk, competence, and work to which he is attracted,
despite his discomfort with its "risks" and "loneliness." Yet it may be
argued that Shapiro's diagrams, like his text, never move beyond the
externalist stance of a positive phenomenology. So far from enacting
the promise of a genetic phenomenology of embodied ambivalence,
Shapiro's series of spatial figures represent rather a positivist prophy-
laxis, a practice of distancing one's troubles, binding them in a clinical
optic whose aesthetics are wholly surrendered to science without
phenomenology.

Shapiro's aesthetic loss is considerable. I want to show how the

Ambivalent Aspects

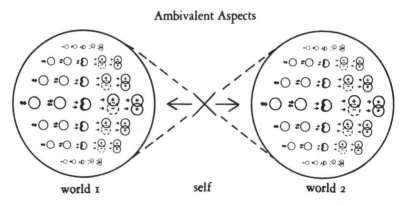

Fig. 10.1. World—self—world. Reproduced by permission of the publisher (from
K. J. Shapiro, *Bodily Reflective Modes*, fig. 12; copyright © 1985 by Duke University.

structure of ambivalence he analyzes impoverishes his textual body, reducing its style to bare contrastive sentences that are incapable of reframing their concerns. To do this, I shall draw comparisons with O'Neill's formulations of the works of Vico and Montaigne, both of whom experienced the same ambivalence between life and science as Shapiro, but each of whom, as O'Neill reads them—and thereby himself—created lasting literatures and methodologies of familized knowledge and sensibility that expand our being. In fairness to Shapiro, I shall later contrast the aesthetics of O'Neill's use of figures in FB and Levin's practice of introducing his chapters with litanies of quotations chosen to invoke the living body of the philosophical tradition to which he responds in thought's dance about the temple of the scriptures.

I return to Shapiro's text. I do so to struggle with the sadness in his distance from it, expressed, as I hear it, in references to BRM, as "this long-term writing project" (BRM, 194, 197) and his confession of alternating commitment and frustration in his expectations of it. I do not mean to denigrate the honesty displayed in this, despite having to insist from the very standpoint of that embodied reflexivity invoked by Shapiro himself that such honesty is not well served by its textualization in the following format:

(a) Original, unambivalent intended object: I want to finish this writing project.
(b) First negation: I do not want to finish this writing project.
(c) Positive embodiment of first negation: I want to be with my family.
(d) Aspect of positive embodiment of first negation: I can fulfill myself through my family.
(e) This aspect negated (second negation): I cannot fulfill myself through my family.
(f) Positive embodiment of second negation: I can fulfill myself by finishing this writing project. (BRM, 196)

Shapiro requires, but does not notice, the textual artifact of the list as a reading device for recycling the sense of sentence (a) in terms of the progression through and conclusion reached in (f). That device is in turn amplified by a diagram (fig. 10.1) that translates the positive and negative sentences in the list in terms of plus and minus signs attached to symbols which, however, can themselves only be read in terms of the text as a legend to the very figure claiming to clarify the text. The result is a conventional scientific text that exemplifies all the abstractive and "extra-somatic" features of a positive rather than embodied reflexivity.

There is the greatest difference in the underlying homotextuality of BRM and that of BRB and FB. The former is ruled by Shapiro's ambition to be received as a phenomenological psychologist in the scientific community with the added hope that this will gladden his family. Thus, his writing subordinates itself to the logical and spatializing practices to which I have drawn attention. By contrast, Levin's text is manifestly an assembly of texts, a liturgical gathering of voices whose effect is to create a tradition or community of recollection in which the mind returns to the dance of being around the body's temple:

> Understanding the texts, we place our body in a stance which supports them and grounds them firmly on the earth where we stand: in brief, we stand *under* the text; we uphold it, too, holding it up to the measure of the sky. *That* is true understanding. (BRB, 215)

Levin's phenomenology is both gay and religious, a happy marriage of "Greekjew," as Joyce would say. Despite its more general claims, BRB remains on the level of love's body when compared with O'Neill's trilevel body politic and his explorations of the biobody, the consumer body, the medical body, and the industrialization of women's bodies, all viewed in terms of a long history of the human family. O'Neill writes as a social scientist, to be sure, just as Levin writes as a philosopher. But FB and BRB are also defiantly religious writings that subordinate their logic and argument to the scriptural task of illumination and celebration—even in the darkest hour. Thus FB is a work of remembrance; starting with a history of the world's body, it pays homage to our giant ancestors who, as Vico says, scared themselves into our civil and divine institutions. FB then turns to society conceived as a body, interpreting the ancient and modern food rituals of the Hebrews and "the MacDonalds." Against the transformation of industrialism, O'Neill defends the familied body, whose labors are shared in mothering and fathering and in a ceaseless struggle to achieve authority against the forces of the state and the economy. Through the apparatus of the therapeutic state, these forces deepen their hold on the human body once our biotechnologies transplant, so to speak, desire, sexuality, health, knowledge and power into the body as a *sociotext*.

In contrast to Shapiro's use of diagrams and Levin's use of citations, O'Neill illustrates various stages of anthropomorphosis that compose *FB* through the use of iconic figures, which play off the contrastive structures that organize the text. Thus "Leaning Lady" (fig. 10.2), herself a body in several pieces, is to be read against the "Smoking Lady" (variously figured alone, independent, and knowledgeable through her choice of cigarette, but for whom the tobacco companies withheld permission to reproduce any photo); their contrast is that of a strong analysis and a weak independence. The contrast is repeated in the complementarity between "Leaning Lady" and the "Christ Figure" (*FB* 72; fig. 10.3), whose wholeness is opposed to the bioanalytics of "Spare-part Man" (*FB* 129; fig. 10.4), to whom, of course "Smoking Lady" is related, however unknowingly. Thus, by means of these figures O'Neill reproduces and defends a history of the world's body under the concept of a radical anthropomorphism that shapes our economy, medicine, and nuclear politics.

Despite his ambition to recast phenomenological psychology, Shapiro approaches the description of his predicament as a writer at home rather narrowly. Given his affection for Merleau-Ponty, he might have been led to Montaigne and his reflections on the relation between public and private life. Before considering what might have come of this turn, I shall show how Giambattista Vico also struggled with his family circumstances, creating from them the *New Science*. In these two authors, Shapiro's problematic is lifted into a great tradition, which is in turn amplified by the literary classics left to us by Vico and Montaigne. It needs to be said, of course, that O'Neill's conception of phenomenological sociology is weighted with this history of familied sensibility and intelligence, which he defends and celebrates as the touchstone of meaning and value. O'Neill thereby foreswears any transcendental and solipsistic reach in scientific writing, seeking instead to redeem thought's necessary alienation in the body's recollection of its familied being.

Giambattista Vico took upon himself the reversal of the great rationalist tradition of philosophy, science, and law descending from Descartes, Bacon, and Grotius. He did so, as he tells us in his *Autobiography*, despite having to work at home in poverty, surrounded by his

Fig. 10.2. Paul Klee, *Leaning,* copyright © 1985 by ADAGP, Montreal.

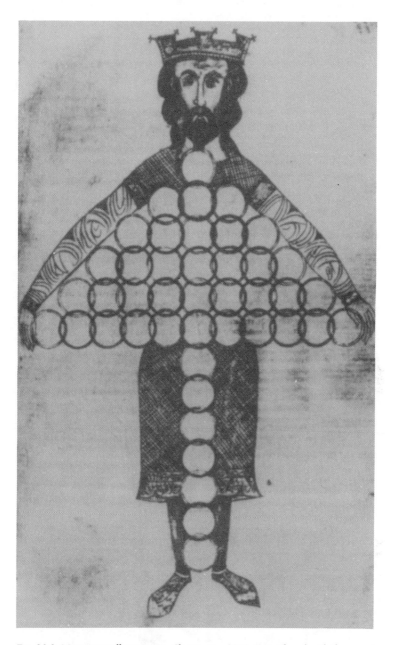

Fig. 10.3. Manuscript illumination, Christ, circa 1341. Reproduced with the permission of the publisher from Alžběta Güntherová and Ján Mišianik, *Illuminierte Handschriften aus der Slowakei* (Prague: Artia).

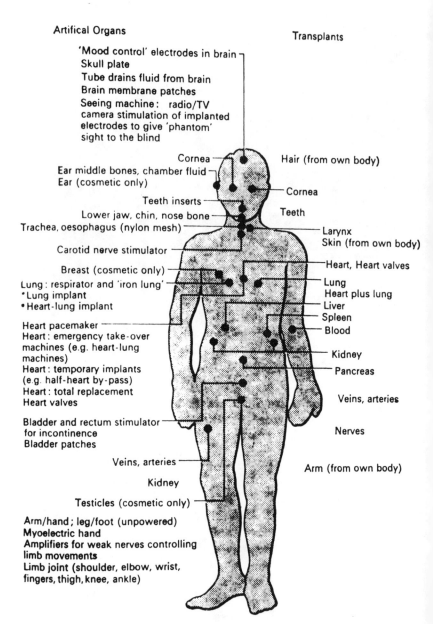

Artifical Organs

Transplants

'Mood control' electrodes in brain
Skull plate
Tube drains fluid from brain
Brain membrane patches
Seeing machine: radio/TV
camera stimulation of implanted
electrodes to give 'phantom'
sight to the blind

Cornea
Hair (from own body)

Ear middle bones, chamber fluid
Ear (cosmetic only)

Cornea

Teeth inserts

Teeth

Lower jaw, chin, nose bone

Trachea, oesophagus (nylon mesh)

Larynx
Skin (from own body)

Carotid nerve stimulator

Breast (cosmetic only)

Heart, Heart valves

Lung: respirator and 'iron lung'
*Lung implant
*Heart-lung implant

Lung
Heart plus lung
Liver
Spleen

Heart pacemaker
Heart: emergency take-over
machines (e.g. heart-lung
machines)
Heart: temporary implants
(e.g. half-heart by-pass)
Heart: total replacement
Heart valves

Blood

Kidney

Pancreas

Bladder and rectum stimulator
for incontinence
Bladder patches

Veins, arteries

Nerves

Veins, arteries

Kidney

Arm (from own body)

Testicles (cosmetic only)

Arm/hand; leg/foot (unpowered)
Myoelectric hand
Amplifiers for weak nerves controlling
limb movements
Limb joint (shoulder, elbow, wrist,
fingers, thigh, knee, ankle)

* = not yet achieved in humans but expected soon

children, and in the face of academic disappointments and political refusals of advancement.[6] In the midst of these things, there rings out the first axiom of the *New Science*, whose own poetry exemplifies the poetic method it lays down for all human learning:

> The most sublime labour of poetry is to give sense and passion to insensate things; and it is characteristic of children to take inanimate things in their hands and talk to them in play as if they were living persons. This philologico-philosophical axiom proves to us that in the world's childhood men were by nature sublime poets.[7]

Together, Vico's *Autobiography* and *New Science* offer us a fable of anxiety, starting from a refusal of Cartesian certainty, wandering at times in darkness like a child in the first forests, but always able to gather the history of its experiences as recollections of the great body and family of mankind. And as surely as the variable fortunes of his health and work drove him back upon his family and children, Vico responded by renewing in himself and in us those bodily beginnings of the world's childhood, whose sensible origins owe nothing to the concepts of rationalist philosophers but everything to their primal poetry. Thus, we owe to Vico's family and his own creative melancholy a great insistence upon the priority of beginnings collected not by philosophers and scientists but in those universal vulgar agreements of religion, marriage, and burial with which humankind has domesticated its fears and adorned itself with civil beauty. Rather than exchange his family and poverty for power and friendship in the Renaissance tradition, Vico's fatherly intuition drew deeply from his home life, from the conversation of his friends around his writing table, and from the babble of his children around his feet. So far from seeing in these things the inflictions of poverty and the loss of philosophical solitude, he turned these familiar sights and sounds into a great poem of the world's civil origins and its sensible education in that tradition of humanity to which we owe all reason and all eloquence.

Fig. 10.4. (*opposite*) Spare-part man. All items other than the lung and heart-lung implants have been achieved and are expected to have a significant clinical impact. Trivial artificial parts such as false teeth are not included; neither are several transplant organs which have been achieved (whole eye) or are often talked about (limbs from other bodies, gonads) because of severe technical or ethical difficulties. Reproduced from Gerald Leach, *The Biocrats* (London, Jonathan Cape; reprint, Penguin, 1972) by permission of Jonathan Cape Ltd.

Here it may be appropriate to point out that O'Neill's *Five Bodies* is constructed from the same sensible materials of embodied history as Vico's *New Science*. It is similarly concerned to defend the common-sense reasoning and values of vulgar institutions against the rationalist culture of the social sciences and their therapeutic expropriation of the family's authority. But whereas Vico envisaged the recycling of our barbarism, O'Neill's faith in the tide of human history is shadowed by the unthinkable limit of our nuclear technology. It is at this zero point of civilization that *FB* reopens the anthropological question, How are we to shape ourselves? Or as he puts it:

> I am concerned to rethink the civic legacy bequeathed to us in the *sociopoetics* of the first humans, whose families and gods have survived most of the history of our own inhumanity and are still alive in the most ordinary places of mankind. If we have anything to fear from humanity's capacity for metamorphosis, it is from the aweful potential we now have to erase all other living forms along with ourselves. The truly unthinkable side of our civilizational discontent is that we may well be the first human society to think of itself as the *last*. Before such a prospect, we are obliged to rethink the human body, to reconstitute its family, its political economy, and its biotechnologies.[8]

At such a critical juncture, it is helpful to think in terms of others who have lived through the zero point in their civilization, bringing out of it a creative work that now stands in that civilized continuity to which we owe our own intelligence and sensibility. For this reason Montaigne's *Essays* come to mind as a text in which the anxiety of influence is weighted between what is due respectively to the self and its family. At the start of his *Essays*, Montaigne suffers from the same distractions of which any of us might complain, and which we explore more fully in chapter 12. Indeed, like Shapiro, that is his essential complaint and the source of much of Montaigne's expressed ambivalence toward his own work. Thus he enters into the work of the essayist as an artless and private exercise, unsure of himself and his public, barely counting on recognition from his own family and neighbors. But gradually Montaigne learns to weight the historical, philosophical, and literary sources on which he first leans against his own experience in life, politics, love, and the family—and always from his reading and writing. In this way, the very form and method of the *Essays* emerge from a practical faith in the reliability of custom, law, the family, and the body, which have shaped human intelligence and sensibility more surely than philosophical reason and dogma.

There is therefore a huge phenomenological distance between the carnal inquiry engaged in the *Essays* and the propositional and spatialized artifacts through which Shapiro achieves orientation in the writing of *BRM*. And, of course, the same is true of *FB* and *BRB* in this respect. *BRM* remains within the externalized and excarnate stance of the positive phenomenologies it claims to avoid. Thus Shapiro risks the adoption of a solipsist standpoint toward self-analysis, and it is here that Vico and Montaigne constitute a more relevant tradition than Husserl, Piaget, and Lévi-Strauss and, for that matter, a less dispersed assembly than Levin's litanies gathered in *BRB*. What Montaigne discovered is that the daily undertaking of the *Essays* had made him and his book consubstantial. Thus, as they grew into the second book, the *Essays* became Montaigne's very child while he himself was born through them:

> To this child, such as it is, what I give I give purely and irrevocably, as one gives to the child of one's body. The little good I have done for it is no longer at my disposal. It may know a good many things that I no longer know and hold from me what I have not retained and what, just like a stranger, I should have to borrow from it if I came to need it. If I am wiser than it, it is richer than I.[9]

Vico's *New Science*, Montaigne's *Essays*—and O'Neill's *Five Bodies*— are plainly the works of family men. To such men, the exercise of solipsism is never tempting, however much advertised by philosophy, art, and science.

We are perhaps now in a position to draw further comparisons with Levin's *The Body Recollection of Being*, which like Shapiro's *Bodily Reflective Modes* is also concerned to re-vision (or deconstruct) phenomenological psychology. To do so, however, Levin has a different sense of the tradition than either Shapiro or O'Neill, being largely concerned to reread Heidegger through Merleau-Ponty's critique of the rationalist bias of transcendental phenomenology. Nothing is to be gained from the conventional exercise of deciding the veracity of these readings; it is their deliberate bias that is of interest. Shapiro and Levin turn to Merleau-Ponty for the concept of embodied reflexivity, but O'Neill has borrowed from Merleau-Ponty in a far wider exploration of the intersubjectivity of knowledge embodiment, work, and politics. What emerges in Levin's rereading is a concept of grounded incarnation that is far more "Jewgreek" than anything in Merleau-Ponty or in O'Neill, for whom the incarnation is a Catholic and Marxist concept. Whether Jew or Catholic, Levin and O'Neill seem to draw on their respective religious traditions in ways that remove them entirely from Shapiro's painful ambition of writing a scientific text for phenomenological psychologists.

In the end, Shapiro seems to suffocate under a narrowed conception of phenomenology to exemplify his conflicts, and *BRM* remains an externalist project whose writing is a burden to its author. By contrast, O'Neill and Levin seem more committed to writing and to the text as redemptive exercises, exemplary of the body's grounded reverberation of being recollected in a tradition, a family, a church or temple. Levin and O'Neill conceive of writing as a sacred gesture, as a ritual of incarnation in which the synesthesia of the senses repeats the convocation of the communal body gathered religiously in the sound, sights, song and dance of the text. From this standpoint, writing defends the tradition and does not simply repeat it. Thus writing does not ignore the new or reject it in favor of the tradition. For this reason, *Five Bodies* is not a defense of the traditional family in the face of its new surroundings. Rather, it is in view of *FB*'s study of the new environment of health, consumption, and work that a concept of critical, familied intelligence is elaborated as a necessary historical, civic, and political competence within our own self-shaping institutions. *FB* starts from the body-text in order to show how it must be continuously re-visioned in terms of the socio-text, whereas *BRB* remains with the task of recollecting the concept of embodiment in view of our forgetfulness of life, or rather its subordination to knowledge. This is assumed in *FB* in order to specify the knowledge and practices that rewrite our bodies in several institutional settings that determine the political economy of the body, knowledge and practice that are spelled out in the present volume.

In conclusion, it occurs to me that, while as a reader I am less disposed toward Shapiro's *BRM* than to Levin's *BRB*, it remains true that Shapiro's predicament catches me more as a writer. And so I have studied Shapiro's book more than Levin's. I have done so because a writer is driven more by the anxiety of reading than by the pleasure of the text. Here, however, we would need a psychoanalysis of the writer's body, such as I consider later in the case of Roland Barthes's practice of "homotextuality," and in my treatment of Montaigne, Descartes, and Freud as symptomatic texts. My preference for such texts might in turn be considered a source of my allergic response to Stanley Fish, Richard Rorty, and Fredric Jameson. Other reviewers may decide upon that!

APPENDIX

Bodily Reflective Modes: A Phenomenological Method of Psychology, by Kenneth Joel Shapiro, Duke University Press, Durham, 1985, pp. 230, $30 Hardback.

The Body's Recollection of Being: Phenomenological Psychology and the Deconstruction of Nihilism, by David Michael Levin, Routledge and Kegan Paul 1985, pp. 390, £9.95.

Both these books are on phenomenological psychology; they emphasize the original role of experiencing one's own body in the human experiencing of others. One author (Levin) is a philosopher, the other (Shapiro) a psychologist, and both claim to be strongly influenced by a 'body-psychology-therapist.' Eugene Gendlin, who for some reason is little treated by either author. To begin with a philosopher:

Levin's book is for Heideggerians, for probably only they could easily understand it; it is a symphony to the greater glory of Heidegger and (unfortunately) the greater mystification of psychology. Two typical chapter headings are: 'The Gathering Round-Dance' and 'The Ground and its Poetising.' This long book has barely a summary to guide the reader but it does include about 600 quotations. It is an over-long hermeneutic expedition into the metaphor of body as in: 'body of tradition', 'embodiment', 'body of the text' and 'body politic'.

Levin believes that Heidegger must, 'to escape the philosophers' study' deal with the very real issue of human suffering and he hopes to do this by way of the psychology of Jung and his disciple Neumann. The archetypes of the Collective Unconscious are given an ultimate root as images in primordial body, and in this way the Unconscious is finally assigned its 'appropriate phenomenology' while philosophy is enriched by the return of conscious awareness to its home in body.

The most quoted (analytical) psychologist, Erich Neumann, and the most respected psychotherapist, Carl Rogers, are rooted in the evolutionary-biological model of mental processes, something which Jung for all his spirituality did not escape and consequently neither does Levin. We might note that the eminent Medard Boss succeeded in allowing the philosophy of Hiedegger to wake up psychotherapy from its complacency by using much clinical material, but we feel that this book is no advance on Medard Boss, whose 'Daseinanalyse and Psychoanalysis' is, in the opinion of the reviewer, a minor masterpiece.

Shapiro's book takes its inspiration not from Heidegger but from Merleau-Ponty, and its point of departure is also sensitivity to the experience of our own body. For example: my stomach sinks at the first ring of the telephone before I know it is the anxiously awaited call. In all this he is anti-structuralist, he is 'not lost as subject in language, his intentions irrecoverable in, or superceded by texts.' He is subject, rather at a preconceptual bodily-feeling level. At this level (of childhood) the 'me' and the 'not-me' are not distinct. It is in this region that according to Shapiro, structure has its pre-conceptual presence. Here are founded the metaphors of everyday speech, e.g. 'in grief I was *empty*'. 'I can *grasp* what you mean, etc. Ella Sharpe, the English psychoanalyst, did a great deal of work in this area and her teacher, Melanie Klein, is approved by Shapiro, who paraphrases her views on ambivalence sympathetically. However, he shrinks from the rich account of this phenomenon given by psychoanalysis to embrace a more easily handled (simple minded) notion of ambivalence in terms of focus and distraction. As a practical application of this theory he takes the example of having mixed feelings about writing an academic paper, but this example lacks the richness that one would hope for in a discussion of ambivalence.

However, the book is well written, compact, provides, helpful definitions, examples and summaries and for this reason it would be a good 'text book' for students in phenomenology from which the teacher could learn a great deal.

Finally we come to both authors' attitudes to psychotherapy. Levin seeks to integrate or colonize it under phenomenology by claiming that 'depth psychology' (as he calls it) was *forced* into using the idea of the Unconscious or as he says the 'unconscious conscious'—a phrase analysed and dismissed by Freud as nonsensical. The phenomenology of body, he declares, could take over the role of this unfortunate Unconscious. Shapiro, too, has the colonizing tendency, claiming, that when the psychoanalyst forgets metapsychology he is a practising phenomenologist!

However neither author succeeds in 'writing out' the Unconscious: Levin replaces it with a Neumann-inspired race memory while Shapiro claims that the ability to form the present in terms of the past ('forming') is the 'royal road' to the structure of behaviour (to use his own words). This recalls, of course, Freud's original sentence that: 'dreams are the royal road to the Unconscious' which includes the idea that the *interpretation* of those dreams is the 'royal road' so we might well ask: is it the interpretation of 'forming' that leads to structure? Would structure then be known by its 'distortions and concealments'—a charge levelled at the Unconscious by Shapiro. So where now is the Subject? Could it be in these distortions and concealments, in the metaphors and metonymies of language?

Ross Shelton
Trinity College, Dublin[10]

John O'Neill, Five Bodies, Ithaca: Cornell University Press, 1985, 181 pp.
Bryan S. Turner, *The Body and Society.* Oxford: Basil Blackwell, 272 pp., $20.95.

John O'Neill's *Five Bodies* is a major work of recent Canadian social theory. Its importance for sociology can only be adequately assimilated, however, in terms of another work, Bryan S. Turner's *The Body and Society.* These books present the fascinating serendipity of two scholars writing on the same subject in what appears to be complete independence from each other. Though apparently unaware of each other's work, Turner and O'Neill have much in common. Each has a commanding grasp of classic and contemporary sociological theory, each articulates the seminal importance of Michel Foucault, and each is what might be called a Commonwealth sociologist, Turner working in Australia and O'Neill in Canada. This last commonality is not as tenuous as it might appear. In presenting the need for a sociology of the body, each suggests a fundamental reorientation of sociological thought. Perhaps such radical calls for reorientation can only come from the periphery—from places off the American/English/Continental theoretical axis.

The two books are different but complementary in the strong sense that the case of each becomes more important in light of the other. It may be best to begin with Turner, since his book is addressed to a distinctly sociological audience. *The Body and Society* is midway between being a scholarly monograph and a text suitable for advanced undergraduate and graduate courses. I myself plan to use Turner to conclude a year-long undergraduate theory course. The book provides an excellent summary of Weber and Marx, with significant bits of Durkheim and Parsons as well, and demonstrates how this material can be creatively adapted to theorize a problem the immediacy of which students will readily grasp: the relation of the body to society. For the advanced student, Turner displays how to use the classics to create theory.

Turner's sociology can be approached through one of his quotations of Foucault: "Countless people have sought the origins of sociology in Montesquieu and Comte. That is a very ignorant enterprise. Sociological knowledge is formed rather in practices like those of the doctors" (p. 49). For Foucault these practices are paradigmatically those in which the body is produced, both as an object of knowledge and, concurrently, as the modality through with power operates.

Foucault's conjunction of power/knowledge asserts that neither term can operate independently of the other. Medical knowledge of the body institutionalizes a power over the body, and that power operates through the unquestionable imperative for increased knowledge. This knowledge is productive: it claims the interest of producing the life of the body. But to be produced the body must be disciplined: trained, subjected to strict regimens (e.g., diet, about which Turner says a good deal), and most important to Foucault, the body must be made an object of surveillance. Hospitals, as any patient realizes, are constructed not to allow the body to rest, but to make it readily accessible to observation, just as Bentham's model prison, the panopticon, was designed to make the bodies of prisoners optimally accessible to the unseen observer. Because the prisoner could not know if he was being observed or not, being observed became the internalized reality of his behavior. But in these exercises of power—whether prison, hospital, military parade ground, factory, or school—the body is not repressed by power, it is produced. This production is double: the body is produced as itself being capable of enhanced productivity, and it is produced as an on-going object of surveillance and discipline.

Both Turner and O'Neill provide useful introductions to Foucault, whose work forms the basis for each of their books. Turner takes this Foucauldian base in a distinctly sociological direction. He rereads the sociological classics, particularly Weber and Marx, in terms of what each has to say about those practices in which the body has been socially determined. For Weber this is primarily the production of the ascetic body, and for Marx it is the labouring body. On this basis Turner takes on no less a task than rewriting the Parsonian problem of social order. For Hobbes, Turner argues, the body is the central point of reference, both as the bodies of individual men and as the body politic of the state. "The problem of order," Turner writes, "resulted from the fact that these bodies, if unchecked, would periodically collide, rather like stars in the firmament. The solution was a sovereign power to regulate the motion of bodies" (p. 89).

What Turner then proposes is "to rewrite Hobbes in order to produce a theory of social order which starts out from the problem of regulating bodies"(p. 90). What follows is a new four-fold taxonomy, generating four new functional prerequisites or "sub-problems" which "every social system has to solve" (p. 91). These are constructed on the vertical columns of populations and bodies (taken from Foucault's distinctions of anatomo-politics and bio-politics, respectively) and the horizontal rows of time and space. Without doing justice to Turner's development of this typology, it may be summarized as generating the problems of (a) *reproduction* of populations over time, (b) *restraint* of bodies in time, (c) *regulation* of populations spacially arrayed, and (d) *representation* of the external, spacial surfaces of bodies. Reproduction is associated with the social practice of patriarchy and finds its principle theorist in Malthus. Restraint is practiced paradigmatically in asceticism as theorized by Weber. Regulation has its paradigm practice in panopticism, but Rousseau, not Foucault, is cited as its principle theorist. Finally representation is practiced in late capitalist commodification, which Goffman describes as face-work.

The reconceptualization allows Turner to present two peripheral sociological specializations, medical sociology and sociology of religion, as core enterprises. They must be core, that is, to a sociology conceived as practices effected on bodies. For Turner, as for O'Neill, medical practice is the empirical activity in which modernity most clearly reveals itself, but contemporary medicine can only be understood as a displacement of traditional concerns of religion. Turner also presents the problem of patriarchy as being central to sociology. Patriarchy, and this argument will return in O'Neill, is conceived less as a problem of sexism— though that is hardly denied—than an organization of the patriarchal household as a production unit. To the extent that patriarchy has broken down this is not to be understood as the "liberation" of women, but rather as the commodification of the body displacing the household production unit. This summary only suggests an argument which deserves the fullest debate.

Turner says a great deal about many topics, but let me suggest that his greatest contribution may be to focus a fundamental antinomy, perhaps even contradiction, of sociological thought. Taking the body as a fundamental point of origin forces us to recognize that sociology must be phenomenological, since embodiment is the phenomenology of the lived body. But sociology must also recognize that "personal experience of embodiment is highly mediated by social training, language and social context" (p. 264). The "social ontology" of the body for which he repeatedly calls will not be arrived at by philosophical reflection but only, as Foucault stated, by the study of practices of the production of bodies and, Turner would add, the phenomenology of bodies so produced. Because sociology itself is so implicated in the discursive practices of power/knowledge by which bodies are produced, the study of the body forces sociology to recognize its quintessentially hermeneutic position.

Five Bodies is addressed not primarily to sociologists but to those whom O'Neill calls "radical humanists" (p. 152). If Turner seeks to reconstitute sociology through a focus on the body, O'Neill presents nothing less than an agenda for a renewed contemporary humanism. We have lost our sense of humanism, O'Neill argues, as we have moved from history as "biotext" to history as "socio-text." As biotext, history was thought with and through the body. In what is perhaps his most impressive chapter, O'Neill revives the proposition from Vico that "human beings think nature and society with their bodies. . . . the divisions of the body yield the divisions of the world and of society . . . classification . . . followed an *embodied logic*" (p. 28). This logic is the basis of later "rationalist" thought, but it has been lost. The biotext has become the sociotext, which takes us back again to Foucault, power/knowledge, and the production of bodies. In the sociotext, human beings no longer think with their bodies, but rather the practices of social science are "designed to rewrite the human body, to reinscribe its mind and emotions" (p. 152).

For O'Neill as for Turner, the essential practices of the sociotext are patriarchy, commodification, and medicine. The latter two are the principle practices of capitalist and technological reinscription of bodies. Patriarchy for O'Neill seems to represent the perversion of what he calls the "familied" body. O'Neill is not the first to call attention to the modernist paradox of the family being simultaneously held up as exemplary of what society values and attacked as a locus of social pathology. His theoretical situation of this paradox allows him to suggest not a nostalgia of the family but a challenge. My own phrasing of this would be, can there be a "familied" body in a society which demands that the needs of the body are for commodities, not relationships?

For O'Neill as for Turner, the essential issue is finally one of the social production of desire. Here again the same antimony poses itself: the body's desire is produced in a social discourse of consumerism, but commodities cannot comfort the body which in its phenomenology is "defamilized." The extension of O'Neill's argument would seem to be that the authentic phenomenology of the refamilized body requires a new societal discourse of the body. As examples of this discourse O'Neill, as radical humanist, gives us James Agee and Dylan Thomas. Hardly new, they remain nonetheless challenging in the recognition of bodily needs their reading demands; still, they cannot be much guidance to what form a renewed sociology can take. To create this discourse within sociology, we need to return to Turner.

In his theorized typology of a sociology of the body, Turner suggests a research program through which sociology as a study of practices can recreate itself; a richer basis for the often euphemistic "further research" could hardly be provided. If Turner shows *how* to create a sociology of the body, O'Neill's polemical style pleads *why* such a sociology is imperative. For Foucault the discovery of the body as the locus of power/knowledge required the burial of humanism as the homocentrism of a body which could not be a centre, only an effect of a discourse. Without sacrificing the insight of the Foucauldian critique, O'Neill has resuscitated humanism. After the complementarity of Turner's and O'Neill's efforts, sociology cannot, and need not, ignore the humanistic claims of the body. What was peripheral is reinscribed as central.

Arthur W. Frank
University of Calgary[11]

CHAPTER 11

Power and the Splitting
(*Spaltung*) of Language
Renaissance Rhetoric and the
Double Intertextuality of Self
and Society

The following exercise involves a review of/commentary on a special issue of *New Literary History* devoted to the topic of Renaissance literature and contemporary theory.[1] The issue contains seven papers from authors who had, of course, independently to focus their work so that they would, broadly speaking, honor the topic while defending their own special knowledge of the Renaissance as well as their sense of how their specialty might be affected by their understanding of current literary criticism. This is a common enough exercise, and our ability to bring it off is good evidence of the commonsense structure of interpretative opinion that is as operative in the literary community as elsewhere. The commentator's task is no different. In this case, however, I was unaware while working on my commentary that several others were engaged in the same task. What may be observed from the published results is that three professors of English, two from the United States and one from West Germany, and a fourth from Canada, a sociologist, were able to approach their task in an extraordinarily complementary way. I shall, therefore, sketch very briefly the argument frames used by each commentator, pointing to the places where each envisages the possibility of the others' approach, and thus situate my own comments (the point being to show that the reader—who can always consult *New Literary History*—acquires competence with these texts through recognition of their method as much as from knowing what they are "about"). The exercise is also useful inasmuch as it displays how a common task is achieved without explicit knowledge of the other practitioners' strategies of interpretation. What emerges is a variety of comments ruled by the "same" texts in which the ration of consensus and difference remains undecidable.

Gordon Broden, then, finds in the papers a concern with the problematic of selfhood as one that connects Renaissance rhetoric with postmodern arguments about structures of impersonal power and techniques of self-fashioning. He reads the contributions through Jakob Burckhardt's *The Civilization of the Renaissance in Italy* as a model, noticing that only Robert Weimann makes reference to it—and even then in a passing dismissal. Yet Broden insists—he promises a book to prove it—that Weimann's concept of *Aneignung* (appropriation) does not differ from Burckhardt's focus on the problematic of the self's definition in a (capitalist) world of proliferating things, and he even insists that Burckhardt foreshadows the Marxist concept of alienation, which Weimann employs. Broden constructs his commentary around a "re-view" of Burckhardt, examining contemporary criticism in the light of its near past—implicitly rejecting "post"–modernism by finding its discoveries where it had abandoned their possibility.

Meredith Skura observes that the critical method of the several papers assumes an abandonment of literature as an exclusive category in favor of the analysis of the text and its context, which requires knowledge not only of history, politics, and economics but also of *psychoanalysis*, which seems called for to deal with the conflicts between the aspirations of self and the civil facade of a censoring, repressive power structure. Since contemporary psychoanalysis no longer deals with a "timeless unconscious," Jacques Lacan's revision of Freud, object-relations psychology and self-psychology have brought psychoanalysis to the same sense of text and context as now obtains with respect to literature. She concludes that these two institutions are ready for a methodological marriage, although she doubts whether contemporary Marxism can be brought into the primal scene of criticism, despite what we have already seen if only with regard to Fredric Jameson.

Claus Uhlig produces his commentary by focusing on the four methodologies that he sees operative in contemporary Renaissance studies. First, there is the view of the Renaissance as a "usable past," whose significance lies in its contribution to projections of present and future history. Second, there is the "historicist" approach, which seeks to reconstruct the distinctive *episteme* of the Renaissance. Third, there is the increasing stress on "interdisciplinarity" in treating Renaissance texts and contexts. Fourth, there remain "traditional positivistic" Renaissance studies. Uhlig then proceeds to fit the various contributions to this fourfold framework, noticing artifactual troubles in each exercise—such as the problem of the relation between art and society and the extent to which later interpretive strategies are required by the already "self-interpreting" texts of the Renaissance. Uhlig's personal preference is for "a kind of enlightened neohistoricism" whose goal is to respect the distinctive *episteme* of the Renaissance arrived at through a cautious interdisciplinarity that respects the whole it seeks to deconstruct.

Against this background, my own commentary unwittingly took the following course:

SELF-INTERPRETING ARTIFACTS AND LIMITED THEORY

I shall begin with Louis Marin's formulation of the question we must put to our contemporary practice of literary criticism the moment we abrogate to it any power of scientific generalization. Marin poses the question, What could be the relation between literary theory and history if by theory one understood a general and exhaustive explanation of the facts? Is there any contemporary theory that might be applied in this way to Renaissance literature? Marin does not think so. He insists that in some sense the object for analysis must already reveal "some rudiments of the theory which it is supposed to illustrate" and cannot stand to its explanatory artifacts as nature stands to science. Every cultural artifact contains a second-degree level, where it "mirrors" its own reading or interpretation. To suppose otherwise is to imagine art as wholly unconscious behavior awaiting an external critic to reveal its sense, the latter possessed of a transhistorical metalanguage given to no preceding generation. Such a theory of art would, of course, reduce us to the silence of stones.

We do not possess a total cultural paradigm. Such a presupposition would, in my view, at best make sense only as a retrospective artifact of analysis—a reverential mode of turning our back on things with the added hope that we might be facing into a future. Of course, we are obliged to treat subcultures, subtexts, institutions, and roles as more likely than not to cohere within a given period or *episteme*. Or else we should have to abandon intelligibility. Today, we favor discontinuity in order to practice a certain cultural charity that is ignored in those very histories of humanity that progress by abstracting from, relegating, and shunting over altogether aspects of history that condemn themselves by not easily fitting the schemas of rationality. Discontinuity is the measure of our wounded humanism.[2] We must suppose that all human conduct is at some level self-expressive and self-explicating in accordance with its own schemas of sense, practicality, and value. The alternative to this view is to treat prior history as a third-world culture that imports the meaning it lacks from a contemporary world marked, curiously enough, by enormous uncertainty about its own cultural status. In short, pure criticism, like pure democracy or pure capitalism, is an imperialist fiction. Culture has no such Archimedean point. What weights on us is the relevance, the call or encroachment, of every other human expression across history, class, and culture. As Marin puts it:

> Both the past text and contemporary theory experience *displacement* [my emphasis]—the former *away from* the otherness of its history *into* the anachronism of theoretical propositions eluding thought, the latter *away from* the alleged atemporality of its propositions and theses *into* the historicity of a pseudohistorical (virtual) development. And in this sense it is true, or at least operational, to say that the past text, as a verbal artifact, develops, through the questioning of contemporary theory, one of its potential profiles; while it can also be said, reversing the process, that contemporary theory uncovers, through the very displacement it forces upon the text by probing it, unsuspected potentialities of the theoretical energy specifically relevant to that text.[3]

Although we cannot pursue it in detail—and this applies to the other essays—Marin's remarkable "reading" of Luca Signorelli's cupola in the St. John sacristy of Notre Dame of Loreto exemplifies both the theoretical and methodological reflexivity he invokes on behalf of any cultural object.[4] We are obsessed with the quest for a bedrock of truth, perception, visibility, speech, and writing. Thus the text becomes a "tortured body," an open wound of signs where writing and reading, commentary and criticism, seek touch and penetration, "blinding and exhaustion." All this is reflected in Signorelli's iconic transformations of the Divine Word into scriptural discourse, into the portrayal of reading and commentary, achieved against the shift of divine presence and absence, movement and rest. Like the icon, Marin's interpretative procedure is an exemplary act of erudition and fidelity that points to its own chiasmus of seeing and believing: "*The* book, the written text, the discourse-text has become *a* body marked by its history, a body not intended for reading, or reading mediated through writing, but for touching in the plainness of its contingent, singular existence—in other words, intended to be shown, taken, and consumed in the act of Faith."[5]

Thus we may think of various literary genres in art, science, and philosophy as generating scenarios in which a discursive inquiry may be followed—or in which the conditions of its utterability may be formulated as rules of human nature or of divine society. Literary and historical consciousness, therefore, are never without *autodeixis*. But this is achieved only through displacement, understood not just as a psychological or life-style achievement—as an ascesis—but as a sense of necessary passage and perspective energizing understanding and explanation. History and literary theory, then, can only be adulterations of one another.

POWER AND RHETORICAL SPLITTING (*Spaltung*)

I must now make a move designed to pursue the central issue—power and the splitting of language—which I shall employ to survey the rest of the contributions, hopefully avoiding unnecessary snares, and without spilling unlimited ink. Remarks on the nature of language and politics, truth and deception, occur in all the essays with particular reference to rhetorical practice, courtly conduct, theater, and publishing. In addition to what can be learned from the substantive analyses pursued by various authors, it seems worthwhile to insist on the inseparability of language and power and to interpret the split (*Spaltung*) generated by the conflict between domination and desire as the source of the rhetorical address of the conditions of truth and illusion, freedom and slavery, deception and authenticity. This rhetorical splitting of language will occur in any human institution—in the family, the state, the church, and the economy. My later discussion of Weimann's paper will return to this issue, refining the argument somewhat.

Power puts language and desire under pressure, according to its various individual and institutional contexts, to raise and to seek answers to the question, Under what conditions is discourse on truth, or love, or freedom, or equality, or identity, or power, or God, possible? It is from this perspective that I read Heinrich Plett's essay on Elizabethan culture and politics.[6] Plett focuses on the court as a center of power seeking to bring discourse, comportment, and ceremonial into line with its political interest. Thus he regards Elizabethan courtly culture—its specific achievements in literature, painting, music, architecture, and ceremonial—as a product of the legitimation needs of the House of Tudor. Every state is obliged to address the sources and maintenance of its own order and disorder, perceived as internal and external supports and threats. For this reason, the imagery of the body and the body politic are nicely suited to the state's purposes, a line of argument that I explore in my book *Five Bodies*. By the same token, the elaboration of bodily imagery, ceremonials, and conduct falls to the work of poets, musicians, and playwrights, and to those who direct etiquette and manners. As Plett points out, the textual production of discourse and comportment suited to courtly needs constitutes a cultural metatext.

Here, a word of interpretation is perhaps required. I think we ought not to consider the texts in question as in any way descriptive of lost behavior. They are rather manuals for the production of such behavior—voice, comportment, vision, motive—and thus descriptive to the extent their prescriptions were honored. That is to say, these "institutes" represent probabilities of conduct honored and dishonored, and are part of the world they otherwise appear to describe from elsewhere. Indeed, it may be suggested that it is this inescapable circumstance that generates the split, observed by Plett, between the courtly arts obliged to serve an establishment of a limited polity and the Humanist address of an unlimited republic of letters. In other words, the political stimulus—not to mention the presumed patronage—given to the arts in any period may well generate the fantasy of an intellectual, artistic, and scientific utopia of free thought and speech, of natural and unconstrained comportment. Such utopias can easily be imagined as pre- and postpolitical constructs; nor is it difficult to allocate texts of this sort. Moreover, we can expect the pressure of politics on the arts and sciences to mark them in an internal way.

Thus we can treat certain self-censoring effects of literature—irony, allegory, and impersonation—as intelligible in the context of the problematics of the concealment and revelation of power. The figure of the courtier will personify these strategies and artifices, just as the topic of love or the fickleness of "my lady" will serve to displace the site of power and its arbitrary use, or the place of fortune in man's life will serve the same function. We can also see how the same political pressures will constrain poetry to those exercises of praise—encomia, genethliaca, epithalamia, or trionfi—that celebrate a lord, prince, or royal house. In general, the pressure of political reality will be aestheticized in the reverse conduct of *sprezzatura* and *grazia*, setting off the courtier's nonchalance, beauty, and elegance from the forces that threaten to destroy it—in the achievement of what Robert Herrick called a "wild civility." For this reason George Puttenham called allegory "the courtly figure":

> The use of this figure is so large, and his vertue of so great efficacie as it is supposed no man can pleasantly utter and persuade without it, but in effect is sure never or very seldome to thrive and prosper in the world, that cannot skilfully put in vse, in so much as not onely every common Courtier, but also the gravest Counsellour, yea and the most noble and wisest Prince of them all are many times enforced to vse it, by example (say they) in his mouth to say, *Qui nescit dissimular nescit regnare*.[7]

The courtly figure, of course, generates a whole army, so to speak, of expectable tropes: enigma, irony, dissemblance, hyperbole, and periphrasis. All of these can, in turn, be personified in social figures (roles) that populate the court. Edmund Spenser's *Faerie Queene* is in this respect a poetic initiation into the secrets and delights of courtly demeanor, as well as the avoidance of hypocrisy and baseness, which threaten to imbalance the court. In such a context, one can expect the paradox pointed to by Plett, namely, the repudiation of both art (*celare artem*) and nature (*celare naturam*), as in Sir Philip Sidney's sonnet cycle *Astrophel and Stella*. This occurs because, with respect to the problem of order and disorder, the court contributes to both sides. It will therefore at times see itself as an art that subdues nature, embracing Orpheus and Hercules as culture heroes, and at times as the source of artificiality and decadence that destroys nature, life, and truth, thereby undermining society and character. Such "splitting" occurs in any institution, as well as in any civilized character, since his or her life cannot be led outside of institutions and their dilemmas of thought, feeling, and expression. Franz Kafka's use of the court figure is surely outstanding for its sustained delimitation of this problematic, as Henry Sussman has shown with such brilliance.[8] Such considerations make it unwise to accept Richard Rorty's view that literature best solves our problems.

We can therefore identify institutional crisis—for example, in the social mobility of Elizabethan society—when the gap between *beau semblant* and *false semblant* widens—and is on everyone's lips. Short of this, the courtier will be obliged to cope, or "cape" with his situation, to change clothes, to mask himself, as Baldassare Castiglione advises, or to construct for himself an *arrière boutique*, such as Montaigne found in the *Essays*. Between Puttenham, Castiglione, and Montaigne there is, however, some difference in the construction of public and private selves. According to Plett, Castiglione and Puttenham address this issue—"vestirsi un altra persona"—in a manner that projects the courtier as an entirely social being, emptied of privacy. He is completely tuned to the decorum of communication, always capable of feigning what the situation dictates, and renders satisfaction through this very display. The principles of his conduct are codified in courtly rhetoric. The result is a stylization of speech and comportment that erases the boundary between reality and appearance, between society and personality, floating everything in the art of dissimulation and masque.

The subtexts of political masque are literature, art, theater, and music, which, so to speak, write themselves upon the body politic. At least this is so for the doctrine of the king's two bodies,[9] as well as for the queen's body and the satellite bodies at court.[10] Later, Oliver Cromwell and his Puritan bodies would call for a new aesthetic—the "plain style" of Protestantism and the spirit of capitalism—which seems also to embrace the dramaturgy of contemporary socialism, however much it may have promised to clothe itself in love's body. As Weimann observes, however, the imagery of Shakespearean theater should not be viewed in purely structuralist terms without a regard for the historical and social junctions in the political process for which it was both a constitutive as well as a descriptive resource.[11] Thus the imagery of the king's "two bodies"—a body natural and a body politic—was employed to carry an argument critical of Elizabeth's virginal disregard of the Stuart succession problem. This exercised her legal advisers, driving them to the construction of plays and masques, put on at the Inns of Court, to convey to the queen their concern that her marriage to the state might be more fruitful in her natural body. Thus the varying imagery of the plays put before Elizabeth portrays her as an impervious goddess, a jealous tyrant opposed to anyone's marriage, and as a helpless nymph pursued by would-be ravishers. Between classical myths and the imagery of the body politic, writers for the court's entertainment and the public theater explored Elizabeth's sovereign separation of her two bodies—especially when she was courting, and later with more resignation.[12]

If we view the functions of rhetoric as a result of the interaction between politics and language, there really can be no question of the disappearance of rhetoric unless our political life collapses. In other words, we have no collective life outside of language and no language outside of society. We are obliged to write and to speak as best we can, exercising a critical tolerance whose institutionalization represents our metascience. Thus rhetoric is far from being the enemy of science. It induces in us a responsibility for language in the twin practices of writing and reading, speaking and listening, which strengthen the republic of letters and thereby foster the body politic.[13] It is only due to the Enlightenment myth of the "two languages" of literature and science that we imagine an unrhetorical, that is, apolitical language of science. Curiously enough, this positivist postulate is more dependent upon a liberal polity (from Karl Popper's "Open Society" to Rorty's "contingent" society) for the preservation of an unvarnished language of scientific inquiry. Thus it is naive to argue that the vocabulary of politics, if suitably cleansed of rhetoric, might give to political society the peace it allegedly brings to the scientific community.[14] It is equally naïve to claim, as does Rorty, that literature is a better basis for liberal politics than philosophy.

Here we may turn Cesare Vasoli's account of Francesco Patrizi's *Della retorica*, with its proposal for a "scientific" discourse that would ground "l'art de bien raisonner."[15] The background of this demand on language is the collapse of the old patrician regimes and the rise of new principalities, including the Hapsburg domination. As well, the Counter-Reformation added to the new political constraints on speech. Under such pressures, Patrizi dreamed of a reversal in the relations between power and language, in which language recovers its sacred and original potency. Eulogy is criticized as an empty sack or bladder, the instrument of flattery and falsity. The lack of correspondence between language and reality is attributed to a divine punishment, our expulsion from a linguistic Eden. Henceforth we live in the "great ruin of human language." The political consequence of the poverty of language is that men and women live in fear and servitude, incapable of naming either the reality that oppresses them or the pristine reality that might liberate them from the "long and numerous chains of words, with which Justice and Peace are bound hand and foot, breast and neck." Thus, Patrizi sought to disentangle oratory and rhetoric from political servitude by finding in them a "universal discourse" that would permit us to treat morals and politics "scientifically." This, of course, required a correction to the whole tradition from Prodicus of Ceos and Georgias to Aristotle, which never sought to remedy the hopelessly metaphorical nature of fallen language. Thus words and ideas remain mere "derivations." Without a true grasp of the origin and essence of things, language serves those in power because they can impose their definition of things and have them accepted, through fear or else through the excitements of pleasure and wonder, but always at the expense of truth and justice. In Patrizi's view, rhetoric is an art appropriate to conditions of political immaturity, where the opinions of the people rule the people. Wherever the people are "free," oratory is their "master."

Patrizi's dream of a universal language, then, is the response to his fantasy of restoring patrician power, the rule of the "wise." Actually, Patrizi brings the same accusation against the Humanist attempt to revive rhetoric in the context of the modern principalities, arguing that it can only serve once again to silence or to enslave the people. Thus the only way around these mutual accusations of political naïveté was to move language onto a restored plane, to ground human speech in a "divine rhetoric" possessed of the same certainty as the "mathematical sciences"—*possente a dire* and *possente a sapere*. It is such a task, as Brian Vickers points out, that was assigned to the poet by Sidney in continuance of the long rhetorical tradition of elocution.[16] This, too, is how we should understand *The Faerie Queene*. It derives from the link between epideictic and ethics, in particular the apportionment of eulogy to virtue and blame to vice. Thus we have a rhetorical strategy as ideally suited to the production of the Renaissance heroic figure as it was to the classical republican hero, as we see from the *Cyropaedia*.

Vickers recounts the historical transmission of epideictic from Aristotle, Virgil, and Horace through Quintilian and Averroës's translation of Aristotle's *Poetics*. He also calls attention to the teaching practices of the schools and universities in keeping alive the thesis of disputation argued *in utramque partem*, the rhetorical combination of *laus* and *vituperatio*.[17] He rightly points to the critical strengths of that tradition, to its creative capacity for seeing both sides of the question, its orientation toward critical moral choices. He nevertheless finds a fundamental fault in the increasing interest during the Renaissance in the analysis of the will and appetites, the psycho-physiological springs of action, and in the mobilization to follow virtue. Here, of course, epideictic was an obvious aid. But it suffered an amputation. To win individuals over to virtue, it is a risk to acquaint them, however vituperatively, with the vices they thereby avoid. In addition, the fictional nature of poetry seemed also to contaminate its own virtue. Worse still, its vigorous separation of good and evil served to undermine the exercise of discriminating between them. The case for poetic justice deteriorates into moral propaganda.

Frank Whigham's approach to the relationship between politics and hermeneutics carries us further into these issues.[18] His phenomenology of courtly behavior is especially important in revealing the effects of power and social mobility on courtly language and behavior. Here the relations between language and the body politic require us to view courtly literature as simultaneously an address and a practical resource in the circumstances it described. The problem addressed in courtly literature, as Whigham summarizes it, was twofold: to preserve the manner of the aristocracy from debasement, while teaching those who acquired it to appear always to have possessed it. Unfortunately, the production of manuals for such purposes made them available to those who knew how to read, the Tudor "new men" whom the king kept in and around the court. Thus the court encouraged a literature of "self-fashioning" in a world where the exercise of power made man uncertain of themselves and their society.

Here we have a source of Renaissance anxiety as potent as any general crisis of skepticism or cosmic depression. In other words, we have a sociological rather than purely metaphysical concern with the distinction between reality and appearance, identity and mask—or, indeed of the "political unconscious." It would be most interesting if it could be shown that this social anxiety generated at the court was a driving force in the Renaissance discovery that human society is generally not under the eye of God and that cosmic order must be grounded in our own orders of discovery. Here we might have a stage-specific contribution to the Protestant anxiety that Max Weber found as a mobilizing spirit in the new order of capitalism. In either case, however, a mechanism would be at work to naturalize this historical achievement. It is an essentially stratifying practice pointed out by Whigham, namely, an emphasis upon style over substance. In other words, both the aristocracy and the bourgeoisie had to repress meritocratic strivings from below, even where this falsified their own histories. To do so, they had to argue that, however their substance might be acquired, their manner was natural to them, or else a matter of predestination, and quite beyond the history of acquisition.

Here, then, civil discourse is fundamentally distorted: when social classes speak to one another they speak only of themselves. The reason for this is that their discourse is stylized or coded to affirm separate and unequal identities.[19] In response to this situation, we can understand how later socialist discourse converges upon the fiction of an ideal speech community.[20] That this extrapolation does not overreach the present discussion can be seen from the Renaissance value placed upon conversation as a site (in the Enlightenment this site is moved to the salon) were identity cannot be concealed. To flee from conversation is to confess baseness, an inability to withstand the judgment of one's peers who accept such rivalry, rewarding it with goodwill or else with scorn and mockery. There is, of course, considerable pressure put upon conversation to degenerate under these circumstances through what Puttenham call *paradiastole*, flattery and related figures, which empty discourse, character, and situation of any trust. Thus the court or the "corridors of power," like the theater, become figures of deception and intrigue. In turn, as men learn to trust their fellows less and less, their language splits into the language of a private self withheld from public discourse. However, Renaissance men seem to have realized that, having abandoned a divine interlocutor, the self outside of court society and civilization risked a barbarism possibly worse than the dangers of society.

It is here that I think Montaigne is an especially relevant figure. His preoccupation with friendship and the conversation of books and equals must be seen in the light of the corruption of men and their language enforced by the tyrant. The latter is a creature of whim and arbitrary decision because he lacks the company of men who, knowing and speaking their own minds, can enable the tyrant or prince to rule himself. The tyrant's predicament is his loneliness, which in Montaigne's view renders him less than human. The worst polity is one in which such a man is dominant. In the essay "Of the Disadvantage of Greatness," Montaigne reflects upon the sickly position of the tyrant, deprived of genuine company and so deprived of the chance to mature emotionally and intellectually: "It is a pity to have so much power that everything gives way to you. Your fortune repels society and companionship too far from you; it plants you too far apart. That ease and slack facility of making everything bow beneath you is the enemy of every kind of pleasure. That is sliding, not walking; sleeping, not living. Imagine man accompanied by omnipotence: he is sunk; he must ask you for hindrance and resistance, as an alms; his being and his welfare are in indigence."[21]

Although Timothy Murray's investigations take the theater as the scene of a Renaissance preoccupation with the arts and morality of counterfeit, he shifts his focus to a critic's concern with issues surrounding textual integrity, ownership, authorship, and the like.[22] It is difficult to redirect this line of inquiry to the broader issue of the relation between political, social, and theatrical morality from which Murray departs. He notes that for contemporaries the difficulties playwrights had with the abuse of their texts was indicative of the general immorality of the theatre and was far from being either an author's or latter-day critic's concern. He also suggests that theatrical infidelity and plagiarism were part of the general crisis of language, a suspicion of texts running from Montaigne to Bacon, Hobbes, and Ben Jonson. But whereas Montaigne wrote the *Essays* and Bacon wrote, in a quite different spirit, *The Advancement of Learning*, Jonson was driven into the print shop to preserve the correspondence between thought and speech—although that possibility dates from much earlier.[23] Here we have three strategies designed to protect us from distraction and servitude. They hardly share the same conception of the relation between language and reality, however, particularly when we restrict ourselves to the level of moral, social, and political reality. Ben Jonson's flight from the theater to the printer's shop strikes one as an unhappy move. It reminds us of Glenn Gould's flight from the concert hall to the recording studio. In each case there is madness in search of a pure text, the quest for authorship without society, except as the latter consists solely of technicians of art, far from the "short-lived bodies" of pleasure and appreciation that may affect an artist, for everyone's good. Happily, Montaigne, who loved himself and his *Essays*, did not harbor either one in quite the same way.

MIMESIS AND *ANEIGNUNG*

Robert Weimann fears that from the standpoint of poststructuralist "antihumanism," Renaissance literary theory might have to be jettisoned, along with the rest of the machinery of mimesis, on the ground that it fails to capture the conflicting forces of desire in literary appropriation.[24] Thus in the work of René Girard, and perhaps Harold Bloom—but certainly in Freud, as we shall see in chapter 14– literary identity is achieved through violence and murder: mimesis is sacrificial, the celebration of a slaughtered tradition.[25] Weimann questions that approach on the ground that it threatens to lose the dialectical relation between the individual and collective appropriation of reality and textuality. Consequently, he argues for a prelegal and preideological concept of appropriation (*Aneignung*), that is, "making things one's own," which permits desire to enter history without submerging it in conflict and rivalry. This fundamental human activity of appropriation is, of course, articulated through a number of historically changing oppositions between society and nature and between the individual and society. But these contrastive structures are always collective appropriations achieved in religion, myth, art, and literature. It is a trope of modernity to schematize that history according to stages of social, political, economic, and psychological development, making individual appropriation their measure. Thus, the Renaissance, like capitalism, is interesting as what we might call a switching point in the modality of appropriation. Specifically, the question of individual appropriation disembeds from the quasi-natural processes of social reproduction. Life, thought, language, perception, power, and property become "alien" contrastive objects for a "self" that can discourse on their individual appropriation. Indeed, the very notion of "self" now falls into this scheme, as we see throughout Renaissance literature.

I would side with Weimann in his disagreement with Girard over the neglect of the subjective moment of discursive production (knowledge, power, and pleasure) in the Renaissance. This moment of individual appropriation (*jouissance?*) is downplayed in favor of the economy of textuality, the propriety of authorship as a juridical subject of property and exchange. The heterogeneity of Renaissance literature requires that we proceed very carefully in establishing the significance of the "author function" in Rabelais, Cervantes, Montaigne, or any of present authors. So many of them exploited mimesis precisely as an opportunity offered by the open manuscript tradition of self-invention, as Weimann nicely shows with regard to Rabelais's fabulous, proliferating text. Like Rabelais, Montaigne also wove the literary corpus into his own body, belly, and laugh.[26] The corporeal metaphors of literary appropriation are continued in the metaphors of procreation in Sidney and Cervantes, as Weimann notes. Authorial power and playfulness are signs that the author's function is not subordinated to the schema of received tradition and society, nor to Girard's unproductive desire, which does not confront its own historical appropriation.

By the same token, Weimann remarks that the reader's function, or reception process, is shifted: "Thus, behind the author's studied politeness, a new aesthetic of reception is positively proposed to his audience. The reader is summoned to appropriate the text individually and yet thereby project his own faculties universally, beyond all particularity of class and station. The dialectic is one of appropriation and objectification, and it allows, together with a new rhetoric, an astonishing flexibility in the relations of author and readers."[27]

Rabelais, Montaigne, and Cervantes were conscious of their need for readers to amplify the circuit of literary appropriation. The act of reading is solicited as coproductive of the text's individuality, as the prologues and prefaces testify. Here Cervantes and Montaigne appeal to the reader's freedom to distinguish fiction and history, nature and society, in tones that are remarkably ahead of Jean-Paul Sartre's later invocation of the reader's freedom as a constitutive feature of literary production.[28] In the present volume chapters on Montaigne and Roland Barthes continue this discussion, which should also be kept in mind with regard to my earlier discussion of the individual's plight in Stanley Fish's interpretative community.

Weimann's argument reminds one of Paul Ricoeur's analysis of the "mixed texture" of the trilogy of feelings—having, power, and worth (*avoir, pouvoir, valoir*)—which are at first nonlibidinal and preconflictual levels of meaning appropriation.[29] These three levels of feeling are constitutive of human praxis; that is, they mobilize the embodied subject's grasp of objectivity and intersubjectivity in the three domains of economics, politics, and culture. Thus human beings acquire their humanity through the feelings appropriate to power and its language of domination, ambition, intrigue, freedom, and equality. The figures of money, the tyrant, and the self are rhetorical expressions of the subject's institutional life, as is shown in some detail in several of the papers under discussion. In turn, the objective institutions of economy, politics, and culture can be invested with overdetermining cathexes from the libidinal stages of the history of desire.

It is inevitable, from the oedipal standpoint, that creativity and procreativity will overlap in the imaginary and symbolic orders. This means, however, that both the psychic and the external worlds are socially mediated. Rather than standing as opposites of one another, both are similar in that they transcend strictly individual experience because they are "structured like a language" (Lacan). Fantasies are, so to speak, social dramaturgies, scenes from a life in which we are actor and audience, caught in a mise-en-scène of desire under censure:

> It is only through a speech that lifted the prohibition that the subject has brought to bear on himself by his own words that he might obtain the absolution that would give him back his desire.
>
> But desire is simply the impossibility of such speech, which, in replying to the first can merely reduplicate its mark of prohibition by completing the split (*Spaltung*) which the subject undergoes by virtue of being a subject only in so far as he speaks.[30]

Thus it is important not to think of language splitting as a simple ego-splitting (*Ichspaltung*).[31] Rather, the recognition and disavowal (*Verleugnung*) in fantasy involves a rhetorical exchange with an audience figure, from whom recognition is required. Just as the patient requires the presence of the analyst, so the poet may invoke the Muse of an ideal reader able to sift out the quadrilateral framework of the fantasy—as who, as whom, as when, as why. Desire seeks recognition, therefore, not only in the infantile stage and familial context but throughout life and in various social contexts, including its therapeutic, literary, revolutionary, and ceremonial settings.[32] In other words, fantasies do not represent a retreat from reality: they invoke an alternative world populated with ideal listeners or readers who will recognize the dreamer and his dream,[33] and, of course, an ideal community in which all this is brought together. That is why we separate ourselves from Rorty's irony, Fish's professional, and Jean Lyotard's sublime—but not from Jameson's utopia, even though we may quarrel along the road.

DOUBLE INTERTEXTUALITY

I want to suggest, then, that there is, so to speak, a double intertextuality—one at the level of literary tradition and influence, in Bloom's sense, and another between the *autotext* and *sociotext*, which raises the text of desire into the text of exchange—religion, politics, and economy—floating the figures of the city, the risen body, marriage, the courtier, the proletarian, and the body politic, as I have developed it in chapter 4. It is this double intertextuality that is explored in rhetoric, hermeneutics, allegory, mimesis, commentary, and ideology criticism. As Northrop Frye shows, this double intertextuality arises because of the civilizational *switch* between desire and society:

> Civilization is not merely an imitation of nature, but the process of making a total human form out of nature, and it is impelled by the force . . . we have . . . called desire. The desire for food and shelter is not content with roots and caves: it produces the human forms of nature that we call farming and architecture. . . . Desire in this sense is the social aspect of . . . emotion, an impulse toward expression which would have remained amorphous if the poem had not liberated it by providing the form of its expression. The form of desire, similarly, is liberated and made apparent by civilization. The efficient cause of civilization is work, and poetry in its social aspect has the function of expressing, as a verbal hypothesis, a vision of the goal of work and the forms of desire.[34]

Thus we need to consider the Renaissance pursuit of identity, or self-fashioning,[35] in relation to such other institutional powers of shaping, identity, and control as the family, state, and church. Sociologically, we can expect those forces to vary between the medieval, Renaissance, and capitalist periods, perhaps shifting in relative dominance but always exerting their particular force. The figures of Christ, the court, and the tutor will variously represent their specific modes of shaping identity, distributing internal and external forces of social control. In short, literature, religion, art and courtly ceremonial, manners and etiquette, all are articulations of the problem of order— its embodiment, so to speak.[36]

From this perspective we can view literature or ceremonial as a trilevel artifact, analyzable into *autotext*, when considered as an item of individual behavior; *sociotext*, when considered as institutional response; *ideotext*, when considered as a self-interpreting response to the issue of connecting autotext and sociotext. Every text, from this point of view, contains all three levels; hence we reject behaviorism and ideologism as two extremes of antireflexivity. Moreover, because we think that, for good sociological reasons, the levels of autotext and sociotext are as inseparable as are the levels of sociotext and ideotext, we are able to reject any simple economism or sociologism of literary and ceremonial conduct. In short, the trilevel text is a tissue of internal relations embedded in a social history that cannot be reduced either to a Freudian family romance or a Marxist class struggle, though these may be relevant figures of interpretation for certain levels of the text,[37] as I argue throughout the present work.

We need to know in detail the institutional locus of power, separation, identity, truth, and counterfeit that figurate a given text. Thus power and authority may be regarded as legitimate or illegitimate sources of control, fashioning social, moral, political, and literary identities that are natural or unnatural; or else they may be construed in pre- and posthistorical utopias of social and individual harmony. In turn, the divisions of power and morality, society and the individual will be internalized as rhetorical figures of language, enriching and impoverishing its reflexivity.

Literature and the arts of ceremonial are rather refractions of the world they display and not simple representations. We must consider their representative force in the activity through which they generate reflection and response to the problematic of power and control, freedom and identity. In this sense, all the arts from literature to manners are, in Giambattista Vico's terms, "severe poems," that is, instruments and resources of "anthropomorphosis" and not merely its embellishment. By the same token, they function on two further levels, as instruments of "sociomorphosis" and of "ideomorphosis." We might say, for example, that Shakespeare's theater is the theater of Elizabethan power operating on all those levels cf individual, collective, and ideological conduct, projecting itself as a cosmos on the world's stage and in the minds of its audience. Its artistic achievement lies in its powers of revelation, exposure, concealment, and celebration of that living theater beyond theater. The same will be true of the theater of literary criticism, and it is for this reason that it engages us.

PART THREE Symptomatic Texts

CHAPTER 12

**The Essayist (Montaigne)
Is Not a *Malade Imaginaire***

It was a melancholy humor, and consequently a humor very hostile to
my natural disposition, produced by the gloom of the solitude into which
I had cast myself some years ago, that first put into my head this day dream
of meddling with writing. And then, finding myself entirely destitute and
void of any other matter, I presented myself to myself for argument and
subject. It is the only book in the world of its kind, a book with a wild
and eccentric plan. And so there is nothing in this job worth noticing but
its bizarreness; for a subject so vain and mean could not have been
fashioned by the best workman in the world into something worthy of
practice.

—Michel de Montaigne[1]

Here, and in the remaining essays, I propose to deal with symptomatic
texts and some exercises in symptomatic criticism. I have espoused
the concept of the literary body as what practices literature. Rather
than defend the institution of criticism as the rock bottom of literature
and even, as Stanley Fish argues, "the very structure of our consciousness," I consider the interpretive community as the locus of a mixed
ratio of *imitatio* and *inventio* through which writers and readers embody themselves in a kind of autobiography, whose origins I explore
in chapter 15 on infant transcription. I begin with Montaigne because
he is the first essayist of the symptomatic text, whose proper sense I
defend against what might be called "sickly criticism." I then move
to Descartes in order to show that the *Meditations* suppress their own
scene of embodied writing and of public discourse in order to enact
the posture of a solitary *cogito* shut off from the world it nevertheless
seeks to reconstruct. A similar posture is struck by Freud, our arch-
symptomatologist, while working up the invention of psychoanalysis.
Here I explore Freud's paranoid framework for the inscription of a
priority claim against the interpretative community of science and
the arts. Finally, I return to Roland Barthes for an exemplary re-
statement of homotextuality, or the self's acquisition of a literary
body, and a declaration of our unfinished joy in reading and writing,

expanded in a primal reading of Giambattista Vico through Freud to James Joyce.

It is as much a literary prejudice as a vulgar one that writing is an idle pastime, the diversion of solitary persons, if not of sickly and misanthropic minds. Pierre Barrière, Michel Butor, Alfred Glauser, and Anthony Wilden[2] have all argued that in writing the *Essays* Montaigne constructed an idol of his friendship for Etienne de La Boétie in order thereby to compensate for his own sickly and irresolute nature. I shall argue, on the contrary, that it is impossible to grasp Montaigne's pleasure in reading and writing unless we consider the *Essays* as a carnal inquiry in which the essayist's sensual and spiritual animation is heightened by Montaigne's very effort of essaying the *Essays*. The limitless quest of the *Essays* is their yield of literary pleasure—and not all a sickly and imaginary solitude. Montaigne's *Essays* are embarked on life. At the same time, they hug the shores of society and custom. Undistracted by metaphysical speculations, they push on steadily in a bodily odyssey, seeking to bring home good sense and sound judgment, avoiding the sirens of fantasy and despair: "I study myself more than any other subject. That is my metaphysics, that is my physics" (3:13, 821).

Montaigne's consubstantiality with the *Essays* in no manner precedes his own writing and reading of them. We therefore cannot grasp Montaigne's *Essays* apart from the constant cross-fertilization between his reading and writing habits.[3] Thus, Montaigne's writing and reading are acts of carnal inquiry, often moody, lazy, and dependent, but also witty, strong, humorous, and gay. Montaigne reads with his body, and he is therefore a religious writer in the only sense that is proper to him or to the word, namely, as a loving effort to keep body and soul together in family life. He wished to preserve in the *Essays* his living tie to this world and the family whom he loved but knew he must one day surely leave. The *Essays* are for this reason plainly the work of a family philosopher. That is why Montaigne is never tempted by the excesses of philosophy and theology. He no more set himself above himself than above his children, or servants or his wife. He kept an open house. He never forgot his own father's generosity in moulding him and he adopted it as the measure of any of his own instructions. Just as families are not kind to moral heroes, Montaigne hunted out any tendency in himself toward the extremes of pride and humility. But this means he had to try to mold himself within the limits of ordinary sense and reasonable folly.

With this in mind, we may see how easily the consubstantiality thesis becomes excessive in regard to the *Essays*. This is the case, I think, with Glauser's brilliant reversal of the metaphor whereby Montaigne claimed to be nothing but a creature of his own literary activity. According to this view, Montaigne lacked any substance before he began to pour himself in the *Essays*. The essayist is then the paradoxical embodiment of what began as sheer fantasy. The *Essays* continued to clothe him so appealingly that Montaigne could never recover his protested nudity and originality. Having borrowed everything for fear of lacking substance, Montaigne became a creature of a literary style whose visceral metaphors gave him the illusion of embodiment. Apart from the light and warmth of the *Essays*, Montaigne was nothing but a cold creature wracked with sickly dreams and uncontrollable fantasies, haunting his tower, sucking life from his books, more like a vampire than a honeybee.

Having begun this way, it is easy enough for Glauser to feed everything into the consubstantiality thesis. Thus, books 1 and 2 are stuffed with a life of action, politics, and war with which Montaigne was otherwise unconnected, being too indecisive, self-indulgent, and generally weak-natured ever to have found himself engaged in real life:

> A writer asserts himself in relation to his life as a man. There is a very clear separation between the mayor and the essayist and the dialogues between them creates a distance that generates the essays. Montaigne would rather deform his own life than the one taking shape in the *Essays*. He acquires worldly graces only through his work. His indifference toward the cares of society is transformed into a strange passion for his own company. These contrasts are the devices of a writer. When he pretends to want to resemble the craftsmen and laborers whom he imagines more happy than university rectors, he forgets, for the moment, that those whom he envies do not write the *Essays*, and for that reason are hardly worth envy.[4]

Relentlessly, Glauser argues that Montaigne never ceased to run away from the void in himself. Travel, writing, and dreaming are the whole of his life, and only in the *Essays* can he invent for himself any substance or any attachment to life and society. Even in old age

Montaigne persisted in recreating the youth, good looks, health, and love he had never possessed. He is, in short, the most vain, the most empty, and the most deformed of all men, dragging out his days as a literary Casanova. The *Essays* are nothing but the mirror of Montaigne's self-spectacle; once the mirror is removed nothing remains. Worse still, having dissolved himself in the mirror's illusion, Montaigne had no qualms at drowning his friend La Boétie in the same pool of narcissism. All this was not achieved, however, without a burden of guilt. Thus Montaigne reached the heights of literary sublimation by romanticizing not only people at home, but also distant denizens of a precivilized state before the very invention of letters—letters that then may discover the innocence of barbarism as the measure of the guilt in literary culture.[5]

Finally, Glauser rests his argument on the claim that the *Essays* are truly a literary illness, alternating between misery and gaiety to suit the fictions of Montaigne's mind, unbridled by anything in the world. Indeed, had Montaigne not poured himself onto the paper, and had he not mummified himself between the pages of the *Essays*, he would have left no single thing of substance. With no real ability for communication or friendship, Montaigne made himself consubstantial with the *Essays*, in which he forged himself upon the world as an unforgettable immoralist:

> Having set out with the honest intentions of a man who also wished to be as true as possible, the work became, despite him, the distorting image of a sincerity that saw itself further and further compromised by the creation of the *Essays*. Sincerity—*sine cera*—turned into something else, became therefore impossible, in the wax of the *Essays*. The honey all his own, of which he speaks, is nothing without the beehive capable of preserving it.[6]

It is hardly necessary to add Barrière's arguments to those of Glauser, who treats the *Essays* in terms of the progressive temptations of retirement, suicide, and diversion, a series of bodily maladies that have writing as their natural by-product. According to this view, the *Essays* are nothing but the prison of a sickly, inactive self overwhelmed with loss and old age. Within the limits of this argument, we do better to consider Wilden's additional arguments on the organizing absence at the center of the *Essays*, since here, too, we have a strong insistence on a historical malaise to account for Montaigne's attachment to the *Essays*. According to Wilden, the image of La Boétie's friendship represents a metasexualization of the plenitude of desire and loss, which generates the *Essays* as a communicative relationship between Montaigne and the *Essays* as well as between Montaigne and his reader. Thus Montaigne's self-formation (*Bildung*) is dependent upon its necessary externalization (*Entäusserung*) in the *Essays*, on the one hand, and the communicative alienation of the self-other relationship in friendship, on the other. The difference is that in the *Essays*, more than in friendship, Montaigne could experiment with the possibility of nonrecognition by the reader as the other of his self-essay. At the same time, Montaigne could gather the certainty of his presence to himself and to posterity through the *Essays*, which made him as much as he made them.

As Wilden would have it, Montaigne succeeded only in making property of himself in the *Essays*, thereby reifying the communicative relationship between plenitude and loss, or between self and friendship. He concludes with the argument that Montaigne could continue as an essayist only by disavowing the search for a plenitude that nevertheless remained the driving force of the *Essays*. According to Wilden, then, the *Essays* are the expression of a double absence—the lack of a transcendent self in their author and the loss of a mirroring self in the friendship of La Boétie:

> What remains of Montaigne's dialectic with La Boétie and with the masters of antiquity is nevertheless our royal road to the essence of Montaigne. In talking to his Self, he is attempting to bridge the gap between conscious demand and unconscious desire, between the symbolic world of discourse and the imaginary world of *jouissance*, between a question which is an answer and an answer which is a question. Only because this is an open-ended dialectic is it possible to *read* Montaigne and thus to escape the myth of the "real" Montaigne.[7]

In my view, the vanity of the *Essays* is not simply a device for embarking upon a quickly self-conscious enterprise, as might appear from Montaigne's preface "To the Reader." Rather, essaying mobilizes a pervasive doubt that struggles to become a literary resource rather than a philosopher's topic. The *Essays* are at once Montaigne's recourse from time and themselves the creature of time, as we know from the cumulative editions of the text. But the growth of the *Essays* is not due to Montaigne's lack of method or of art, nor to a patchwork attempt to appear more methodical and artful than he had earlier thought possible. True thought is not more ahead of itself than life is outside itself. Therefore thought is like our living, and finds its way from day to day, and not without us. For this reason we cannot subject our reading of the *Essays* to any principled interpretation, and far less to any radical subjectivism of imagination and illness. The *Essays* are a daily resolve, like the body's needs, or like love and friendship, which we cannot serve merely in principle but must attend to here and now, according to their seasons. The *Essays* are Montaigne's body, his constant companion, the double of his life. The *Essays* are therefore not articulated according to any regulative philosophical or artistic principles, though they establish an unrepentant claim upon literary authority or moral truth.

If Montaigne concentrated upon himself, it is with a steady attachment to his friend La Boétie, to his family, to his city, and to the voices from the past with whom he conversed in his library. He considered himself a small note in the collective and largely anonymous history of mankind, of which literature and art yield us only a fractured sounding. What is mature in Montaigne is not his scepticism or his relativism, it is rather his ability to hold life's attachments at a distance in order to consider how it is we are nevertheless beholden to everything and everyone around us. Montaigne is not an idle subjectivist, sunk in fantasy or carried away by endless imaginary projects. He knew himself to be among the most variable of spirits, most changeable in his moods, irresolute and without method in the discharge of his affairs. For all this, the *Essays* are not a series of vile confessions, even though they insist on self-observation and inquiry. Rather, they "rebound" from everything that oppresses the mind and the body, whether through the negation of positivity or an affirmation in place of negativity, ruled, of course, by Montaigne's experience with things and himself.

The *Essays* do not play with dialectics; they are rooted in the carnal ambiguity of our relation to ourself, to our reason, sense, body, and language. In each case, we must avoid the pursuit of absolute distinctions, of complete certainty and clarity, since these belie our own mixed composition. In exchange for forgoing any transcendental flight or excess, there opens up to the essayist a mundane presence of the literary self to the embodied self, to which the essayist must faithfully apprentice himself. It is through writing that Montaigne came to build up something like a model of himself in order to ground the otherwise wholly metaphorical enterprise of the self-portrait: "Thus, reader, I am myself the matter of my book; you would be unreasonable to spend your leisure on so frivolous and vain a subject." (from "To the Reader").

Nothing is contradicted by Montaigne's denial (*Verleugnung*) of the necessity of the *Essays*. Montaigne's pleasure in writing, which he translates into the scene of an exotic country where "in the sweet freedom of nature's first laws, I assure you I should very gladly have portrayed myself here entire and wholly naked," is forthright. At the same time, his literary pleasure is compromised in the recognition of the writer's concession to prevailing standards of public decency. The preface, then, announces a potential split in the *Essays* between the writer's desire and the reader's own curiosity unless in the pleasure of reading they both ally themselves in the incarnate union of book and self. At the same time, the *Essays* are Montaigne's happy credo— into which he could pour himself while simultaneously standing at a Sunday distance from them. They accumulate from a working pleasure in reading and writing and from the joy of finding a reader capable of exercising his own literary competence with the *Essays* as a continuous bodily inscription. Such pleasure lies outside any literary organization. Hence Montaigne's topics and titles in the *Essays* serve only as strategies of pleasure, taking a page from a book or a poem in order to go on writing a book or a poem in order to go on reading a book or a poem.[8] And so the *Essays* find readers who find readers like friends seeking one another, by word of mouth.

Everything of Montaigne has been subject to that same reinscription begun by himself in the text of the Bordeaux copy of the *Essays*. Just as Montaigne was never content with the printed page, continuously altering a word, a punctuation mark, inserting lines, paragraphs, and pages, so, too, everything around him was subject to the same reinscription. Thus, in his own day Christianity was being rewritten by Luther and Calvin, altering its ancient text with novel readings that shook Montaigne's faith, as it shook his beloved France. The princes served by Montaigne had need of him, though not ultimately, because of the changes they were engaged in by rewriting principalities into the constitution of an absolute monarchy. Time, too, has covered the family home in Bordeaux with the graphics of local commerce, just as history has left of the seigneurial domain only a tower and few bare rooms, whose significance survives only through those who love them enough to continue that original reinscription that was Montaigne's passion for writing.

For this reason it is as impossible for us to recapture Montaigne as it was for himself. What we see in the text of the *Essays*, that is, in the marginal additions—are they additions, and to what are they additions?—is Montaigne's own abandonment to the joy of writing. Imagine the sheer strength of the hand that so carefully illuminated the margins of the *Essays*, repeating a holy tradition of writing found now in the stream of human consciousness.[9] It is only weaker minds, because less joyful, that insist on reinscribing the text of the *Essays* into the orderly schemas that are suited to our secular faith in science's assembly of clear thought. Such exercises achieve nothing but the worst democratization of Montaigne's thought—neither popular nor singular. They make of Montaigne a mind without any distinction but its faults; they humble him in favor of minor professionals and the feeble breed of their students. They produce interpretations without heart and merely add to books the books that make it impossible for anyone to understand the love of books. This is, of course, a jealous claim. It requires care because it risks intruding on the friendship of Montaigne, making love's enemies where perhaps he might not have chosen.

In keeping to ordinary things, the *Essays* stay closer to life than to the ceremony of literature and madness. That is to say, they treat of things from within their ordinary concerns and without first mounting any elaborate schema to serve philosophy, theology, or literature. This means that Montaigne was able to avoid the extremes of either subjectivizing his literary task or else pushing it toward anonymity. He was able to display his writing and reading as a course of work, capable to a point, subject to revision without radical alteration, and always achieving its purpose as far as it goes. The *Essays* feed upon themselves in the sense that they improvise the skills of reading and writing required for composing their material at hand. But they never pretend to absolute literary autonomy. Montaigne wished to be seen and heard as a craftsman, not as the medium of art for art's sake. Here, as elsewhere, we encounter the problem of literary authority.

The artist's temptation—what leads him on and what may lead him astray, or into sheer imitation—is the museum, the tradition of writing or painting or thinking that precedes him, which seduces him and makes him want to continue its past. To survive, the artist must concentrate on his own work, the essay or the canvas. Only this matters, and yet it must also provide for the movement from work to work, essay to essay, which is the artist's life. Montaigne was never far away from his books, from his philosophers, historians, and poets. He moved among them like a bee among the flowers, alighting here and there, a buzzing, busy presence borrowing what he needed in order to remake himself in the *Essays*. Thus he combined work and pleasure, leaving for his readers the same bodily and spiritual recreation, provided they are capable.

When he speaks of his nonchalance, and even of his ignorance, Montaigne speaks of that necessary creative ignorance without which the thinker, writer or, artist could not get underway. This, of course, is not a complete ignorance, since the work of art, once it is underway, must connect with its own conventions and seek a public for its intelligibility or its visibility. Montaigne therefore worked at the *Essays* indirectly, and only gradually, with here and there a quick sally, centering on its own vocation. He requires his reader like a friend to undertake the same break with the conventions he needs to relativize in order to experience himself in recreation. To achieve this, Montaigne employed paradox and a style that awakens the reader's instincts, or his bodily ties to language and community, whereby the author and reader discover their mutual incarnation in the pleasure of literature. Montaigne frequently shifts from the impersonal to the personal voice, from the past to the present, from *obiter dicta* to the testimony of his own eyes, ears, and body, and by means of these shifts he heightens the literary company between himself and his reader.

By requiring of him his own literary competence, the *Essays* exercise the reader, and do not simply subordinate him before an exaltation of literary language. Montaigne's style is therefore essential to the liberty of discourse and friendship which excludes tyranny. It required, too, the solitude represented by his library tower. There he fostered the silence that permits writers to choose their words. By contrast, the tyrant—at times played by the literary critic—monopolizes talk, fearing the liberty of discussion, or else he subordinates the arts to his pleasure, denying them any more serious revelation. Hence, also, his insistence on the publication of his private thoughts, since thoughts without hope of a public cannot be free. For the same reason, the *Essays* take their time, walk when they want to, and run when they like, always free to turn to any side that attracts their author, yet never losing themselves for want of their own direction.

Nevertheless, Montaigne does seem to deprecate his enterprise as an essayist and to be at particular pains to forewarn his reader against attaching any significance to what he reads in the *Essays*. Montaigne speaks of the difficulty he experienced in giving shape to his thoughts. He complained of their fleeting nature and of their vagueness. Thoughts come upon him suddenly and do not stay; they lie upon him like an ill humor. It is he who is in the grip of ideas, laboring at them to give them some sort of shape and definition.

Montaigne was no Cartesian. For him ideas are not the clear and distinct constructs of a disembodied mind proceeding in accordance with logical or mathematical rules. There is an embodied state of ideas to which any thoughtful man is beholden, as we shall see in the following chapter on Descartes. To begin with, our ideas are no clearer than any mood or passion of ours. Indeed, even our passions are not given to us without devotion. Thus jealousy, or envy, or voluptuousness, require all our strength and imagination, and may even demand that we develop great cunning if not intelligence on their behalf. By the same token, we cannot devote our minds to serious thought without passion and labor. Montaigne was beholden to thought's embodied way. It is not because his was a prescientific mind that he found thought difficult. Nor was he hesitant because he was not a trained philosopher or theologian. Above all, it is not because he was weak in character, easily distracted, and secretly given to failure in order to preserve face as a gentleman of leisure.

Montaigne found thinking difficult because he rejected the easy assembly of philosophy and theology careless of humanity's embodied state, and because he could not ignore that the practice of science in his day only made itself foolish in its pronounced omnipotence. The thinking self is not outside thought's embodied practices, and the same is true of the reading self or of the self in pursuit of writing. Montaigne's *Essays* are the consequent exploration of the exchanges between sources, texts, language, and the self that inhabits them in order to explore its own dimensions. For this reason, we must locate Montaigne's bodily troubles in writing and reading as natural effects of the romance of books. Whereas other critics have seen faults in Montaigne's methods of reading and composition, with the purpose of displaying their own higher morality in these matters, we argue that it is precisely in the way that the essayist works that he gradually establishes himself as the most serious of all writers, the one most concerned with the bodily regimen of literature and its lively uses.

It is in the light of this problematic that we must approach Montaigne's defensiveness with regard to his choice of the essay form. For after all, he did not choose to write history or poetry. Montaigne wrote essays; he did not write poor history or bad poetry. He wrote in his own fashion, rather than forgo writing because he held any previous model or genre of the art in too high esteem. Moreover, Montaigne wrote conscious of his own incapacities, quirks, mannerisms, and modes of thought and speech. Therefore writing was as essential to him as it was to Petrarch or to Rabelais—it was a daily undertaking that he could no more go without than any other bodily function. He lived the *Essays*, and waited upon them like the very days of his life for the trail of meaning that life acquires only over its course, and in no other way than at its own expense:

> Who does not see that I have taken a road along which I shall go, without stopping and without effort, as long as there is ink and paper in the world? I cannot keep a record of my life by my actions; fortune places them too low. I keep it by my thoughts. Thus I knew a gentleman who gave knowledge of his life only by the workings of his belly; you would see on display at his home a row of chamber pots, seven or eight days' worth. That was his study, his conversation; all other talk stank in his nostrils.
> Here you have, a little more decently, some excrements of an aged mind, now hard, now loose, and always undigested. And where shall I make an end of describing the continual agitation and changes of my thoughts, whatever subject they light on, since Didymus filled six thousand books with the sole subject of grammar? (3: 9, 721)

Having discovered the impossibility of any definitive revelation, the artist and essayist have nevertheless to avoid the traps of narcissism and relativism, of willful contradiction and ultimate self-defeat. Thus, we see in the self-portraits of Rembrandt, as in the *Essays* of

Montaigne, the gradual dominance of the author's look, mocking, suspicious, candid, proud, humble, and caught in the farce. With all the strength of natural inquisitiveness and self-scrutiny these portraits throw back the pain of living, of aging and dying. In both cases, there is a progressive deepening of the expressive potentials of the baroque, away from theatrical dispersion, toward the inner concentration of the soul's body. In the portraits of 1648, *Rembrandt Drawing Himself by the Window*,[10] we have, as in Montaigne's comments on his own activity as a writer, a subversion of the myth of representation by means of a reflection endlessly reflected upon, unless gathered religiously in each of us. We are face to face with the mystery of creative work, with its virtuosity of affecting us long after its author has left his hand upon it.

So Montaigne opened up his life to the *Essays*, writing them into his flesh and bones, sinking them into every corner of his life. He thereby found a language that is visceral and vital, spreading out on the page, tensed and calm, poised and effervescent. At their very best the *Essays* seize life itself, balancing it in a moment of leisure where the activity of reading and writing vibrates in harmony with all of life and nature. Thus, the essayist confronts the waiting page like any other clearing in which he enters himself as a question, searching for the opportunity to develop his own bodily capacities of movement and sensation. The writer's fingers move over the page, into the words, cutting a furrow whose fruit lies ahead, blossoming into the sentence and the paragraph, from page to page. Writing is a dance, a transformation of the body, lifting and moving ahead of itself, yet tired, tiring, and forever trying to hide its necessary pauses.

Writing is music, chasing its own rhythms, shaping the body's strength into word after word, upon which there supervenes the sounding sense of a line coming into and after being. Therefore writing, like the dance, or like music, requires a regime, a bodily art of concentration and dispersal; a continuous poise and ever-ready rhythm. Writing is a bodily assumption of the virtual sense of the waiting page, and a necessary fall into meaning. The page, then, is at the essayist's fingertips and really not a space in any coordinate sense, or a material on which he writes; it is an unfolding of time's body and the necessity of thought's speech waiting upon the same assumption in the reader's sensible, sounding body. Thus, in writing and reading we fulfill the body's capacity for subtility, lifting its weight, displacing it into the ubiquity of thought. At the same time, the page produces the paradox of thought's diaspora to the very extent that it concentrates a writer or reader on himself, bent upon the page and rapt in the pleasures and pains of writing and reading.

In the *Essays* we see that the art of writing does not raise the writer above his body into some spiritual realm half traced on the page. The writer's fingers and the page are a working ensemble, an alternation of intelligible space and spatialized intelligence that permits Montaigne to speak of the consubstantiality between himself and his book. We rightly speak of the body of literature. And that is the sense of Montaigne's consubstantiality with the *Essays*, namely, a lively bond from which he drew the strength to write his life, whether in sickness or in health—but never succumbing to a literary illness. As such, Montaigne became the model for Barthes's literary body explored earlier in chapter 5 and later in chapter 16 where we examine Barthes's homotexuality. These two modes of the literary self stand in sharp contrast with the Cartesian model of inquiry to which we now turn.

CHAPTER 13

Mecum Meditari
Descartes Demolishing Doubt,
Building a Prayer

I am thinking of the Cartesian *cogito*; I want to finish this work; and I can
feel the coolness of the paper under my hand and I can see the trees of
the boulevard through the window. My life is constantly thrown headlong
into transcendent things; it passes wholly outside of me. The *cogito* is
either this thought which took shape three centuries ago in the mind of
Descartes, or the meaning of the texts he has left to us, or else it is an
external truth which breathes through them; in any case, it is a cultural
being to which my own thought reaches out but does not quite embrace,
just as my body, in a familiar surrounding, finds its orientation and makes
its way among objects without needing to have them expressly in mind.
—Maurice Merleau-Ponty[1]

It now happens that my own thoughts are turned toward the *cogito*
through a chain of events and present circumstances that continue
the cultural life of the *cogito* enriched for me by the gentle and
persistent reflections of Merleau-Ponty, to whom I owe much of my
philosophical and literary culture.[2] At this very moment, I too write
on a cool page across which the winter sunlight falls; the trees outside
my window stand dark against the blue sky, and my neighbors'
houses seem to nudge closer against the cold. This moment of peace
was not there at the start of this work; it has arisen only now, as the
shape of what I may have accomplished needs defiant assertion to
make itself a beginning. But I must set aside the naughty genius of
fiction, of plans and of logic. I have worked on this essay without a
study, away from home, with few books, at other times with many.
My thoughts have not always been my own, were rarely clear, and,
like myself, have had to settle for their present circumstance and
predicaments. I have made several journeys and rebuilt my home in
the past year, whose time in my life I cannot tell. Rather than separate
me from my task, as at times it seemed, these travels have drawn me
to myself; and whereas the task of rebuilding a home might have
made this work impossible, it rather revealed to me, as to Descartes,
those anxieties that arise with things to be torn down, and it has
shown me those hopes from whose roots things may grow up. And

just as the peasants I have seen set a tree upon the scaffolding of a new house, for the sake of its life, I set this essay above my present cares for the sake of the prayer I find in the *Meditations*.

Although Chaim Perelman generally treats Descartes as a protagonist of the view that all rhetorical practices must be stripped away from the language of science, he has also a better sense for the inescapable rhetoric of Cartesian discourse itself. Thus he notices Descartes's imagery of the "chain of ideas," or of "walking slowly and carefully," "fearful of falling."[3] I propose to show how extensive these concerns are in shaping the aims and resolution of the *Meditations*. To the extent I am capable of this exposition, I believe the way is open to further studies of philosophical discourse as a proper object of rhetorical argument.[4] Thus it is important to pay careful attention to how Descartes conceives the site of philosophical work.[5]

What motivates him to want to demolish and to rebuild the world around him? Surely, it is madness to reject the accumulated experience of the senses and of the great articulations of our language in which we think and perceive things, events, and relationships largely as do our fellow beings. Who cannot see that the great edifice and landscape of our senses and common experience is a work that exceeds each one of us; that is has been painstakingly built up by countless generations who have added to it without a single plan, who have made repairs here and there without any thought of tearing everything down to start anew? Who else would entertain the general destruction of our beliefs and opinions in the ordinary business of our lives and institutions, of which they are the common currency, unless he thought himself in possession of some great design for mankind? Such a person, if not mad, would need to be a god, or a philosopher, or else an engineer and architect, if not all of these at once. Above all, to begin such a work of demolition, he would need to be sure that the voice that inspired him was not that of the Devil tempting him with the powers of creation. And yet, if this voice comes rather from God, how can Descartes be sure of the proportion between the divine mind and his own?

"I am quite alone." Descartes persuades himself that in withdrawing from the world, he has nevertheless a secure place in the world from which to undertake "this general overview of my opinions." Descartes, then, means to conduct an assault on himself, to attack the common man in himself with the agile arguments of the philosopher he has become through espousing doubt. Even so, he senses that he has neither the time nor the strength for doubting every one of his beliefs. In other words, it would be unreasonable for an embodied thinker to embark upon a philosophical life that would exceed the limits of ordinary living, which in fact prescribes the uses of certainty and doubt within the framework of "corporeal nature in general." So far from being an object in the world of which his senses might be mistaken, or merely an image of itself as in a painting, Descartes acknowledges that his body is rather a mode of perceptual knowledge, reflexively aware of its waking and sleeping states, and as such, the constitutive ground of our being in the world:

> But, although the senses sometimes deceive us, concerning things which are barely perceptible or at a great distance, there are perhaps many other things one cannot reasonably doubt, although we know them through the medium of the senses, for example, that I am here, sitting by the fire, wearing a dressing gown, with this paper in my hands, and other things of this nature. And how could I deny that these hands and this body belong to me, unless perhaps I were to assimilate myself to those insane persons, persons whose minds are so troubled and clouded by the black vapours of the bile that they constantly assert that they are kings, when they are very poor; that they are wearing gold and purple, when they are quite naked; or who imagine that they are pitchers or that they have a body of glass. But these are madmen, and I would not be less extravagant if I were to follow their example.[6]

Indeed, to say we exist, or that there is a world, or that we have a body, is to say very much the same thing. Moreover, to say any of these things is ordinarily strange because they articulate the same perceptual faith in much the same way as each of our senses articulates the same body and its world. Questions about the infallibility of our senses, like questions about the purity of our morals, ought never to be abstracted from the ordinary contexts of our living under pain of separating us from our fellow humans—and, worst of all, from ourselves. Whoever seeks absolute certainty, or absolute trust, risks either having to withdraw from the world or being viewed as insane. The grammar of reasonableness in matters of perception and trust is fractured by the lunatic. Wholesale infringements of any local grammar and its institutional practices—rather than minor offenses readily confessed and repaired—will put any of us beyond the pale.

Such exclusion is a sanctioned practice of everyday life and is incurred by children, loved ones, students, workers, and officials as ordinary members of society.[7] To invoke and to respond to such sanctions, and not to be ignorant or indifferent to them, is the ordinary mark of one's moral worth, if not of one's rational status. Thus to claim that no one knows anything or sees or hears anything for certain, or that we are asleep when we think we are awake, or hate when we think we love, or that everything might be other than what we ordinarily take it to be, is to exceed even madness—for the lunatic lacks all such distinctions.

Descartes does not consider himself mad. Yet he entertains the project of ridding himself of all beliefs, opinions, judgments, and experiences that are his only in virtue of his commonsense knowledge of things and persons. He means to withdraw from public life and discourse in order to reconstruct the foundations of his knowledge and language. Aware of the huge scope of his project, Descartes tells us that he had to wait until he had achieved a sufficient maturity and leisure in order to begin the general destruction of his previous opinions and to lay fresh foundations, so as to establish something firm and constant in the sciences. Such an ambitious project of demolition might just as well founder upon the corrosive anxiety it engenders rather than lead to a new edifice of confidence and certainty. Indeed, as we shall see later, Descartes could torture himself over his sinful pride in separating himself from the common faith and practices of his fellow men. And in replying to the objections raised against his methodical doubt, he appears more moderate than either the *Discourse* or the *Meditations* give the impression.

Thus he concedes that most of his knowledge has come to him through his senses, or through the senses of others whom he trusted, and especially through language as a thesaurus of things and relationships which are the articulation of our surrounding world. In such a world we may, of course, be mistaken, deceived and misinformed. These experiences, however, do not entirely invalidate our senses. Nor do they cause us to replace trust with wholesale mistrust in our relations to others. Above all, we have no recourse from language, generally speaking. We cannot get rid of words as though they were useless rubble entirely unsuited to the foundations of knowledge and intercourse. Commonsense practice insists rather upon making distinctions. Instead of tearing down the edifice of our senses and society, or withdrawing from the world of discourse, we learn to distinguish occasional errors, deceptions, and misinformation from universal error, deceit, and ignorance. In short, commonsense language, knowledge, and values are that great edifice of our lives which we take them to be precisely because they cannot be toppled over by any single error, or deception, or ignorance.

Such objections were well known to Descartes. We shall argue that they weighed upon him, making him fearful of wandering from the common path and anxious that his work might fall in ruins rather than stand firm in our memory. Not only his critics but he himself could ridicule his solitary pretentions. Thus, anyone who forsakes all fellowship because of a single disappointment must be considered childish—if not infantile, since every child has to learn to accommodate to the lapses of those in whom it trusts. And anyone who abandons reading because he has found one book to correct another must rather be considered foolish than wise, since he who claims to read must in fact be able to evaluate the competing claims in what he reads through what he reads. And so it is with all our senses— their competence with the objects of sight, sound, touch, and taste is never entirely at stake in any single operation. Rather, their corrigibility is proper to their exercise and, so to speak, intrinsic to their practical reflexivity.

Much of the commentary on the *cogito*, apart from that of Jaakko Hintikka,[8] misses the fact that Descartes does not argue from the *cogito* to the *sum*. Had he done so, then the commentary on his arguments for making the copula of thought and existence would be unavoidable. Whatever the challenge offered to philosophers by the Cartesian doubt, none of them any less than Descartes himself hesitates to urge that their own practices of argument, doubt, and validation can render the intelligibility of Descartes's copulation of thought and existence clear to their fellow philosophers. However this is done—and the approaches are quite varied[9]—what needs to be noticed is that commentators on the *Meditations* treat them as the occasion for a return to analysis without anxiety, that is, as a pretext for showing how any challenge to the certainty that we live knowledgeably cannot exceed the rhetorical practice of philosophy without religion. I think, however, that we can set such commentary aside in favor of trying to understand the *Meditations* in terms of their proper discourse type, that is, as a psychological essay[10] in which Descartes weighs up what it is from his conscious experience he can assert as public knowledge or science.

In order to carry out such an exploration he needs to imagine himself doubly set apart from the flow of his experience: (a) in the isolation of his study; and (b) in reflective isolation from his senses, perception, and judgment. Thus, Descartes imagines that it might be possible to reconstruct his experience and to rearticulate it without relying on commonsense discourse, thereby laying the foundations of certain knowledge, which others might similarly enjoy, supposing they were to submit themselves to the rigors of philosophical meditation rather than to easy imitation. It is essential to the *Meditations* that the rhetorical effects of social isolation determine the philosophical effect of sensory and perceptual withdrawal by a freely inquiring mind. At the same time, the rhetoric of social withdrawal is transgressed through the philosophers' language, which continues to articulate the public discourse on the difference between waking and dream states, between certainty and uncertainty, between sight and blindness. In this way, the philosopher abrogates to his imagined private experience the authority of public knowledge, as well as its pragmatics of proof and refutation, which he conscripts through the reader's collusion.

It is (only) a rhetorical effect of the philosopher's doubt that appears to separate him from the world of fellow beings and discourse. However much Descartes continues to objectify things in a cognitive space projected from his desk, the philosopher never leaves the greater world within which his meditations make use of his body, the page, the room, the fireside and the desk whose existence presupposes the work of others greater in number and talents than the reader or writer of the *Meditations*. Thus what we witness in the *Meditations* is rather a theater of doubt[11] in which Descartes's struggles with the evil genius (*un certain mauvais génie*) is resolved by calling in a deus ex machina, that is, a God who could not possibly allow the philosophical seduction of Descartes by his fantasy of universal doubt. However much Descartes pretends to remove all the props from the stage, he cannot remove the personal/public I, eye (*je vois*) *je*, or *jeu* (play) in the *cogito*, which always leaves the reader on stage.

Even when Descartes appears to have withdrawn body and soul, he remains with the audience all the while as the masked narrator—*larvatus prodeo*[12]—leading the reader on toward the divine goal of the *Meditations*—*larvatus pro deo?*

The *cogito*, as Merleau-Ponty observes, is in effect a textual cogito, that is, a verbal effect that absorbs to itself the universality of an anonymous discourse in which language holds us while effacing itself, just as our body veils the tacit *cogito* through which we are already worldly creatures before any thematization of subject and object relations:

> the true formula of this *cogito* should be: "One thinks, therefore one is." The wonderful thing about language is that it promotes its own oblivion: my eyes follow the lines on the paper, and from the moment I am caught up in their meaning, I lose sight of them. The paper, the letters on it, my eyes and body are there only as the minimum setting of some invisible operator. Expression fades out before what is expressed, and this is why its mediating role may pass unnoticed, and why Descartes *nowhere* mentions it. *Descartes, and a fortiori has reader, begin their meditation in what is already a universe of discourse.*[13]

The *Meditations* are surrendered to the ineluctable nature of language, to the play within the play written at the philosopher's table by a thinking body whose fantasy of its nonexistence merely reveals the limits of its "inexistence" distributed as (rhetorical) effects of writing and reading, nowhere else. Thus the *Meditations* cannot reconstruct egological experience elsewhere than within the pragmatics of intersubjective discourse. Language has no outside nature, no origins, but only a structure and history of reciprocity in which you and I amplify each other's discourse and intelligence, enlarging our general culture:

> I should be unable even to read Descartes' book, were I not, before any speech can begin, in contact with my own life and thought, and if the spoken *cogito* did not encounter within me a tacit *cogito*. This silent *cogito* was the one Descartes sought when writing his *Meditations*. He gave life and direction to all those expressive operations which, by definition, always miss their target since, between Descartes' existence and the knowledge of it which he acquires, they interpose the full thickness of cultural acquisition.[14]

What this means is that it is only the *cogito* as a *performance*, and not as a *perception*, that unites thought and being. It is only by means of my exploration of things, persons, and language that I acquire an inner perception of self; and certainty is built upon these first uncertain relations to our world:

> Certainty derives from the doubt itself as an act, and not from these thoughts, just as the certainty of the thing and of the world precedes any thetic knowledge of their properties. . . . The *cogito* is the recognition of this fundamental fact. In the proposition: "I think, I am", the two assertions are to be equated with each other, otherwise there would be no *cogito*. Nevertheless we must be clear about the meaning of this equivalence: it is not the "I am" which is pre-eminently contained in the "I think", not my existence which is brought down to the consciousness which I have of it, but conversely the "I think", which is reintegrated into the transcending process of the "I am", and consciousness into existence.[15]

Despite the rhetorical persuasions of the *Meditations*, the very problematic of the *cogito* is never wholly Cartesian. Rather, the *cogito* presupposes a long history of previous philosophical discourse, sustained by others, which will be taken up in future from time to time, as it has in the past which bequeathed to us its question. Viewed in this way, the *cogito* does not found philosophical discourse, and could not possibly do so, except through a retrospective fiction of the historians of philosophy, whose practice of periodization are themselves only a further convention within the philosophical community. There is, of course, a "Cartesian" *cogito*. But it is available only as a particular inflection of the philosopher's question which, has its peculiar style because it starts from an obsessive anxiety of grounds that marks Cartesian discourse. Now it may well be that Descartes's anxiety is amplified by his intention to expropriate public discourse in a self-sufficient proclamation of the authorial subject whose voice reechoes the Creator's word/world.

Here we cannot decide on the larger frame of the *Mediations*. All the same, we should not overlook their articulation with Descartes's other works, *The World, Dioptrics, Geometry*, and the *Discourse on Method*, which in turn raise further questions about the motives of their hidden author.[16] Perhaps Descartes's anxiety is doubly bound to the expropriation of the *vox populi* and of the vox dei. In other words, Descartes's anxiety of method may not be so much the effect of the doubt in the *cogito* as the undertaking of an equation between the voices of God and of Science proclaimed in the name of Descartes—which thereby becomes fearfully unwritten. This, I believe, is the larger framework for which all Descartes's writings are pretexts. It is against this horizon that we may explore the lesser anxieties and their resolution in the *Meditations*.

Descartes, as we have seen, approaches the *cogito* without trust in the commonsense world of perception and belief. He is troubled by "false opinions," "insecure principles," "things which are not entirely certain and indubitable," "things which seem manifestly false." He is tempted to conclude that because "I have sometimes found that these senses played me false . . . it is prudent never to trust entirely those who have once deceived us." Yet, rather than leave things under the shadow of universal doubt and suspicion, Descartes resolves "to begin afresh from the foundations," "to establish something firm and constant in the sciences." His strategy is then not to exhaust his energies in a critical review of everyone of his opinions, but more like an engineer to demolish the edifice of his beliefs by attacking it at a point whose fall brings down everything else with it: "Because the destruction of the foundations necessarily brings down with it the rest of the edifice, I shall make an assault first on the principles on which all my former opinions were based."[17]

Where did Descartes's anxiety over certainty begin? Was it from childhood disappointments with elders whom he trusted absolutely and whose ordinary fallibility and weakness could not sustain the infantile wish for parental omnipotence?[18] Are, then, Descartes's military and engineering metaphors the sublimated aggression in a long-standing plan to overthrow the parental edifice at its weakest point and to plant just there something as firm and unshakable as the thinking phallus—the thought-self of the *cogito/sum*? We cannot overlook Descartes's rhetorical expansion of doubt and uncertainty in himself and in others as a particular style of the *cogito*.[19] Thus, we may contrast the private practice of the *Meditations* with Socrates' public practice of his ignorance in the marketplace, where he found the occasions for those dialogues, which could just as well be enjoyed in a drinking bout like the *Symposium*. Fellowship is essential to the Socratic turn away from nature as a place of truth, justice, and beauty and is not breached even at Socrates' trial.

But Descartes declares no such faith in common practice. He considers his fellow men to be like shifting sand and their company to be avoided in favor of his own thoughts, just as an engineer lays the footings of his buildings according to his own design, rejecting everything he was not inspected for himself. Alternatively, in the *Discourse on Method* Descartes pictures himself as a single-minded traveler, sticking to the main road and not wandering off, turning in circles and going nowhere—which is the way of his fellow men whose opinions always lead them astray. But whether as architect or traveller, Descartes always goes *alone*, following a path "so remote from the normal way that I thought it would not be helpful to give a full account of it in a book written in French and designed to be read by all and sundry, in case weaker intellects might believe that they ought to set out on the same path."[20]

Descartes's solitary vocation, whether as architect or as traveler, merely serves to heighten his anxieties about the security of his foundations and his steps along the right road to certainty. Having questioned the common practice of building roads and houses, everything sinks into the shifting sands of opinion, and the Cartesian *cogito* becomes the butt of the Jesuit Pierre (rock) Bourdin's parody on its fear of sliding foundations. The *Discourse on Method* and the *Meditations* reveal a profound nausea, an obsession with mud, sand, ruins, falling, straying, and blindness, against which their author pleads for solidity, security, and certainty. It is (no) accident that in one of his dreams on the night of 10 November 1619 Descartes sees himself struggling to walk, holding himself to one side (the left) because he fears falling into a precipice (on the right).[21] Dragging himself along (under the burden of sin, or shame at the weakness of his limbs or his ambitions) he heads for the safety of the college chapel beckoning to him on the road. But a wind whirls him around on one foot, and when he tries to turn back to greet a man he has passed on the road, it hurls him against the chapel. The chapel image reminds us, in turn, of Descartes's mock rebuttal of Bourdin in which the master builder rebukes the mason who presumed to criticize him for pretending to demolish everything and not make use of a single stone at hand when constructing the foundations of his building:

> Now the very church alone which the Architect has already built proves that all this is the silliest nonsense. For it is quite clear that in it the foundations have been most firmly laid, and that the Architect has destroyed nothing which was not worthy of destruction; and that he has

never departed from the precepts of others unless he had some better plan; that the building soars to a great height without threatening to fall; finally that he has constructed not out of nothing, but out of the most durable material, not nothing but a stable and well-built church to the glory of God. But all this together with other matters in which my critic has suffered from delusions, can be seen clearly enough from the Meditations alone which I published. . . . And certainly all such similes are equally out of place when talking of the Method of inquiring into truth.[22]

Between dream and parody, we discover Descartes's desire for the one true foundations of all belief, the church built upon that rock— Peter/Petrus/Pierre—that was to outlast the sands of time. Thus the *Discourse* and the *Meditations* lay out the road to the site where the foundations can be laid for the philosopher's chapel, in which one of the world's lasting meditations on the one true God is performed *per omnia saecula saeculorum*. Here, with all his senses, passions, loves, hates, errors, and opinions, closed in upon himself, like a little chapel closed in upon itself from the outside world, closed to the sky and its stars, closed to the sights and sounds of the earth, Descartes meditates on the impossibility of thinking and feeling nothingness as the god term of creation. *Ex nihilo nihil*. And since he himself has no idea of himself as either the formal or eminent cause of the world around him, Descartes rests his finitude in the infinite being of God. Thus Descartes, the anxious architect, the anxious traveler, and perhaps the anxious child, discovers in his God that certain paternity with which the craftsman imprints every object of his own making.

And, in truth, it is not to be thought strange that God, in creating me, should have put in me this idea to serve, as it were, as the mark that the workman imprints on his work; nor is it necessary that his mark should be something different from the work itself. But, from the mere fact that God created me, it is highly credible that he in some way produced me in his own image and likeness, in which the idea of God is contained, by means of the same faculty by which I apprehend myself; that is to say, when I reflect upon myself, not only do I know that I am an imperfect, incomplete and dependent being, and one who tends and aspires unceasingly towards something better and greater than I am, but I also know, at the same time, that he upon whom I depend possesses in himself all the great attributes to which I aspire, and the ideas of which I find in me, not merely indefinitely and potentially, but actually and infinitely, and that he is thus God.[23]

The *Meditations*, then, are nothing else than the road Descartes had to take that would lead to the place where doubt is cut across by faith. Anyone who makes the same pilgrimage, who begins by leaving his everyday surroundings, courting the terrors of the road, will find himself beckoned by a wayside chapel where, if he contemplates his own nature, he will find the certain mark of God upon him—*imago dei*. The *Meditations*, as everyone recognizes, are not ruled by any order of logic. What motivates them is Descartes's life-long quest for a reliable truth, which after all his travels and studies led him back to the chapel of his youth. There, in a profound meditation on the source of his being, Descartes discovered—*pura et attenta mentis inspectio*—in the purity and virginity of his intellect, that he was conceived by God, whose inseparable creature he remained, despite all uncertainty, doubt, and error of his own making. Therefore, we do not read the *Meditations* because they contain a method for their reading—such readings generally disappoint those philosophers who continue nevertheless to insist on such practice. We begin to read the *Meditations* when we are able to face the uncertainty of the boundaries between philosophy and religion. Once this step is taken, we can only comment on the *Meditations* with the same humility that is to be found in them—but without any hope of redeeming ourselves in such greater prayer as rises—*ad majorem dei gloriam*—from them.

Here, then, in my study, at work on the *Meditations*, I am no more alone than were Descartes or Montaigne or Merleau-Ponty. The same shining world surrounds me as it did them once before, while the silence of my study murmurs with their voice in the turning pages of my reading, and their time runs into mine through this hand writing:

> I shall now close my eyes, stop up my ears, turn away all my senses, even efface from my thought all images of corporeal things, or at least, because this can hardly be done, I shall consider them as being vain and false; and thus communing only with myself, and examining my inner self, I shall try to make myself, little by little, better known and more familiar to myself.[24]

> Claudam nunc oculos, aures obturabo, avocabo omnes sensus, imagines etiam rerum corporalium omnes vel ex cogitatione mea delebo, vel certe, quia hoc fieri vix potest, illas ut inanas et falsas nihili pendam, meque solum alloquendo et penitius inspiciendo, meipsum paulatim mihi magis notum et familiarem reddere conabor.[25]

CHAPTER 14

Science and the Founding Self

Freud's Paternity Suit in the Case of the Wolf Man

Psychoanalysis is my creation . . . even today no one can know better than I do what psychoanalysis is.

—Sigmund Freud[1]

The inseparability of truth and paradox is currently accepted as the best way to ventilate the institutionalized truth of philosophy, literature, politics, and psychoanalysis. Beyond the eye of God, we lack any observer standpoint not implicated in its own look. Blindness and insight overlap in the reflexive spot of bad faith that now rules not only our everyday lives but also our artistic and scientific lives. Ethics and criticism are now largely in the business of teaching us how to live with paradox rather than to seek formalistic exclusions of moral and logical contradictions. Psychoanalysis, especially, offers itself as an instrument of paradoxy inasmuch as the analyst triangulates every dyad in which each partner is failed by his or her observations of the other, who returns the question of desire.

By the same token, that is, by the same *symbolon* of desire, the analyst's impartial standpoint is tragically caught in those revisions of the unconscious play worked by transference and countertransference, of which the "Dora" case is the most lasting testimony.[2] Here, however, I propose to show how Freud institutionalized his own vision of the observational data in which psychoanalytic theory is grounded as the bedrock of its arguments and as the "rock"—recall the analysis of this claim in Descartes—upon which the movement of psychoanalysis is founded. Since these arguments determine much of the tragedy of ex-communication in Freud's relations with his colleagues, we shall re-present their rhetorical articulations in the case of the Wolf Man—itself a candidate for the primal scene of psychoanalysis.[3]

The modern self appears to be the subject in and of a double fiction in which it is able to split so as to appear to disappear while invoking its creative resistance to any firm stand. Such strategies, however, remain tied to the text and artifacts that continue to nurture the fictions of self-weaning. The question of the maternity or of the paternity of our fictions shapes their beginning and may rule their establishment. But the cycle of these things requires that the artist generate himself or herself as his or her own father/mother fiction, turning, turning, time again. Thus the text has no single voice not because it has no voice of its own, or has only the voice of law and convention, but because its voice is familied and intergenerational. It thereby inhabits a community of art and science whose figure is Oedipus, provided we understand Oedipus as a figure of intergenerational blindness and insight and not as a single moment of self-discovery.

Freud's discourse is self-consciously a founding discourse. It is concerned from the very beginning with its own authority. Yet Freud is never free from dependency upon his own father figures (Josef Breuer), his doubles (Wilhelm Fliess) and his own mythopoesis (Moses, Napoleon). Psychoanalysis oscillates between a master discourse and lover's discourse as Freud pursues the paternity and the plentitude of thought and language, which his own theory of the unconscious shows to be unattainable.[4] What Freud never brought down from Mount Sinai was the tablets of observation uncontaminated by theory. Psychoanalytic evidence is not the product of "observation alone." Instead, it always involves the work of "interpretation" subject to the paradox of self-observation:

> Every science is based on observations and experiences arrived at through the medium of our psychical apparatus. But since *our* science has as its subject that apparatus itself, the analogy ends here. We make our observations through the medium of the same perceptual apparatus, precisely with the help of the breaks in the sequence of "psychical events": we fill in what is omitted by making plausible inferences and translating it into conscious material. In this way we construct, as it were, a sequence of conscious events complementary to the unconscious psychical processes. *The relative certainty of our psychical science* is based on the binding force of these inferences. *Anyone who enters deeply into our work will find that our technique holds its ground against any criticism.*[5]

With such considerations in mind, I propose to show how Freud conducts his own paternity suit on behalf of his discovery of the science of psychoanalysis. For reasons of economy, I restrict myself by and large to the case of the Wolf Man, which Freud considered the bedrock of his science. We are interested in tracing how Freud's discursive practices frame a scientific priority claim within a family history that is constructed in terms of a double science-fiction, that is, the reconstruction of the primal scene and its forebear in the primal horde. It does not degrade Freud's claim to speak of it in terms of the notion of science fiction. Properly speaking, this term captures the uncanny truth of both science and literature at the place where the creative self struggles with the paradigm discourse or model figure against which it seeks to appropriate its own claim to invention. The case history of the Wolf Man is inseparable from the history of the psychoanalytic movement and is solidly interwoven with Freud's account of the movement's history, where in turn the findings of the case history are made central doctrine. There we encounter Freud's "insistence upon the letter" (of the Law)—to paraphrase Lacan ever so slightly. Freud's claims for the truth of the central dogmas of psychoanalysis, despite his invocation of scientific dialogue, in fact produced a sacralization of the Freudian text, together with an excom-municative voice that has ruled over the quarrelsome family of psy-choanalysts ever since the movement was founded.

Here, of course, we must try to interpret the insistence of the letter not in terms of Freud's notable repetition compulsion but rather in view of the text's inability to resist our rereading of it as a legal fiction in which Freud's insistence upon scientific priority "in the case that is now before us" requires him to act the personae of judge, jury, and victim in what I shall call the Trial Scene.[6] At this point, I must remind the reader of Stanley Fish's analysis of Freud's rhetorical procedure in the case of the Wolf Man. Although Fish does not follow Freud's detailed quasi-legal argument, he nicely sets aside Peter Brooks's defense of the radically modernist indeterminacy of the case history[7] by demonstrating that its masterful closure is established before the case even opens:

> One is tempted to say that the story Freud tells is doubled by the story of the telling or that his performance mirrors or enacts the content of the analysis; but, in fact, it is the other way around: the content of the analysis mirrors or enacts the drama of the performance, a drama that is already playing itself out long before it has anything outside itself to be "about," and playing itself out in the very terms that are here revealed supposedly for the first time, the terms of the preservation and concealing of masculine

self-esteem and aggression. It is a commonplace of psychoanalysis that surface concerns are screens for concerns that are primarily sexual; what I am saying is that in the case of the Wolf-Man (where the commonplace was established historically) the concerns of infantile sexuality are screens for the surface concerns that Freud acknowledges but then apparently sets aside. What Freud presents as mere preliminary material—his prospective discussion of evidence, conviction, and independence—is finally the material that is being worked through, even when the focus was ostensibly shifted elsewhere, to the patient and his infantile prehistory. The real story of the case is the story of persuasion, and we will be able to read it only when we tear our eyes away from the supposedly deeper story of the boy who had a dream.[8]

In Freud's view, the pursuit of science constitutes the highest form of the sublimated self. In practice, Freud's scientific self is highly paternal and supremely political in the management of rival theories in the psychoanalytic movement. The case of the Wolf Man will be examined to show how the Freudian self is constituted in the primal scene of psychoanalysis and its psychopolitics. In this respect, it is interesting to observe that Freud prefaces the section of the history of the psychoanalytic movement that brings his case against Alfred Adler and Carl Jung with a quotation from Goethe: "Mach es Kurz! / Am Jüngsten Tag ist's ein Furz! [Cut it short! / On the Day of Judgment it is no more than a fart!]."

As Ernest Jones points out in a note (SE, 14:42), this is God the Father's reply to Satan's complaints about Napoleon. Jones notices the irony that Freud may as well be replying to himself as to his critics. By the same token, Freud may be identified with either God the Father or Napoleon. Although Jones notices that Jüngsten (last) would not be capitalized in German, he muses that the error might derive from the pun on Jung's name and that Freud's history proclaims a Last Judgment.

In fact, Freud reserves the Last Judgment for himself. Whereas he had at first wished that Jung would secure his immortality as a youthful incorporation of the old man, his rejection by Jung led him to a fantasy of being murdered and incorporated by Jung (a displacement of both Freud's own aggression and his homosexual feelings). Since Freud's death did not materialize, he pictures himself being rediscovered and immortalized by some later reader. It requires "little creative power," as he might have said, to see how Freud worked these experiences into the structure of *Totem and Taboo* (1914), where the murder and incorporation of the father by his sons binds them forever in a community of (un)creative repetition.[9] In the same vein, the father's monopoly over the women forbidden to the sons is represented as Freud's theoretical defense of "lady" psychoanalysis[10] against violation by the jealous sons, even though he had contemplated slipping into this lady's past to allow Jung to enjoy her future. But on no account would he let Adler near the "goddess libido," whom he had offended and for which she must be avenged by Freud.[11]

The issue of the inability to conclude, of which Freud complains in the case of the Wolf Man, is nicely caught in Lacan's remarks on the relation between recollection and reconstruction.[12] The case of the Wolf Man exhibits all the power and pleasure of paternal deferral in reaching this bedrock of psychoanalysis. It is the textual model of anal eroticism. The patient's verbalization of his history opens up a Pandora's box. In its legal sense, *verbaliser* means "to write a traffic ticket." *Pandore* is a slang term for "policeman." *Verbaliser* also means "to talk too long," as we are prone to do in order to justify ourselves— or to retain the coherence of our self-deception.

At issue in the primal scene is the deferred action (*Nachträglichkeit*), which requires repeated restructuring of the events as exemplified in the case history's own narrative. This is Freud's testament (numbers refer to page and paragraph of the text cited; my emphasis throughout):

(281.1) Freud compares the difference between himself and the critics of psychoanalysis with the difference between "the whale and the polar bear," unable to "wage war" because they cannot meet on any common ground. The critics refuse to recognize the postulates of psychoanalysis and consider that its results are "artefacts." The situation is aggravated more recently by the formation of another kind of "opposition" that claims "in their own opinion at all events" to accept the techniques and results of psychoanalysis but consider they are "justified" in drawing different conclusions from its materials.

(281.2) *"As a rule . . . theoretical controversy is unfruitful."* Thus the latter group, departing from the basic materials of psychoanalysis, risk becoming "intoxicated" with their "own" assertions.

Freud therefore decides, rather than engage in theoretical controversy, to "combat dissentient interpretations" (Adler and Jung) by "testing" them on the case history of the Wolf Man.

(281.3) The case makes the following admittedly "improbable" claims:
(a) That a child at age one and a half is capable of perceiving and remembering the events of the primal scene
(b) That it is possible at the age of four for a deferred revision of this material to penetrate the understanding
(c) That any procedures could succeed in bringing into consciousness coherently and convincingly the details of the primal scene as experienced and understood in the above circumstances.

So far, then, we see Freud representing challenges to his own view through a series of images ranging from military combat to political opposition until raised by himself to the level of a scientific contest.[13] Furthermore, Freud represents this progression in civilized agony as a movement from animal indifference to the properly human recognition of differences under the rule of law. To do so requires that Freud subject himself to the fair representation of the opposition view and to a balanced account of the issues at stake. The result is a further discursive construct within the case history, which attempts to model itself on a scientific dialogue with elements of cross-examination:

(282.1) Freud replies that *"anyone* who will take the trouble of pursuing analysis into these depths by means of the prescribed techniques *will convince himself"* of the claim in (c) above, and that any analyst stopping short of the depth approach "has *waived his right* of forming a judgement on the matter."
(282.2) With regard to the claims in (a) and (b) above, Freud insists that any doubts about them derive from "a *low estimate of the importance* of early infantile impressions," which "would involve the disappearance of much that has formed part *of the most intimate characteristics of analysis,* though also, no doubt, of much that raises resistance to it and alienates the confidence of *the outside"*

Here Freud's terms for the discussion of the significance of infantile experiences place any potential critic in a limbo land between (a) anyone's ability to convince himself of the validity of depth analysis, and (b) rejection of the most intimate teaching of psychoanalysis and thus loss of membership in the movement: becoming an outsider.

There follows a number of admonishments regarding the implications for the therapeutic practice of psychoanalysis arising from the differential evaluation of infantile materials and their effect upon later life experience (282.4–284.1) Freud then raises what he considers will be the most damaging self-criticism at the heart of the whole matter, namely, the "constructed" nature of the primal scene:

> (284.2) "[t]hese scenes from infancy are not reproduced during the treatment as recollections, *they are the products of construction.*" Many people will certainly think that this single admission elicits the whole dispute.

Freud proceeds to remark upon his compulsion to direct his own case—in effect reproducing the symptomatology of the text we are now trying to document.—

> (284.3) "I am anxious not to be misunderstood."

It is possible, then, that Freud's insistence on the "infantile factor" merely introduces fantasies or dreams of his own, quite apart from the argument that he has reworked the patient's memories to impose the suggestion of the primal scene on impressionable patients. And if, as readers, we are worried about our own suggestibility in the face of Freud's rhetorical persuasion, we must carefully attend to the following response and its internal repetitions:

> (286.2) "*Let it be clearly understood* . . . on the part of those who take the view opposed to mine . . . that they are phantasies not of the patient but of the analyst himself. . . . An analyst, indeed, who hears this reproach, *will comfort himself* by recalling *how gradually* the construction of this phantasy which he is supposed to have originated came about . . . *how* independently of the physician's incentive . . . *everything seemed to converge upon it, and how later* remarkable results radiated out from it . . . *how not only* the larger problems . . . but the smallest peculiarities in the history. . . . *And he will disclaim* . . . the amount of ingenuity necessary for the concoction."

Here, Freud pictures himself as one enslaved by the hard work of science, itself a figure of patient determination by independently evolving facts of the case. Carried away by his own rhetoric, Freud disavows any ingenious construction on his part, despite his admission that the primal scene is not a fact of recollection but one "divined—constructed—gradually and laboriously from an aggregate of indications" (285.1). He concludes with the complaint that between himself and "an adversary who has not experienced the analysis himself" there will be no possibility of a decision between the charge of subtle self-deception directed at Freud and his own counter-charge of obtuseness of judgment (286.2).

So far Freud has conducted the case for and against the centrality of the construct of the primal scene as though it were a matter of defending the scientific status of psychoanalysis before an actual audience of critics or before an internalized figure of science with whom any practicing scientist will find himself in dialogue. Such a figure represents the conscience of the scientist and requires of him that he split his own self into a triad of scientific personae charged with presenting, refuting, and judging the merits of an argument reached either by theoretical deduction or by experimental induction. Freud was sufficiently aware of the role of theoretical constructs in the mediation of theory and experimental practice not to simply award the prize on the basis of a narrow-minded positivism. By the same token, he very well understood that theoretical invention must prove its efficacy by enabling us to reenvisage a field of hitherto uncolligated facts.

Having said this, it is time now to populate Freud's argument with the persons of Jung and Adler, since it is their "antagonistic views" (287.2) that Freud is specifically concerned to combat. We should notice, however, that it is the father of psychoanalysis himself who identifies the aggression of his sons and who interprets any difference of opinion as a succession struggle that justifies him in excommunicating, if not symbolically murdering, the sons. Certainly, Freud reserves to himself the potency of a founding theorist, charging Adler and Jung with prematurity and infantile narcissism. Their feeble speculative hypotheses about regression and egoism as central to psychic behavior reduce the practice of psychoanalysis to an easy therapeutic technique, while their personal revolt permits the wider society to reject everything that is truly revolutionary and inconvenient in the advance of psychoanalysis (287.2). Freud then disposes of Jung with a clever pun on his name, which is followed up with the priority claim whose rhetorical construction I have been documenting up to this point:

(287.3– "It is worth remarking that *none of the factors* which are addressed
288.1) by the opposing view in order to explain these scenes from
infancy *had to wait for recognition until Jung brought them forward
as novelties.*"

The joke is that, so far from needing Jung (Youth) to make the case
for the infantile factor, psychoanalysis in fact requires the "old man"
not only to see such "novelties" before the young man—

(281.1) "[A]ll of this (employed, moreover, in the same context, though
perhaps with a slightly different terminology) had *for years*
formed an integral part of *my own theory*"—

but to see even better that the infantile factor is operative through a
movement back and forth (*nachträglich*) whose construction requires
all the strength of the founding theorist of psychoanalysis. Any other
interpretation of the materials of the primal scene depends on ex-
tracting details as a clue to the whole story—*pars pro toto*—thereby
reducing the proper temporality of the narrative that is constructed
through the primal scene as an event that interprets its own pre- and
posthistorical significance in the infant neurosis. Freud's rivals are,
so to speak, primitive synecdochalists. Their rebellious immaturity
derives from their analytic incapacity to sustain the deferral to which
the origins and etiology of a neurosis are subject.[14]

As further proof of this, Freud renews his defense with a further
"supplement and rectification" of materials held back—literally in
square brackets (291.3–295)—that contains his irritation with Jung's
"twisted reinterpretations" of the primal scene. Thus Freud proposes
one more reading of the primal scene in terms of Jung's theory of
regressive symbols:

(292.2) "Allowing the assumption that the child observed a copulation,
and was convinced of the reality of castration, and that from his
later preference for *coitus a tergo, more ferarum,* this must have
been the parental position—it may still be argued that the child
transferred a later observation of animal copulation in place of
the parental act, by way of inference."

(292.2) "*Colour is lent to this view* by such facts that the wolves in the
dream were actually sheep-dogs, as drawn by Wolf Man; that the
number three refers to the times he saw the dogs copulating; that
on a summer afternoon the child did see his parents in bed but
in an "innocent" scene—but, that he wished to see their "love-

making" and so he transferred the animal copulation to the bedroom scene."

(293.1) *"It is at once obvious how greatly the demands on our credulity are reduced.* Jung's theory would remove the disagreeable scene of parental copulation; the child's memory would only have to go back to the fourth year. . . . *Young though he was,* the transposition of his impressions at four years to an imaginary trauma at eighteen months was possible . . . provided he was in bed in his parent's bedroom.

Here Freud puns on Jung's name, after "coloring" the young man's story of an even younger man's story designed to resist the old man's theory that the young man in question was even younger, that is, eighteen months old at the time of the primal scene—and not, of course, simply in the parental bedroom but in a privileged observer position due to the *coitus a tergo.* What is at stake on this point emerges in the next paragraph, which is marked with the same rhetorical insistence I have noted previously:

(294.3) "Scenes of observing sexual intercourse between parents at a very early age (whether they be real memories or phantasies) are *as a matter of fact* by no means rarities in the analysis of neurotic mortals. *Possibly* they are no less frequent among those who are not neurotics. *Possibly* they are part of the regular store in the— conscious or unconscious—treasury of their memories. But *as often* as I have been able by means of analysis to bring out a scene of this sort . . . it has related to *coitus a tergo* which *alone* offers the spectator a possibility of inspecting the genitals."

Here Freud forms an alliance with the infant inspector of genitals against the young pretenders, Jung and Adler. Their notion of "masculine protest" presupposes the history of the sexual differentiation of the subject, whose discovery by Freud it refuses to recognize. Adler externalizes a source of conflict that Freud insists is internal to the unity of the subject. As a result, Adler reduces the ego to "the ludicrous part of the clown in the circus who by his gestures tries to convince the audience that every change in the circus ring is being carried out under his orders. But only the youngest of the spectators are deceived by him."[15]

Once again, Freud's text re-presents the very features of a deferred narrative, which is constitutive of the claims of the power of psychoanalysis to reconstruct unconscious processes and the temporal demands they make on the analyst. The patient's ability to fashion a narrative through which he or she can recall past events under analysis involves a double construction on the part of the patient and the analyst. Thus the construction of the "primal scene" is not literally an event of the past, but through it past events begin to pattern in such a way that the construct is justified. In other words, recollection does not involve memory so much as a creative fiction that struggles with the patient's will to forget the past. The case history, then, is necessarily a *science-fiction,* a reading of signs from the past that cannot be remembered because it is their language that has been lost and that must be imaginatively re-created. That task would exceed the patient and make analysis interminable without the analyst's ability to give the history closure, that is, a fictional rather than a remembered finale.

Jung and Adler split with Freud because, in the founder's view, they were unable to sustain the split identity (*Spaltung*) in the infantile sexual theorist who accomplishes a double identification in the primal scene, namely, with the "active" man and the "passive" woman. Admittedly, Freud himself does not always honor this doubling of the narrative in the case of the Wolf Man. His own narcissism may well have been a disturbing factor in his efforts to "decide" the case. But here I must defer any conclusion, availing myself of Freud's own exit. He concludes the Trial Scene, as I have called it, with a series of rhetorical questions regarding his advocacy of such an absurd construct as the primal scene and his unwillingness to admit that he has virtually withdrawn its claims:

(295.1) "I will admit something else instead: I intend on this occasion to close the discussion of the reality of the primal scene with a *non liquet.* This case history is not yet at an end; in its further course a factor will emerge which will shake the certainty we seem at present to enjoy."

The founding theorist dismisses us with the promise of more to come. We shall advance in understanding by moving further back in human history where, like the infant theorist, we can fill in the gaps in individual truth with prehistoric truth. Thus, each one of us steps not once but twice into the great river of time's unconscious.

It cannot be denied that Freud constructed a curious double bind for the psychoanalytic community, inasmuch as his remarks on philosophy as a form of paranoia and religion as an obsessional neurosis serve, on the one hand, to reject the rival theorist as a paranoiac and, on the other hand, to bind his murderous sons to him under pain of excommunication from the psychoanalytic movement. Despite Freud's insistence on the paranoid style of systematic theorizing and his own fortitude in proceeding with fragmentary studies, he nevertheless kept to himself the authority of psychoanalysis—the synecdochal key, so to speak. He alone knew how the parts fitted to the whole; he alone knew that the whole could not be grasped in any time other than the time of the unconscious. Thus Freud bound his follows to a double narcissism, that is, to a theory that was his alone as its progenitor and one that he loved as himself, if not as a mistress.

What separated Freud from Jung and Adler was the tenacity with which he held to the pruning of the infantile materials specific to the individual case history and its detailed symbolic structure—such as that found in the case of the Wolf Man—interpreted as the sexual precipitate at the rock bottom of analysis. Freud insists that the puzzle has no pieces that can be inserted apart from the history in which and to which they are found to belong. The case history necessarily unfolds the elements that, so to speak, fictionalize it as a compelling account of the vicissitudes of a family illness. Thus it is essential that Freud does not abstract psychoanalytic theory from the case history and that the inextricable links between observation and interpretation are preserved in the case history as a science-fiction whose pragmatics Freud had in fact to discover for himself. This is the heart of Freud's paternity claim with respect to psychoanalysis. It entitled Freud to reject any version of psychoanalytic practice in which observation and interpretation are separated from the workings of the unconscious and the mechanisms or tropologies of desire that affect the psyche, stratifying, splitting and narrativizing it in a language that can be deciphered only as the analysand surrenders to analysis. The case history as Freud prescribed it—though not entirely without violation—seeks to inscribe itself within a history that is already there, in fact, into a double history of the individual and of humankind, so that the case history has no abstract, theoretical primacy but rather retraces anyone's story, his or her story. To remark on violations in this is to keep in mind that Freud reworks the practices of observation and interpretation, of reading and writing, in terms of his own finding/ founding mythology and to remember that Freud's case is never inseparable from the patient's case history, nor from the history of the psychoanalytic movement.

In the case histories, events and their reconstruction are separable only as a rhetorical effect: the facts are laid out in all their non-sense to the point where common sense becomes giddy and must call in the theorist. However outrageous, incomplete, and contradictory, the hypothesis that yields even partial understanding will have saved us from the paralysis of facts. Freud can then move in his deus ex machina and erect a theater in which a symptom can be traced via the myth of Oedipus at the same time that a technical language of the history and structure of the psyche is precipitated in a supplementary drama of the history of the psychoanalytic movement. The oedipal myth structures the case histories by binding the subject to the primal scene in which everyone's identity is achieved only through sexual difference at the same time that the history of that structure of difference circulates the sexes intergenerationally to build kinship structures that repeat the exchange of sons and daughters-in-law. Incest violates both a structure and a history, so that where incest occurs the structure must be reconfirmed through the exposure of the history, as in the myth of Oedipus. Castration is the retrospective cut, marking the separation of the generations as a phallic *coupure,* which in turn recapitulates the separation from the mother-breast rendered absent through the paternal presence.

Castration redistributes, so to speak, love (hate) for the mother and hate (love) for the mother in a fully developed oedipal complex. From this standpoint, the pre-oedipal phase or pregenital stage, where the mother-infant-body begins to differentiate, already implies the paternal "third," or "other," or "Law," forbidding the "ourobolic" absorption of the mother-by-the-child-by-the-mother. The Freudian vision requires the complete victory of the Father over the mother. As such it imposes a biblical reading on the Greek myth while suppressing both the earlier Minoan-Mycenean myth and the Christian mystery of the Holy Family. Freud privileges the body of the Law (castration) over the lore of the (maternal) body. He privileges paternal sublimation over maternal seduction. Psychoanalysis is a biblical science.

What emerges from Freud's conflicts with Jung and Adler is not simply a succession of writings through to the so-called later cultural writings, often considered *ultra vires*. Rather, Freud's collegial conflicts are constitutive of the standpoints he developed around racism, narcissism, the maternal body, totemism, and monotheism. It is impossible to separate the institutional history of the International Psycho-Analytic Association from the internal history that is constitutive of the thematics in the main series of Freud's texts from 1910 onwards. This must be kept in mind in the reconstruction of any history or periodization of Freud's texts, or of the "mind" of Freud, as Peter Homans has argued so brilliantly.[16] In short, this is another aspect of "the domestic economy of the mind," which I am currently exploring in a larger study with reference to the five case histories.

Freud certainly conscripted others to his vision of psychoanalysis. But he did so because he himself was bound, like Odysseus, to a psychoanalytic theory of vision. That is to say, the discovery that founds psychoanalysis is what the unconscious sees and speaks otherwise. There is a blind spot (castration) in human vision that determines psychic reality through mechanisms of speech and symptomatology revealed in the case histories. He who does not see this does not understand psychoanalysis. That is Freud's edict. The weak theorist sees beyond his blind spot. He does not see what precisely (because it is likely to be overlooked or disavowed) constitutes his object of observation while resisting, distorting, and misleading his vision. The strong theorist is patient with these operations. He internalizes them in the figures and narrative of the properly Freudian case history. In the same way, Freud's conception of psychoanalysis is not driven by any overview of its goals. Rather, his writings constantly revise themselves, return to their own oversight, struggle with horizons not taken, advance by retrospective insight, always deepening a chosen furrow. Here the theorist seeks not to overlook what is overlooked by the patient, whose vision is blocked by what his parents in turn have wished invisible. The split in the family economy renders what is witnessed in the primal scene invalid—an incommunicable source of illness on the side of the voyeur calling for all the communicative art of the soothsayer.

The compulsion, drive or instinct for knowledge (*Wisstrieb*) can hardly turn away from any mirror in which its own economy, sacrifice, adventure and elegance might be reflected. It is also possible, however, that there is a devil in the past between knowledge and the soul's Faustian thirst to know. In this case, the theorist will be driven to destroy, to revise, or to disown his own theories until he can sell himself to himself in the highest of all bids. In this, the theorist's soul endlessly postpones the terror of certainty, which would be death, in exchange for the continuous revision and re-creation of himself born through doubt and uncertainty. Here, then, Freud's primal scene is the foundation of the theoretical life that begins with the infant's "indecision" in the encounter with sexual difference. The inability to see what is there to be seen—the absence of the phallus upon the mother-body—further compounds the disavowal (*Verleugnung*) at the heart of theory. It is then quite possible for the theorist to think of himself as any figure—Moses, Hannibal, Napoleon, to mention Freud's favorites—whose vision is extraordinarily unlimited by what is either evident or obvious.[17] The theorist is prepared to suffer in order to see otherwise. But his pride is that he will have been devoured by his own thoughts turned against him like Actaeon's dogs, with which he shared the chase until a forbidden sight turned the chase into a deadly one.

Whether it is the primal scene or Diana's bath, the passionate theorist is pursued by his unwillingness to abandon the love of inquiry that separates him from the chorus of convention. For it cannot be the sight of Diana that inspires Actaeon but the question he might have put to her and that she might have returned to him, remembering that she herself was once a huntress. What does Life (*Eros*) want from Death (*Thanatos*)? What does the Mind want from the Unconscious? All of human culture derives from these questions. But there is a risk that its rituals mortify the questions with answers that have lost their inspiration. Here psychoanalysis is no more exempt from mortification than the rest of human culture. Indeed, if the practice of psychoanalysis turns against Freud himself, it is because the founding father succeeded in oedipalizing his followers to such an extent that, as Lacan might have put it, they now chew upon its *corps morcelé* with as little thought as the average communicant, oblivious of that "other scene" to which the theorist is always directed.

CHAPTER 15

The Mother Tongue
*Semiosis and Infant
Transcription*

> All around me men are working
> but I am stubborn, and take no part.
> The main difference is this:
> I prize the breasts of the mother.
> —*Tao Te Ching*

I suppose we can take it that there can be no such thing as we have
in mind by the "search for meaning" if meaning is the work of either
a transcendental ego or of a subjectless structure of language.[1] Or else
we are obliged to reintroduce the life of language and the mind
through deep and surface structures. Although these moves, as I see
it, displace logical meaning with the pragmatics of sense making as
a biographical and social institution, they fail to analyze the embodied
work of language and meaning, which throughout our lives operates
both infralinguistically and translinguistically. We use and are used
by language like any other human institution. By the same token, our
language makes reference to its own plight, being self-referential or
metalinguistic. But language achieves no extra metaphysic in this
regard, since everything about language is in language.

Language, once we have it, is like our second body, that is, the
body we have but do not think. In this aspect, we are had by language
and our body, and in living them we are intimate with a life that is
not our own and yet no one else's:

> We shall need to reawaken our experience of the world as it appears to
> us in so far as we are in the world through our body, and in so far as we
> perceive the world with our body. But by thus remaking contact with the
> body and with the world, we shall also rediscover ourself, since, perceiving
> as we do with our body, the body is a natural self and, as it were, the
> subject of perception.[2]

Because our language becomes second nature to us, we ordinarily
communicate and are ordinary communicants through its possession
by-and-of-us. Because this is so, we rarely think of our language,

however much or little we think in our language. Even so, even our most ordinary use of language is reflexive with its everyday formulation of its category, rule, person, place, timing, and turn-taking practices, as we have learned from speech act theory and conversation analysis.[3] Once we shift from everyday language and its situated practices to the languages of our culture, political, economic, technical, scientific and literary institutions, we are more conscious of the need to rethink these languages if we are ever to think in them as competent communicants. Unless we are to remain bound to the normal practices or disciplinary paradigms of these institutional languages, we need to find in ourselves the creative anxiety to break with their influence, and to marginalize and deconstruct their un-thought, unspeakable, and invisible side.[4]

For most of us, then, and for all of us most of the time, the search for meaning is over and done. This is so, not because we live unexamined lives, but precisely because our everyday language contains a great catechism with which we try to understand ourselves and our world. Indeed, as I see it, our everyday language contains a vulgar cosmology, metaphysics, psychoanalysis, and sociology re-quired throughout the history and family of our lives, repeating that first "severe poem" of the world, which Giambattista Vico discovered us in. Thus, our everyday language turns upon "the monumental tropes of birth, marriage, and death, as well as love, labor, and knowledge, through which we explore the collective and individual meaning of our lives sedimented in our religions, arts, sciences, and commonsense.[5]

Here my purpose is to explore the acquisition of our first body and its infant (*infans*) articulation of language and meaning. I am concerned, then, with the infant's embodied search for meaning, with an originary semeosis arising from within the mother-infant body (or *matrix*) articulated in the mother-tongue (*la langue maternelle*). This is the level of language before language that is still not silence and not yet speech. It nevertheless involves a huge labor between mother and infant, like that between every mother animal who feeds and cares for her helpless offspring, making their bodies from her own body long after they have struggled from the womb and until they are recognizably members of their own kind. It is within this tradition of maternal love and infant *poiesis* that we discover the originary matrix of language and meaning.

I propose to locate the problematic of the search for meaning in the embodied inquiry that is aroused in the *matrix* (the mother-infant body). To do so, we need to reconsider Freud's theory of the vicissitude of the instincts to determine the deviation (*clinamen*) through which the biological body, so to speak opens to the psychic body. Here we may be guided by Paul Ricoeur's observations:

> Freud is in line with those thinkers for whom man is desire before being speech; man is speech because the first semantics of desire is distortion and he never completely overcomes this initial distortion. If this is so, then Freud's doctrine would be animated from beginning to end by a conflict between the "mythology of desire" and the "science of the physical apparatus"—"science" in which he always, but in vain, tried to contain the "mythology," and which, ever since the "Project," was exceeded by its own contents.[7]

I am going to argue that there is an "originary surface," which I shall call the *flesh,* where the primitive language of the body is transcribed into the first language of the mind. Moreover, I want to stress that the circuit between the biological and the psychic body intertwines with the circuit between the mother and infant body. Thus the first language or mother tongue arises in the overlap of the flesh and the matrix. I do not expect my argument to be entirely convincing. This is not so much because of its modest empiricism as a recognition from the start that the argument requires more knowledge of psychoanalytic theory and neurophysiology than I can presently lay claim to, especially when one considers that there is a continuous development of contemporary brain theory[8] with more relevance to psychoanalysis than earlier states of the science available to Freud. Freud himself wavered in deciding the final worth of the attempt to ground psychoanalysis in the biology and physics of his day. But even in his "Project for a Scientific Psychology" (1895) he seems always to have been aware that the "physical apparatus" could not be closed off in what Ricoeur calls "an energetics without hermeneutics."[9] The real psychoanalytic discovery is that of the "surface" or flesh in which the symbolic processes (semeosis) are inscribed and where, so to speak, our hermeneutical life has its proper origin. It is here, too, that Freud's theory of sexuality and its clinical evidence are to be located, so that finally there is a radically hermeneutical turn in psychoanalysis away from the early theories of neurophysiology. In Ricoeur's words:

> Psychoanalysis never confronts one with bare forces, but always with forces in search of meaning. This link between force and meaning makes instinct a psychical reality, or, more exactly, the limit concept at the frontier between the organic and the psychical. The link between hermeneutics and economics may be stretched as far as possible—and the theory of affects marks the extreme point of that distention in the Freudian metapsychology: still the link cannot be broken, for otherwise the economics would cease to belong to psychoanalysis.[10]

In his *Three Essays on the Theory of Sexuality* (1905) and various summary reformulations, Freud argues that whereas hunger is the model of desire—or, as we should say, of the flesh—it is sexuality that is the model of every desire. To argue this, as Jean Laplanche shows,[11] Freud had literally to prop up (*étayer, anlehnen*) his theory of sexuality against the theory of life. In other words, Freud leaned on biology to underwrite psychoanalysis. Here Freud's metapsychology repeats at its own level a disciplinary anaclisis motivated by his attempt to analyze the fundamental mother-infant dependency. To find in the beginning of life the origins of sexuality as life's own *clinamen,* or deviation, Freud leans the psychoanalysis of sexuality on the biology of the sexual drives—with a difference that results in the theory of the generalized sexuality of the infant:

> The first organ to emerge as an erotogenic zone and to make libidinal demands on the mind is, from the time of birth onwards, the mouth. To begin with, all psychical activity is concentrated on providing satisfaction for the needs of that zone. Primarily, of course, this satisfaction serves the purpose of self-preservation by means of nourishment; but physiology should not be confused with psychology. The baby's obstinate persistence in sucking gives evidence at an early stage of a need for satisfaction which, though it originates from and is instigated by the taking of nourishment, nevertheless strives to obtain pleasure independently of nourishment and for that reason may and should be termed sexual.[12]

As I see it, we can accept the theory of sexual *clinamen,* provided we see that it is the body as flesh whose destiny is "organized" as the site and sequence of erotogenous zones—mouth, tongue, anus, urethra, genitals—according to Freud's libidinal theory. It is the flesh that is already in semeosis from the embryo's first signs of uterine life[13] to the mother-infant oral (mouth/breast), sucking, gurgling, biting, clinging, urethral, and anal communion.

I want to argue that semiosis is an articulation or figuration of the flesh, which is the receptacle (*chora*)[14] of all inscription, trace, and textuality. The flesh is the receptacle of lived presence and absence as well as of lived temporality of its own mobility or desire. In this sense, the flesh is not a passive tablet of experience, of dreams, or of pleasure and pain. Rather, the flesh prefigures every figuration, trace and gesture through a continuous difference that is the mark or sign of life itself. This token of life is presymbolic. That is to say, it is the very ground of the possibility of symbolism, of the distinction between presence and absence.

The flesh is always a sign of itself, except when dead. As *nature morte,* the flesh is a hostage to the realism that cannot grasp it when living. This is because the living flesh is never fully present to itself, while continuously yearning for its absent states of desire. The flesh is difference, the in-between of presence and absence, satisfaction and desire. It continues to be this difference from the first sign of life until the last sign of death, and in all its rhythms of desire, lack, abjection, incorporation and satisfaction, the flesh repeats or represents itself as its own icon. The flesh is the proper transcript of its own vicissitudes, of its instincts, pleasure, desire, sexuality, love, pain and suffering. It is this transcript that every living being records for itself and that it must continuously decipher in reading its own experience, instincts, dreams, likes and dislikes. The daily transcriptions of the flesh provide us with the soul's reading.

I am adopting Freud's suggestion that the psychic ego be regarded as both the surface of the bodily ego and its projection in order to stress the continuity of the body organ and the psychic apparatus of the ego. This is because I think the psychoanalytic conception of the ego is otherwise reduced to a species of faculty psychology abstracted from the essential Freudian discovery of the precipitation of internal objects in the constitution of the total subject. In other words, I think the primary processes remain open on the body to the level of consciousness as its other scene. I think it can be argued, in this spirit, that the basic *clinamen* in the instincts toward the drives, hence from death to life, occurs in two phases, described by Laplanche in the following terms:

> (1) Metaphorization of the aim, which shifts intake of milk in response to hunger (*saugen*) in the incorporation of the mother breast in pleasure sucking (*lutschen*);
>
> (2) *The metonymization of the object,* which substitutes milk for what is next to it, namely, the breast, so that the infant rediscovers not the lost object but its metonym.[15]

In the *Project for a Scientific Psychology* (1895) Freud considered that it is in this second phase that perception and judgment are differentiated, to be taken up later in language. Here at the breast the infant is already engaged in separating the wishful cathexis of a memory and a perceptual cathexis similar to it, while learning to deal with a constant perceptual component, on the one hand, and a variable perceptual component, that is, between thing and predicate, on the other. Freud again takes up this process at the stage of the feeding infant:

> Let us suppose, for instance, that the mnemic image wished for (by a child) is the image of the mother's breast and a front view of its nipple, and that the first perception is a side view of the same object, without the nipple. In the child's memory there is an experience, made by chance in the course of sucking, that with a particular head-movement the front image turns into the side image. This side image which is now seen leads to the (image of the) head-movement: an experiment shows that its counterpart must be carried out; and the perception of the front view is achieved.
>
> There is not much judgement about this as yet; but it is an example of the possibility of arriving, by a reproduction of cathexes, at an action which is already one of the accidental offshoots of the specific action.[16]

Equally interesting are Freud's observations in the "Project" regarding the first phase of the metaphorization of sucking into sensual sucking with respect to the intercorporeal basis of cognition. Here the mother's body is the first object of theoretical interest, the first source of satisfaction. Thus the infant has to learn without the overlap (matrix) of its mother's body and its own body to recognize movements arising from the mother body as a constant structure or thing, and sensations or motor images arising from within its own body. Due to the helplessness of the early infant body, its ability to fulfill specific action in the external world requires the mother's mediation called for in the infant's cry,[17] which as an internal discharge requires the secondary function of communication, allowing the mother to begin the work of imputing moral motives[18] to the infant as the basis for its later socialization. There too, Freud locates the origin of speech:

> Speech innervation is originally a path of discharge . . . operating like a safety valve, for regulating oscillations . . . it is a portion of the path to *internal change,* which represents the only discharge till the *specific action* has been found. . . . This path acquires a secondary function from the fact that it draws the attention of the helpful person (usually the wished for object itself) to the child's longing and distressful state; and thereafter it serves for *communication* and is thus drawn into the specific action.[19]

At this stage too, the early processes of cognition and communication link up in the perception of (a) objects that make the infant cry; (b) crying that characterizes an object. Thus cognition involves a linking up of unconscious memories and objects of perceptual attention, including some that arouse a sound image, and later objects that will be associated with intentional sounds. "Not much is now needed," says Freud, "in order to invent speech."[20] Indeed, there is considerable evidence to show that the infant oral stage affects the formation of the so-called soft consonants and vowels (*L, M, I*) with effects of sweetness and plenitude associated with sucking.[21]

Despite Freud's observations, we think experience would show that a sucking infant does not look at the breast. Rather, it experiences the breast and nipple in its mouth. But this means that its eyes are elsewhere, and typically towards the mother's face. Here the visual percept of the face (the gaze) and the oral experience of the breast and nipple overlap with other cutaneous experiences, as well as with clinging and releasing responses. Indeed, a considerable coordination between oral and visual experience is required to bring the infant's sucking response to focus on the nipple. Once this is achieved, a conduit opens between the infant's inside body and the world of external bodies:

> The experience of relief from unpleasure through its nipple which fills the newborn's mouth (remember the disparity of sizes!), and the milk streaming from it, is only one part of the picture, a passive experience. The act of sucking and of deglutition is the infant's first active co-ordinated muscular action. The organs involved are the tongue, the lips and the cheeks. Accord-

ingly, these are also the muscles which are the first ones to be brought under control, a fact which makes the later smiling response possible. Similarly these will be the first surfaces used in tactile perception and exploration. They are particularly well suited for this purpose because in this single organ, the mouth cavity, are assembled the representatives of several of the senses in one and the same area. These senses are the sense of touch, of taste, of temperature, of smell, of pain, but also the deep sensibility involved in the act of deglutition. Indeed, the oral cavity lends itself as no other region of the body to bridge the gap between inner and outer perception.[22]

While the demarcation of inside and outside experience between the mother and infant bodies may be progressively elaborated in perceptual operations, it can only begin as a tactile experience of the flesh in which any part of the experience can stand for the whole. Thus infant vision and infant orality overlap in the madonna/infant smile. I therefore venture the suggestion that in the infant's play with the breast, that is, in the *clinamen* from *saugen* to *lutschen* there occurs a shift from biological passivity to nonpathological mastery of the maternal *fort/da* which Freud discusses in *Beyond the Pleasure Principle,* but locates much later. I think the issue here is not one of chronology but, as Maurice Merleau-Ponty might have said, of the acquisition of a structure of behavior, a competence with continuous manifestations in accordance with the stages of the developing corporeal schema. If this is at all the case, then it would permit us, on another occasion, to analyze the transference of the smile between the infant and mother as a constitutive feature of the Madonna and Child iconology.[23] Here again, we find some support for such an enterprise in Ricoeur's remark on Freud's analysis of Leonardo's *Mona Lisa:*

> With Freud, we said that the lost archaic object has been "denied" and "triumphed over" by the work of art which recreates the object or rather creates it for the first time by offering it to all men as an object of contemplation. The work of art is also a *fort-da,* a disappearing of the archaic object as fantasy and its reappearing as a cultural object. Thus, does not the death instinct have as its normal, nonpathological expression, the disappearance-reappearing in which the elevation of fantasy to symbol consists?[24]

I wish to suggest further that in the shift from *saugen* to *lutschen* the infant experiences, well before Lacan's mirror stage, essentially the same internal precipitation of the forms of the Other by shifting from the mother-breast to his own tongue and thumb. Freud himself speaks of the derivation of the ego from the body's sensations arising from its own exploration of its cutaneous surface, that is from the flesh as an inside/outside source of sensations that are the basis for the differentiation of perception and judgment with respect to the (un)pleasure principle and the reality principle.

Freud thus indicates clearly the two meshing observations of the ego from the "surface": on the one hand, the ego is the surface of the physical apparatus, a specialized organ continuous with it; on the other hand, it is the projection or metaphor of the body's surface, a metaphor in which the various perceptual systems have a role to play.[25]

Furthermore, I am implying that this surface of flesh between the body and the ego means that the prelibidinal ego is not from the very start in conflict with the primary process of sexuality, though this conflict may be "organized" at higher or later levels of ego development. I think that the infant's perception of the mother-body is wholly absorbed with her expressive face, smile, and voice, which is, of course, a total-body response communicated in the way she holds and handles the infant's body and its expressive responses. Here, again, we have a surface of exchange in the communicative flesh recognized immediately in the mother/infant body. At the same time, this surface is not simply an undifferentiated overlapping of sensations. Rather, it is already an "organizer," in Spitz's sense, of the psychological development of the infant.

Here it may be worthwhile to record Ricoeur's observations on the difficulty of the solipsism involved in Freud's use of the term *pleasure* as opposed to *satisfaction*. Although I continue that use, I insist on the familization of the flesh and matrix to provide the proper sense of the psychic operations of pleasure. Apart from this difference, therefore, my argument is faithful to Ricoeur's interpretation of the necessary distinction:

There are numerous reasons in Freud's writings for having doubts about our knowledge of the nature of pleasure. In the first place it should not be forgotten that the earliest formulation of the pleasure principle is closely connected with a representation of the psychical apparatus which, as we have repeatedly emphasized, is solipsistic in nature. The topographic-economic hypothesis is solipsistic by construction but this characteristic never attaches to the clinical facts that the hypothesis translates—the relation to the mother's breast, the father, the family constellation, authorities—nor to the analytic experience, dramatized in the transference, in which interpretation takes place. The very notion of impulse or instinct, more basic than all the auxiliary representations of the topography, is distinct from the ordinary notion of instinct inasmuch as an instinct in the Freudian sense involves other persons. Hence, the final meaning of pleasure cannot be the discharge of tensions within an isolated apparatus; such a definition applies only to the solitary pleasure of autoerotic sexuality. Ever since the "Project" Freud used the word "satisfaction" (*Befriedigung*) for that quality of pleasure that requires the pleasure of others.[26]

Auguste Bonnard has called attention to the primal significance of the tongue in the organization of the body ego and object cathexis. As soon as one reflects on it, what we must see is that the infant's world is, so to speak, in its mouth. Here the world of insides and outsides is experienced with the tongue, tasting, sucking, spitting, gurgling, touching, touched. It is, of course, an icon of the flesh. As an exploratory organ whose modality is nonvisual, the primal significance of the tongue is enormous from the beginning of life and throughout childhood. The tongue, rather like the ear and the skin, is probably well ahead of the eye in the infant experience of inside and outside world. To do its work, the tongue is equipped with the richest supply of cranial nerves, enabling it to operate at the command of both the highest and most primitive nerve centres. It is the infant's major scanner for the organization of its good-and-bad experiences of objects, self, and others:

It is to be assumed that the pre-genital, non-visual, self-comforting mechanisms of the tongue are at the intra-oral service of all small infants. Most of these, however, seem destined by their normality of response to prefer to grasp and savour, and thus include the outside, whether it be the missing nipple or their own thumb, at their lips, by which they restore their circle of balanced quiescence. This more usual type of responsive activity, whereby the tongue acts as a sensory bridge, reaching out from inside the self to experience of external objects, suggests the likelihood of its physical role being that of mediator in the maturational progression from primary to secondary narcissism. Dawning awareness of the recurring source of intrusions into the mouth, preferably desirable and "harnessed" by the tongue, would provide an important prototype for object cathexis.[27]

Far more than a terminological quibble is at issue in the *clinamen* whereby "instinctual" pleasure is sexualized. If the circuit of pleasure could be closed at the biological level, then the infant would never acquire symbolic behavior. Without the maternal mediation of the infant's bodily needs, and the radical contingency of satisfaction and dissatisfaction, the symbolizing of desire would never arise, and the infant would never acquire speech. Freudian desire always speaks to the other before itself. Its demands are, so to speak, on recognition and are rhetorical rather than physical. The semantics of desire, then, are necessarily *familized*, for good and evil. Here, again, the consequences are clearly expressed in Ricoeur's comment:

> The intersubjective structure of desire is the profound truth of the Freudian libido theory; even in the period of the "Project" and Chapter 7 of the *Traumdcutung*, Freud never described instincts outside of an intersubjective context; if desire were not located within an interhuman situation, there would be no such thing as repression, censorship, or wish-fulfillment through fantasies; that the other and others are primarily bearers of prohibitions is simply another way of saying that desire encounters another desire—an opposed desire. The whole dialectic of roles within the second topography expresses the internalization of a relation of opposition, constitutive of human desire; the fundamental meaning of the Oedipus complex is that human desire is a history, that this history involves refusal and hurt, that desire becomes educated to reality through the specific unpleasure inflected upon it by an opposing desire.[28]

The infant flesh is destined from the very beginning to embody the very inquiry that is constructive of a living being. The exploration of its own internal and external boundaries and testing of all experience/information that enters/exits its orifices and skin surfaces entirely absorbs the infant in its own carnal knowledge. The flesh, then, is neither a biological nor a psychic ground from the start. It becomes both in the mother-infant feeding relation, as the instinct to survive, which is then diverted into a "pleasure sucking"[29] whose object is neither milk nor the breast but its own autoeroticism:

> Thus the first object of the oral component of the sexual instinct is the mother's breast which satisfies the infant's need for nutrition. In the act of sucking for its own sake the erotic component, also gratified in sucking for nutrition, makes itself independent, gives up the object in an external person, and replaces it by a part of the child's own person. The oral impulse becomes *auto-erotic*, as the anal and other erotogenic impulses are from the beginning. Further development has, to put it as concisely as possible, two aims: first, to renounce auto-eroticism, to give up again

the object found in the child's own body in exchange again for an external one; and secondly, to combine the various objects of the separate impulses and replace them by one single one. This naturally can only be done if the single object is again itself complete, with a body like that of the subject; nor can it be accomplished without some part of the auto-erotic impulse excitations being abandoned as useless.[30]

From its earliest days, the infant body entertains the possibility of becoming the partial body or the "body bit" (*corps morcelé*) of its mother or as its (as yet undifferentiated) self. "Partial objects include breast, penis, and numerous other elements related to bodily life (excrement, child, etc.), all of which have in common the fundamental characteristics of being, in fact or in fantasy, *detached* or *detachable*."[31] To some extent, this is given in the infant's somatic experience of its body with organs whose drives are represented in its mental life as though they had a source outside/inside itself, which it has yet to integrate in a whole-body image. Thus the hunger drive attaches the sucking infant to the mother's breast for her milk. But soon the infant internalizes its need for milk by diverting it towards the very pleasure of sucking, thereby psychosexualizing a biological drive or instinct, and replacing the partial mother body with its own partial body (tongue, thumb). "We call this action "pleasure sucking" (German: *lutschen,* signifying the enjoyment of sucking for its own sake—as with a rubber 'comforter'); and as when it does this the infant again falls asleep with a blissful expression we see that the action of sucking is sufficient in itself to give it satisfaction."[32]

It should be noted that the infant's stage of autoeroticism does not precede his attachment to the mother-breast. Rather, it represents the rediscovery of this lost object in his own body, from which he will have again to be detached in favor of a whole body whose image is for-himself-and-for-others. Here, the mirror phase, the castration and Oedipus complexes are the circuits of the familized yet individual body. But this lies beyond the scope of the present analysis.[33] For the present what I wish to discern in these vicissitudes of the flesh is the capacity of the body as flesh for differentiating its somatic experience of organ and object perception, which it represents in a mental field. Thus the body and the mind are two scenarios of the flesh. Indeed, we might argue that the mind is a scenario opened up by the sexualization of the biological body.

Through sexualization, if I understand Freud rightly, the biological body is opened up from the closed circuit of the instincts into the general economy of a purely expressive drive which can be harnessed, so to speak, to the organization of the erotogenic zones and libidinal stages. Simultaneously, this articulation of the sexualized body is the basis for the familization of the infant body through the subordination of the semiotic matrix (mother-infant body) to the symbolic patrix, that is, the order of language and society invoked in-the-name-of-the-father—the castration complex (the "*non du père*") and the Oedipus complex (the *nom du père*). This schema is set forth clearly in Freud's *Outline of Psychoanalysis*, repeating the anaclisis of theory and experience in the double history of infant sexuality and its science:

A child's first erotic object is the mother's breast that nourishes it; love has its origin in attachment to the satisfied need for nourishment. There is no doubt that, to begin with, the child does not distinguish between the breast and its own body; when the breast has to be separated from the body and shifted to the "*outside*" because the child so often finds it absent, it carries with it as an "*object*" a part of the original narcissistic libidinal cathexis. The first object is later completed into the person of the child's mother, who not only nourishes it but also looks after it and thus arouses in it a number of other physical sensations, pleasurable and unpleasurable. By her care of the child's body she becomes its first seducer. In these two relations lies the root of a mother's importance, unique, without parallel, established unalterably for a whole lifetime as the first and strongest love-object and as the prototype of all later love-relations—for both sexes. In all this the phylogenetic foundation has so much the upper hand over personal accidental experience that it makes no difference whether a child has really sucked at the breast or has been brought up on the bottle and never enjoyed the tenderness of a mother's care. . . . And for however long it is fed at its mother's breast, it will always be left with a conviction after it has been weaned that its feeding was too short and too little.
This preface is not superfluous, for it can heighten our realization of the intensity of the Oedipus complex. When a boy (from the age of two or three) has entered the phallic phase of his libidinal development, is feeling pleasurable sensations in his sexual organs and has learned to procure these at will by manual stimulation, he becomes his mother's lover. He wishes to possess her physically in such ways as he has divined from his observations and intuitions about sexual life, and he tries to seduce her by showing her the male organ which he is proud to own. In a word, his early awakened masculinity seeks to take his father's place with her; his father has hitherto in any case been an envied model to the

boy, owing to the physical strength he perceives in him and the authority with which he finds him clothed. His father now becomes a rival who stands in his way and whom he would like to get rid of. . . . The boy's mother has understood quite well that his sexual excitation relates to herself. Sooner or later she reflects that it is not right to allow it to continue. She thinks she is doing the correct thing in forbidding him to handle his genital organ. . . . At last his mother adopts the severest measures; she threatens to take away from him the thing he is defying her with. Usually, in order to make the threat more frightening and more credible, she delegates its execution to the boy's father, saying that she will tell him and that he will cut the penis off. Strange to say, this threat operates only if another condition is fulfilled before or afterwards. In itself it seems too inconceivable to the boy that such a thing could happen. But if at the time of the threat he can recall the appearance of female genitals or shortly afterwards he has a sight of them—of genitals, that is to say, which really lack this supremely valued part, then he takes what he has heard seriously and, coming under the influence of the *castration complex,* experiences the severest trauma of his young life.[34]

We must abandon the myth of biological satisfaction. The infant never experiences biological sufficiency as its "natural" state. On the contrary, the sexual order is the necessary supplement[35] of the infant's organic functions, as though self-preservation were always less than self-love, requiring it rather than being in conflict with it. Despite its risk, infant integrity is sought on the level of psychology rather than biology. But this means that there must be a surface of exchange between life and love, which I have called the flesh. I suggest that the infant semiosis already begins with the diversion (*clinamen*) of the biological instinct of survival into the relatively autonomous pursuit of "pleasure sucking." Through the *clinamen* of pleasure the biological body is eroticized in all its organs, and its internal and external surfaces; its orifices become zones of self-affecting and, therefore, self-interpretative flesh—the semiotic body. It is on this body that the communicative exchanges between infant and mother, as well as the infant's articulation of the boundary between its own insides and outsides, are registered.

Infant sexuality, then, so far from being the perversion of a natural body, is the first inscription of the natural body in the semiotic process that articulates the infant body with meaning, language, and symbolism. In other words, the perversion of the infant's feeding instinct by the purely sexual drive to unbound pleasure shifts the biological body into phase with the communicative body, the body for itself and for others. The constructs of the biological and neurophysiological body are abstracted from the libidinal body, that is, from the double contexture of the flesh and the matrix within which there opens up the semantic of desire. Psychoanalysis, as we understand it, is a movement within language back towards the first language of the body, traced on the body's mind well before intentionality is ruled by desire. Psychoanalysis is therefore an infant science, more patient than any of our other sciences.

CHAPTER 16

Homotextuality

Barthes on Barthes, Fragments
(RB), with a Footnote

Fragments: *Roland Barthes by Roland Barthes (RB)*
Why fragments? Passages. Images. Texts. Paragraphs. Stars. Constellations. Turning up for their own sake; for the sake of it—the pleasure of *id.*
    Woven. Written. Without design. Uncopied. Copious. Words. Somebody is writing. Whose body?
    Write about yourself. Whenever was that? The child's body amid larger bodies. Surrounded, seen, handled, hungered, caressed, cross. Other bodies, every body, some bodies, no bodies. Mother there, father gone, grandmother, grandfather. Incorporate. Prehistory.
    Proper talk. Gossip. Piano. Woman's talk. Programs. Contracts. Bills. The dead body of language. Boredom. Silence. Retreat. Waiting. Generation. Acting. Illness. Records. The written body. Ritual of science. Dangers of childhood. Parents. Absence. Custom.
    When is the body my body? Death. Sickness. Family photos. Childhood. Vacations.
    Paradoxical. Contrary. Cut outs. Fragments. Free, discreet, generous texts. Dislocation. Mutations. Text on text. Language on language. Without a center. Without repetition. Abolition. Language. Society. Bourgeois contract. Political discourse. Sacrifice. Public bodies. Literary bodies. Mythologies.
    Decomposition. Play. Perversion.
    Writing as surplus value. Seminal play. The spume. Irrigation.
    Ink. Writing upon writing, text upon text. Barthes on Barthes. Page upon page; word without end. The play within the play. By degrees, transgression. Foreground/background. Gendered. Dialectics. Dissolution of paradigms, of sexual and semantic conflict into fragments, shimmers, slips and drifts. Improvisation of meaning and sexuality:

> Who knows if this insistence on the plural is not a way of denying sexual duality? The opposition of the sexes must not be a law of Nature; therefore, the confrontations and paradigms must be dissolved, both the meanings and the sexes be pluralized: meaning will tend toward its multiplication,

its dispersion (in the Theory of the Text), and sex will be taken into no typology (there will be, for example, only *homosexualities,* whose plural will baffle any constituted, centered discourse, to the point where it seems to him virtually pointless to talk about it)." (*RB,* 169).

Sowing words. Sowing seed. Polysemy. Proliferation. A sea of ink. Pen. Man. Ship. Floating. Cruising. Adrift. Butterfly. La Papillon. *Theory of literary fragments:* Limitations. Openings, desire, foreplay. Promiscuous starts without the traps of conclusion, contracted consummation. Jottings from nowheres, *hors-texte.* Condensations. Scraps of my life; daily narcissims: "Production of my fragments. Contemplation of my fragments (correction, polishing, etc.). Contemplation of my scraps (narcissism)." (*RB,* 15).

He wanted to write himself in *RB.* But always there crept in the maxims. Were these to reassure others that this fragmentary creature had, after all, a bottom nature? Or were they there to appease his own fears, to calm his passion for extravagance by catching himself in words that hang on him like old clothes? To wrap himself in a patchwork, a quilt of rhapsodic thoughts, starting from no center, at all costs avoiding a scene.

To really write *RB* he would need to get past his mirror image, to slip past his mother. But he cannot do this because *RB* is the blind spot from which all this is seen. To see himself in depth is a task he poses for others. This book (*RB*) is therefore only the book of the self's resistance to his own life—a novel without a proper name. To the extent that it subverts even this achievement, it does so by occasionally shrugging off its own corpus in favor of the writer's working body—such as it is:

> To write the body
> Neither the skin, nor the muscles, nor the bones nor
> the nerves, but the rest: an awkward, fibrous, shaggy,
> raveled thing, a clown's coat. (*RB,* 180)

Literature's two bodies: one whole, a corpse with integrity, respected; the other fragmented, teasing and tormented; delirious, drifting in a tide of words. But with a vision of the feminine flood; cycle of life; therefore waiting, *voyeur.*

Barthesian fragments: textual cuts, circumcisions; women's robes; flowing, feminized. Writing, bleeding on the virgin page; cave artist of the womb's passages.

Literary labor, conceived in envy of speechless fertility. Speak, mother, to tell me who I am. Silence, waiting. Therefore *literary couvade:* reenter the mother's body through the inking wound, germinate words, words, words. Risk of birth, risk of death to heal the polemic of language. Seek literary bliss: resurrection of the fragmentary, broken text. Writer's body in the grip of its own myth. Logos of literary pregnancy: to take hold of the new body's beginnings. Flesh, smile, language. Mother. Home. But wait. Begin a watch, daily zigzag on the page to keep the wound open.

A Footnote.[1]

We read books with our bodies. We write with our bodies too. Because we do so, we read and write our bodies as conversible, storyable experiences of living, loving, waiting, sensing ourselves and one another. We live, then, between two bodies: the literary body, which reads and writes that other body of literature so that we can hardly know one apart from the other:

> No object is in a constant relationship with pleasure (Lacan apropos of Sade). For the writer however, this object exists: it is not the language: it is the *mother tongue.* The writer is someone who plays with his mother's body (I refer to Pleynet on Lautréamont and Matisse): in order to dismember it, to take it to the limit of what can be known about the body: I would go so far as to take bliss in a *disfiguration* of the language, and opinion will strenuously object, since it opposes "disfiguring nature."[2]

Poets celebrate this; novelists, essayists, and critics make hard work of it. At least, that was so until writers discovered themselves as poets. They did not, of course, admit this readily. The discovery could at first be attributed to language itself. That is to say, the poetic, playful, and pleasurable in language could be said to be *of* language: the autonomy of language thereby found as an infantile pleasure, hereronomous. In this way, literary pleasure could be contained by literary work: a division of literary labor. This is perhaps a necessary arrangement. We do not, and should not, easily abandon the work of realism through which we have fashioned so much of the world and ourselves. What is done is done. Moreover, we have built this world much as we have fenced our fields, built our homes and all the other machinery of our living. Indeed, we rightly celebrate these achievements in the realisms of our science and literature. Yet in the life of the arts and sciences there must therefore be periods of rejection, innovation, and iconoclasm.

Everything Barthes wrote exploited and subverted the formats that fasten the literary body to outworn ideologies of production and consumption. Like Rabelais, he was a literary transvestite,[3] trying anything, one costume after another, one body after another, dividing, multiplying himself, in pursuit of pleasure: "So far as much of the best, of the most original in modern art and literature is autistic, i.e., unable or unwilling to look to a reality of 'normality' outside its own chosen rules, so far as much of the modern genius can be understood from the point of view of a sufficiently comprehensive, sophisticated theory of games, there is in it a radical homosexuality."[4]

Barthes's literary principles were ludic rather than destructive: unmasking, unveiling, undressing—but never exceeding the strip-tease itself. He had a dread of dead language and of the social institutions that make literature a corpse rather than a living body of filiations and flashes that articulate the sheer pleasures of reading and writing. He struggled to generalize writing, to de-oedipalize the text. Childlike, he wished to set afloat all specific languages, to unmoor interpretation from its literary models, to let it drift pleasurably in the mother tongue. In other words, always more words, Barthes improvised a further state in the physiology of literature,[5] lodging interpretation once and for all in the literary body.

> Apparently Arab scholars, when speaking of the text, use this admirable expression: the certain body. What body? We have several of them; the body of anatomists and physiologists, the one sciences sees and discusses: this is the text of grammarians, critics, commentators, philologists (the pheno-text). But we have also a body of bliss consisting solely of erotic relations, utterly distinct from the first body: it is another contour, another nomination; thus with the text; it is no more than the open list of the fires of language (those living fires, intermittent lights, wandering features strewn in the text like seeds and which for us advantageously replace the "*semina aeternitatis*," the "*zopyra*," the common notions, the fundamental assumptions of ancient philosophy). Does the text have a human form, is it a figure, an anagram of the body? Yes, but of our erotic body. The pleasure of the text is irreducible to the physiological need.[6]

To understand this conception of the literary body, we cannot hang onto an unrevised conception of language, mind, and embodiment.

When we speak of the autonomy of language and literature we should be careful not to reintroduce the very separation that this notion is intended to heal with respect to the instrumentalist conception of language and embodiment. We do not have language at our disposal. As embodied beings we live in language. As such we have no privileged position with respect to language, any more than we have with respect to time. Indeed, it is this double bind that is properly understood in the recognition of the autonomy of language. Yet we are not caught in the web of language like helpless flies. We achieve a certain distance with respect to it; thus the polarities of synchrony and diachrony may be taken as vibrations in the web, points at which the code turns into a message. We may use the linguistic web to see ourselves caught in it and struggling to be free from it; the web thereby having served its purpose. Thus in the theater of Antonin Artaud, Bertolt Brecht, Eugene Ionesco, and Samuel Beckett the voice is no longer used in order to repeat or enact a thought, as though the body were merely the soul's servant. Speech is rather an originating gesture that sets the body thinking, as it is forced to do, for example, when confronted with alien things, madness, and otherwise exotic cultures. Thus Beckett can employ only Mouth or Voice or Footsteps, and Brecht can bring forth thought from color, because these devices create meaning for an embodied community that is deprived of its audience/viewer transcendence by these very effects/affects. The mind is bracketed in such theater; only the body can anticipate the action. Not, of course, the Cartesian body, atrophied by its superior mind, no better than the debris that surrounds and eventually overwhelms our living. Rather, the gestural body, before the spectacle, before the conventions of language and the conformist text. The gest as gist; the meaning thereby deeded in a public act available to anyone present: corporate community.

The web of language is therefore both a necessary structure and a temporary event: metalanguage as the pact between language and the writer that provides the space within which the writer can maneuver. A writer's language, like his or her body, carves out a virtual space in which neither words nor objects ever have any absolute closure, but rather each releases the other in exhaustible systems of meaning, which the writer brings to recognition through style, that is to say, in practical sketches of the writer's world. None of this is necessary for a disembodied mind. But the writer dwells in language precisely because he or she is an embodied being: familied and thereby social. Our embodied presence to the world and others is the wedge of difference that generates and elides time and distance but without any totaling of the histories and geographies of language and perception.[7]

Barthes called for a thoroughly structuralist approach to literature, as in his own study of fashion,[8] or in Claude Lévi-Strauss's studies of myth.[9] Yet he regarded literature as an endless interrogation, a fracturing—like Orpheus, forbidden to look back on the truth to which it believes itself allied. He considered literary realism hopelessly inarticulate about its necessary choices; in short, it cannot tell of its alliance with the unreality of language through which it works its very realism.[10] Barthes also rejected the mythology of scientific discourse. He regarded its objectivism and realism as rhetorical achievements that effect the neutrality of science in a referential code whose grammatical decoys—absence of first-person referee/third-person agency—can just as well be appropriated in literary discourse. From the other side, literary discourse, so far from being a purely subjective achievement, can be analyzed in terms of objective units of discourse, intelligible progression and resolution, as well as conventional taxonomies and classification of things, persons, and events that fulfill its sense and expressivity. In Barthes's view, however, structuralism is not exempt from taking a stand on its own use of language. In other words, structuralism is neither presumptively nor uniquely on the side of the scientific mode of discourse. Indeed, Barthes considered it necessary for structuralism to compromise its analytic intent with its historicist experience of language, in order to accommodate its own lateness.

By turning to the activity of writing, we once again confront the options of subjective and objective discourse, and with the artificiality of the dominance of scientific over nonscientific language once released from the constraints of the hierarchical conventions of realism and objectivism, the writer is obliged to explore the pleasure of the text without any sense of its frivolity or constrained pedagogy. Indeed, it is the task of structuralism to reveal to science the scandal of language, namely, that after so many years of abuse it still remains sovereign, and is no longer in need of the technical alibis furnished to science by the humanities in its seeming defense.

The fragmentary mode that Barthes chose for his own work was designed to show by incongruity the design of "real" books, to reveal the material format of consequential thought, the idea flowing through the words in sustained narrativity punctuated with reasonable stops and starts: essential paraphrase. Above all, literary realism subordinates detail to a general schema, guaranteeing that readers will always know where they are and what to look for; everything worked out. Hence the importance of literary genres for the orderly passage of truth in kinds. These two movements come together in the activity of structuralism—a movement of deconstruction in order to reproduce the function of structure: the production of meaning and value.[11] The benefit of this notion is that it undercuts literary positivism, inasmuch as the latter sacrifices the productive intention of the work to the establishment of its external biographical and circumstantial facts. Positivist history paradoxically rejects the lived, embodied historicities of literature by locating the author's intention and sources in formative influences found elsewhere and otherwise than how the author conceived them to be. It misses the radical literary deformation or misreading[12] through which a work acquires "sources" as embodied "resources" and thereby structures itself. As such, the work must first be interpreted from within, and then as an attempt to put meaning in the world as one of its languages or styles.

Every literary work is caught in this tension between language and literature, that is, between literature as the parasite of language and as its life-giving transfusion of new meaning an intelligibility. Barthes contrasted language and style. For the writer, language is not so much an instrument of expression as a horizon, a setting of familiar bodily experiences within which the writer speaks much like anyone else. Literature must bend to style, that is, the writer's specific carnal imagery, vocabulary, and timing: "Thus under the name of style a self-sufficient language is evolved which has its roots only in the depths of the author's personal and secret mythology, that subnature of expression where the first coition of words and things takes place, where once and for all the great verbal themes of his existence come to be installed."[13] It is in this corporeal infralanguage that Barthes discovered his own writing, as well as that of Jules Michelet and Jean Racine. To be consequent, he could hardly work in any other fashion if he were to realize the project of *Roland Barthes by Roland Barthes*.

Style, then, is the corporeal bond between the man and his text— what I am calling, therefore, *homotextuality*—or between woman and her text—*gynema*. It is founded in the writer's personal myths, which work in him or her like the four humors, or in those places where the flesh and the world experience the metamorphosis of expression and carnal being.[14]

Barthes had no patience with the claim that literature expresses anything other than language; there is no prelinguistic expression, no first words. The author's job is to work with language that has already been used, stereotyped, and settled a thousand times, layer upon layer of convention, law, and common sense. Hence fragmentation offers at least one device for blocking meaning until it overflows this very artifice in whatever direction it cares to take.[15] Inasmuch as the author sinks into the tautological resonances of language upon language, he or she loses the self and the world in the task of writing, which somehow—not as sheer instrument or material—restores both the world and the writer. Thus an author can never present a doctrine, or evidence, or even commitment, since the literary labor involved in their production obliges him more heavily to their flawed creation: "an author is a man who wants to be an author" (*RB*).

Like Montaigne, whom we considered earlier, Barthes "rolled around" in his literary body, enjoying its moments, its slackness, its dispersions—essential diaspora—its tastes, its moods, its rejections, as well as its loves, even when impossible. It is with this in mind that we must understand Barthes's choice of writing fragments rather than books. Literary fragments reveal the writer the way a woman's dress reveals her body. The pleasure is in the artful choice, arrangement, moment, movement—understatement. He played with texts as women play with dress, multiplying their bodies, each woman every woman, shimmering—other woman. Barthes found his own passion for fragmentation in other writers. In the Marquis de Sade, Charles Fourier, and Saint Ignatius of Loyola, he discovered the same pleasure in segmentation (the body of Christ, the body of the victim, the human soul). He intended nothing transcendental in this trinity: merely three fetishisms of the text, pleasuring word upon word through an excess of classification:

> our three authors deduct, combine, arrange, endlessly produce rules of assemblage; they substitute syntax, *composition* (a rhetorical, Ignation

word) for creation; all three fetishists, devoted to the cut-up body, for them the reconstitution of a whole can be no more than a summation of intelligibles: nothing indecipherable, no irreducible quality of ejaculation, happiness, communication: nothing is that is not spoken.[16]

No official reading; Barthes sought only the "man" in the text. Like Montaigne he has no other physics, no other metaphysics. No concern, then, with the official sites and alibis of literary interpretation: history, class, biography. Look only for the excess in writing: the stolen goods of literature. The necessary method, therefore, is to unglue the text, fragment it; to let socialism, faith, and evil through the net (for others to fish) catching smaller pleasures in the text—a method he hoped for and that he applied to himself as well as to Sade, Fourier, Loyola, and Michelet:

> Were I a writer, and dead, how I would love it if my life, through the pains of some friendly and detached biographer, were to reduce itself to a few details, a few preferences, a few inflections, let us say: to "biographemes" whose distinction and mobility might go beyond any fate and come to touch, like Epicurean atoms, some future body, destined to the same dispersion; a marked life, in sum, as Proust succeeded in writing his in his work, or even in a film, in the old style, in which there is no dialogue and the flow of images (that *flumen orationis* which is perhaps what makes up the "obscenities" of writing) is intercut, like the relief of hiccoughs, by the barely written darkness of the intertitles, the casual eruption of another signifier: Sade's white muff, Fourier's flowerpots, Ignatius's Spanish eyes.[17]

Thus, he materialized the problem of biography. That is to say, he cut into the hermeneutical problem by going for the humoral imagination that furnishes the thematic unities in an author's work, whether of Michelet or of himself. His readings, therefore, are like the palmist's readings, finding repetitive themes in auguries of the flesh and matter, condensations of living. Thus, he gave to Michelet's vast corpus a carnal history, discovering an incessant metamorphosis between the historian's working, suffering, animal, fluid body and the ravages of the body politic suffering the history of France.[18] The rhythms of the history of France held Michelet in the same obsession as the rhythm of life he worshiped in the female cycle. History appeared to him like a living body whose trajectory ran through all sorts of intermediate stages of life, matter, vegetation, character, and spirit, culminating in the moralization of nature. At its highest point, therefore, history appeared to Michelet to reproduce itself in a gendered struggle between Grace, the woman—at times sleepy (Turkey), or bored (Napoleon), or playful (Richelieu)—and Justice, the forceful male (Satan, Luther, the French Revolution). Just as the grand principles of history are sexualized in Michelet's discourse, so all the major figures of history are bodily types, dry, cold, ruled by the basic humors of the world's body. For this reason, the most enduring historical figures are women. Their bodies are historical bodies: eternal rhythm of blood and life, magic and religion, dominance and submission. The highest unity of history is therefore prefigured in the androgyne, the marriage of the heart and reason, and realized in the revolutionary deliverance of the people.

We shall not enjoy any work of Barthes's without first perusing the table of contents from which its pickings are offered. And we would miss the feast if we were to insist upon ordering the items into a *menu fixe*. The items are ordered alphabetically as in an encyclopedia precisely because they obey no order. They constitute a treasury of discourse, of endless little chats for anyone who picks out an item. Only a madman—a nerveless reader—would use Barthes's text in an orderly fashion. As with titles, so with books. Barthes never wrote one. He started many, enjoyed the foreplay, postponed consummation. Hence book on book—*metabook*—permitting readers to choose a passage and proceed at their own pace; stops, starts, gaps, flashbacks, abridgments, footnotes—above all, never saying anything that cannot as well be said later at another turn; reader and writer waiting for another, like lovers.

Barthes explains his procedures as the only way a literary lover can proceed with any hope of finding a listener, or reader. The lover discourses, runs ahead of himself, as did Barthes, to where he and his lover will be, carried upon futures of speech that indeed embody his love like a dancer's feet. The lover's discourse, therefore, is exclamatory rather than descriptive of what loving he experiences. The lover's discourse is a hallucination of his feelings toward the beloved whom he always beholds otherwise: "Amorous *dis-cursus* is not dialectical; it turns like a perpetual calendar, an encyclopaedia of affective culture (there is something of Bouvard and Pecuchet in the lover)."[19] Thus, Barthes points out that his discourse draws languorously on books, conversations, friends, and his own life, but without any authoritative purpose. For if he were to proceed in anything but a fragmentary fashion, he would encounter the institutional sirens of the love story and, worse still, of the philosophy of love. Consequently, for the table of contents in *A Lover's Discourse, Fragments,* he chooses "an *absolutely insignificant* order,"[20] namely, that of titles in an alphabetic order; foreclosing the will to possess his lover:

The table of contents is disturbed by the English translation and the page sequence, which upsets the left/right, down/up, arrangement. Fortunately, this effect also restores the disorder invited by the alphabetical arrangement. In such tokens, the writer, like a lover, abandons any concern with integrity. This would be an impossible demand on the reader's own passion. Like lovers, both reader and writer want to get to their satisfaction any way they can, on each occasion this way rather than that, skipping within an order motivated by pleasure. Barthes's fragmentary method therefore consciously provides for the same literary liberties to be taken with his text as he himself took with other texts. Literary pleasure cannot be controlled any more than a lover's discourse; it awaits the reader's picking:

> Tmesis, source or figure of pleasure, here confronts two prosaic edges with one another; it sets what is useful to a knowledge of the secret against what is useless to such knowledge; Tmesis is a seam or flaw resulting from a simple principle of functionality; it does not occur at the level of the structures of languages but only at the moment of their consumption; the author cannot predict Tmesis: he cannot choose to write *what will not be read*. And yet, it is the very rhythm of what is read and what is not read that creates the pleasure of the great narratives: has anyone ever read Proust, Balzac, *War and Peace*, word for word? (Proust's good fortune: from one reading to the next, we never skip the same passages.)[21]

Only the lover is caught in the act of discourse, in figures articulated according to varying moods, hours, places, memories—the need to integrate them being specifically absent; as though a lover could discourse upon what love is finally. If we still need to ask what made Barthes write, we should see in our own question nothing else than a sign of fatigue that the writer does not know: writing made him write, as love makes a lover talk. He was feminized by writing, wore it like a wound: "A gentle hemorrhage which flows from no specific point in my body." As a writer he could double himself like an hermaphrodite and thereby solace his exclusion from the conjugalities of class, convention, and family. He became a lover-in-waiting, comparing himself to the window prostitutes of Hamburg and Amsterdam. Fragments like lovers have beginnings only: they do not tell of their end. Yet as a writer Barthes excluded himself through the force of a gift that he knew his lover could not embrace, like talk, which indeed touches the flesh directly without binding it to conventions of passion, sincerity, and desire. Writing, however, begins only with the lover's absence: therefore he made himself mother and child of his own desire in order to bear the wound of a lover writing:

> Faced with the death of his baby son, in order to write (if only scraps of writing), Mallarmé submits himself to parental division:
>
>> Mère, pleure
>> Moi, je pense.
>>
>> Mother, weep
>> While I think.
>
> But the amorous relation has made me into an atopical subject—undivided: I am my own child: I am both mother and father (of myself, of the other): how would I divide the labour?[22]

The writer can no more live with a passive reader than with a passive lover; the writerly text demands to be manhandled, misread, fragmented, and rewritten, step-by-step, from any point and always open to digressions.

In S/Z Barthes pluralizes a text of Balzac. In other words, he overwhelms the paternal and proprietary culture of the classical text in a riot of reading/writing that rushes in on the text from all sides, thereby destroying its orderly confrontation. Barthes's plural readings require the fragmentary method, chopping up the sacred text into any number of *lexias,* which then function to tell a story like an astrological reading that cannot be told without one body perusing another, fragments of life furnishing fragments of meanings from day to day.[23] Thus a text can no more be sensibly read as a whole than it would make sense to read one's horoscope for the year, rather than to read oneself into it according to one's moods, hopes, and fears—for the fun of it, even—but daily, since the sense of each fragment, like a haiku, lies in what we bring to it, not in its relation to other fragments. The horoscope is therefore an autoscope; and the self is not read otherwise than from day to day. Reading therefore does not deliver our lives; it is living that makes us readers. Once our readings are free from the practices of totalization, unity, and survey, we are at liberty to read things together in our own fashion. Hence Barthes can collect Sade, Fourier, and Loyola despite their differences and without benefit of any conventional colligation. In each figure, Barthes treats the text as a pretext for challenging interpretative stereotypes that otherwise function to censor the underlying literary joy in the Ignatian, Fourierist, and Sadean texts whereby they achieve coexistence:

> Reading texts and not books, turning upon them a clairvoyance not aimed at discovering their secret, their "contents," their philosophy, but merely their *happiness of writing*, I can hope to release Sade, Fourier, Loyola from their bonds (religion, utopia, sadism); I attempt to dissipate or elude the moral discourse that has been held on each of them; working, as they themselves worked only on languages, I unglue the text from its purpose as a guarantee: socialism, faith, evil, whence (at least such is the theoretical intent of these studies) I force the displacement (but not to suppress; perhaps even to accentuate) of the text's social responsibility.[24]

Barthes's literary subversions displace the pleasures of the social contract—security, house, province, family—indeed, the pleasures of classical culture. His literary criticism therefore upsets the established, progressive history of literary monuments. Its goal is to restore the body of literature to its blissful exercise by destroying the myth of the disembodied reader/writer whose pleasure is returned through the observance of our cultural dualisms of male/female, mind/body, power/weakness. Hence his fascination with the transitional, the neither/nor, with tenderness, grace, charm, childhood, between vanity and lucidity. And so throughout *S/Z* the sexual constellations revolving around the castrato La Zambinella are starred for the story's fortune, its reversals of shape, grammar, and discourse, whose instability foretells the death of Sarrasine while serving the narrator with a necessary delaying device with which to thicken, suspend, and finally deliver his story. In this way, the storyteller exchanges desire for a body with desire for the textual body, each receiving the other's wound.

The textual body fascinates with a promised but undeliverable unity, like the arms, legs, eyes, hair of the striptease artist who never goes beyond a ritual of fetishized gestures.[25] The reality she promises us, like that of literature, is the splendid deception of the man/woman, La Zambinella, more beautiful than any woman—even in the eyes of women. With truth and beauty, the desire to abide with the spectacle is stronger than the rationalist striptease, whatever philosophers think. To see things truly and beautifully is to see truth and beauty; for disappointment is always on hand, and more easily entertained. The castrato, being castrated, reveals not his own condition (who cannot identify with a limited being?) but the excessive condition of the woman beyond men-and-women whom both love (can so love themselves) to love. Hence the spectacle of La Zambinella frightened by a snake. We love her, and when we can no longer be deceived by her, we shall die, like Sarrasine, or go home.

The fragmentary method pursued by Barthes pushes reading and writing into the closest possible relation. It is a risk that has fascinated several remarkable writers. It should be noted that Barthes's alphabetical table of contents plays on Flaubert's *Dictionary of Received Ideas*. It may also be worthwhile, then, to speculate on Barthes's fragmentary method as an exercise in which he played his own Bouvard to Pecuchet, lovingly tying reading to writing and writing to reading, thereby turning the world into a library, or a single copybook. The encyclopedic labors of Bouvard and Pecuchet, like Flaubert's own unremitting labor in the research for his work, destroy the realistic version of knowledge by pushing it to its logical extreme: removing choice and composition in deference to the authority of realist science.[26] The chimera of organized knowledge turns into the fantasia of the library as a labyrinth of internal references from which the reader cannot retrieve his steps.[27] Indeed, in Jorge Luis Borges's reflections on this theme the reader might as well be blind:

> In my eyes there are not days. The shelves stand very high, beyond the reach of my years, and leagues of dust and sleep around the tower. Why go on deluding myself? The truth is that I never learned to read, but it comforts me to think that what's imaginary and what's past are the same to a man whose life is nearly over, who looks out from his tower on what was once city and now turns back to wilderness.[28]

Like the modern university, the library externalizes the world's knowledge, but is incapable of generating the creative subjects it dooms to wander through its texts, except as they retreat into photocopying. Paradoxically, these literary clones are indeed guilty of plagiarism, if by that we understand reproduction without the bodily labor and love of the copyist. The latter may seem more foolhardy. Yet he is the model for Flaubert, for Barthes, and for Borges, each superficially repeating himself and others without end; each wasting efforts on works that might be judged below their literary and scientific talents. But this is less likely, if we give a moment's reflection to the demonic side of writing. I have in mind the desperation quickened by fitting fragments to a whole; to a chapter, to a book; to the next book. The anxiety in modern writing does not derive from its concern with the achievement of realism but rather from the mirroring of the text as intertext, like the self's discovery of its intrinsically othering mirror image.[29] The book that opens up the world opens up the world of books. For a while, sainthood surrenders to ignorance and stupidity multiplies. But Bouvard and Pecuchet learn not to learn from their reading and joyously return to themselves—copyists twinned in the pleasures of the text.[30]

Like Flaubert, Barthes wished to destroy the concept of literature as a museum by dissolving its archeological presuppositions, its placement of texts according to genre, specimen, and period.[31] His study of Racine, in particular, challenged the literary establishment by shifting the temporality of texts out of the literary museum into the lived time of the literary body, whose thematics are opposed to the official anthropocentrism of the cultural establishment. Thus, while Barthes's fragments superficially resemble the fragments of the museum, they are radically indifferent to its chronology and catalog. They are rather morsels or tidbits, things cherished in the literary corpus, to be enjoyed by the reader/writer as one body enjoys another.

In the modern period language is sharply divided between prose and poetry.[32] This division reflects the struggle between art and society, between pleasure and utility; it serves the liberation of literary production. Its danger, however, is that it easily turns over into the literary alienation of art for art's sake. Alternatively, it may be employed to turn the study of literary production to the embodied work of reading and writing, and to the patient effort of integrating literary labor with literary pleasure. Here we witness the metamorphoses of "man" and "woman" writer—of homotextuality and gynema—with a limit, we would argue, in the embodied grounds of literary praxis: a "man" or "woman" becoming reading-and-writing. Thus, as we have seen, Barthes never separated the text from its corporeal thematics, its radical biography. Though without privilege—being a familied body—the literary body is the theater stage on which the totalitarian and subversive powers of language and poetry are played out.

In this struggle, the sketch, phase, fragment, parenthesis, and unfinished work clings to life, to the renewable body, rejecting the literary monument, the literary corpse of received ideas, motive, character. In this conflict the fragment as used by Barthes does not destroy the body of literature; it renders it polymorphous, pleasurable, at once readerly and writerly, coproductive of literary community. Ultimately, therefore, Barthes escapes the intransitivity to which poetry is condemned through the simple contrast with prosaic reference.[33] The bodily praxis of literature is inconceivable on the theory that the author is wholly metamorphosed into the writer. This is the old ghost returned to the word machine. Rather, all language is half prose, half poetry, like the embodied soul whose emblem it is. No central, official self, to be sure. Yet not totally empty. Embodied, moved, fixed, drifting, androgyne, prostitute, lover, writer. Like Montaigne earlier, Barthes disclaimed any literary strength or scholarly endurance. He could demean himself as little better than a copyist, without voice or center, a literary eunuch. Yet Barthes never surrendered to the literary system. He remained an outsider in the way a child must live outside his mother's body, fascinated. No other incorporation, no other patrimony ever removed him from this margin. Even when he chose a lover, he remained on the outside of a body he knew writing could never possess. All of his other bodies, drifting in literary promiscuity, were flights from our uterine body, expectant, faithful:

(As a child, I didn't forget: Interminable days, abandoned days, when [the] Mother was working far away; I would go, evenings, to wait for her at the Ubis bus stop, Sèvres-Babylone; the buses would pass one after the other, she wasn't in any of them.)[34]

CHAPTER 17

Vico Mit Freude Rejoyced
A Primal Reading

True there was in nillohs dieybos as yet no lumpend papeer in the waste
and mightmountain Penn still groaned for the micies to let flee. All was
of ancientry. You gave me a boot (signs on it!) and I ate the wind. I
quizzed you a quid (with for what!) and you went to the quod. But the
world, mind, is, was and will be writing its own wrunes for ever, man,
on all matters that fall under the ban of our infrarational senses.

—James Joyce[1]

Vico, Joyce, and Freud constitute a glad company of jubiliant somatol-
ogists (scientists of the infrarational senses), awakening the world's
sleeping history to the body's dance down from the mountaintops,
out of the primal forest into the familied self, all civil, murderous,
and sinful. In Freud, our history begins in the infantile body struggling
with pleasure and pain, incestuous and patricidal, without the circumcisions of law and language that signify the *logos* of self and
society written into the flesh. In Joyce, the world's body is as old as
in Vico it once was young. In Joyce, too, the family is the discontent
of our civilization and of ourselves, to paraphrase Freud. In Vico, the
family is the sensuous form of our civilization, the first bond of our
divinity and the continuous history of our incorporation outside the
mind of the mind. Thus, Vico and Joyce may also be compared in
Freud's vision of the history and civilization of our carnal knowledge,
steeped in murder and castration, or those dreams without which the
gods overwhelm our humanity and deprive us of the sublimations of
family. This, then, will serve us for our scene of writing in which the
copulations of Vico/Joyce, of Joyce/Freud, of Freud/Vico are read in
triads each of the other, that is, as each other's race and ruin.

So let us assume that if Vico influenced Joyce, he did so happily;
that is, by circumstance. By the same trope, we may assume that if
Joyce has any influence on Vico, it is we who are its circumstance.
This is so because neither Vico nor Joyce—and in virtue of them,
we ourselves—consider language anything else than the beneficent
milieu of our life and civil institutions. Vico and Joyce are our fore-

bears because they lifted language upon itself, tearing it from the settled tropes of rationalism and realism, separating it from the authority of its traditional receptions in philosophy, religion, science, and literature, as well as in the church, state, and family. They overturned language by turning it upon itself, bringing forth enlightened reason from the poetic bodies of Vico's giants, and in Joyce's night poetry rewriting the world's body in anybody's everybody eating, dreaming, loving, repeating world without end the dream body's beginnings.

> Our wholemole millwheeling vicociclometer, a tetradomational gazebocroticon (the "Mamma Lujah" known to every schoolboy scandaller, be he Mattey, Markey, Lukey or John-a-Donk), autokinatonetically preprovided with a clappercoupling smeltingworks exprogressive process (for the farmer, his son and their homely codes, known as eggburst, eggblend, eggburial and hatch-as-hatch can) receives through a portal vein the dialytically separated elements of precedent decomposition for the verypetpurpose of subsequent recombination so that the heroticisms, catastrophes and eccentricities transmitted by the ancient legacy of the past, type by tope, letter from litter, word at ward, with sendence of sundance, since the days of Plooney and Columcellas when Giacinta, Pervenche and Margaret swayed over all-too-ghoulish and illyrical and innumantic in our mutter nation, all, anastomosically assimilated and preteridentified paraidiotically, in fact, the sameold gamebold adomic structure of our Finnius the old One, as highly charged with electrons as hophazards can effective it, may be there for you, Cockalooralooraloomenos, when cup, platter and pot come piping hot, as sure as herself pits hen to paper and there's scribings scrawled on eggs. (FW 614–15)

Vico and Joyce are twin poets and like-minded because they assumed the world's incarnation, slipping past divinities without a human face, into the forests, along rivers, out to the open cycle of the sea-sky into the thundering, rain-driven waters of life. All the same and all the difference between the two poets, there is a family resemblance explored by each as dayside and nightside of the world's incorporation. Thus in Vico the family is the content of civilization. In the recollection of birth, marriage, and death, the beginnings, middlings, and endings of our bodies are civilized in a spectacle that draws the gods to mankind, anthropomorphizing them and religiously binding them to the civil institutions of mankind, while man-shaping all of nature in the civic languages of beauty, order, truth, and justice. Like Freud, Vico's familization of world history humbles the conceits of rationalist philosophy and theology with the first poetry of those awkward sensate bodies whose language shone beyond the beasts and flora, turning the thunderous crack of the sky into Jove's voice. Before such poetry there is neither divinity nor humanity. All our civility is therefore beholden to those self-fearing giants who tamed their monstrous bodies in the institutions of civil speech, giving to themselves laws, customs, religion, ritual, and myth, seeding the sky with signs in which they could interpret their own future humanity.

> In this fashion the first theological poets created the first divine fable, the greatest they ever created: that of Jove, king and father of men and gods, in the act of hurling the lightning bolt; an image so popular, disturbing, and instructive that its creators themselves believed in it, and feared, revered, and worshipped it in frightful religions. . . . They believed that Jove commanded by signs, that such signs were real words, and that nature was the language of Jove. The science of this language the gentiles universally believed to be divination, which by the Greeks was called theology, meaning the science of the language of the gods. . . .
>
> That such was the origin of poetry is finally confirmed by this eternal property of it: that its proper material is the credible impossibility. It is impossible that bodies should be minds, yet it was believed that the thundering sky was Jove.[2]

In Joyce, the world is weary, repetitive, and rotten like an old body. Its authority is empty and ridiculous, like the church, the state, and the army. The world's philosophers, theologians, artists, and scientists are divided against themselves just as murderously as the madmen of nationalism and racism. Like a silted river sunk upon itself, unable to breathe or to spawn and find the open sea, life itself is unsure of its course. Men and women eke out their days in small places and in times that weigh on the heart and the mind in senseless repetitions of authority without creation. Joyce himself is the great exile from such a world. Yet no one has done more to attach himself to its banality or to spin out its great platitudes in such art that one can hardly think outside of its nonsense. Joyce's exile makes us all Dubliners, all figures in a tavern keeper's history of "everybody you anywhere." In Joyce, prose and poetry rub shoulders like the people he saw in the pubs, courthouses, churches, and whorehouses of Dublin. To capture such a parade of palaver, Joyce had to turn the world's voice into a self-sounding script, beginning without a beginning and ending with no end.

> There's where. First. We pass through grass behush the bush to. Whish! A gull. Gulls. Far calls. Coming, far! End here. Us then. Finn, again! Take. Bussortlhee, mememormee! Till thousandsthee. Lps. The keys to. Given! A way a lone a last a loved a long the riverrun, past Eve and Adam's, from swerve of shore to bend of bay, brings us by a commodius vicus of recirculation back to Howth Castle and Environs. (*FW*, 628–3)

Like Vico, Joyce pushed the question of origins-and-ends up the great Nile of language, mythology, and religion, dredging in the rivers of memory and the sandscripts of time for the first signs of self and civilization. Thus, Howth Castle environs (HCE) is the surrounding of the beginning without ending of the ending without beginning of everything in the lives of Molly and Bloom. It is the setting for Bloom and Gerty's distant-desire, and of the eternal ebb and flow of love and sorrow in the hearts of the men at church who pray for peace and consolation to the Virgin Mary, Star of the Sea. HCE is properly a Viconian *topos,* that is, a place in which men and women are the self-fashioned circumstance of their own sense and nonsense. As such, HCE is variously self, place, history, self's other, and other as self. Hence, HCE tropes upon Everyman, the Christ figure, the father figure, Joyce's own figure, and everybody since the Fall into the sense and sintalk of language.

> The fall (bababadalgharaghtakamminarronkonnbronntonnerronntuonn-thunntrovarrh ounawnskawntoohoohoordenenthurnuk!) of a once wall-strait oldparr is retaled early in bed and later on life down through all christian minstrelsy. The great fall of the offwall entailed at such short notice the pitjschute of Finnegan, erse solid man, that the humptyhillhead of humself promptly sends an unquiring one well to the west in quest of his tumptytumtoes: and their upturnpikepointandplace is at the knock out in the park where oranges have been laid to rust upon the green since devlinsfirst loved livvy. (*FW*, 3)

Vico's first men were giants of their own poetry forged from their own fearful bodies. They gave us the voices of the gods, vulgar tongues, civil mythologies, and that universal dictionary of the human mind from which we construct all our later arts and sciences. Because our giant ancestors thought the world with their bodies, as do small children, they were obliged to see the world's construction in terms of a religious poetry whose vulgar metaphysics gave to God the power of their own ignorance of things otherwise. They thereby lifted their fear and ignorance from the earth in order to be ruled by heavenly divinities and by kings and heroes whose power over them bound them to the first stages of civilized life.

> The most sublime labor of poetry is to give sense and passion to insensate things; and it is characteristic of children to take inanimate things in their hands and talk to them in play as if they were living persons. This philologico-philosophical axiom proves to us that in the world's childhood men were by nature sublime poets (*NS* 186–187)

Suffer now Vico's little children to come to Freud. By what axioms of linguistic psychoanalysis does the helpless infant theorist bring his discontents to civilization? By little cries he learns to rejoin the giant mother's breast coming and going from himself, separating pleasure and pain, self and unself, world-inside and world outside.[3] Then by tying the mother-body to a string, to throw and catch away joy and misery in a game of self-mastery—*Fort! Da!* Here, then, in the cradle of civilization, the infantile sexual theorist separates self from love's oceans, and turns against the breasts of the earth to stand erect in the cracked mirror of himself. Thus, once outside the womb, the world's children had to learn to shelter themselves and to protect themselves from the violence of nature and one another. Needing therefore to amplify their own organs, the young men discovered fire-based technology by imiting the infantile pleasure they took at extinguishing their first fires in piddling wars. They thereby laid the foundations of hearth and home, marrying themselves to women, cooking, and children.

> It is as though primal man had the habit, when he came in contact with fire, of satisfying an infantile desire connected with it; by putting it out with a stream of his urine. The legends that we possess leave no doubt about the originally phallic view taken of tongues of flame—a theme to which western giants, Gulliver in Lilliput and Rabelais' Gargantua, still hark back—was therefore a kind of sexual act with a male, an enjoyment of sexual potency in a homosexual competition. The first person to renounce this desire and spare the fire was able to carry it off with him and subdue it to his own use. By damping down the fire of his own sexual excitation, he had tamed the natural force of fire. This great cultural conquest was thus the reward for this renunciation of instinct. Further, it is as though woman had been appointed guardian of the fire which

was held captive on the domestic hearth, because her anatomy made it impossible for her to yield to the temptation of this desire.[4]

But the young boys had yet another lesson to learn in order to civilize their instincts for "penisolate war" and to favor exchange of the phallus with and for the ladies, making homes and making babies. To familize their homosexual desires, the young men had to educate their sense of smell. On the one hand, they had to learn to be disgusted by their own excreta and, on the other hand, to treat menstruation with the same abhorrence. Thus, by learning to repress their anal eroticism and to find the female clean only out of menstruation, the young men were recruited to heterosexual lovemaking with impregnable girls, thereby strengthening the religious bond of family and fertility.

Freud's speculations on the civilizational reshaping of the primal bodies of the world's children deepen Vico's civil reconstruction of the stages of anthropomorphism that reshaped our giant ancestors. The difference between Freud and Vico is that Freud derives society from lawless bodies, as their second nature, whereas Vico argues that society was natural to the first humans, whose feelings, minds, and bodies were so divinely disposed that our humanity and all its civil institutions could develop from them. Vico argues that it is a rationalist conceit that our ancestors were lawless, unbridled creatures. Rather, they were disposed from the beginning to impose a powerful rule over themselves, so that it is only in later stages of society that humans become disordered creatures of vice, cruelty, and sickness. Thus, the first humans, huge and grotesque like the cyclopes," imposed on themselves almighty gods and patriarchs to bring themselves into the family state and to lay the ground for the city-state and its aristocratic families, led by proud and magnanimous men like Achilles, or such brave and just men as Aristides and Scipio Africanus. We can see, therefore, that all later humanity is beholden to those primal creatures who bound themselves to the rites of religion, marriage, and burial, celebrating the cycle of fertility in nature and ourselves, thereby bringing sexuality of the bestial wilderness into civil society. Moreover, the first humans achieved their domestication without divine intelligence of things but in virtue of a "wholly corporeal imagination." This means that it was their bodies that served them as the self-shaping institution of civility, which, because of their sensible disposition, in turn disposed them toward a pragmatic poetry whose first tasks were:

To invent sublime fables suited to the popular understanding;
To perturb to excess, with a view to the end proposed;
To teach the vulgar to act virtuously, as the poets have taught themselves.
(*NS* 376)

Our giant poets, then, first conceived of the world as a great body in which all smaller bodies are generated and divided according to the self-proliferating imagery of the body's metaphorical language. With such poetry our god-fearing ancestors tamed themselves and the wild beasts into domesticity, and moved the very stones to turn themselves into the walls of Thebes.

These were the stones which Deucalion and Pyrrha, standing before the temple of Themis (that is, in the fear of divine justice) with veiled heads (the modesty of marriage), found lying before their feet (for men were at first stupid, and *lapis,* stone, remained Latin for a stupid person) and threw over their shoulders (introducing family institutions by means of household discipline), thus making men of them. (NS 523)

Before the founding of the civil institution of the family, our forebears could not have assumed our present human shape. Thus, divine providence ordained that they first roamed the earth as giants suited to the wilderness and only after they had settled in caves, and then in huts, cultivating the fields and a settled population, could they assume the proper shape of humankind. Here, however, Vico's story is all too civil, and we must turn to Freud for the missing murderous link that binds our past and future history in consciousness of sin. Thus, we recollect that our primal father hoarded wives and excluded his sons from manhood. Brothered by their love and hatred of their father's power and cruelty, the sons bonded together to murder him, sharing his wives with their guilt. Having consummated patricide and incest in a sacrificial meal of the father's body, torn "limb from lamb," the sons acquired a collective conscience without which the laws of the family and the state would be constantly undermined. For humans are not law-abiding because they have a conscience. Rather the opposite is true; humans have a conscience because they are lawbreakers. Thus, Freud's great discovery of the bloody formation of primal conscience must be added to Vico's civil account of the giant bodies whose civil imaginations first shaped us.

> One day the brothers who had been driven out came together, killed and devoured their father and so made an end of the patriarchal horde. United, they had the courage to do and succeeded in doing what would have been impossible for them individually. (Some cultural advance, perhaps, command over some new weapon, had given them a sense of superior strength.) Cannibal savages, as they were, it goes without saying that they devoured their victim as well as killing him. The violent primal father had doubtless been the feared and envied model of each one of the company of brothers: and in the act of devouring him they accomplished their identification with him, and each one acquired a portion of his strength. The totem meal, which is perhaps mankind's earliest festival, would thus be a repetition and a commemoration of this memorable and criminal deed, which was the beginning of so many things—of social organizations, of moral restriction and of religion.[5]

In Joyce's creation all authority begins well but degenerates into dreadful patriarchy, lechery, incest, and exploitation. Thus, parent and child become the scene of one another's crimes, each devouring the other, in accordance with Freud's "eatupus complex" (FW, 128). The father must be murdered if the mother's sons are to survive and life to go on, remembering him.

> His Thing Mod have undone him: and his madthing has done him man. His beneficiaries are legion in the part he created: they number up his years. Greatwheel Dunlop was the name was on him: behung, all we are his bisaacles. As hollyday in his house so was he priest and king so that: ulvy came, envy saw, ivy conquered. Lou! Lou! They have waved his green boughs o'er him as they have torn him limb from lamb. For his muerification and uxpiration and dumnation and annuhulation (FW 58).

HCE goes falling through history, his murder tumbling language over itself, setting the Viconian cycle spinning through is "muertification and uxpiration and dumnation and annuhulation." At the same time, Joyce's translation of the fall into a history of patricide and degenerate sexual pratfalls is reflected in the internal structure of his language, spelling, and syntax. The Joycean family generates a history of guilt that can be retold from any point in the history of anyone, of any authority, at any age and in any place. The story itself is never-ending, because after the Fall language has lost its closure. Like HCE's stammer, our language is forever separated from pristine reality and never again can anything be named according to its divinity. Separated from the face of God, his children are condemned to spy on the primal scene, hoping thereby to discover their origins.

> Pharoah with fairy, two lie, let them! yet they wend it back, qual his lief, himmertality, bullseaboob and rivishy divil, light in hand, helm on high, to peekaboo durk the thicket of slumbwhere, till their hour with their scene be struck for every and the book of the dates be close, he clasp and she and she seegn her tout d'adieu, Pervinca calling. Soloscar hears. (O Sheem! O Shaam!), and gentle Isad Ysut gag, flispering in the nightleaves flattery, dinsiduously, to Finnegan, to sin again and to make grim grandma grunt and grin again while the first grey streaks steal silvering for to mock their quarrels in dollymount tumbling (*FW*, 580)

In the postlapsarian world, language and identity separate forever despite the realist fictions of civilization, family, and property. Vico's enormous insight is to have seen that patriarchy civilizes male and female sexuality and provides identity where there would only be promiscuity. Thus, patricide and incest are figures of disorder, horrible to speak because their very names upset the symbolic order whose authority derives from the father. In Joyce and Freud, Vico's great civilizational insight is undone as a permanent human achievement; it must be reappropriated as a personal myth reenacted in everyone's family, in a tale without end so long as anyone anywhere abides. Meantime, all our talk is errant, wandering and in error, forever trying to join sin to sense, like the *Wake* itself, or Freud's own incomplete case histories.

We are assembling a theory of civilization whose complex inscription is the work of language, tools, and bodies gathered in civil institutions and rituals that have opened up an unending cycle of life, labor, and language. Vico, Joyce, and Freud are the principal theorists of this civil grammatology in which we have rewritten ourselves. From them we learn that civilization is the work of language and tools which open and honor the earth's fertility as love opens a woman and honors her maternity. For this reason, men settle in marriage and gather their families religiously in rituals that celebrate the fertility of their women, crops, and animals, as well as their own virility. Just as the first men were sky writers, so they were also concerned to write upon nature. Horticulture and agriculture are therefore elements of our primal grammatology, each playing on the difference of male and female, earth and sky, of dilation and enclosure.

A terricolous vivelyonview this; queer and it continues to be quaky. A hatch, a celt, an earshare the pourquose of which was to cassay the earthcrust at all of hours, furrowards and bagawards, like yoxen at the turnpaht (FW, 18).

So the human race could not have spread itself without the miscege- nation of the world fourfolding in the allaphbed of HCE. Divinely, heroically, and demotically recycled in the nick of the name, Here Comes Everybody, we may unearth the very elements of this civil grammatology:

A *hatch:* the tool; language as a tool
A *celt:* a primitive chisel; the Celtic language
An *earshare:* the ploughshare; opening and seeding the earth; "for the lands ploughed at that time were the first altars of the world." (NS, 549)

Turning still, HCE tumbles and falls like Humpty Dumpty all down history, as egg, primate father, son, city, a holy and unholy stam- mering of sense and sin. Wanderer, profligate, builder, procreator, pervert, HCE is the phallic monument, "the fanest of our truefalluses" (FW, 506) that must stand and must fall, as families stand and fall in their own turn.[6]

E A man, erect, King of the Castle; falling to
E A monument, long ago the place of fertility rites, the penal jail of Mountjoy, or into
E An insect upon its back, an earwig, kicking helplessly at the air—at its former erection and fertility

Everyman, by Shem and Shaun, and Everywoman repeats this cycle of erection, falling, and death, as does all of nature, all of history. The seed of this cycle is life itself, its plurability, self-impregnating and self-destructing. The figure of this cycle may be read everywhere in nature. It is a figure with two sides of the same. By the same token, Anna Livia Plurabelle (ALP) may be designated as an isosceles triangle $\triangle$, or as the letter Delta, the rich alluvial tract at the mouth of the river, source of teeming life.[7] The ALP mother's skirts also hide the vulva, ∇, source of wonder, origin of the arts and sciences of self-inquiry. Shem and Shaun, as "daughtersons" of HCE and ALP, are, respectively, less than E, the city founder, and △, the creative mother. Thus, Shaun is closer to E but without his sexual energy—[—a politician without a penis. Shem the artist is repulsed by E and drawn to △ but lacks her solid bottom—∧. Merry, marry all these signs!

In Joyce, the world goes round with the word to become flesh, sinned into sense like the lamb of God, *agnus dei qui tollis peccata mundi,* to forgive our sins wordloosed over the seven seas, over the seven hills, the seven cardinals of vice and virtue. Everybody falls, falling, but to nowhere in language, to no center, no line, no man, no woman, no child, no king, no court, no church, no bed, no sense but word-sense wafted like incense up and away into the nonsense of it all. Heaven falling from monkey to man, from hieroglyph to alphabet, from Hellas to Ireland, from north men to south men, from quantity to quality, from truth to untruth—all our continuities are originally "a sham and a low shame"—but not apart from the penman's forge, self-signed dirt of self-creation. Thus, Joyce forges his own self-text, stealing but never expropriating the languages of the world, making them into his own body, his own tongue and talk in cheek, like food and drink disgustingly transubstantiated into the Christ-body of everybody's unheavenly body.

HIC EST ENIM CORPUS MEUM

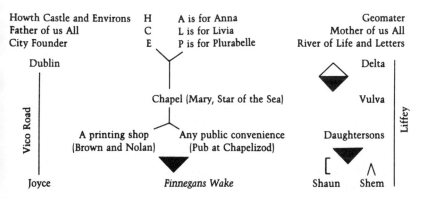

Fig. 17.1. Hic est enim corpus meum

292 • SYMPTOMATIC TEXTS

Then, pious Eneas, conformant to the fulminant firman which enjoins on the tremylose terrian that, when the call comes, he shall produce nichthemerically from his unheavenly body a no uncertain quantity of obscene matter not protected by copriright in the United Stars of Ourania or bedeed and bedood and bedang and bedung to him, with this double dye, brought to blood heat, gallic acid on iron ore, through the bowels of his misery, flashly, faithly, nastily, appropriately, this Esuan Menschavik and the first till last alshemist wrote over every square inch of the only foolscap available, his own body, till by its corrosive sublimation one continuous present tense integrument slowly unfolding all marryvoising mood-moulded cyclewheeling history (thereby, he said, reflecting from his own individual person life unlivable, transaccidentated through the slow fires of consciousness into a dividual chaos, perilous, potent, common to all-flesh, human only, mortal) but with each word that would not pass away the squidself which he had squirt-screened from the crystalline world waned chagreenold and doriangrayer in its dudhud. This exists and isits after having been said we know. (*FW*, 185–86)

In Joyce, our scatology turns into eschatology in order to recreate God's dirt, to turn bread and wine into godsbody, to reinscribe the cycles of urination, defecation, and copulation in the world's most sacred body of literature, that is, in the soundscript common to all flesh, human only, mortal, to be sure, yet whose song does not pass away. How did our forefathers fall, then? And where to in what language did they call to one another in their fall? It is an old story, the same old story, the same for its sin, sinned the same to make the same old city, and river run from father to son, echoing. In Joyce, the Viconian and Freudian cycles of language, law, and mythology are reinscribed in the lifecycle of love, corruption, death, and rebirth lived by each of us in a simple moment of daydreaming, or in the unfathomable nightspeech of unconscious sleep. The kings and heroes of history, the gods and goddesses of the mythical past, turn "collideorscopically" in the evershifting bits and pieces of talk and tale told by anyone on any occasion at all. The imaginative unity sustaining the Viconian and Joycean cycles—as in Freud—is a vision of the alternating currents of the body thinking itself as mind and of the mind's constant reembodiment. Thus, the mind and the body love one another and each engenders the other like parent and lover. This is how God loves Himself. It is also how the most ordinary living is made great in each of us.

It is the artist who is the figurative type of this great split and copulation in the world's body and spirit. Stephen Dedalus as a young artist has not to make a portrait of himself but to acquire a body. Stephen's reincarnation makes his self-portrait possible because the body is the universal image, the portrait of anyone. That is the solution to the sphinx's riddle—without a body, a man is nobody. Amen. By the same token, it is only in love's body that the artist can leave the virgin womb of his imagination. To skirt the guardian Scylla and Charybdis separating mind and body, in order to father and mother himself, Dedalus must be deflowered in order to blossom in artful imitation of nature's self-rejoicing cycle of love and unlove, of "earth's fatigue made grave approach."[8] Later, it is in Bloom's body, all dream and flowering mind, that the cycle of world history is caught in a Dublin day, waking, eating, walking, drinking, talking, pissing, and ejaculating upon the great mysteries of our faith in one another. Bloom's walk around the city is a walk around himself and around the world. Remember. At the sea's edge, between bay and promontory, between life and death, the men gather in mother church to pray to Mary, Star of the Sea, virgin protector of the drunken sailor whoring the world's women. Outside the same church, its prayers rising to the Blessed Virgin, Bloom and Gerty MacDowell join land and sea in their body's desire, rising, Bloom's preying answering, answering to a maidenhood's prayer, until each explodes in the other like the Roman candles in the summer sky. These two, then, breathless within the breathless crowd, stargazing, each in each, wrapt in the body's communion, coming into one another at a prayerful distance, in she-opening, himlooking celebration of the mystery—*Hic est enim corpus meum:*

And she saw a long Roman candle going up over the trees up, up, and, in the tense hush, they were all breathless with excitement as it went higher and higher and she had to lean back more and more to look after it, high, high, almost out of sight, and her face was suffused with a divine, an entrancing blush from straining back and he could see her other things too, nainsook knickers, the fabric that caresses the skin, better than those other pettiwidth, the green, four and eleven, on account of being white and she let him and she saw that he saw and then it went so high it went out of sight a moment and she was trembling in every limb from being bent back so far back he had a full view high up above her knee no-one ever not even on the swing or wading and she wasn't ashamed and he wasn't either to look in that immodest way like that because he couldn't resist the sight of the wondrous revealment half offered like those skirt-dancers behaving so immodest before gentlemen looking and he kept on looking, looking. She would fain have cried to him chokingly, held out her snowy slender arms to him to come, to feel his lips laid on her white brow the cry of a young girl's love, a little strangled cry, wrung from her, that cry that has rung through the ages. And then a rocket sprang and bank shot blind and O! then the Roman candle burst and it was like a sigh of O! and everyone cried O! in raptures and it gushed out of it a stream of rain gold hair threads and they shed and ah! they were all greeny dewey stars falling with golden, O so lovely! O so soft, sweet, soft![9]

Bloom, then, worships at the shrine of Gerty MacDowell, hoping to receive her body and blessing like the sailors at the Benediction in the Star of the Sea church, each upon each building castles in the sand, to make the very earth dream it shall not pass away. Nor is there any outsider's fetish in these blessings, statues, flowers, and knickers of our Lady among the kiddies and the candles. For Gerty is not without poetry any more than old Bloom is without a bit of the artist. While Gerty's youth yearns for uniqueness and Bloom's age thirsts for repetition, the two are not opposites. Bloom insists on a sort of communion with Gerty—"Still it was a kind of language between us."[10] He can guess that Gerty is in her cycle and that someday her daydreams will lead her in the family way and nightly to the rest of life's repetitions. In turn, this reminds him of his marriage with Molly and her magnetic attraction for other men, whom Bloom helps on their way like the good Samaritan. Even sleeping at opposite ends of the earth, Bloom and Molly are joined in a single bed and body of wisdom "expressed in the words *because, bottom* (in all senses bottom button, bottom of the class, bottom of the sea, bottom of his heart), *woman, yet,*"[11] that are spun out in the eight great sentences that tie Molly's birthday to Our Lady's birthday and Bloomsday to every day—*copula felix!*

Bloom is the divine nobody. His daydreams repeat Vico's cycle of history as father-and-son cycles of sin, corruption, copulation, ignorance, and violence. Bloom's paternity is alternately certain and uncertain, kingly, heroic, demogogic, castrate, and meek as Christ on a breakfast tray. His thoughts are the timewarped and spacespun stars flung out of the world's mass of memory, dayfathered dubliners, night dreams flashed into the shining word—*Kyrie eleison!* Everything, everyone is carried along in the wake of these shameful thoughts drifting through the litter of the world's languages, in "singsigns to sound sense," miscegenating, marrying, muddying, *mutatis mutandis*. Bloom becomes Shem becomes Joyce the Plagiast Penman squid-squirting his "once current puns, quashed quotatoes, messes of mottage, unquestionable issue papers, seedy ejaculations, limerick damns, crocodile tears, spilt ink" (*FW*, 183).

Do not look, then, but listen now for Vico's resounding cycles of rise and fall, rejoiced in riverrun, wordloosed seas of imaginative birth and death. Sieved through the unconscious self-twinning of artist and philistine, into man and woman, into epicycles of logos and flesh, Vico's history of language has become a Joycean history of everybody who learns to listen to their body in order to see. From age to age, the world of language turns upon itself so long as love makes the world go round, from shore to shore, in tales transported by letter-litter of everyone, everywhere.

> (Stoop) if you are abcedminded, to this claybook, what curios of signs (please stoop), in this allaphbed! Can you rede (since We and Thou had it out already) its world? It is the same told of all. Many. Miscegenations on miscegenations. Tieckle. They lived und laughed ant loved end left. Forsin. (*FW*, 18)

Thus, Reason is returned to understanding the gestures of that sensuous language which first opened the field and family of sense and nonsense, and to that continuous history of literature, poetry, and music which is renewed in *Finnegans Wake*. To end, let us return to our beginning. What did we want when we started to read Vico in terms of Joyce and Freud? First of all, we had resolutely to set aside a reading of each according to the conventional canon. We did so because of a sense of family between Joyce and Vico, sufficiently explored, and even between Joyce and Freud, however refused.[12] Our decision to treat Vico, Joyce, and Freud as a literary family is nevertheless not willful. It produces a primal scene of interpretation constructed by treating Freud as a crib to the copulation of Vico and Joyce engendering the great body of history. In turn, this first scene may be varied so as to triangulate it from the side of Joyce and Vico, providing alternative insights into history's primal scene. We thereby ground interpretation in psychoanalysis as a domestic science first conceived by Vico and revisioned in Joyce and Freud. The question of origins is now seen as an inquiry from the infantile theorist addressed to the maternal body of history, source of life, language, and literature:

Subtend to me now! Pisk! Other serpumstances beiug ekewilled, we carefully, if she pleats, lift by her seam hem and jabote at the spidsiest of her trickkikant (like thousands done before since fillies calpered. Ocone! Ocone! the maidsapron of our ALP., fearfully! till its neither nadir is vortically where (allow me aright to two cute wrinkles) its naval's napex will have no beandbe. You must proach near mear for at its dark. Lob. And light your mech. Jeldy! (FW, 297)

From the self-heating world of matter (*mater*) sparked by the penile shaft redoubling the world's fever, there flows *inter faeces et urinas,* the river of life and language in which thoughts become gods and tots—and that's the start of all the difference before, behind, and between us.

Lok! A shaft of shivery in the act, anilanciant. Cold's sleuth! Vayuns! Where did thots come from? It is infinitesimally fevers, resty fever, risy fever, a coranto of aria, sleeper awakening, in the smalls of one's back presentiment, gip, and again, geip, a flash from a future of maybe maha-mayability through the windr of a wondr in a wildr is a weltr as a wirbl of a warbl is world. (FW, 597)

So we find in Vico, Freud, and Joyce a sacramental history of the world's first infant body, drawn from the primal forest to the primal scene. Such a history involves the reconstruction and recreation of the language of the world's first children to find in play and poetry that hinge of displacement and dilation from which the tale can be retold.

Begin to forget it. It will remember itself from every sides, with all gestures, in each our word. (FW, 614)

Notes

Chapter 1. On the Practice of Literary Politics

1. Richard Rorty, *Contingency, Irony, and Solidarity*, 45.
2. Ibid., 94.
3. Richard Rorty, "The Priority of Democracy to Philosophy," in *Reading Rorty: Critical Responses to* Philosophy and the Mirror of Nature (and Beyond), ed. Allan R. Malachowski (Oxford: Basil Blackwell, 1990), 293.
4. Barbara Herrnstein Smith, *Contingencies of Value: Alternate Perspectives for Critical Theory*, 149.
5. Ibid., pp. 183–184. Emphasis added.
6. Jeffrey L. Sammons, *Literary Sociology and Practical Criticism*.
7. Rorty, *Contingency*, 28.
8. Nancy Fraser, "Solidarity or Singularity? Richard Rorty between Romanticism and Technology," in *Unruly Practices: Power, Discourse, and Gender in Contemporary Social Theory*, 104. See also Edward Davenport, "The New Politics of Knowledge: Rorty's Pragmatism and the Rhetoric of the Human Sciences," *Philosophy of the Social Sciences* 17, no. 3 (September 1987): 377–94.
9. John O'Neill, *For Marx against Althusser, and Other Essays*.
10. David Carroll, *Paraesthetics: Foucault, Lyotard, Derrida*.
11. Jürgen Habermas, *The Philosophical Discourse of Modernity: Twelve Lectures*; John Rajchman, "Habermas's Complaint," *New German Critique* 45 (Fall 1988): 163–91.
12. Roland Barthes, "Science versus Literature," in *Introduction to Structuralism*, 413.
13. Maurice Merleau-Ponty, *Signs*, 59.
14. John O'Neill, *The Communicative Body: Studies in Communicative Philosophy, Politics, and Sociology*.
15. John O'Neill, *Sociology as a Skin Trade: Essays towards a Reflexive Sociology*.
16. O'Neill, *The Communicative Body*, part 2.
17. Susan R. Horton, "The Institution of Literature and the Cultural Community," in *Literary Theory's Future(s)*, 296.
18. "*Gynesis*—the putting into discourse of 'woman' as that *process* diagnosed in France as intrinsic to the condition of modernity; indeed, the valorization of the feminine, woman, and her obligatory, that is, historical connotations, as somehow intrinsic to new and necessary modes of thinking, writing, speaking. The object produced by this process is neither a person nor a thing, but a horizon, that toward which the process in tending: a *gynema*." Alice A. Jardine, *Gynesis: Configurations of Woman and Modernity*, 25.
19. Roland Barthes, *The Pleasure of the Text*, 14; my emphasis.

Chapter 2. Is There a Class in This Text?

1. Stanley Fish, *Is There a Text in This Class? The Authority of Interpretative Communities*; Fish, *Doing What Comes Naturally: Change, Rhetoric, and the Practice of Theory in Literary and Legal Studies*, chap. 14, "Consequences."
2. James Atlas, "The Battle of the Books," *The New York Times Magazine*, 5 June 1988, 25; Terry Eagleton, "The Idealism of American Criticism," in *Against the Grain: Essays 1975-1985*; Frederick Crews, "Whose American Renaissance?" *The New York Review of Books*, 27 October 1988.
3. Robert Scholes, *Textual Power: Literary Theory and the Teaching of English*, 150.
4. On the nature of political foreclosure (to adapt Lacan's usage), see John O'Neill, "Sociological Nemesis: Parsons and Foucault on The Therapeutic Disciplines," in *Sociological Theory in Transition*, 21–35; Paul Lauter, "Race and Gender in the Shap-

ing of the American Literary Canon: A Case Study From the Twenties." *Feminist Studies* 9, no. 3 (Fall 1983): 435–63; Lauter, "Working-Class Women's Literature: An Introduction to Study," in *Women in Print*, 109–34; Gregory S. Jay, *America the Scrivener: Deconstruction and the subject of Literary History*, chap. 9, "The Subject of Pedagogy: Lessons in Psychoanalysis and Politics."

5. Jean-François Lyotard, *The Postmodern Condition: A Report on Knowledge*; for a careful critical evaluation, see Meaghan Morris, "Postmodernity and Lyotard's Sublime," *Art and Text* 16 (Summer 1984): 44–67.

6. Fish, *Doing What Comes Naturally*, 155–56.

7. Ibid., 553.

8. Stanley Fish, "Interpreting the Variorum," in *Reader-Response Criticism: From Formalism to Post-Structuralism*, ed. Jane P. Tompkins, 174.

9. Edward W. Said, *The World, The Text, and the Critic*.

10. Fredric Jameson, *The Political Unconscious: Narrative as a Socially Symbolic Act.*

11. Said, *The World, the Text, and the Critic*, 17–19.

12. John O'Neill, *Making Sense Together: An Introduction to Wild Sociology.* This work is republished in *The Communicative Body.*

13. Said, *The World, the Text, and the Critic*, 22.

14. Ibid., 23.

15. Ibid., 50–51.

16. Ibid., 229.

17. John O'Neill, *Plato's Cave: Desire, Power and the Specular Functions of the Media*; Geoffrey H. Hartmann, "Ghostlier Demarcations: The Sweet Science of Northrop Frye," in his *Beyond Formalism: Literary Essays 1958–1970*, 24–61.

18. Jameson, *The Political Unconscious*, 289.

19. Ibid., 290–91.

20. John O'Neill, *Five Bodies: The Human Shape of Modern Society.*

21. Jameson, *The Political Unconscious*, 74; see also Cornel West, "Ethics and Action in Fredric Jameson's Marxist Hermeneutics," in *Postmodernism and Politics*, 123–44.

22. Geoffrey H. Hartmann, *Criticism in the Wilderness: The Study of Literature Today.*

Chapter 3. Baudelairizing Postmodernism

1. Paul de Man, *Blindness and Insight: Essays in the Rhetoric of Contemporary Criticism*, 186.

2. Fredric Jameson, "Baudelaire as Modernist and Postmodernist: The Dissolution of the Referent and the Artificial 'Sublime,' " in *Lyric Poetry: Beyond New Criticism*, 247–65; Subsequent page references are noted parenthetically in the text.

3. Jean Baudrillard, "The Ecstasy of Communication," in Hal Foster, ed., *The Anti-Aesthetic: Essays on Postmodern Culture.*

4. For an exposition of a rival textual method than that used here, see Maurice Delcroix and Walter Gaerts, eds., *"Les Chats" de Baudelaire: Une Confrontation de methodes.*

5. Paul de Man, "Literary History and Literary Modernity," in *Blindness and Insight*, 142–65.

6. Walter Benjamin, "The Paris of the Second Empire in Baudelaire," in *Charles Baudelaire: A Lyric Poet in the Era of High Capitalism*, 79–80.

7. Charles Baudelaire, "Le Cygne," in *Les Fleurs du Mal*, 269 (91). Richard Howard's translation, *The Flowers of Evil*, was published by David R. Godine in 1982. The number in brackets refers to the English translation here and below.

8. See, for example, the review by Richard Sieburth in the *Yale Review*, winter, 1983, 263–72.

9. Baudelaire, *Les Fleurs du mal*, 239 (61–62).

10. Paul Van Tieghem, "L'Automne dans la poésie ouest-européenne, de Brockes à Lamartine," in *Mélanges d'histoire littéraire gégérale et comparée: Offerts à Fernard Baldensperger*, 2:337–48.

11. G. M. Hyde, "The Poetry of the City," in *Modernism, 1890–1930*, 337–48.

12. "Techne and Ge-stell in the Setting of the Origin of the Work of Art," in *The Piety of Thinking: Essays by Martin Heidegger*, trans. by James G. Hart and John C. Maraldo, 160–65; David Haliburton, *Poetic Thinking: An Approach to Heidegger*, chap. 2, "Art as Origin."

13. Karl Marx, "Economic and Philo-

sophical Manuscripts," in David McLellan, trans., *Karl Marx: Early Texts*, 154.

14. Terry Eagleton, "Fredric Jameson: The Politics of Style," in *Against the Grain*, 65–78.

15. Scholes, *Textual Power*, 80–85.

16. O'Neill, *The Communicative Body*.

17. Julia Kristeva, "From One Identity to an Other," in *Desire in Language: A Semiotic Approach to Literature and Art*, 124–47.

18. John O'Neill, "The Mother-Tongue: The Infant Search for Meaning," *University of Ottawa Quarterly* 55, no. 4 (1985): 59–72.

19. Baudelaire, *Les Fleurs du mal*, 235 (58). Compare Barbara Johnson's reading of the ethics, economics, and poetics in this poem in "Poetry and Its Double: Two *Invitations au voyage*," in *The Critical Difference: Essays in the Contemporary Rhetoric of Reading*, 23–51.

20. Ibid.

21. Jean Prévost, *Baudelaire: Essai sur la création et l'inspiration poétiques*, 194–95.

22. Baudelaire, *Les Fleurs du mal*, 239 (62).

23. Ibid., 233 (56).

24. Michel Butor, *Histoire extraordinaire: Essai sur une rêve de Baudelaire*; Jean-Paul Sartre, *Baudelaire*; Leo Bersani, *Baudelaire and Freud*.

25. Charles Baudelaire, "Mon Coeur mis à nu," in *Oeuvres complètes*.

26. Edmund Burke, *A Philosophical Enquiry into the Origin of Our Ideas of the Sublime and Beautiful*, lxxxi–cxx.

Chapter 4. Religion and Postmodernism

1. Daniel Bell, *The Cultural Contradiction of Capitalism*; Bell, "Liberalism in the Postindustrial Society," and "Beyond Modernism, beyond Self," in *The Winding Passage: Essays and Sociological Journeys*, 228–44 and 275–302, respectively.

2. Bell, *Cultural Contradictions*, 20.

3. Ibid., 28–29.

4. Ibid., 155.

5. O'Neill, *Plato's Cave*.

6. Daniel Bell, "The Return of the Sacred? The Argument on the Failure of Religion," in *The Winding Passage*, 334–35.

7. The "translation" of Lyotard's minor

"report" for the Quebec government on modern science, which appeared more than a decade ago, is astonishing proof of how literary politics feed off unexamined sources (see chap. 6).

8. Jürgen Habermas, "Modernity: An Incomplete Project," in *The Anti-Aesthetic*, 3–15.

9. Jameson is well informed about events on the contemporary cultural scene. His observations on art, photography, and architecture are as much part of the arts of bricolage as commentaries upon them. Hence it is a matter of (in)convenience to try to keep up with Jameson's essays. See, for example, his "Pleasure: A Political Issue"; pp. 1–14 in *Formations of Pleasure*; and "Architecture and the Critique of Ideology," pp. 51–87 in *Architecture Criticism Ideology* (Princeton: Princeton Architectural Press, 1985).

10. Fredric Jameson, "Postmodernism; or, The Cultural Logic of Late Capitalism," *New Left Review* 146 (1984): 52–92.

11. Fredric Jameson, "Postmodernism and Consumer Society," in Hal Foster, ed., *The Anti-Aesthetic*, 113.

12. I choose these because one may as well.

13. John O'Neill, "The Disciplinary Society: From Weber to Foucault," *British Journal of Sociology* 37, no. 1: (1987): 42–60.

14. Foster, *The Anti-Aesthetic*.

15. Jean Beaudrillard, "The Ecstasy of Communication," in Foster, *The Anti-Aesthetic*, 129.

16. Marshall Berman, *All That Is Solid Melts into the Air: The Experience of Modernity*; John O'Neill, "Marxism and Mythology," in *For Marx*.

17. Jean-François Lyotard, "Le désir nomme Marx." in *Economie libidinale*, 117–88.

18. Herbert Marcuse, *Eros and Civilization: A Philosophical Inquiry into Freud*, 193–94.

19. Fredric Jameson, *Marxism and Form: Twentieth-Century Dialectical Theories of Literature*, 113–14.

20. Ibid., 100–101.

21. Jameson, *The Political Unconscious*, 19–20.

22. Ibid., 285.

23. *Ibid.,* 290–91.
24. *Ibid.,* 295.
25. O'Neill, *Five Bodies.*
26. Henri Lefebvre, *Le manifeste différentialiste.*
27. Marx, "Economic and Philosophical Manuscripts."
28. Thomas G. Bergin and Max H. Fisch, trans. *The New Science of Giambattista Vico,* 142–44.

Chapter 5. Breaking the Signs

1. John O'Neill, "From Phenomenology to Ethnomethodology: Some Radical 'Misreadings,' " *Current Perspectives in Social Theory* 1 (1980): 7–20.
2. Barthes, "Science versus Literature," 413.
3. Barthes, *The Pleasure of the Text,* 9–10.
4. Roland Barthes, "Myth Today," in *Mythologies,* 116–34.
5. Rosalind Coward and John Ellis, *Language and Materialism,* 28.
6. Barthes, *Mythologies,* 132.
7. Roland Barthes, "To Write: An Intransitive Verb?" in *The Structuralist Controversy: The Languages of Criticism and the Sciences of Man,* 143.
8. Roland Barthes, *Le Grain de la voix: Entretiens, 1962–1980,* 190.
9. Jacques Derrida, *Writing and Difference.*
10. John O'Neill, "Situation, Action and Language," in *Sociology as a Skin Trade,* 81–95. See also Dominick La Capra, *A Preface to Sartre* (Ithaca, N.Y.: Cornell University Press, 1978), chap. 2, "Literature, Language, and Politics: Ellipse of What?" La Capra shows how Sartre later rethought his position in the light of Barthes's views.
11. Roland Barthes, "The Tasks of Brechtian Criticism," in *Critical Essays,* 74.
12. Roland Barthes, "Literature and Signification," in *Critical Essays,* 268.
13. Roland Barthes, *Writing Degree Zero and Elements of Semiology,* 33–34.
14. Ibid., 87.
15. Maurice Merleau-Ponty, *The Prose of the World.*
16. Barthes, *Writing Degree Zero,* 10.
17. Ibid., 11.
18. Ibid., 16.
19. Michel Butor, "La Fascinatrice," *Les*

Cahiers du Chemin 4 (15 October 1968); 20–55.
20. Roland Barthes, *Michelet par lui-même,* 17.
21. Ibid., 18.
22. Ibid., 31.
23. *Roland Barthes by Roland Barthes,* 69.
24. Ibid., 161.
25. Ibid., 160.
26. John O'Neill, "Decolonization and the Ideal Speech Community: Some Issues in the Theory and Practice of Communicative Competence," in *Critical Theory and Public Life,* 57–76.
27. *Roland Barthes by Roland Barthes,* 175.

Chapter 6. Marxism and the Two Sciences

1. Anthony Giddens, *New Rules of Sociological Method,* 162.
2. Frederick Engels, "Letter to Heinz Starkenburg, 25 January 1894," in *Karl Marx: Selected Works* (Moscow: Foreign Language Publishing House, 1935).
3. Karl Marx, *Capital: A Critique of Political Economy,* 12.
4. Barry Gruenberg, "The Problem of Reflexivity in the Sociology of Science," *Philosophy of the Social Sciences* 8 (1978): 321–43; Jonathan R. Cole and Harriet Zuckerman, "The Emergence of a Scientific Specialty: The Self-Exemplifying Case of the Sociology of Science," in *The Idea of Social Structure: Papers in Honor of Robert K. Merton.*
5. Ludwig Wittgenstein, *On Certainty;* Aaron V. Cicourel, *Method and Measurement in Sociology;* Harold Garfinkel, *Studies in Ethnomethodology.*
6. Jürgen Habermas, *Communication and the Evolution of Society;* Karl-Otto Apel, *Towards a Transformation of Philosophy.*
7. Talcott Parsons, *The Social System.*
8. See Thomas J. Fararo, "Science as a Cultural System," in *Explorations in General Theory in Social Science: Essays in Honor of Talcott Parsons.*
9. Richard D. Whitley, "Black Boxism and the Sociology of Science: A Discussion of the Major Developments in the Field," in *Sociology of Science.*
10. Ibid., 192.
11. Alvin W. Gouldner, *The Dialectic of Ideology and Technology: The Origins, Gram-*

mar, and Future of Ideology; Gouldner, *The Future of the Intellectuals and the Rise of the New Class*.

12. Jürgen Habermas, *Knowledge and Human Interests*, 62.

13. Trann Overend, "Enquiry and Ideology: Habermas' Trichotomous Conception of Science," *Philosophy of the Social Sciences* 8 (1978): 1–35.

14. Kostas Axelos, *Alienation, Praxis, and Techne in the Thought of Karl Marx*.

15. Karl Marx, *Early Texts*, trans. and ed. David McLellan (Oxford: Basil Blackwell, 1971), p. 154; my emphasis.

16. Charles Rachlis, "Marcuse and the Problem of Happiness," *Canadian Journal of Political and Social Theory* 2 (1978): 63–88.

17. Peter Sedgwick, "Natural Science and Human Theory: A Critique of Herbert Marcuse," in *The Socialist Register*.

18. Herbert Marcuse, *One-Dimensional Man: Studies in the Ideology of Advanced Industrial Society*, 266.

19. Jürgen Habermas, *Toward a Rational Society: Student Protest, Science and Politics*, 93.

20. Ibid., 88.

21. Jürgen Habermas, *Legitimation Crisis*.

22. Theodor Adorno, et al., *The Positivist Dispute in German Sociology*.

23. See John O'Neill, "Scientism, Historicism and the Problems of Rationality," in *Modes of Individualism and Collectivism*.

24. Brian Fay, *Social Theory and Political Practice*, 43.

25. Karl R. Popper, *The Poverty of Historicism*; Popper, *The Open Society and Its Enemies*.

26. Robert Lane, "The Decline of Politics and Ideology in a Knowledgeable Society," *American Sociological Review* 31 (1966): 647–61; Daniel Bell, *The Coming of Post-Industrial Society* (New York: Basic Books, 1976).

27. Ben Agger, "Marcuse and Habermas on New Science," *Polity* 10 (1976): 158–81; William Leiss, "Technological Rationality: Marcuse and His Critics," in *The Domination of Nature*; Norman Stockman, "Habermas, Marcuse and the *Aufhebung* of Science and Technology," *Philosophy of the Social Sciences* 8 (1978): 15–35.

28. H. T. Wilson, *The American Ideology:*

Science, Technology, and Organization as Modes of Rationality in Advanced Industrial Societies, 84.

29. John O'Neill, "Merleau-Ponty's Critique of Marxist Scientism," *Canadian Journal of Political and Social Theory* 2 (1978): 31–62; H. T. Wilson, "Science, Critique and Criticism: The 'Open Society' Revisited," in *On Critical Theory*.

30. Max Weber, "Science as a Vocation," in *From Max Weber: Essays in Sociology*.

31. Robert K. Merton, "Paradigm for the Sociology of Knowledge," in *The Sociology of Science: Theoretical and Empirical Investigations*.

32. M. D. King, "Reason, Tradition, and the Progressiveness of Science," *History and Theory* 10 (1971): 3–32.

33. M. J. Mulkay, "Conformity and Innovation in Science," in *Sociology of Science*; Rolf Klima, "Scientific Knowledge and Social Control in Science: The Application of a Cognitive Theory of Behaviour to the Study of Scientific Behaviour," in *Social Processes of Scientific Development*; Gernot Bohme, "The Social Function of Cognitive Structures: A Concept of the Scientific Community within a Theory of Action," in *Determinants and Controls of Scientific Development*.

34. Warren O. Hagstrom, *The Scientific Community*; Norman W. Storer, *The Social System of Science*; Diana Crane, "The Gate-Keepers of Science: Some Factors Affecting the Selection of Articles for Scientific Journals," *The American Sociologist* 2 (1967): 195–201; Harriet Zuckerman, "The Code of Science," *Studium generale* 23 (1970): 942–61; Derek J. de Solla Price, *Little Science, Big Science*; Jerry Gaston, *Originality and Competition in Science: A Study of the British High Energy Physics Community*; Jonathan R. Cole and Stephen Cole, "Scientific Output and Recognition: A Study in the Operation of the Reward System in Science," *American Sociological Review* 32 (1967): 377–90.

35. Karin D. Knorr, "Producing and Reproducing Knowledge: Descriptive or Constructive? Toward a Model of Research Production," *Social Science Information* 16 (1977): 669–96.

36. Imre Lakatos, "Falsification and the Methodology of Scientific Research Pro-

grammes," in *Criticism and the Growth of Knowledge*, 91–95.

37. Herminio Martins, "The Kuhnian 'Revolution' and Its Implications for Sociology," in *Imagination and Precision in Political Analysis: Essays in Honor of Peter Nettl*.

38. Abraham Kaplan, *The Conduct of Inquiry*.

39. Pierre Bourdieu, "The Specificity of a Scientific Field and the Social Conditions of the Progress of Reason," *Social Science Information* 14 (1975): 19–47.

40. Karin D. Knorr and Dietrich W. Knorr, *From Scenes to Scripts: On the Relationship between Laboratory Research and Published Papers in Science*.

41. Knorr, "Producing and Reproducing Knowledge," 671.

42. Bernard d'Espagnat, "The Quantum Theory and Reality," *Scientific American* 241 (1979): 158–81.

43. Yaron Ezrahi, "The Political Resources of Science," in *Sociology of Science: Selected Readings*.

44. Wolfgang Van den Daele and Peter Weingart, "Resistance and Receptivity of Science to External Direction: The Emergence of New Disciplines under the Impact of Science Policy," in *Perspectives on the Emergence of Scientific Disciplines*.

45. Ibid., 248.

46. Ibid., 265.

Chapter 7. The Disciplinary Production of Natural and Social Science Arguments

1. Joseph Gusfield, "The Literary Rhetoric of Science: Comedy and Pathos in Drinking Driver Research," *American Sociological Review* 41 (1976): 16–34.

2. As early as 1975, I began to treat the written page as having identifying rhetorical features that carry, so to speak, its disciplinarity. A number of works have appeared that take the analysis of literary and scientific discourse in various directions. Here I should acknowledge Ken Morrison's dissertation, "Reader's Work" (York University, Toronto, 1976). Mention should be made of the following works, each of which would contain a further lineage that would in part overlap. See Ben Agger, *Reading Science: A Literary, Political and Sociological Analysis*;

Charles Bazerman, *Shaping Written Knowledge: The Genre and Activity of the Experimental Article in Science*; David Birch, *Language, Literature, and Critical Practice: Ways of Analysing Text*; Richard Brown, *Society as Text: Essays on Rhetoric, Reason and Reality*; Bryan S. Green, *Literary Methods and Sociological Theory*; Karin D. Knorr-Cetina, *The Manufacturing of Knowledge: An Essay on the Constructivist and Contextual Nature of Science*; Bruno Latour, *Science in Action*; Michael Mulkay, *The Word and the World: Explorations in the Form of Sociological Analysis*; Donald M. McCloskey, *The Rhetoric of Economics*; J. S. Nelson, A. Megill, and D. McCloskey, *The Rhetoric of the Human Sciences: Language and Argument in Scholarship and Public Affairs*; Herbert W. Simons ed., *Rhetoric in the Human Sciences*; and Stuart Peterfreund, ed., *Literature and Science: Theory and Practice*. Going to press, I have just found an early study of science article abstracts, Myrna Gopnik, *Linguistic Structures in Scientific Texts*.

3. Gerald Holton, "On the Role of Themata in Scientific Thought," *Science* 188 (1975): 333.

4. Thomas S. Kuhn, *The Structure of Scientific Revolutions*.

5. Michael Polyani, *Personal Knowledge: Towards a Post-Critical Philosophy*.

6. Bruno Latour and Steve Woolgar, *Laboratory Life: The Social Construction of Scientific Facts*.

7. Knorr, "Producing and Reproducing Knowledge."

8. Ludwik Fleck, *Genesis and Development of a Scientific Fact*.

9. Carl Hempel, "The Function of General Laws in History," in *Theories of History*, 344–56.

10. John Ziman, *Public Knowledge: The Social Dimension of Science*.

11. See *Contemporary Sociology* 8 (1979): 789–824, a special issue on the major journals in American sociology, with articles on the *American Journal of Sociology, American Sociological Review*, and *Social Forces*, and essays dealing with accountability and the review process; and see especially Ben Agger, *Socio(onto)logy: A Disciplinary Reading* (Urbana: University of Illinois Press, 1989).

12. Robert K. Merton and Harriet Zucker-

man, "Patterns of Evaluation in Science: In-stitutionalization, Structure and Functions of the Referee System," *Minerva* 9 (1971): 66–100.

13. J. R. Cole and S. Cole, "Scientific Output and Recognition"; S. Cole and J. R. Cole, "Visibility and the Structural Bases of Awareness of Scientific Research," *American Sociological Review* 33 (1968): 397–413; Paul D. Allison and John A. Stewart, "Pro-ductivity Differences among Scientists," *American Sociological Review* 39 (1974): 596–606.

14. D. E. Chubin and S. Moitra, "Content Analyses of References: Adjunct or Alterna-tive to Citation Counting?" *Social Studies of Science* 5 (1975): 423–31; D. E. Chubin, "On the Use of the Science Citation Index in Sociology," *American Sociologist* 8 (1973): 187–191; A. Bayer and J. Folger, "Some Correlates of a Citation Measure of Produc-tivity in Science," *Sociology of Education* 39 (1966): 381–90.

15. H. Small and B. C. Griffith, "The Structure of Scientific Literatures (I)" *Science Studies* 4 (1974): 17–40; B. C. Griffith et al., "The Structure of Scientific Literatures (II)," *Science Studies* 4 (1974): 339–65.

16. Merton, *The Sociology of Science*.

17. Knorr and Knorr, *From Scenes to Scripts*.

18. Michael A. Overington, "A Critical Celebration of Gusfield's 'The Literary Rhet-oric of Science,'" *American Sociological Re-view* 62 (1977): 170–73.

19. J. J. Waller, "Identification of Problem Drinkers among Drunken Drivers," *Journal of the American Medical Association* 200 (1967): 124–30.

20. Kenneth Burke, *A Grammar of Mo-tives*.

21. Gusfield, "The Literary Rhetoric of Science," 23.

22. Harold Garfinkel, " 'Good' Organiza-tion Reasons for 'Bad' Clinic Records," in *Studies in Ethnomethodology*, 186–207; Aaron V. Cicourel, *Method and Mea-surement*.

23. Louis Althusser and Etienne Balibar, *Reading "Capital"*; Harold Bloom, *The Anxi-ety of Influence: A Theory of Poetry*; Bloom, *A Map of Misreading*; Pierre Macherey, *A Theory of Literary Production*.

24. Talcott Parsons, *The Structure of Social Action: A Study in Social Theory with Special Reference to a Group of Recent European Writers*.

25. Joseph A. Schumpeter, *History of Eco-nomic Analysis*.

26. Harvey Sacks, "Sociological Descrip-tion," *Berkeley Journal of Sociology* 8 (1963): 1–16.

27. Thomas P. Wilson, "Normative and Interpretative Paradigms in Sociology," in *Understanding Everyday Life*, 57–79.

28. Harvey Sacks, Emmanuel A. Scheg-loff and Gail Jefferson, "A Simple Systemat-ics for the Organization of Turn-Taking for Conversation," *Language* 50 (1974): 696–735.

29. D. H. Hamblin, "The Counsellor and Alienated Youth," *British Journal of Guidance and Counselling* 2 (1974): 87–95.

30. Caroline W. Bynum, "Feminine Names for God in Cistercian Writing: A Case Study in the Relationship of Literary Language and Community Life."

31. Digby C. Anderson, "Some Organiza-tional Features in the Local Production of a Plausible Text," *Philosophy of the Social Sciences* 8 (1978): 119.

32. Stephen Toulmin, *The Uses of Ar-gument*.

33. Harvey Sacks, "On the Analyzability of Stories by Children," in *Directions in So-ciolinguistics: The Ethnography of Communi-cation*, 325–45; Michael Moerman, "Analy-sis of Cue Conversation: Providing Accounts, Finding Breaches and Taking Sides," in *Studies in Social Interaction*, 170–228.

34. Lakatos, "Falsification."

35. G. Nigel Gilbert, "The Transforma-tion of Research Findings into Scientific Knowledge," *Social Studies of Science* 7 (1977) 229–300.

36. Bynum, "Feminine Names for God," 9–10; my emphasis on negatives.

37. Albert Hofstadter, "The scientific and literary uses of language," in *Symbols and Society: Fourteenth Symposium of the Confer-ence on Science, Philosophy, and Religion*, 291–335.

38. Barry Barnes, *Scientific Knowledge and Sociological Theory*.

39. J. H. Hexter, *The History Primer*.

40. Paolo Freire, *The Pedagogy of the Oppressed*; O'Neill, "Decolonization."

41. John O'Neill, "The Mutuality of Accounts: An Essay on Trust," in *Theoretical Perspectives in Sociology*, 369–80; Karl-Otto Apel, *Analytic Philosophy of Language and the Geisteswissenschaften*.

42. Clause Mueller, *The Politics of Communication: A Study in the Political Sociology of Language, Socialization, and Legitimation*; J. A. Barnes, *Who Should Know What? Social Issues, Privacy and Ethics*; Dorothy E. Smith, "The Social Construction of Documentary Reality," *Sociological Inquiry* 44 (1974): 257–68.

Chapter 8: A Realist Model of Scientific Knowledge

1. These insights I share with my colleague Ken Morrison, whose own work has revealed some of the fascinating technical detail of the organizational formats of what he calls discipline-specific inquiry and its pedagogic practices. See Kenneth L. Morrison, "Reader's Work"; Morrison, "Some Properties of 'Telling-Order Designs' in Didactic Inquiry," *Philosophy of the Social Sciences* 11 (1981): 245–62; and Morrison, "Some Researchable Recurrences in Disciplinary Specific Inquiry," in *Interactional Order: New Directions in the Study of Social Order*, 148–158.

2. Alfred Schutz and Thomas Luckmann, *The Structures of the Life-World*, 302–3.

3. Roy Bhaskar, *A Realist Theory of Science*.

4. Roy Bhaskar, *The Possibility of Naturalism: A Philosophical Critique of the Contemporary Human Sciences*.

5. Bhaskar, "Rorty, Realism and the Idea of Freedom"; Martin Hollis, "The Poetics of Personhood," in *Reaching Rorty*, 244–56. It would be a challenging exercise to show how the Rorty reader packages the critical collection required to produce "Rorty" as a teachable object for the philosophers he has disowned.

6. Bruno Latour, "The Three Little Dinosaurs; or, A Sociologist's Nightmare," *Fundamenta Scientiae*, 1 (1980): 79–85.

7. Martin Hollis, *Models of Man: Philosophical Thoughts on Social Action*.

8. John O'Neill, *Perception, Expression,*

and *History: The Social Phenomenology of Maurice Merleau-Ponty*.

9. Alfred Schutz, *Reflections on the Problem of Relevance*.

10. Schutz and Luckmann, *The Structures of the Life-World*, 156.

11. O'Neill, "From Phenomenology to Ethnomethodology."

12. Hans Georg Soeffner, "Common Sense and Science: Observations about a Common Misunderstanding of Science," *Newsletter of the International Society for the Sociology of Knowledge* 8 (1982): 9–23.

13. Giddens, *New Rule of Sociological Method*.

14. Schutz and Luckmann, *The Structures of the Life-World*, 122.

15. Ibid., 286.

16. Bhaskar, *A Realist Theory*, 22.

17. Ibid., p. 117.

18. Apel, *Analytic Philosophy*.

19. Fleck, *Genesis and Development*.

20. Latour, "Three Little Dinosaurs," 82.

21. Latour and Woolgar, *Laboratory Life*.

22. Michael E. Lynch, "Technical Work and Critical Inquiry: Investigations in a Scientific Laboratory," *Social Studies of Science* 12 (1982): 499–533.

23. Karin D. Knorr-Cetina, "Tinkering towards Success: Prelude to a Theory of Scientific Practice," *Theory and Society* 8 (1979): 347–76.

24. Morrison, "Reader's Work."

25. Anderson, "Some Organizational Features."

26. Fleck, *Genesis and Development*; Karin D. Knorr-Cetina, *The Manufacture of Knowledge: An Essay on the Constructivist and Contextual Nature of Science*; Latour and Woolgar, *Laboratory Life*; Steve Woolgar, "Discovery: Logic and Sequence in a Scientific Text (I)," in *The Social Process of Scientific Investigation*.

27. Richard Rorty, *Philosophy and the Mirror of Nature*.

28. Martin Heidegger, *On the Way to Language*; Merleau-Ponty, *The Prose of the World*; Jacques Derrida, *Of Grammatology*.

29. Kenneth L. Morrison, "Stabilizing the Text: The Institutionalization of Knowledge in Historical and Philosophic Forms of Argument." *Canadian Journal of Sociology* 12, no. 3 (1987): 242–74.

30. Hollis, *Models of Man*, 4.
31. Ibid., 5.
32. Ibid., 4–5, 6, 191–95.
33. Ibid., 6.
34. Ibid., 7.
35. Ibid.
36. Ibid.
37. Ibid., 10.
38. Ibid.
39. Ibid., 12.
40. Ibid.
41. Ibid., 14.
42. Ibid., 15.
43. Ibid.
44. Ibid., 16–18.
45. Ibid., 19.
46. Ibid., 19–20.
47. Ibid., 20–21; my emphasis.

Chapter 9. Deconstructing Fort/Derrida

1. My text preserves as nearly as possible its play upon its own play as a commentary at the Workshop on Archaeology of Deconstruction, Twenty-third Annual Conference of the Society for Phenomenology and Existential Philosophy (SPEP), held at Georgia State University and Emory University, Atlanta, Georgia, 18–20 October, 1984. I have removed personal details; I am concerned only to reproduce the conventions of philosophical practice as generally observed but usually unthematic features of the institution of philosophy, within which we nevertheless strive to arouse philosophical desire. What follows, however, should alert readers to the liability of an apology for one's own practice.
2. John O'Neill, *Essaying Montaigne: A Study of the Renaissance Institution of Writing and Reading.*
3. Herman Rapaport, "Staging Mont Blanc," in *Displacement: Derrida and After*, 59–73.
4. Susan Handleman, "Jacques Derrida and the Heretic Hermaneutic," in *Displacement*, 98–129.
5. John R. Searle, "Reiterating the Differences: A Reply to Derrida," *Glyph* 1 (1977): 198–208; Jacques Derrida, "Limited Inc.," *Glyph* 2 (1977): 162–254.
6. Immanuel Kant, *Prolegomena to Any Future Metaphysics*, p. 24.
7. Ibid., 116.

8. See n. 2.
9. Jacques Derrida, "Living On: Borderlines," in *Deconstruction and Criticism*, 76–176.
10. Barbara Johnson, "Taking Fidelity Philosophically," in *Difference in Translation*, 142–48.
11. Jacques Derrida, "Coming into One's Own," in *Psychoanalysis and the Question of the Text*, 114–47.

Chapter 10. Three Men in a Text

1. David Michael Levin, *The Body's Recollection of Being: Phenomenological Psychology and the Deconstruction of Nihilism*; Joel Shapiro, *Bodily Reflective Modes: A Phenomenological Method of Psychology*; John O'Neill, *Five Bodies.*
2. O'Neill, *The Communicative Body.*
3. O'Neill, *For Marx.*
4. See chap. 17.
5. O'Neill, "Sociological Nemesis," 21–35.
6. John O'Neill, "Vico on the Natural Workings of the Mind," in *Phenomenology and the Human Sciences*, 117–25.
7. Bergin and Fisch, *The New Science of Giambattista Vico*, paragraphs 186–87.
8. O'Neill, *Five Bodies*, 11–12.
9. *The Complete Works of Montaigne: Essays, Travel Journal, Letters*, 293.
10. *Journal of the British Society for Phenomenology* 17 (May 1986): 201–3.
11. *Canadian Journal of Sociology* 13, no. 4 (Fall 1988): 450–54.

Chapter 11. Power and the Splitting (*Spaltung*) of Language

1. *New Literary History* 14, no. 3 (Spring 1983); the commentaries by Gordon Broden, Meredith Skura, Claus Uhlig, and myself are to be found on pp. 665–710.
2. Michel Foucault, *The Order of Things: An Archaeology of the Human Sciences.*
3. Louis Marin, "On the Interpretation of Ordinary Language: A Parable of Pascal," in *Textual Strategies: Perspectives in Post-Structuralist Criticism*, 239–59.
4. Louis Marin, "Toward a Theory of Reading in the Visual Arts: Poussin's *The Arcadian Shepherds*," in *The Reader in the Text*, 293–324.

5. Louis Marin, "The Iconic Text and the Theory of Enunciation: Luca Signorelli at Loreto (Circa 1479–1484)," *New Literary History* 14, no. 3 (Spring 1983): 589.

6. Heinrich F. Plett, "Aesthetic Constituents in the Courtly Culture of Renaissance England," *New Literary History* 14, no. 3 (Spring 1983): 589.

7. George Puttenham, *The Arte of English Poesie*, 186, cited in Plett, *Aesthetic Constituents*, 602–3.

8. Henry Sussman, "The Court as Text: Inversion, Supplanting, and Derangement in Kafka's *Der Prozess*," *PMLA* (1977): 41–55; Sussman, "The All-Embracing Metaphor: Reflections on Kafka's 'The Burrow,'" *Glyph* 1 (1977): 100–131.

9. Ernest Kantorowicz, *The King's Two Bodies*.

10. Norbert Elias, *The Civilizing Process: The History of Manners*.

11. Robert Weimann, "Metaphor and Historical Criticism: Shakespeare's Imagery Revisited," in *Structure and Society in Literary History: Studies in the History and Theory of Historical Criticism*, 188–233.

12. Marie Axton, *The Queen's Two Bodies: Drama and the Elizabethan Succession*.

13. John O'Neill, "Time's Body: Vico on the Love of Language and Institution," in *Giambattista Vico's Science of Humanity*, 333–39.

14. Barthes, "Science versus Literature," 410–16.

15. Cesare Vasoli, "Francesco Patrizi and the 'Double Rhetoric,'" *New Literary History* 14, no. 3 (Spring 1983): 531–51.

16. Brian Vickers, "Epideictic and Epic in the Renaissance," *New Literary History* 14, no. 3 (Spring 1983): 497–538.

17. Walter D. Ong, *Fighting for Life: Context, Sexuality and Consciousness*, chap. 4, "Academic and Intellectual Arenas."

18. Frank Whigham, "Interpretation at Court: Courtesy and the Performer-Audience Dialectic," *New Literary History* 14, no. 3 (Spring 1983): 589.

19. Basil Bernstein, "Social Class, Linguistic Codes and Grammatical Elements," *Language and Speech* 5 (1962): 221–40.

20. Habermas, *Communication and the Evolution of Society*.

21. Montaigne, *The Complete Works*, trans. Donald M. Frame.

22. Timothy Murray, "From Foul Sheets to Legitimate Model: Antitheater Text, Ben Jonson," *New Literary History* 14, no. 3 (Spring 1983): 641–64.

23. Elizabeth L. Eisenstein, *The Printing Press as an Agent of Change: Communications and Cultural Transformations in Early-Modern Europe*, 122–26.

24. Robert Weimann, "'Appropriation' and Modern History in Renaissance Prose Narrative," *New Literary History* 14, no. 3 (Spring 1983): 459–96.

25. René Girard, *Violence and the Sacred*; Bloom, *The Anxiety of Influence*.

26. O'Neill, *Essaying Montaigne*.

27. Weiman, "Appropriation and Modern History," 484.

28. Jean-Paul Sartre, *What Is Literature?*

29. Paul Ricoeur, *Freud and Philosophy: An Essay on Interpretation*, 536–41.

30. Jacques Lacan, "The Direction of the Treatment and the Principles of Its Power," in *Ecrits: A Selection*, 269.

31. Jean Laplanche and J.-B. Pontalis, *The Language of Psycho-Analysis*, 427–29.

32. John O'Neill, "The Specular Body: Merleau-Ponty and Lacan on Infant Self and Other," in *The Communicative Body*, 58–73.

33. Meredith Ann Skura, *The Literary Use of the Psychoanalytic Process*.

34. Northrop Frye, *The Anatomy of Criticism: Four Essays*, 105–6.

35. Stephen Greenblatt, *Renaissance Self-Fashioning: From More to Shakespeare*.

36. John O'Neill, "The Hobbesian Problem in Marx and Parsons," in *Explorations in General Theory in Social Science*, 295–308.

37. John O'Neill, "The Paradox of Communication: Reading the *Essays* Otherwise," in *Essaying Montaigne*.

Chapter 12. The Essayist (Montaigne) Is Not a *Malade Imaginaire*

1. Montaigne, *The Complete Works*, book 2, essay 8, p. 278; hereafter cited in the text.

2. Pierre Barrière, *La vie intellectuelle en Périgord 1550–1800*; Michel Butor, *Essais sur les "Essais"*; Alfred Glauser, *Montaigne paradoxale*; Anthony Wilden, "Par divers moyens on arrive à pareille fin: A Reading

of Montaigne," *Modern Language Notes* 83 (1968): 577–97; Wilden, "Montaigne on the Paradoxes of Individualism: A Communication about Communication," in *System and Structure: Essays in Communication and Exchange*, 88–109.

3. John O'Neill, *Essaying Montaigne*.

4. Glauser, *Montaigne paradoxale*, 19.

5. Ibid., 23.

6. Ibid., 152–53.

7. Wilden, "Par divers moyens," 597.

8. Roland Barthes, *Le plaisir du texte*.

9. Cassiodorus Senator, *An Introduction to Divine and Human Readings*.

10. Jean Paris, "Tel qu'en lui-même il se voit," in *Rembrandt*, 97–121.

Chapter 13. *Mecum Meditari*

1. Maurice Merleau-Ponty, *Phénoménologie de la perception* (Paris: Gallimard, 1945), 423; *Phenomenology of Perception*, 369.

2. O'Neill, *The Communicative Body*.

3. Chaim Perelman, "Analogie et métaphore en science, poésie et philosophie," in his *Le Champ de l'argumentation*, 271–83.

4. See chapters 6, 7, and 8.

5. For a classical quarrel on this, see Michel Foucault, *Folie et déraison*, and Jacques Derrida, "Cogito and the History of Madness," in *Writing and Difference*, 31–63.

6. René Descartes, *Discourse on Method and The Meditations*, 96; Descartes, *Meditationes de prima philosophia, méditations Metaphysiques*, 19–20.

7. John O'Neill, *The Communicative Body*, part 2; Walter Benn Michaels, "The Interpreter's Self: Peirce on the Cartesian 'Subject,' " in *Reader-Response Criticism: From Formalism to Post-Structuralism*, 185–200.

8. Jaakko Hintikka, "Cogito, ergo sum: Inference or Performance?" in *Descartes: A Collection of Critical Essays*, 108–39, also Hiram Caton, *The Origins of Subjectivity: An Essay on Descartes*, 140–43. For critical positions, see F. Feldman, "On the Performatory Interpretation of the *cogito*," *Philosophical Review* 82 (1973): pp. 345–63, and Bernard Williams, *Descartes: The Project of Pure Inquiry*, chap. 3, "*Cogito* and *sum*."

9. See the papers in *Descartes: A Collection of Critical Essays*; L. J. Beck, *The Metaphysics of Descartes: A Study of the Meditations*; and

Anthony Kenny, *Descartes: A Study of His Philosophy*.

10. O'Neill, *Essaying Montaigne*.

11. Robert Champigny, "The Theatrical Aspect of the Cogito," *Review of Metaphysics* 12 (1959): 370–77; Ralph Flores, "Cartesian Striptease," *Substance* 39 (1983): 75–88.

12. Jean-Luc Nancy, "Larvatus pro Deo," *Glyph* 2 (1977): 14–36, and *Ego sum*.

13. Merleau-Ponty, *Phenomenology of Perception*, 400–401.

14. Ibid., 402.

15. Ibid., 383.

16. Timothy J. Reiss, "Cartesian Discourse and Classical Ideology," *Diacritics* 6, no. 4 (Winter 1976): 19–27; also his "The *concevoir* Motif in Descartes," in *La cohérence intérieure: Etudes sur la littérature française du xviie siècle, présentées en hommage à Judd D. Hubert*, 203–22; and his *The Discourse of Modernism*; as well as Michel Serres, "Knowledge in the Classical Age: La Fontaine and Descartes," in *Hermes: Literature, Science, Philosophy*, 15–28.

17. Descartes, *Discourse on Method and The Meditations*, 96.

18. Iago Galston, "Descartes and Modern Psychiatric Thought," *Isis* 35 (Spring 1944): 118–28; Stephen Schonberger, "A Dream of Descartes: Reflections on the Unconscious Determinants of the Sciences," *International Journal of Psychology* 20 (January 1939): 43–57.

19. Nathan Edelman, "The Mixed Metaphor in Descartes," *The Romantic Review* 41 (1950): 167–78; G. Nador, "Métaphores de chemins et de labyrinthes chez Descartes," *Revue d'histoire de la philosophie* 152 (1962): 37–51; Sylvie Romanowski, L'Illusion chez Descartes: La structure du discours cartésien.

20. Descartes, *Meditationes de prima philosophia* 7: 7.

21. Henri Gouhier, *Les Premières pensées de Descartes: Contribution à l'histoire de l'Anti-Renaissance*; Norman Kemp Smith, *New Studies in the Philosophy of Descartes: Descartes as Pioneer*, 3–39.

22. René Descartes' "Objections 7, Third Question: Whether a Method Can Be Devised Anew," in *The Philosophical Works of*

Descartes, trans. Elizabeth S. Haldane and G. R. T. Ross (Cambridge: Cambridge University Press, 1934), 2:325–44.

23. René Descartes, *Discourse on Method and The Meditations*, 130; *Meditationes de prime philosophia*, 51–52.

24. Descartes, *Discourse on Method and The Meditations*, 113.

25. Descartes, *Meditationes de prima philosophia*, 34.

Chapter 14: Science and the Founding Self

1. Sigmund Freud, "On the History of the Psycho-Analytic Movement," in *Standard Edition of the Complete Psychological Works* (hereafter *SE*), 14:7. No one can study the issue of the scientist's ambivalence toward his motives for priority claims without consulting Robert K. Merton, "The Ambivalence of Scientists" (1963), in *The Sociology of Science*, 382–412, and George Weisz, "Scientists and Sectarians: The Care of Psychoanalysis," *Journal of the History of the Behavioral Sciences* 11, no. 4 (October 1975): 350–64.

2. Sigmund Freud, "Fragment of an Analysis of a Case of Hysteria" (1905 [1907]), in *Case Histories*, vol. 1.

3. Sigmund Freud, "From the History of an Infantile Neurosis" (1918 [1914]), in *Case Histories*, vol. 2. I devoted my seminar, "Theory of the Text" (1987) to a complete textual analysis of "Wolf Man." The results require a full-length monograph and are part of my larger study of the five case histories, *The Domestic Economy of the Mind*, forthcoming.

4. Samuel Weber, *The Legend of Freud*. See, however, George B. Hogenson, *Jung's Struggle With Freud*, for the contrary argument that Freud grounded his authority in silence and the primal authority of the law of the dead father.

5. Sigmund Freud, "An Outline of Psycho-Analysis," in *SE*, 23: 159.

6. Freud, "From the History of an Infantile Neurosis," 281–95. References are to page and paragraph sequence on those pages.

7. Peter Brooks, "Fictions of the Wolf Man: Freud and Narrative Understanding,"

in his *Reading for the Plot: Design and Intention in Narrative*.

8. Stanley Fish, "Withholding the Missing Portion: Psychoanalysis and Rhetoric," in *Doing What Comes Naturally*, 537.

9. Barry Silverstein, " 'Now Comes a Sad Story': Freud's Lost Metapsychological Papers," in *Freud: Appraisals and Reappraisals*, 1:143–98; Robin Ostow, "Autobiographical Sources of Freud's Social Theory: *Totem and Taboo, Group Psychology and the Analysis of the Ego*, and *Moses and Monotheism Revisited*," *Psychiatric Journal of the University of Ottawa*, 1977, 169–80.

10. Patrick Mahony, "The Budding International Association of Psychoanalysis and Its Discontents: A Feature of Freud's discourse," in *Psychoanalysis and Discourse*, 157–92.

11. Paul E. Stepansky, *In Freud's Shadow: Adler in Context*, 185–89; Stepansky, "The Empiricists Rebel: Jung, Freud and the Burdens of Discipleship," *Journal of the History of the Behavioral Sciences* 12 (1976): 216–39.

12. Jacques Lacan, "The Function and Field of Speech and Language in Psychoanalysis," in *Ecrits*, 48–50, pp. 107–8, n. 14.

13. Walter J. Ong, "Academic and Intellectual Arenas," in *Fighting for Life*, 118–48.

14. Freud, *Case Histories*, 2: 277–78, n. 2. See also Jean Laplanche, *Life and Death in Psychoanalysis*, 41–44.

15. *SE*, 14: 53.

16. Peter Homans, "Disappointment and the Ability to Mourn: De-idealization as a Psychological Theme in Freud's Life, Thought, and Social Circumstances, 1906–1914," in *Freud: Appraisals and Reappraisals*, 2: 3–102.

17. William J. McGrath, *Freud's Discovery of Psychoanalysis: The Politics of Hysteria*.

Chapter 15: The Mother Tongue

1. Richard M. Zaner, *The Context of Self: A Phenomenological Inquiry Using Medicine as a Clue*.

2. Merleau-Ponty, *Phenomenology of Perception*, 206.

3. John R. Searle, *Speech Acts: An Essay in the Philosophy of Language*.

4. Bloom, *The Anxiety of Influence*.

5. O'Neill, *Making Sense Together*.

6. Sigmund Freud, "Instincts and Their Vicissitudes" (1915), in *SE*, 14: 111–40.

7. Ricoeur, *Freud and Philosophy*, 313.

8. Lawrence, C. Kubie, "Some Implications for Psycho-Analysis of Modern Concepts of the Organization of the Brain," *Psychoanalytic Quarterly* 22 (1953): 21–68; Mortimer Ostow, "A Psychoanalytic Contribution to the Study of Brain Function," *Psychoanalytic Quarterly* 23 (1954): 317–423; Paul D. Maclean, "Psychosomatic Disease and the 'Visceral Brain,'" *Psychosomatic Medicine* 11, no. 6 (November–December 1949): 338–53.

9. Ricoeur, *Freud and Philosophy*, 69.

10. Ibid., 151.

11. Laplanche, *Life and Death in Psychoanalysis*; see also S. Lebovic and M. Soulé, *La Connaissance de l'enfant par la psychanalyse*, 292ff.

12. Sigmund Freud, *An Outline of Psycho-Analysis*, 10–11; see also John Bowlby, "The Child's Tie to His Mother: Review of the Psychoanaytical Literature," in *Attachment and Loss*, 1:361–78.

13. Davenport Hooker, "Reflex Activities in the Human Fetus," in *Child Behaviour and Development*, 17–28.

14. Kristeva, *Desire in Language*, 133–34.

15. Laplanche, *Life and Death in Psychoanalysis*, 137.

16. Sigmund Freud, "Project for a Scientific Psychology," (1905), in *SE*, 1:328–29.

17. Hans Tischler, "Schreien, Lallen und erstes Sprechen in der Entwicklung des Sauglings," *Zeitschrift für Psychologie* 160, nos. 3–4 (April 1957): 210–63.

18. Freud, "Project for a Scientific Psychology," 318.

19. Ibid., 366.

20. Ibid., 367.

21. Ivan Fonagy, "Les Bases pulsionnelles de la phonation," *Revue françise de psychoanalyse* 34, no. 1 (1970): 101–36; 35, no. 4 (1971): 543–91.

22. René A. Spitz, "The Primal Cavity: A Contribution to the Genesis of Perception and Its Role for Psychoanalytic Theory," *The Psychoanalytic Study of the Child* 10 (1955): 221.

23. Julia Kristeva, "Motherhood according to Giovanni Bellini," in *Desire in Language*, 236–70.

24. Ricoeur, *Freud and Philosophy*, 322.

25. Laplanche, *Life and Death in Psychoanalysis*, 82.

26. Ricoeur, *Freud and Philosophy*, 322.

27. Augusta Bonnard, "The Primal Significance of the Tongue," *International Journal of Psycho-Analysis* 41 (1960): 301–7.

28. Ibid., 307.

29. H. M. Halveson, "Infant Sucking and Tensional Behaviour," *Journal of Genetic Psychology* 53 (1938): 365–430.

30. Sigmund Freud, "Development of the Libido and Sexual Organization," in *A General Introduction to Psychoanalysis*, 338.

31. Laplanche, *Life and Death in Psychoanalysis*, 13.

32. Freud, *A General Introduction to Psychoanalysis*, 322.

33. John O'Neill, "The Specular Body: Merleau-Ponty and Lacan on Infant Self and Other," in *The Communicative Body*, 55–73.

34. Freud, *An Outline of Psychoanalysis*, 45–47.

35. Derrida, *Of Grammatology*.

Chapter 16: Homotextuality

1. This, then, is an example of itself. The following notes are more dutiful. Like pallbearers, they carry the weight of the literary corpus honored through them. Think, then, of the internal citations (*RB*) as the caryatids of temple literature.

2. Roland Barthes, *The Pleasure of the Text*, p. 37.

3. Sandra M. Gilbert, "Costumes of the Mind: Transvestism as Metaphor in Modern Literature," *Critical Inquiry* 7, no. 2. (Winter 1980): 391–417.

4. George Steiner, "Eros and Idiom," in *On Difficulty and Other Essays*, 117.

5. O'Neill, *Essaying Montaigne*.

6. Barthes, *The Pleasure of the Text*, 16–17.

7. John O'Neill, *The Communicative Body*; Merleau-Ponty, *Signs*, 96.

8. Roland Barthes, *Système de la mode*.

9. Claude Lévi-Strauss, *Mythologiques: Le cru et la cuit*, *Mythologiques: Du miel aux cendres*, and *Mythologiques: L'origine des manières de table*.

10. Roland Barthes, "Literature Today: Answers to a Questionnaire in *Tel Quel*," in *Critical Essays*, 151–61.

11. Roland Barthes, "The Structuralist Activity," in *Critical Essays*, 213–20.

12. Bloom, *A Map of Misreading*.

13. Barthes, *Writing Degree Zero*, 10.

14. *On Poetic Imagination and Reverie: Selections from the Works of Gaston Bachelard*.

15. Barthes, *Critical Essays*, pp. xi–xxi.

16. Roland Barthes, *Sade/Fourier/Loyola*, 4.

17. Ibid., 9.

18. "La Sorcière," in *Critical Essays*, 103–15; Linda Orr, "A Sort of History: Jules Michelet's 'La Sorcière,'" *Yale French Studies* 59 (1980): 119–36.

19. Barthes, *A Lover's Discourse: Fragments*, 7.

20. Barthes, *Pleasure of the Text*, 10–11.

21. Barthes, *A Lover's Discourse*, 99.

22. Barthes, *Pleasure of the Text*, 99.

23. Roland Barthes, *S/Z*. The method of "starring" the text can be found in Jean-Pierre Richard, *L-Univers imaginaire de Mallarme*.

24. Barthes, *Sade/Fourier/Loyola*, 9, my emphasis.

25. Roland Barthes, "Striptease," in *Mythologies*, 84–87.

26. Jorge Luis Borges, "Of Exactitude in Science," in *A Universal History of Infamy*.

27. Jorge Luis Borges, *The Book of Sand*.

28. Jorges Luis Borges, "The Keeper of the Books," in *In Praise of Darkness*, 75.

29. Jacques Scherer, *Le "Livre" de Mallarmé: Premiers recherches sur des documents inédits*.

30. Michel Foucault, "Fantasia of the Library," in *Language, Countermemory, Practice: Selected Essays and Interviews*, 109.

31. Eugenio Donato, "The Museum's Furnace: Notes Toward a Contextual Reading of *Bouvard and Pecuchet*," in *Textual Strategies*, 223–24.

32. John O'Neill, "Language and the Voice of Philosophy," introduction to Merleau-Ponty, *The Prose of the World*, xxv–xxvi.

33. For a comparison of Barthes and Blanchot in these terms, see Tzvetan Todorov, "Reflections on Literature in Contemporary France," *New Literary History* 10, no. 3 (Spring 1979): 511–31.

34. Barthes, *A Lover's Discourse*, 14–15. In *La Chambre Claire* Barthes deals with his mother's death. See Tzvetan Todorov, "The Last Barthes," *Critical Inquiry* 7, no. 3 (Spring 1981): 449–54. For nice symptomatic readings of Barthes, see Reda Bensmaia, *The Barthes Effect: The Essay as Reflective Text*; Steven Ungar, *Roland Barthes: The Professor of Desire*; and Patrizia Lombardo, *The Three Paradoxes of Roland Barthes*.

Chapter 17. Vico mit Freude Rejoyced

1. James Joyce, *Finnegans Wake*, 19–20; hereafter cited in the text as *FW*.

2. Bergin and Fisch, *The New Science of Gianbattista Vico*, pars. 379, 383; hereafter cited in the text as *NS*.

3. Sigmund Freud, *Beyond the Pleasure Principle* (1920), *SE*, vol. 18.

4. Sigmund Freud, *Civilization and Its Discontents* (1930), in *SE*, 21:37.

5. Sigmund Freud, *Totem and Taboo* (1912–13), in *SE*, 13:141–42.

6. Roland McHugh, *The Sigla of "Finnegans Wake,"* chap. 1; E see also Margaret C. Solomon, *Eternal Geomater: The Sexual Universe of "Finnegans Wake."*

7. Anthony Burgess, *Joysprick: An Introduction to the Language of James Joyce*; 18–20.

8. James Joyce, *Ulysses*, 282.

9. Joyce, *Ulysses*, 364.

10. Ibid., 370.

11. Richard Ellmann, *Ulysses on the Liffey*, 164.

12. A. Walton Litz, "Vico and Joyce," in *Giambattista Vico: An International Symposium*, 245–55; Sheldon R. Brivic, *Joyce between Freud and Jung*; Brivic, "Time as an Organizing Principle in the Fiction of James Joyce" and "Joycean Psychology," in *Joyce Centenary Essays*, 70–81 and 106–16, respectively.

Bibliography

Adorno, Theodor, Hans Albert, Rolf Dahrendorf, Jürgen Habermas, Harold Pilot, and Karl R. Popper. *The Postivist Dispute in German Sociology*. Translated by Glyn Adey and David Frisby. London: Heineman, 1976.

Agger, Ben. "Marcuse and Habermas on New Science." *Polity* 10 (1976): 158–81.

———— *Reading Science: A Literary, Political, and Sociological Analysis*. New York: General Hall, 1989.

Allison, Paul D., and John A. Stewart. "Productivity Differences among Scientists." *American Sociological Review* 39 (1974): 596–606.

Althusser, Louis, and Etienne Balibar. *Reading "Capital."* New York: Pantheon, Books, 1970.

Anderson, Digby C. "Some Organizational Features in the Local Production of a Plausible Text." *Philosophy of the Social Sciences* 8 (1978): 113–35.

Apel, Karl-Otto. *Analytic Philosophy of Language and the Geisteswissenschaften*. Doldrecht: D. Reidel, 1967.

———— *Towards a Transformation of Philosophy*. London: Routledge & Kegan Paul, 1980.

Atlas, James. "The Battle of the Books." *The New York Times Magazine*, 5 June 1988, 25.

Axelos, Kostas. *Alienation, Praxis, and Techne in the Thought of Karl Marx*. Austin: University of Texas Press, 1976.

Axton, Marie. *The Queen's Two Bodies: Drama and the Elizabethan Succession*. London: Royal Historical Society, 1977.

Bachelard, Gaston. *On Poetic Imagination and Reverie: Selections from the Works of Gaston Bachelard*. Translated by Collete Gaudin. Indianapolis: Bobbs-Merrill, 1971.

Barnes, Barry. *Scientific Knowledge and Sociological Theory*. London: Routledge & Kegan Paul, 1974.

Barnes, J. A. *Who Should Know What? Social Issues, Privacy, and Ethics*. New York: Penguin, 1979.

Barrière, Pierre. *La Vie intellectuelle en Périgord, 1550–1800*. Bordeaux: Editions Delmas, 1936.

Barthes, Roland. *Critical Essays*. Translated by Richard Howard. Evanston, Ill.: Northwestern University Press, 1972.

———— *Le Grain de la voix: Entretiens, 1962–1980*. Paris: Editions du Seuil, 1981.

———— *A Lover's Discourse: Fragments.* Translated by Richard Howard. New York: Hill & Wang, 1978.

———— *Le Plaisir du texte.* Paris: Editions du Seuil, 1973.

———— *Michelet par lui-même.* Paris: Editions du Seuil, 1954.

———— *Mythologies.* Translated by Annette Lavers. London: Paladin, 1973.

———— *The Pleasure of the Text.* Translated by Richard Miller. New York: Hill & Wang, 1975.

———— *Roland Barthes by Roland Barthes.* Translated by Richard Howard. New York: Hill & Wang, 1977.

———— *Sade/Fourier/Loyola.* Translated by Richard Miller. New York: Hill & Wang, 1976.

———— "Science versus Literature." In *Introduction to Structuralism,* edited by Michael Lane. New York: Basic Books, 1970.

———— *Système de la mode.* Paris: Editions du Seuil, 1967.

———— *S/Z.* Translated by Richard Miller. New York: Hill & Wang, 1974.

———— "To Write: An Intransitive Verb?" In *The Structuralist Controversy: The Languages of Criticism and the Sciences of Man,* edited by Richard Macksey and Eugenio Donato. Baltimore: Johns Hopkins University Press, 1970.

———— *Writing Degree Zero and Elements of Semiology.* Translated by Annette Lavers and Colin Smith. Boston: Beacon Press, 1970.

Baudelaire, Charles. *Les Fleurs du Mal.* Translated by Richard Howard. Boston: David R. Godine, 1982.

———— "Mon Coeur Mis à nu." In *Oeuvres complètes,* edited by Y.-G. Le Dantec and Claude Pichois. Paris: Gallimard, 1961.

Bayer, A., and J. Folger. "Some Correlates of a Citation Measure of Productivity in Science." *Sociology of Education* 39 (1986): 381–90.

Bazerman, Charles. *Shaping Written Knowledge: The Genre and Activity of the Experimental Article in Science.* Madison: University of Wisconsin Press, 1988.

Beaudrillard, Jean. "The Ecstasy of Communication." In *The Anti-Aesthetic: Essays on Postmodern Culture,* edited by Hal Foster, 128. Port Townsend, Wash.: Bay Press, 1983.

Beck, L. J. *The Metaphysics of Descartes: A Study of the Meditations.* Oxford: At the Clarendon Press, 1965.

Bell, Daniel. *The Coming of Post-industrial Society.* New York: Basic Books, 1976.

———— *The Cultural Contradictions of Capitalism.* New York: Basic Books, 1976.

———— *The Winding Passage:* Essays and Sociological Journeys. Cambridge, Mass.: ABT Books, 1980.

Benjamin, Walter. "The Paris of the Second Empire in Baudelaire." In *Charles Baudelaire: A Lyric Poet in the Era of High Capitalism,* Translated by Harry Zohn. London: NLB, 1973.

Bensmaia, Reda. *The Barthes Effect: The Essay as Reflective Text*. Minneapolis: University of Minnesota Press, 1987.

Bergin, Thomas G., and Max H. Fisch, trans. *The New Science of Giambattista Vico*. Ithaca, N.Y.: Cornell University Press, 1968.

Berman, Marshall. *All That Is Solid Melts into the Air: The Experience of Modernity*. New York: Simon & Schuster, 1982.

Bernstein, Basil. "Social Class, Linguistic Codes, and Grammatical Elements." *Language and Speech* 5 (1962): 221–40.

Bersani, Leo. *Baudelaire and Freud*. Berkeley and Los Angeles: University of California Press, 1977.

Bhaskar, Roy. *The Possibility of Naturalism: A Philosophical Critique of the Contemporary Human Sciences*. Atlantic Highlands, N.J.: Humanities Press, 1979.

———. *A Realist Theory of Science*. Hassocks, Sussex: Harvester Press, 1978.

———. "Rorty, Realism and the Idea of Freedom." In *Reading Rorty: Critical Responses to "Philosophy and the Mirror of Nature" (and Beyond)*, edited by Alan R. Malachowski. Oxford: Basil Blackwell, 1990.

Birch, David. *Language, Literature, and Critical Practice: Ways of Analysing Text*. London: Routledge & Kegan Paul, 1989.

Bloom, Harold. *The Anxiety of Influence: A Theory of Poetry*. New York: Oxford University Press, 1973.

———. *A Map of Misreading*. New York: Oxford University Press, 1975.

Bohme, Gernot. "The Social Function of Cognitive Structures: A Concept of the Scientific Community within a Theory of Action." In *Determinants and Controls of Scientific Development*, edited by Karin D. Knorr, Harmon Strasser, and Hans Georg Zilian. Dordrecht: D. Reidel, 1975.

Bonnard, Augusta. "The Primal Significance of the Tongue." *International Journal of Psycho-Analysis* 41 (1960): 301–7.

Borges, Jorge Luis. *The Book of Sand*. Translated by Norman Thomas di Giovanni. New York: Dutton, 1977.

———. "The Keeper of the Books." In *In Praise of Darkness*. Translated by Norman Thomas di Giovanni. New York: 1974.

———. "Of Exactitude in Science." In *A Universal History of Infamy*, translated by Norman Thomas di Giovanni. New York: Dutton, 1972.

Bourdieu, Pierre. "The Specificity of a Scientific Field and the Social Conditions of the Progress of Reason." *Social Science Information* 14 (1975): 19–47.

Bowlby, John. "The Child's Tie to His Mother: Review of the Psychoanalytical Literature." In his *Attachment and Loss*, vol. 1. New York: Basic Books, 1969.

Brivic, Sheldon R. *Joyce between Freud and Jung*. Port Washington, N.Y.: Kennikat Press, 1980.

———. "Time as an Organizing Principle in the Fiction of James Joyce," and "Joycean Psychology." In *Joyce Centenary Essays*, edited by Richard F. Epstein. Carbondale: Southern Illinois University Press, 1983.

Brooks, Peter. *Reading for the Plot: Design and Intention in Narrative*. New York: Knopf, 1984.

Brown, Richard. *Society as Text: Essays on Rhetoric, Reason and Reality*. Chicago: University of Chicago Press, 1987.

Burgess, Anthony. *Joysprick: An Introduction to the Language of James Joyce*. London: André Deutsch, 1973.

Burke, Edmund. *A Philosophical Enquiry into the Origin of Our Ideas of the Sublime and Beautiful*. Edited by J. T. Boulton. London: Routledge & Kegan Paul, 1958.

Burke, Kenneth. *A Grammar of Motives*. New York: Prentice-Hall, 1945.

Butor, Michel. *Essais sur les "Essais."* Paris: Gallimard, 1968.

——— "La Fascinatrice." *Les Cahiers du Chemin* 4 (15 October 1968): 20–55.

——— *Histoire extraordinaire: Essai sur une rève de Baudelaire*. Paris: Gallimard, 1961.

Bynum, Caroline W. "Feminine Names for God in Cistercian Writing: A Case Study in the Relationship of Literary Language and Community Life." Paper presented at Colloquium on Consciousness and Group Identification in High Medieval Religion, York University, Toronto, 7–9 April, 1978.

Carroll, David. *Paraesthetics: Foucault, Lyotard, Derrida*. New York: Methuen, 1987.

Cassiodorus Senator. *An Introduction to Divine and Human Readings*. Translated by Leslie Webber Jones. New York: Octagon Books, 1966.

Caton, Hiram. *The Origins of Subjectivity: An Essay on Descartes*. New Haven, Conn.: Yale University Press, 1973.

Champigny, Robert. "The Theatrical Aspect of the Cogito." *Review of Metaphysics* 12 (1959): 370–77.

Chubin, D. E. "On the use of the Science Citation Index in Sociology." *American Sociologist* 8 (1973), 187–89.

Chubin, D. E., and S. Moitra. "Content Analyses of References: Adjunct or Alternative to Citation Counting?" *Social Studies of Science* 5 (1975): 423–31.

Cicourel, Aaron V. *Method and Measurement in Sociology*. New York: Free Press, 1969.

Cole, Jonathan R., and Stephen Cole. "Scientific Output and Recognition: A Study in the Operation of the Reward System in Science." *American Sociological Review* 32 (1967): 377–90.

Cole, Jonathan R., and Harriet Zuckerman. "The Emergence of a Scientific Specialty: The Self-Exemplifying Case of the Sociology of Science." In *The Idea of Social Structure: Papers in Honor of Robert K. Merton*, edited by Lewis A. Coser. New York: Harcourt, Brace, Jovanovich, 1975.

Cole, S., and J. R. Cole. "Visibility and the Structural Bases of Awareness of Scientific Research." *American Sociological Review* 33 (1968): 397–413.

Coward, Rosalind, and John Ellis. *Language and Materialism*. London: Routledge & Kegan Paul, 1977.

Crane, Diana. "The Gate-Keepers of Science: Some Factors Affecting the Selection of Articles for Scientific Journals." *The American Sociologist* 2 (1967): 195–201.

Crews, Frederick. "Whose American Renaissance?" *New York Review of Books*, 27 October 1988.

Davenport, Edward. "The New Politics of Knowledge: Rorty's Pragmatism and the Rhetoric of the Human Sciences." *Philosophy of the Social Sciences* 17, no. 3 (September 1987): 377–94.

Delcroix, Maurice and Walter Gaerts, eds. *"Les Chats" de Baudelaire: Une confrontation de méthodes.* Namur: Presses Universitaires de Namur, 1980.

de Man, Paul. *Blindness and Insight: Essays in the Rhetoric of Contemporary Criticism.* New York: Oxford University Press, 1971.

Derrida, Jacques. "Coming into One's Own." In *Psychoanalysis and the Question of the Text*, edited by Geoffrey H. Hartman. Baltimore: Johns Hopkins University Press, 1978.

—— "Limited Inc." *Glyph* 2 (1977): 162–254.

—— "Living On: Borderlines." In *Deconstruction and Criticism*, edited by Harold Bloom, Paul de Man, Jacques Derrida, Geoffrey H. Hartman, and J. Hillis Miller. New York: Seabury Press, 1979.

—— *Of Grammatology.* Translated by Gayatri Chakrovotly Spivak. Baltimore: Johns Hopkins University Press, 1974.

—— *Writing and Difference.* Chicago: University of Chicago Press, 1978.

Descartes, René. *Discourse on Method* and *The Meditations.* Translated by F. E. Sutcliffe. Harmondsworth, England: Penguin, 1968.

—— *Meditationes de prima philosophia, Méditations metaphysiques.* With French translation by the Duc de Luynes. Paris: Librairie Philosophique J. Vrin, 1970.

—— *The Philosophical Writings of Descartes.* Translated by Robert Stoothoff and Dugald Murdoch. Cambridge: Cambridge University Press, 1984.

d'Espagnat, Bernard. "The Quantum Theory and Reality," *Scientific American* 241 (1979): 158–81.

de Solla Price, Derek J. *Little Science, Big Science.* New York: Columbia University Press, 1963.

Donato, Eugenio. "The Museum's Furnace: Notes toward a Contextual Reading of *Bouvard and Pecuchet.*" In *Textual Strategies: Perspectives in Post-Structuralist Criticism*, edited by Josue V. Harari. Ithaca, N.Y.: Cornell University Press, 1979.

Eagleton, Terry. *Against the Grain: Essays, 1975–1985.* London: Verso, 1986.

Edelman, Nathan. "The Mixed Metaphor in Descartes." *The Romantic Review* 41 (1950): 167–78.

Eisenstein, Elizabeth L. *The Printing Press as an Agent of Change: Communications and Cultural Transformations in Early-Modern Europe.* New York: Cambridge University Press, 1979.

Elias, Norbert. *The Civilizing Process: The History of Manners.* New York: Urizen Books, 1978.

Ellmann, Richard. *Ulysses on the Liffey*. London: Faber and Faber, 1972.

Ezrahi, Yaron. "The Political Resources of Science." In *Sociology of Science: Selected Readings*, edited by Barry Barnes. Harmondsworth, England: Penguin, 1972.

Fararo, Thomas J. "Science as a Cultural System." In *Explorations in General Theory in Social Science: Essays in Honor of Talcott Parsons*, edited by Jan J. Loubser, Rainer C. Baum, Andrew Effrat, and Victor Meyer Lidz. New York: Free Press, 1976.

Fay, Brian. *Social Theory and Political Practice*. London: Allen & Unwin, 1975.

Feldman, F. "On the Performatory Interpretation of the *cogito*." *Philosophical Review* 82 (1973): 345–63.

Fish, Stanley. *Doing What Comes Naturally: Change, Rhetoric, and the Practice of Theory in Literary and Legal Studies*. Durham, N.C.: Duke University Press, 1989.

———. *Is There a Text in This Class? The Authority of Interpretative Communities*. Cambridge: Harvard University Press, 1980.

Fleck, Ludwik. *Genesis and Development of a Scientific Fact*. Edited by Thaddeus J. Trenn and Robert K. Merton. Translated by Fred Bradley and Thaddeus J. Trenn. Chicago: University of Chicago Press, 1979.

Flores, Ralph. "Cartesian Striptease." *Sub-Stance* 39 (1983): 75–88.

Fonagy, Ivan. "Les Bases pulsionnelles de la phonation." *Revue française de psychoanalyse* 34, no. 1 (1970): 101–36; 35, no. 4 (1971): 543–91.

Foster, Hal, ed., *The Anti-Aesthetic: Essays on Postmodern Culture*. Port Townsend, Wash.: Bay Press, 1983.

Foucault, Michel. "Fantasia of the Library." In *Language, Countermemory, Practice: Selected Essays and Interviews*, edited by Donald F. Bouchard. Ithaca, N.Y.: Cornell University Press, 1980.

———. *Folie et déraison: Histoire de la folie à l'age classique*. Paris: Librairie Plon, 1961.

———. *The Order of Things: An Archaeology of the Human Sciences*. New York: Vintage Books, 1973.

Fraser, Nancy. *Unruly Practices: Power, Discourse, and Gender in Contemporary Social Theory*. Minneapolis: University of Minnesota Press, 1989.

Freire, Paolo. *The Pedagogy of the Oppressed*. New York: Herder & Herder, 1972.

Freud, Sigmund. *Beyond the Pleasure Principle*. (1920). Vol. 18 of *Standard Edition of the Complete Psychoanalytical Works*. London: Hogarth Press, 1961.

———. *Civilization and its Discontents* (1930). Vol. 21 of *Standard Edition*. London: Hogarth Press, 1963.

———. "Development of the Libido and Sexual Organization." In *A General Introduction to Psychoanalysis*, translated by Joan Rivière. New York: Washington Square Press, 1960.

———. "Fragment of an Analysis of a Case of Hysteria" (1905 [1907]). In *Case Histories*, vol. 1. Harmondsworth, England: Penguin, 1980.

———— "From the History of an Infantile Neurosis" (1981 [1914]). In *Case Histories*, vol. 2. Harmondsworth, England: Penguin, 1981.

———— "Instincts and their Vicissitudes" (1915). In *Standard Edition*, vol. 14. London: Hogarth Press, 1957.

———— "On the History of the Psycho-Analytic Movement." In *Standard Edition*, vol. 14. London: Hogarth Press, 1961.

———— "An Outline of Psycho-Analysis." In *Standard Edition*, 23:159. London: Hogarth Press, 1961.

———— "Project for a Scientific Psychology" (1905). In *Standard Edition*, 1:328–29. London: Hogarth Press, 1966.

———— *Totem and Taboo* (1912–13). Vol. 13 in *Standard Edition*. London: Hogarth Press, 1950.

Frye, Northrop. *The Anatomy of Criticism: Four Essays*. Princeton, N.J.: Princeton University Press, 1957.

Galston, Iago. "Descartes and Modern Psychiatric Thought." *Isis* 35 (Spring 1944): 118–28.

Garfinkel, Harold. *Studies in Ethnomethodology*. Englewood Cliffs, N.J.: Prentice-Hall, 1967.

Gaston, Jerry. *Originality and Competition in Sciences: A Study of the British High Energy Physics Community*. Chicago: University of Chicago Press, 1973.

Giddens, Anthony. *New Rules of Sociological Method*. London, Hutchinson; New York: Basic Books, 1976.

Gilbert, Nigel G. "The Transformation of Research Findings into Scientific Knowledge." *Social Studies of Science* 6 (1976): 281–306.

Gilbert, Sandra M. "Costumes of the Mind: Transvestism as Metaphor in Modern Literature." *Critical Inquiry* 7, no. 2 (Winter 1980): 391–417.

Girard, René. *Violence and the Sacred*. Baltimore: Johns Hopkins University Press, 1977.

Glauser, Alfred. *Montaigne paradoxale*. Paris: A. G. Nizet, 1972.

Gopnik, Myrna. *Linguistic Structures in Scientific Texts*. The Hague: Mouton, 1972.

Gouhier, Henri. *Les Premières pensées de Descartes: Contribution à l'histoire de l'Anti-renaissance*. Paris: Librairie Philosophique J. Vrin, 1958.

Gouldner, Alvin W. *The Dialectic of Ideology and Technology: The Origins, Grammar, and Future of Ideology*. New York: Seabury Press, 1976.

———— *The Future of the Intellectuals and the Rise of the New Class*. New York: Seabury Press, 1979.

Green, Bryan S. *Literary Methods and Sociological Theory*. Chicago: University of Chicago Press, 1988.

Greenblatt, Stephen. *Renaissance Self-Fashioning: From More to Shakespeare*. Chicago: University of Chicago Press, 1980.

Griffith, B. C., H. Small, V. A. Stonehill, and S. Day. "The Structure of Scientific Literatures (II)." *Science Studies* 4 (1974): 339–65.

Gruenberg, Barry. "The Problem of Reflexivity in the Sociology of Science." *Philosophy of the Social Sciences* 8 (1978): 321–43.

Gusfield, Joseph. "The Literary Rhetoric of Science: Comedy and Pathos in Drinking Driver Research." *American Sociological Review* 41 (1976): 16–34.

Habermas, Jürgen. *Communication and the Evolution of Society.* Boston: Beacon Press, 1979.

——— *Knowledge and Human Interests.* Boston: Beacon Press, 1971.

——— *Legitimation Crisis.* Boston: Beacon Press, 1975.

——— "Modernity: An Incomplete Project." In *The Anti-Aesthetic: Essays on Postmodern Culture,* edited by Hal Foster. Port Townsend, Wash.: Bay Press, 1983.

——— *The Philosophical Discourse of Modernity: Twelve Lectures.* Translated by Frederick Lawrence. Cambridge: MIT Press, 1987.

——— *Toward a Rational Society: Student Protest, Science, and Politics.* Boston: Beacon Press, 1970.

Hagstrom, Warren O. *The Scientific Community.* New York: Basic Books, 1965.

Haliburton, David. *Poetic Thinking: An Approach to Heidegger.* Chicago: University of Chicago Press, 1981.

Halveson, H. M. "Infant Sucking and Tensional Behaviour." *Journal of Genetic Psychology* 53 (1938): 365–430.

Hamblin, D. H. "The Counsellor and Alienated Youth." *British Journal of Guidance and Counselling* 2 (1974): 87–95.

Handleman, Susan. "Jacques Derrida and the Heretic Hermaneutic." In *Displacement: Derrida and After,* edited by Mark Krupnik. Bloomington: Indiana University Press, 1983.

Hart, James G., and John C. Maraldo, trans. *The Piety of Thinking: Essays by Martin Heidegger.* Bloomington: Indiana University Press, 1976.

Hartman, Geoffrey H. *Criticism in the Wilderness: The Study of Literature Today.* New Haven, Conn.: Yale University Press, 1980.

——— "Ghostlier Demarcations: The Sweet Science of Northrop Frye." In *Beyond Formalism: Literary Essays, 1958–1970,* 24–61. New Haven, Conn.: Yale University Press, 1970.

Heidegger, Martin. *On the Way to Language.* Translated by Peter D. Hertz. New York: Harper & Row, 1971.

Hempel, Carl. "The Function of General Laws in History." In *Theories of History,* edited by Patrick Gardiner. Glencoe, Ill.: Free Press, 1956.

Herrnstein Smith, Barbara. *Contingencies of Value: Alternate Perspectives for Critical Theory.* Cambridge, Mass.: Harvard University Press, 1988.

Hexter, J. H. *The History Primer.* New York: Basic Books, 1971.

Hintikka, Jaakko. "Cogito, ergo sum: Inference or Performance?" In *Descartes: A Collection of Critical Essays,* edited by Willis Doney, 108–39. Notre Dame, Ind.: University of Notre Dame Press, 1968.

Hofstadter, Albert. "The Scientific and Literary Uses of Language." In *Symbols and Society: Fourteenth Symposium of the Conference on Science, Philosophy, and Religion*, edited by Lyman Bryson, et al. New York: Cooper Square, 1964.

Hogenson, George B. *Jung's Struggle with Freud*. Notre Dame, Ind.: University of Notre Dame Press, 1983.

Hollis, Martin. *Models of Man: Philosophical Thoughts on Social Action*. New York: Cambridge University Press, 1977.

———— "The Poetics of Personhood." In *Reading Rorty: Critical Responses to "Philosophy and the Mirror of Nature" (and Beyond)*, edited by Alan R. Malachowski. Oxford: Basil Blackwell, 1990.

Holton, Gerald. "On the Role of Themata in Scientific Thought." *Science* 188 (1975): 333.

Homans, Peter. "Disappointment and the Ability to Mourn: De-idealization as a Psychological Theme in Freud's Life, Thought, and Social Circumstance, 1906–1914." In *Freud: Appraisals and Reappraisals*, vol. 2, edited by Paul E. Stepansky, 3–102. Hillsdale, N.J.: Analytic Press, 1988.

Hooker, Davenport. "Reflex Activities in the Human Fetus." In *Child Behaviour and Development*, edited by Roger G. Barker, Jacob S. Kounin, and Herbert F. Wright. New York: McGraw-Hill, 1943.

Horton, Susan R. "The Institution of Literature and the Cultural Community." In *Literary Theory's Future(s)*, edited by Joseph Natoli. Champaign: University of Illinois Press, 1989.

Hyde, G. M. "The Poetry of the City." In *Modernism, 1890–1930*, edited by Malcolm Bradbury and James MacFarlane, 337–48. Harmondsworth, England: Penguin Books, 1976.

Jameson, Fredric. "Baudelaire as Modernist and Postmodernist: The Dissolution of the Referent and the Artificial 'Sublime.' " In *Lyric Poetry: Beyond New Criticism*, edited by Chaviva Hosek and Patricia Parker, 247–65. Ithaca, N.Y.: Cornell University Press, 1985.

———— *Marxism and Form: Twentieth-Century Dialectical Theories of Literature*. Princeton, N.J.: Princeton University Press, 1972.

———— "Pleasure: A Political Issue." In *Formations of Pleasure*. Formations Editorial Collective. London: Routledge & Kegan Paul. 1983.

———— *The Political Unconscious: Narrative as a Socially Symbolic Act*. Ithacan, N.Y.: Cornell University Press, 1981.

———— "Postmodernism and Consumer Society." In *The Anti-Aesthetic: Essays on Postmodern Culture*; edited by Hal Foster. Port Townsend, Wash.: Bay Press, 1983.

———— "Postmodernism; or, The Cultural Logic of Late Capitalism." *New Left Review* 146 (1984): 52–92.

Jardine, Alice A. *Gynesis: Configurations of Woman and Modernity*. Ithaca, N.Y.: Cornell University Press, 1985.

Jay, Gregory S. *America the Scrivener: Deconstruction and the Subject of Literary History*. Ithaca, N.Y.: Cornell University Press, 1990.

Johnson, Barbara. *The Critical Difference: Essays in the Contemporary Rhetoric of Reading*. Baltimore: Johns Hopkins University Press, 1980.

——— "Taking Fidelity Philosophically." In *Difference in Translation*, edited by Joseph F. Graham. Ithaca, N.Y.: Cornell University Press, 1985.

Joyce, James. *Finnegans Wake*. Centennial Edition. New York: Viking Press, 1982.

——— *Ulysses*. London: Penguin Books, 1971.

Kant, Immanuel. *Prolegomena to Any Future Metaphysics*. The Paul Carus translation extensively revised by James W. Ellington. Indianapolis: Hackett Publishing Company, 1977.

Kantorowicz, Ernest. *The King's Two Bodies*. Princeton, N.J.: Princeton University Press, 1957.

Kaplan, Abraham. *The Conduct of Inquiry*. San Francisco: Chandler Publications, 1964.

Kellner, Douglas, ed. *Jameson/Postmodernism/Critique*. Washington, D.C.: Maisonneuve Press, 1990.

Kenny, Anthony. *Descartes: A Study of His Philosophy*. New York: Random House, 1968.

King, M.D. "Reason, Tradition, and the Progressiveness of Science." *History and Theory* 10 (1971): 3–32.

Klima, Rolf. "Scientific Knowledge and Social Control in Science: The Application of a Cognitive Theory of Behaviour to the Study of Scientific Behaviour." In *Social Processes of Scientific Development*, edited by Richard Whitley. London: Routledge & Kegan Paul, 1974.

Knorr, Karin D. "Producing and Reproducing Knowledge: Descriptive or Constructive? Toward a Model of Research Production." *Social Science Information* 16 (1977): 669–96.

Knorr, Karin D., and Dietrich W. Knorr. *From Scenes to Scripts: On the Relationship between Laboratory Research and Published Papers in Science*. Research Memorandum 132. Vienna: Institute for Advanced Studies, 1978.

Knorr-Cetina, Karin D. *The Manufacture of Knowledge: An Essay on the Constructivist and Contextual Nature of Science*. New York: Pergamon, 1981.

——— "Tinkering towards Success: Prelude to a Theory of Scientific Practice." *Theory and Society* 8 (1979): 347–76.

Kristeva, Julia. *Desire in Language: A Semiotic Approach to Literature and Art*. Edited by Leon S. Roudiez. Translated by Thomas Gora, Alice Jardine, and Leon S. Roudiez. New York: Columbia University Press, 1980.

Kubie, Lawrence C. "Some Implications for Psycho-Analysis of Modern Concepts of the Organization of the Brain." *Psychoanalytic Quarterly* 22 (1953): 21–68.

Kuhn, Thomas S. *The Structure of Scientific Revolutions*. Chicago: University of Chicago Press, 1962.

Lacan, Jacques. "The Direction of the Treatment and the Principles of Its Power." In *Ecrits: A Selection*, translated by Alan Sheridan. New York: Norton, 1977.

Lakatos, Imre. "Falsification and the Methodology of Scientific Research

Programmes." In *Criticism and the Growth of Knowledge*, edited by Imre Lakatos and Alan Musgrave. Cambridge: Cambridge University Press, 1970.

Lane, Robert. "The Decline of Politics and Ideology in a Knowledgeable Society." *American Sociological Review* 31 (1966): 647–61.

Laplanche, Jean. *Life and Death in Psychoanalysis*. Translated by Jeffrey Mehlman. Baltimore: Johns Hopkins University Press, 1976.

Laplanche, Jean, and J.-B. Pontalis. *The Language of Psycho-Analysis*. Translated by D. Nicholson-Smith. New York: Norton, 1973.

Latour, Bruno. *Science in Action*. Cambridge, Mass.: Harvard University Press, 1987.

———— "The Three Little Dinosaurs; or, A Sociologist's Nightmare." *Fundamenta scientiae* 1 (1980): 79–85.

Latour, Bruno, and Steve Woolgar. *Laboratory Life: The Social Construction of Scientific Facts*. Beverly Hills, Calif.: Sage, 1979.

Lauter, Paul. "Race and Gender in the Shaping of the American Literary Canon: A Case Study from the Twenties." *Feminist Studies* 9, no. 3 (Fall 1983): 435–63.

———— "Working-Class Women's Literature: An Introduction to Study." In *Women in Print*, edited by Joan E. Hartman and Ellen Messer-Davidow. Opportunities for Women's Studies Research in Language and Literature, vol. 1. New York: HLA, 1982.

Lebovic, S., and M. Soulé. *La Connaissance de l'enfant par la psychoanalyse*. Paris: Presses Universitaires de France, 1970.

Lefebvre, Henri. *Le manifeste différentialiste*. Paris: Gallimard, 1970.

Leiss, William. *The Domination of Nature*. Boston: Beacon Press, 1972.

Levin, David Michael. *The Body's Recollection of Being: Phenomenological Psychology and the Deconstruction of Nihilism*. London: Routledge & Kegan Paul, 1985.

Lévi-Strauss, Claude. *Mythologiques: Le Cru et la cuit*. Paris: Librairie Plon, 1964.

———— *Mythologiques: Du Miel aux cendres*. Paris: Librairie Plon, 1967.

———— *Mythologiques: L'Origine des manières de table*. Paris: Librairie Plon, 1968.

Litz, A. Walton. "Vico and Joyce." In *Giambattista Vico: An International Symposium*, edited by Georgio Tagliacozzo and Hayden V. White. Baltimore: Johns Hopkins University Press, 1969.

Lombardo, Patrizia. *The Three Paradoxes of Roland Barthes*. Athens: University of Georgia Press, 1989.

Lynch, Michael E. "Technical Work and Critical Inquiry: Investigations in a Scientific Laboratory." *Social Studies of Science* 12 (1982): 499–533.

Lyotard, Jean-François. *Economie libidinale*. Paris: Editions de Minuit, 1974.

———— *The Postmodern Condition: A Report on Knowledge*. Translated by Geoff Bennington and Brian Massumi. Minneapolis: University of Minnesota Press, 1984.

McCloskey, Donald M. *The Rhetoric of Economics*. Madison: University of Wisconsin Press, 1985.

McGrath, William J. *Freud's Discovery of Psychoanalysis: The Politics of Hysteria*. Ithaca, N.Y.: Cornell University Press, 1986.

Macherey, Pierre. *A Theory of Literary Production*. London: Routledge & Kegan Paul, 1978.

McHugh, Roland. *The Sigla of "Finnegans Wake."* Austin: University of Texas Press, 1976.

Maclean, Paul D. "Psychosomatic Disease and the 'Visceral Brain.' " *Psychosomatic Medicine* 11, no. 6 (November–December 1949): 338–53.

McLellan, David, trans. *Karl Marx: Early Texts*. Oxford: Basil Blackwell, 1971.

Mahony, Patrick. *Psychoanalysis and Discourse*. London: Tavistock, 1987.

Marcuse, Herbert. *Eros and Civilization: A Philosophical Inquiry into Freud*. New York: Vintage, 1962.

———— *One-Dimensional Man: Studies in the Ideology of Advanced Industrial Society*. Boston: Beacon Press, 1964.

Marin, Louis. "On the Interpretation of Ordinary Language: A Parable of Pascal." In *Textual Strategies: Perspectives in Post-Structuralist Criticism*, edited by Josue V. Harari, 239–59. Ithaca, N.Y.: Cornell University Press, 1979.

———— "The Iconic Text and the Theory of Enunciation: Luca Signorelli at Loreto (circa 1479–1484)." *New Literary History* 14, no. 3 (Spring 1983): 553–96.

———— "Toward a Theory of Reading in the Visual Arts: Poussin's *The Arcadian Shepherds*." In *The Reader in the Text*, edited by Susan R. Suleiman and Inge Crosman, 293–324. Princeton, N.J.: Princeton University Press, 1980.

Martins, Herminio. "The Kuhnian 'Revolution' and Its Implications for Sociology." In *Imagination and Precision in Political Analysis: Essays in Honor of Peter Nettl*, edited by A. H. Hanson, T. Nossiter, and Stein Rokken. London: Faber, 1972.

Marx, Karl. *Capital: A Critique of Political Economy*. Translated by Samuel Moore and Edward Aveling, Chicago: C. H. Kerr, 1906.

Merleau-Ponty, Maurice. *Phenomenology of Perception*. Translated by Colin Smith. London: Routledge & Kegan Paul, 1962.

———— *The Prose of the World*. Translated by John O'Neill. Evanston, Ill.: Northwestern University Press, 1973.

———— *Signs*. Translated by Richard C. McCleary. Evanston, Ill.: Northwestern University Press, 1964.

Merton, Robert K. *The Sociology of Science: Theoretical and Empirical Investigations*. Chicago: University of Chicago Press, 1973.

Merton, Robert K., and Harriet Zuckerman. "Patterns of Evaluation in Science: Institutionalization, Structure, and Functions of the Referee System." *Minerva* 9 (1971): 66–100.

Michaels, Walter Benn. "The Interpreters' Self: Peirce on the Cartesian 'Subject.'" In *Reader-Response Criticism: From Formalism to Post-Structuralism*, edited by Jane P. Tomkins. Baltimore: Johns Hopkins University Press, 1980.

Moerman, Michael. "Analysis of Cue Conversation: Providing Accounts, Finding Breaches, and Taking Sides." In *Studies in Social Interaction*, edited by David Sudnow. New York: Free Press, 1972.

Montaigne, Michel de. *The Complete Works: Essays, Travel Journal, Letters.* Translated by Donald M. Frame. Stanford, Calif.: Stanford University Press, 1948.

Morris, Meaghan. "Postmodernity and Lyotard's Sublime." *Art and Text* 16 (Summer 1984): 44–67.

Morrison, Kenneth L. *"Reader's Work*: Devices for Achieving Pedagogic Events in Textual Materials for Readers as Voices to Sociology." Ph.D. diss., York University, Toronto, 1976.

———— "Some Properties of 'Telling-Order Designs' in Didactic Inquiry." *Philosophy of the Social Sciences* 11 (1981): 245–62.

———— "Some Researchable Recurrences in Disciplinary Specific Inquiry." In *Interactional Order: New Directions in the Study of Social Order*, edited by David T. Helm. New York: Irvington, 1989.

———— "Stabilizing the Text: The Institutionalization of Knowledge in Historical and Philosophic Forms of Argument." *Canadian Journal of Sociology* 12, no. 3 (1987): 242–74.

Mueller, Claus. *The Politics of Communication: A Study in the Political Sociology of Language, Socialization, and Legitimation.* New York: Oxford University Press, 1973.

Mulkay, M. J. "Conformity and Innovation in Science." In *Sociology of Science*, edited by Paul Holmes. The Sociological Review Monograph Series, no. 18. Keele, U.K.: University of Keele Press, 1972.

Mulkay, Michael. *The Word and the World: Explorations in the Form of Sociological Analysis.* London: Allen and Unwin, 1985.

Murray, Timothy. "From Foul Sheets to Legitimate Model: Antitheater Text, Ben Jonson." *New Literary History* 14, no. 3 (Spring 1983): 641–64.

Nador, G. "Métaphores de chemins et de labyrinthes chez Descartes." *Revue d'histoire de la philosophie* 152 (1962): 37–51.

Nancy, Jean-Luc. *Ego Sum.* Paris: Flammarion, 1979.

———— "Larvatus pro Deo." *Glyph* 2 (1977): 14–36.

Nelson, J. S., A. Megill, and D. McCloskey. *The Rhetoric of the Human Sciences: Language and Argument in Scholarship and Public Affairs.* Madison: University of Wisconsin Press, 1987.

O'Neill, John. *The Communicative Body: Studies in Communicative Philosophy, Politics, and Sociology.* Evanston, Ill.: Northwestern University Press, 1989.

———— "Decolonization and the Ideal Speech Community: Some Issues in the Theory and Practice of Communicative Competence." In *Critical Theory and Public Life*, edited by John Forester. Cambridge: MIT Press, 1985.

———— "The Disciplinary Society: From Weber to Foucault." *British Journal of Sociology* 37, no. 1 (1987): 42–60.

———— *Essaying Montaigne: A Study of the Renaissance Institution of Writing and Reading.* London: Routledge & Kegan Paul, 1982.

———— *Five Bodies: The Human Shape of Modern Society.* Ithaca, N.Y.: Cornell University Press, 1985.

———— *For Marx Against Althusser, and Other Essays.* Lanham, Md.: University Press of America, 1982.

———— "From Phenomenology to Ethnomethodology: Some Radical 'Misreadings.' " *Current Perspectives in Social Theory* 1 (1980): 7–20.

———— "The Hobbesian Problem in Marx and Parsons." In *Explorations in General Theory in Social Science: Essays in Honor of Talcott Parsons*, edited by Jan C. Loubser, *et al.*, 295–308. New York: The Free Press, 1976.

———— *Making Sense Together: An Introduction to Wild Sociology.* New York: Harper & Row, 1974.

———— "Merleau-Ponty's Critique of Marxist Scientism." *Canadian Journal of Political and Social Theory* 2 (1978): 31–62.

———— "The Mutuality of Accounts: An Essay on Trust." In *Theoretical Perspectives in Sociology*, edited by Scott G. McNall. New York: St. Martin's Press, 1979.

———— *Perception, Expression, and History: The Social Phenomenology of Maurice Merleau-Ponty.* Evanston, Ill.: Northwestern University Press, 1970.

———— *Plato's Cave: Desire, Power and the Specular Functions of the Media.* Norwoods, N.J.: Ablex, 1991.

———— "Scientism, Historicism and the Problems of Rationality." In *Modes of Individualism and Collectivism*, edited by John O'Neill. London: Heinemann, 1973.

———— "Sociological Nemesis: Parsons and Foucault on the Therapeutic Disciplines." In *Sociological Theory in Transition*, edited by Mark L. Wardell and Stephen P. Turner, 21–35. Boston: Allen & Unwin, 1986.

———— *Sociology as a Skin Trade: Essays Towards a Reflexive Sociology.* London: Heinemann, 1972.

———— "Time's Body: Vico on the Love of Language and Institution." In *Giambattista Vico's Science of Humanity*, edited by Giorgio Tagliacozzo and Donald Phillip Verene. Baltimore: Johns Hopkins University Press, 1976.

———— "Vico on the Natural Workings of the Mind." In *Phenomenology and the Human Sciences*, edited by J. N. Mohanty, 117–25. Denver: Philosophical Topics, 1982.

Ong, Walter D. *Fighting for Life: Context, Sexuality and Consciousness.* Ithaca, N.Y.: Cornell University Press, 1981.

Orr, Linda. "A Sort of History: Jules Michelet's 'La Sorcière.' " *Yale French Studies* 59 (1980): 119–36.

Ostow, Mortimer. "A Psychoanalytic Contribution to the Study of Brain Function." *Psychoanalytic Quarterly* 23 (1954): 317–423.

Ostow, Robin. "Autobiographical Sources of Freud's Social Theory: *Totem and Taboo, Group Psychology and the Analysis of the Ego* and *Moses and Monotheism Revisited.*" *Psychiatric Journal of the University of Ottawa* (1977): 169–80.

Overend, Trann. "Enquiry and Ideology: Habermas' Trichotomous Conception of Science." *Philosophy of the Social Sciences* 8 (1978): 1–35.

Overington, Michael A. "A Critical Celebration of Gusfield's 'The Literary Rhetoric of Science.' " *American Sociological Review* 62 (1977): 170–73.

Paris, Jean. *Rembrandt*. Paris: Librairie Hachette, 1965.

Parsons, Talcott. *The Social System*. Glencoe, Ill.: Free Press, 1951.

———. *The Structure of Social Action: A Study in Social Theory with Special Reference to a Group of Recent European Writers*. New York: Free Press of Glencoe, 1964.

Perelman, Chaim. *Le Champ de l'argumentation*. Brussels: Presses Universitaires de Bruxelles, 1970.

Peterfreund, Stuart, ed. *Literature and Science: Theory and Practice*. Boston: Northeastern University Press, 1990.

Plett, Heinrich F. "Aesthetic Constituents in the Courtly Culture of Renaissance England." *New Literary History* 14, no. 3 (Spring 1983): 597–622.

Polyani, Michael. *Personal Knowledge: Towards a Post-Critical Philosophy*. London: Routledge & Kegan Paul, 1973.

Popper, Karl R. *The Open Society and Its Enemies*. 2 vols. New York: Harper & Row, 1963.

———. *The Poverty of Historicism*. Boston: Beacon Press, 1957.

Prévost, Jean. *Baudelaire: Essai sur la création et l'inspiration poétiques*. Paris: Mercure de France, 1964.

Puttenham, George. *The Arte of English Poesie* (1589). Edited by Gladys Doidge Willcock and Alice Walker. 1936; reprint, Cambridge: Cambridge University Press, 1970.

Rachlis, Charles. "Marcuse and the Problem of Happiness." *Canadian Journal of Political and Social Theory* 2 (1978), 63–88.

Rajchman, John. "Habermas's Complaint." *New German Critique* 45 (Fall 1988): 163–191.

Rapaport, Herman. "Staging Mont Blanc." In *Displacement: Derrida and After*, edited by Mark Krupnik. Bloomington: Indiana University Press, 1983.

Reiss, Timothy J. "Cartesian Discourse and Classical Ideology." *Diacritics* 6, no. 4 (Winter 1976): 19–27.

———. "The *Concevoir* Motif in Descartes." In *La Cohérence intérieure: Etudes sur la littérature française du xviie siècle, presentées en hommage à Judd D. Hubert*, edited by J. van Baelen and David L. Rubin. Paris: Jean-Michèle Place, 1977.

———. *The Discourse of Modernism*. Ithaca, N.Y.: Cornell University Press, 1982.

Richard, Jean-Pierre. *L'Univers imaginaire de Mallarmé*. Paris: Editions du Seuil, 1961.

Ricoeur, Paul. *Freud and Philosophy: An Essay on Interpretation.* Translated by Denis Savage. New Haven, Conn.: Yale University Press, 1970.

Romanowski, Sylvie. *L'illusion Chez Descartes: La Structure du discours cartésien.* Paris: Klincksieck, 1974.

Rorty, Richard. *Contingency, Irony, and Solidarity.* Cambridge: Cambridge University Press, 1989.

——— *Philosophy and the Mirror of Nature.* Princeton: Princeton University Press, 1979.

Sacks, Harvey. "On the Analyzability of Stories by Children." In *Directions in Sociolinguistics: The Ethnography of Communication,* edited by J. J. Gumperz and D. Hymes. New York: Holt, Rinehart and Winston, 1972.

——— "Sociological Description." *Berkeley Journal of Sociology* 8 (1963): 1–16.

Sacks, Harvey, Emmanuel A. Schegloff, and Gail Jefferson. "A Simple Systematics for the Organization of Turn Taking for Conversation." *Language* 50 (1974): 696–735.

Said, Edward W. *The World, the Text, and the Critic.* Cambridge, Mass.: Harvard University Press, 1983.

Sammons, Jeffrey L. *Literary Sociology and Practical Criticism.* Bloomington: Indiana University Press, 1977.

Sartre, Jean-Paul. *Baudelaire.* Paris: Gallimard, 1947.

——— *What is Literature?* Translated by Bernard Frechtman. New York: Harper & Row, 1965.

Scherer, Jacques. *Le "Livre" de Mallarmé: Premiers recherches sur des documents inédits.* Paris: Gallimard, 1957.

Scholes, Robert. *Textual Power: Literary Theory and the Teaching of English.* New Haven, Conn.: Yale University Press, 1985.

Schonberger, Stephen. "A Dream of Descartes: Reflections on the Unconscious Determinants of the Sciences." *International Journal of Psychology* 20 (January 1939): 43–57.

Schumpeter, Joseph A. *History of Economic Analysis.* New York: Oxford University Press, 1954.

Schutz, Alfred. *Reflections on the Problem of Relevance.* Edited by Richard M. Zaner. New Haven, Conn.: Yale University Press, 1970.

Schutz, Alfred, and Thomas Luckmann. *The Structures of the Life-World.* Translated by Richard M. Zaner and H. Tristram Englehardt, Jr. Evanston, Ill.: Northwestern University Press, 1973.

Searle, John R. "Reiterating the Differences: A Reply to Derrida." *Glyph* 1 (1977): 198–208.

——— *Speech Acts: An Essay in the Philosophy of Language.* Cambridge: Cambridge University Press, 1969.

Sedgwick, Peter. "Natural Science and Human Theory: A Critique of Herbert Marcuse." In *The Socialist Register,* edited by Ralph Miliband and John Saville. New York: Monthly Review Press, 1966.

Serres, Michel. *Hermes: Literature, Science, Philosophy.* Edited by Josue V. Harari and David F. Bell. Baltimore: Johns Hopkins University Press, 1982.

Shapiro, Kenneth Joel. *Bodily Reflective Modes: A Phenomenological Approach for Psychology.* Durham, N.C.: Duke University Press, 1985.

Silverstein, Barry. " 'Now Comes a Sad Story': Freud's Lost Metapsychological Papers." In *Freud: Appraisals and Reappraisals,* vol. 1, edited by Paul E. Stepansky. Hillsdale, N.J.: Analytic Press, 1986.

Simons, Herbert W., ed. *Rhetoric in the Human Sciences.* London: Sage, 1989.

Skura, Meredith Ann. *The Literary Use of the Psychoanalytic Process.* New Haven, Conn.: Yale University Press, 1981.

Small, H., and B. C. Griffith. "The Structure of Scientific Literatures (I)." *Science Studies* 4 (1974): 17–40.

Smith, Dorothy E. "The Social Construction of Documentary Reality." *Sociological Inquiry* 44 (1974): 257–68.

Smith, Norman Kemp. *New Studies in the Philosophy of Descartes: Descartes as Pioneer.* London: Macmillan, 1966.

Soeffner, Hans Georg. "Common Sense and Science: Observations about a Common Misunderstanding of Science." *Newsletter of the International Society for the Sociology of Knowledge* 8 (1982): 9–23.

Solomon, Margaret C. *Eternal Geomater: The Sexual Universe of "Finnegans Wake."* Carbondale: Southern Illinois University Press, 1969.

Spitz, René A. "The Primal Cavity: A Contribution to the Genesis of Perception and Its Role for Psychoanalytic Theory." *The Psychoanalytic Study of the Child* 10 (1955): 216–24.

Steiner, George. "Eros and Idiom." In *On Difficulty and Other Essays.* New York: Oxford University Press, 1978.

Stepansky, Paul E. "The Empiricists Rebel: Jung, Freud, and the Burdens of Discipleship." *Journal of the History of the Behavioral Sciences* 12 (1976): 216–39.

——— *In Freud's Shadow: Adler in Context.* Hillsdale, N.J.: Analytic Press, 1983.

Stockman, Norman. "Habermas, Marcuse, and the *Aufhebung* of Science and Technology." *Philosophy of the Social Sciences* 8 (1978): 15–35.

Storer, Norman W. *The Social System of Science.* New York: Holt, Rinehart and Winston, 1966.

Sussman, Henry. "The All-Embracing Metaphor: Reflections on Kafka's 'The Burrow.' " *Glyph* 1 (1977): 100–131.

——— "The Court as Text: Inversion, Supplanting, and Derangement in Kafka's *Der Prozess.*" *PMLA* 92 (1977): 41–55.

Tischler, Hans. "Schreien, Lallen und erstes Sprechen in der Entwicklung des Sauglings." *Zeitschrift für Psychologie* 160, nos. 3–4 (April 1957): 210–63.

Todorov, Tzvetan. "The Last Barthes." *Critical Inquiry* 7, no. 3 (Spring 1981): 449–54.

———— "Reflections on Literature in Contemporary France." *New Literary History* 10, no. 3 (Spring 1979); 511–31.

Tompkins, Jane P., ed. *Reader-Response Criticism: From Formalism to Post-Structuralism.* Baltimore: Johns Hopkins University Press, 1980.

Toulmin, Stephen. *The Uses of Argument.* Cambridge: Cambridge University Press, 1969.

Ungar, Steven. *Roland Barthes: The Professor of Desire.* Lincoln: University of Nebraska Press, 1983.

Van den Daele, Wolfgang, and Peter Weingart. "Resistance and Receptivity of Science to External Direction: The Emergence of New Disciplines under the Impact of Science Policy." In *Perspectives on the Emergence of Scientific Disciplines,* edited by Gerald Lemaine et al. The Hague: Mouton, 1976.

Van Tieghem, Paul. "L'Automne dans la poésie ouest-européene, de Brockes à Lamartine." In *Mélanges d'histoire littéraire générale et comparée: Offerts à Fernand Baldensperger,* 2:337–48. Paris: Librairie Ancienne Honoré Champion, 1930.

Vasoli, Cesare. "Francesco Patrizi and the 'Double Rhetoric.'" *New Literary History* 14, no. 3 (Spring 1983): 531–52.

Vickers, Brian. "Epideictic and Epic in the Renaissance." *New Literary History* 14, no. 3 (Spring 1983): 497–538.

Waller, J. J. "Identification of Problem Drinkers among Drunken Drivers." *Journal of the American Medical Association* 200 (1967): 124–30.

Weber, Max. "Science as a Vocation." In *From Max Weber: Essays in Sociology,* edited by H. Gerth and C. Wright Mills. New York: Oxford University Press, 1958.

Weber, Samuel. *The Legend of Freud.* Minneapolis: University of Minnesota Press, 1982.

Weimann, Robert. "'Appropriation' and Modern History in Renaissance Prose Narrative." *New Literary History* 14, no. 3 (Spring 1983): 459–96.

———— *Structure and Society in Literary History: Studies in the History and Theory of Historical Criticism.* Charlottesville: University of Virginia Press, 1975.

Weisz, George. "Scientists and Sectarians: The Care of Psychoanalysis." *Journal of the History of the Behavioral Sciences* 11, no. 4 (October 1975): 350–64.

West, Cornel. "Ethics and Action in Fredric Jameson's Marxist Hermeneutics." In *Postmodernism and Politics,* edited by Jonathan Arac, 123–44. Minneapolis: University of Minnesota Press, 1986.

Whigham, Frank. "Interpretation at Court: Courtesy and the Performer-Audience Dialectic." *New Literary History* 14 no. 3 (Spring 1983): 623–40.

Whitley, Richard D. "Black Boxism and the Sociology of Science: A Discussion of the Major Developments in the Field." In *Sociology of Science,* edited by Paul Halmes. The Sociological Review Monograph Series, no. 18. Keele, U.K.: University of Keele Press, 1972.

Wilden, Anthony. "Par divers moyens on arrive à pareille fin: A Reading of Montaigne." *Modern Language Notes* 83 (1968): 577–97.

———— *System and Structure: Essays in Communication and Exchange.* London: Tavistock, 1972.

Williams, Bernard. *Descartes: The Project of Pure Inquiry.* Atlantic Highlands, N.J.: Humanities Press, 1978.

Wilson, H. T. *The American Ideology: Science, Technology, and Organization as Modes of Rationality in Advanced Industrial Societies.* London: Routledge & Kegan Paul, 1977.

———— "Science, Critique and Criticism: The 'Open Society' Revisited." In *On Critical Theory*, edited by John O'Neill. Lanham, Md. University Press of America, 1989.

Wilson, Thomas P. "Normative and Interpretative Paradigms in Sociology." In *Understanding Everyday Life*, edited by Jack D. Douglas. London: Routledge & Kegan Paul, 1971.

Wittgenstein, Ludwig. *On Certainty.* New York: Harper & Row, 1969.

Woolgar, Steve. "Discovery: Logic and Sequence in a Scientific Text (I)." In *The Social Process of Scientific Investigation*, edited by K. Knorr, R. Krohn, and R. Whitley. Dordrecht: D. Reidel, 1980.

Zaner, Richard M. *The Context of Self: A Phenomenological Inquiry Using Medicine as a Clue.* Athens: Ohio University Press, 1981.

Ziman, John. *Public Knowledge: The Social Dimension of Science.* (Cambridge: Cambridge University Press, 1968).

Zuckerman, Harriet. "The Code of Science." *Studium Generale* 23 (1970): 942–61.

Index